EARTH SCIENCE DAYBOOK

In Collaboration with NSTA

TEACHER'S EDITION

GREAT SOURCE
EDUCATION GROUP
A Houghton Mifflin Company

Acknowledgments
Teacher's Edition Reviewers

Charles M. Harmon
Los Angeles Unified School District
Los Angeles, California

Maxine Rosenberg
Curriculum Consultant
Newton, Massachusetts

Dwight Sieggreen
Hillside Middle School
Northville, Michigan

Thomas Vaughn
Arlington Public Schools
Arlington, Massachusetts

Credits

Writing: Bill Smith Studio
Editorial: Great Source: Fran Needham, Marianne Knowles, Susan Rogalski; Bill Smith Studio
Design: Great Source: Richard Spencer; Bill Smith Studio
Production Management: Great Source: Evelyn Curley; Bill Smith Studio
Cover Design: Bill Smith Studio

National Science Teachers Association: Tyson Brown, Carol Duval, Juliana Texley, Patricia Warren

Photos
Page *iv*: PhotoDisc; PhotoSpin; **1:** PhotoDisc; **2:** Corel; PhotoDisc; **3:** PhotoDisc; **4:** PhotoDisc; **8:** PhotoDisc; **9:** © Wampler Gaylon/CORBIS SYGMA; **11:** Painet; **12:** NASA; **13:** NASA; **14-15:** PhotoDisc; **16a:** NASA; **16b:** Corel; **17:** NASA; **18-19:** PhotoDisc; **20:** BSS; **20:** NASA; **22:** Corel; **22-23:** PhotoDisc; **24:** © Reuters New Media/CORBIS; **24:** © Reuters New Media/CORBIS; **25:** Corel; **26-27:** Corel; **28-29:** Corel; **30:** PhotoDisc; **32-33:** Corel; **34-35:** PhotoDisc; **36-37:** PhotoDisc; **38-39:** PhotoDisc; **40:** UCMP Berkley; **41:** ArtToday; **42-43:** PhotoDisc; **44:** PhotoDisc; **45:** PhotoSpin; **46-47:** PhotoDisc; **48:** © Layne Kennedy/CORBIS; **50:** Peter Sterling/taxi/Getty Images; **51:** Corel; **52:** Bettmann/CORBIS; **54-55:** PhotoSpin; **55:** PhotoSpin; **56:** Bettmann/CORBIS; **57:** PhotoSpin; **57:** Bettmann/Corbis; **58-59:** PhotoDisc; **60:** Bettmann/CORBIS; **61:** PhotoSpin; **62:** ArtToday; **63:** PhotoDisc; **64-65:** PhotoDisc; **66-67:** Corel; **68-69:** PhotoDisc; **71:** USGS; **73:** © Bettman/CORBIS; **74-75:** BSS art; **77:** Princeton University/USGS; **81:** NOAA Central Library; **82:** PhotoDisc; **83:** Corel; **84-85:** PhotoDisc; **86:** © Pedro Ugarte/ AFP/CORBIS; **87:** PhotoDisc; **88-89:** PhotoDisc; **90-91:** PhotoDisc; **92:** PhotoDisc; **93:** Corel; **94:** PhotoDisc; **97:** S. Mukerji, IDRC; **98-99:** PhotoDisc; **101:** PhotoDisc; **102-103:** PhotoDisc; **107:** PhotoDisc; **108-109:** PhotoDisc; **108a:** Friends of Quabbin; **108b:** Friends of Quabbin; **108c:** Les Campbell; **111:** PhotoDisc; **112-113:** PhotoDisc; **114:** Corel; **116-117:** PhotoDisc; **118:** ArtVille; **119:** Corel; **120-121:** PhotoDisc; **122:** Corel; **124:** PhotoDisc; **125:** W. James Ingraham, Jr/Beachcombers' Alert; **126-127:** PhotoSpin; **128:** PhotoSpin; **128:** PhotoSpin; **129:** PhotoDisc; **130-131:** Corel; **132-133:** PhotoDisc; **133:** PhotoDisc; **134:** © Tom Stewart/CORBIS; **135:** PhotoDisc; **136:** NOAA Central Library; **138:** PhotoSpin; **140-141:** Corel; **142:** NASA/GSFC/LaRC/JPL, MISR Team; **144-145:** Corel; **146:** Corel; **148:** NASA; **148-149:** PhotoDisc; **150:** NOAA Central Library; **151:** Les Nagey; **151:** NOAA Central Library; **152-153:** PhotoDisc; **154:** Corel; **156-157:** PhotoDisc; **158-159:** PhotoDisc; **160:** © Layne Kennedy/CORBIS; **161:** PhotoDisc; **162-163:** PhotoDisc; **165:** Connecticut Historical Society; **166-167:** Corel; **168-169:** PhotoDisc; **170:** Corel; **171:** Corel; **171:** Corel; **172-173:** Corel; **174:** Corel; **175:** Corel; **176:** PhotoDisc; **177:** © Roger Ressmeyer/CORBIS; **178:** NASA; **179:** MIT Lincoln Laboratory; **180-181:** BSS; **182a:** University of Hawaii; **182b:** NASA; **184:** NASA; **186-187:** PhotoDisc; **188:** PhotoDisc; **189:** NASA; **190-191:** Corel; **192:** Corel; **192-193:** NASA; **194-195:** PhotoDisc; **196:** PhotoDisc; **199:** NASA; **200-201:** PhotoDisc; **202:** NASA; **205:** PhotoDisc; **206:** PhotoDisc; **208:** NASA/MSFC; **212:** PhotoDisc; **214:** NASA

Cover: All images PhotoDisc

Illustrations: Thomas Gagliano, Technical Illustration; Page 10 map, Dan Stuckenscheider

*sci*LINKS® is a registered trademark of the National Science Teachers Association. The *sci*LINKS® service includes copyrighted materials and is owned and provided by the National Science Teachers Association.
All Rights Reserved.

Copyright © 2003 by Great Source Education Group, Inc. All rights reserved.

Permission to reproduce pages 225–231 of this book is granted to the users of *Earth Science Daybook*. No other part of this work may be reproduced or transmitted in any form or by any means electronic or mechanical, including photocopying and recording, or by any information storage retrieval system without the prior written permission of Great Source Education Group, Inc., unless such copying is expressly permitted by federal copyright law. Address inquiries to Permissions, Great Source Education Group, Inc., 181 Ballardvale Street, Wilmington, MA 01887.

Great Source®, *Write Source*®, and *ScienceSaurus*® are registered trademarks of Houghton Mifflin Company.

All registered trademarks are shown strictly for illustrative purposes and are the property of their respective owners.

Printed in the United States of America.
International Standard Book Number: 0-669-49251-5

1 2 3 4 5 6 7 8 9 10 —DBH— 10 09 08 07 06 05 04 03

Why NSTA Worked On These Books

Scientists write letters, argue incessantly, make mistakes, suffer from jealousy, exhibit both vanity and generosity—all while striving in diverse ways to enlarge human understanding. Among the most important skills they possess is the ability to communicate ideas, defend them against critics, and modify their own positions in the face of contravening evidence. Every literate person—every scientifically literate person—must do this.

The National Science Teachers Association (NSTA) is pleased to participate in the publication of these Science Daybooks because they bring together science, reading, and writing. Most important: The primary sources in the Daybooks—first-hand accounts that scientists and researchers use to communicate their ideas—firmly place science in the context of human endeavor.

What NSTA Did

From the outset, NSTA staff and members collaborated with Great Source editors and developers to ensure that the Daybooks were created from a teacher's perspective and were based on the National Science Education Standards. We helped link important topic areas with primary sources. We suggested activity ideas at the pilot stage and reviewed those submitted by authors during development. We reviewed the teaching plans that accompany student lessons and supported these plans with tips, warnings about misconceptions, and brief activities taken from articles in *Science Scope*—NSTA's middle school peer-reviewed journal. NSTA also provides the *sci*LINKS® extensions that appear throughout the book, directing readers to Web sites that offer further information, additional lessons, and activities.

What Is NSTA

NSTA is the largest organization in the world committed to promoting excellence and innovation in science teaching and learning for all. To address subjects of critical interest to science educators, the NSTA Press publishes projects of significant relevance and value to teachers of science—books on best teaching practices, books that explain and tie in with the National Science Education Standards, books that apply the latest science education research, and classroom activity books. NSTA also considers novel treatments of core science content and is especially eager to publish works that link science to other key curriculum areas such as mathematics and language arts. Hence this project.

Let Us Hear From You

We hope teachers and students benefit from this innovative approach to learning science. Tell us what you think of this joint effort by e-mailing daybooks@nsta.org. For more information about NSTA, please visit our Web site at www.nsta.org.

Planning Guide — 5
Scope and Sequence — 6

UNIT 1 Earth's Surface — 8

Chapter 1
WHAT EARTH LOOKS LIKE

Opener — 10A

1. **Paradise Island!** *Topographic maps can be used to describe Earth's surface.* — 10
2. **The View From There** *Pictures from space help us map Earth.* — 12
3. **Viewing Earth With Two "Eyes"** *New technologies can lead to maps that reveal new kinds of information about Earth.* — 16

Chapter 2
ROCK ON!

Opener — 20A

4. **Rock Clocks** *Scientists' understanding of the rock cycle helps them investigate the age of planet Earth.* — 20
5. **Crystal Conclusions** *Experimenting can lead to exciting new evidence when a scientist has the right "attitude."* — 24
6. **Pebble Poetry** *The physical properties of a pebble can be used to write a poem.* — 28

Chapter 3
ENERGY RESOURCES

Opener — 30A

7. **Digging Up Energy** *Coal and other fossil fuels are nonrenewable energy resources.* — 30
8. **The Heat Is On** *Geothermal energy is a renewable energy source.* — 34
9. **Energy Choices** *Each energy source has its advantages and disadvantages.* — 38

Chapter 4
FOSSIL HUNTERS

Opener — 40A

10. **She Sells Seashells** *A successful fossil hunter has to be in the right place at the right time.* — 40
11. **Markers of Time** *A fossil hunter who thinks scientifically about Earth's past is more than collector.* — 44
12. **Against All Odds** *Amateur fossil hunters can make important scientific contributions.* — 48

UNIT 2 Dynamic Earth 50

Chapter 5 — CONSERVING SOIL
Opener — 52A

13 **Blown Away** Wind, drought, and people's actions can cause soil erosion. — 52

14 **Dust in the Wind** The Dust Bowl of the 1930s was a natural disaster that affected farmers and farmland. — 56

15 **Saving the Land** Soil conservation helps prevent soil erosion. — 60

Chapter 6 — CHANGING SHORELINES
Opener — 62A

16 **Shifting Sands** Shorelines and beaches are constantly changing. — 62

17 **Saving a Lighthouse** Structures built along shorelines are at risk of destruction. — 66

18 **Investigating Erosion** Scientists gather data to inform the public about the dangers of building on coastlines. — 70

Chapter 7 — THE PUZZLE OF EARTH'S CRUST
Opener — 72A

19 **Fitting the Continents Together** Wegener's theory of continental drift was not accepted by other scientists at first. — 72

20 **Explaining How Continents Move** New information convinced scientists that continents could move. — 76

21 **Using New Technology** The newest technologies help confirm the theories of Wegener and Hess. — 80

Chapter 8 — VOLCANOES
Opener — 82A

22 **The Pressure Builds** Volcanoes erupt when gases and magma trapped below Earth's surface are released. — 82

23 **Rivers of Fire** A lava flow and a pyroclastic flow have different properties. — 86

24 **Can Eruptions Be Predicted?** Scientists are improving their methods of predicting volcanic eruptions. — 88

UNIT 3 Water on Earth 92

Chapter 9	Opener	94A
THE WATER CYCLE	**25 Round and Round It Goes** *You can trace water's movement from any point in the water cycle to any other point.*	94
	26 Fog Catchers *Fresh water can be collected from fog.*	96
	27 To Fog or Not to Fog *Fog collection does not work everywhere.*	100

Chapter 10	Opener	104A
BOUNTIFUL RIVER	**28 Coming Together** *A watershed is an area of land that catches precipitation and channels it into a river, lake, or marsh.*	104
	29 Flooding a River *Some dams are built across rivers to create water reservoirs for distant communities.*	106
	30 Restoring a River *Sometimes a compromise can resolve conflicting needs for water.*	110

Chapter 11	Opener	114A
WATER WATCH	**31 Freshwater Worries** *People around the world have problems with their supply of fresh water.*	114
	32 Hold the Salt *Desalination can be used to obtain fresh water from salt water.*	118
	33 One Cool Idea *Towing icebergs is an unusual solution to water shortages.*	122

Chapter 12	Opener	124A
CURRENT EVENTS	**34 Ocean Rivers** *Surface ocean currents flow in predictable paths.*	124
	35 Beachcomber Scientist *Science ideas and tools sometimes come from unexpected places.*	128
	36 Electricity from the Sea *Ocean currents can be harnessed to generate electricity.*	130

UNIT 4 Weather and Climate   134

Chapter 13 — **Opener** — 136A

THE ATMOSPHERE

37 **Feeling the Pressure?** *A barometer measures the pressure of air on objects.* — 136

38 **Up, Up, and Away** *Air pressure and temperature decrease as altitude increases.* — 138

39 **Thar She Blows!** *Differences in air pressure produce winds.* — 142

Chapter 14 — **Opener** — 146A

STORMY WEATHER

40 **Predicting a Storm** *Meteorologists use many forms of data to forecast weather.* — 146

41 **A Storm Like No Other** *When weather systems collide, unusually powerful storms can form.* — 150

42 **At Sea in a Storm** *Many factors influence how people react to dangerous weather.* — 154

Chapter 15 — **Opener** — 156A

WEIRD WEATHER

43 **Down Tornado Alley** *Most tornadoes occur in a specific region of the United States.* — 156

44 **Hail Hail!** *Hailstorms can occur anywhere but pose the greatest risk in the Plains states.* — 160

45 **Digging Out** *Snowstorms were more difficult to predict and deal with in the past than they are today.* — 164

Chapter 16 — **Opener** — 166A

CLIMATE CHANGE

46 **Ancient Climates** *Tree rings can provide information about climate conditions in Earth's past.* — 166

47 **On Thin Ice** *The Inuit people are experiencing the effects of climate change.* — 170

48 **Meltdown?** *Scientists disagree about whether global warming is affecting Arctic ice.* — 172

3

UNIT 5 Astronomy 176

Chapter 17 — **Opener** — 178A
ROCKS AND ICE IN ORBIT

49 **Close Encounters** Scientists try to predict the orbits of asteroids that come close to Earth. — 178

50 **Off Track** Sometimes a comet changes course as it orbits the sun. — 182

51 **Capturing Comet Dust** Studying comet dust can help us understand the history of our solar system. — 184

Chapter 18 — **Opener** — 188A
SOLAR SYSTEM NEWS

52 **Planet Status** Astronomers sometimes disagree about how to classify some objects in space. — 188

53 **Martian Water** Water may have once flowed freely on Mars. — 192

54 **Moon Make-Up** The densities of moons in our solar system can be used to determine the percentages of rock and ice that make them up. — 196

Chapter 19 — **Opener** — 198A
PICTURING THE UNIVERSE

55 **A Star's Life** The brightness and temperature of distant stars provide clues about their life cycles. — 198

56 **Planet Search** Astronomers have found many planets orbiting stars beyond our solar system. — 202

57 **Images From Energy** Radio waves from space can be converted into visual images. — 206

Chapter 20 — **Opener** — 208A
EXPLORING SPACE

58 **Sailing Through Space** Scientists are investigating whether sunlight could be used to push a space probe beyond our solar system. — 208

59 **In Freefall** Astronauts train for space travel by flying in freefalling airplanes. — 212

60 **Why Explore Space?** Some people think space exploration is a waste of time and money; others disagree. — 214

Glossary — 218
Rubric — 225
Copymasters — 226
Index — 232
Credits — 236

How to Use This Book

The Great Source *Life Science, Earth Science, and Physical Science Daybooks* are designed to be flexible resources for you to use with your students. Here are a few suggestions for incorporating them into your science curriculum.

Use the *Science Daybooks* as the core of your science program. Throughout the *Science Daybooks,* the lessons reference *ScienceSaurus®*, a middle school science handbook, and *sciLINKS®*, to provide a complete foundation for a middle school science curriculum. *ScienceSaurus* is a comprehensive reference aligned with the *National Science Education Standards* (grades 5–8), and models scientific investigation and inquiry. The *sciLINKS* Web site provides students with a logical next step to the process of finding out more. With the *Science Daybooks,* we initiate this process by providing students with snippets of readings from "real" science materials. These engage them in the discovery process, and help them apply what they've learned in extended activities. These readings were carefully selected to provide meaningful investigations into every area described by the *National Science Education Standards*. However, unlike a textbook approach that requires students to read about an array of science topics, the *Science Daybooks* allow the students to "get specific" and do the science.

For example, when we study soil erosion, students gain a basic understanding of factors that affect erosion by referencing topics 188, 191, and 192 in *ScienceSaurus*. Then, in one of 12 *Earth Science Daybook* lessons from the Dynamic Earth Unit, students focus on the history of farming practices in the Great Plains that led to the Dust Bowl. They read excerpts from Willa Cather's *O Pioneers!* and John Steinbeck's *The Grapes of Wrath* to learn about farming on the Great Plains before and after the Dust Bowl. They interpret a map and draw conclusions. Students go to the *sciLINKS®* Web site and enter the keyword "Wind Erosion" and connect to a vast number of appropriate Web sources providing additional research information, case studies, and activities. And, they can do additional research and design their own investigations using the models and guidelines found in the *ScienceSaurus* (topics 001–019 and 410–426) and experience the process of "full inquiry," as outlined in the *National Science Education Standards*.

Supplement your existing science program. The units and topics in the *Science Daybooks* match up with those in most current textbooks. Pick and choose units or chapters as you teach those topics during the year.

Extend science after school or during the summer. It can be difficult to do everything you would like in science class. You may want to extend students' science time to after school. The wealth of extended activities in the *Science Daybooks* allows students (as individuals and/or small groups) to pursue different investigations throughout the year and report their findings to the class. Many of the activities were culled from the best of NSTA's *ScienceScope,* a professional journal for middle school science teachers.

Prepare students for high-stakes assessments with opportunities to write and communicate about science. Most often, state assessments require students to read, comprehend, and write about both fiction and nonfiction passages. The *Science Daybooks* promote critical reading, writing, and thinking about science.

Weave into an integrated science curriculum. Since the *Science Daybooks* are small, inexpensive, and portable, a set of three books can be purchased for the students in the first year of a three-year integrated science curriculum. Determine the units to teach in each of the three years, and pass the books along to the next-level teacher at the end of the year.

There are many ways to make good use of the *Science Daybooks* in your classroom. In whatever way you choose to use them, be assured that these materials provide a foundation for a complete and effective curriculum for the middle school grades.

Earth Science Scope and Sequence

Correlation with National Science Education Standards, Grades 5–8

	Unit 1				Unit 2		
CHAPTER ▶	Ch. 1	Ch. 2	Ch. 3	Ch. 4	Ch. 5	Ch. 6	Ch. 7
LESSON ▶	1 2 3	4 5 6	7 8 9	10 11 12	13 14 15	16 17 18	19 20 21

Unifying Concepts and Processes

	1	2	3	4	5	6	7	8	9	10	11	12	13	14	15	16	17	18	19	20	21
Systems, order, and organization															•				•	•	
Evidence, models, and explanation	•	•	•	•	•	•				•	•	•							•	•	•
Change, constancy, and measurement								•	•				•	•	•	•	•	•			•
Evolution and equilibrium										•	•	•				•					
Form and function	•																				

Science as Inquiry

Abilities necessary to do scientific inquiry						•				•											
Understanding about scientific inquiry		•	•		•							•						•	•	•	•

Physical Science

Properties and changes of properties in matter																					
Motion and forces																•	•				
Transfer of energy									•												

Life Science

Regulation and behavior																					

Earth and Space Science

Structure of the earth system	•	•	•	•	•	•	•	•	•				•	•	•	•	•	•	•	•	•
Earth's history				•	•	•				•	•	•							•	•	•
Earth in the solar system		•	•																		•

Science and Technology

Abilities of technological design																					•
Understanding about science and technology		•	•							•	•									•	•

Science in Personal and Social Perspectives

Personal health																					
Populations, resources, and environments							•	•	•				•	•		•					
Natural hazards																•	•	•		•	
Risks and benefits																					
Science and technology in society											•					•	•	•			•

History and Nature of Science

Science as a human endeavor					•					•	•	•							•	•	
Nature of science					•					•	•	•									
History of science										•	•				•				•	•	

	UNIT 3					UNIT 4				UNIT 5			
Ch. 8	Ch. 9	Ch. 10	Ch. 11	Ch. 12	Ch. 13	Ch. 14	Ch. 15	Ch. 16	Ch. 17	Ch. 18	Ch. 19	Ch. 20

Chapters span pages 22–60.

Unifying Concepts and Processes

Science as Inquiry

Physical Science

Life Science

Earth and Space Science

Science and Technology

Science in Personal and Social Perspectives

History and Nature of Science

UNIT 1 Earth's Surface

About the Photo
The rock formations in Utah's Bryce Canyon fascinate people with their extraordinary shapes. Students may wonder how such unusual shapes could have been formed. Explain that over millions of years, wind and ancient rivers eroded the land, removing softer rock layers and sculpting others into these spectacular formations, called "hoodoos."

About the Charts
A major goal of the *Science Daybooks* is to promote reading, writing, and critical thinking skills in the context of science. The charts below describe the types of reading selections included in this unit and identify the skills and strategies used in each lesson.

UNIT 1 Earth's Surface

Tiny things can lead to huge discoveries.
Who knew that you could learn about the extinction of dinosaurs by looking at microscopic crystals? Streaky layers in crystals are evidence of a major meteorite impact on Earth millions of years ago. Dust in the air may have blocked sunlight, killing plants. Plant-eating dinosaurs would have starved first, and then meat-eating dinosaurs.

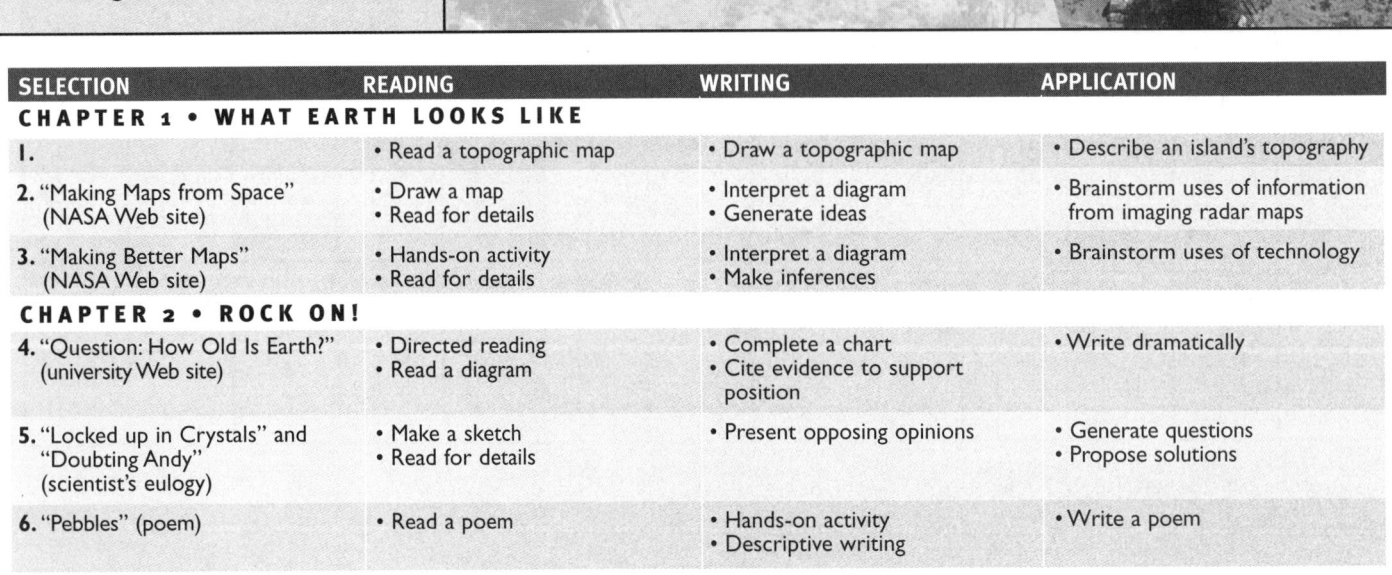

In this unit you'll learn about Earth's surface and the stories it tells. Space-age technology is providing new ways to map the surface. By examining rocks, scientists can make inferences about the age and history of our planet. You'll explore some sources of energy that are hidden deep below the surface. And you'll find out how fossils—the remains and traces of ancient organisms—help tell Earth's stories.

SELECTION	READING	WRITING	APPLICATION
CHAPTER 1 • WHAT EARTH LOOKS LIKE			
1.	• Read a topographic map	• Draw a topographic map	• Describe an island's topography
2. "Making Maps from Space" (NASA Web site)	• Draw a map • Read for details	• Interpret a diagram • Generate ideas	• Brainstorm uses of information from imaging radar maps
3. "Making Better Maps" (NASA Web site)	• Hands-on activity • Read for details	• Interpret a diagram • Make inferences	• Brainstorm uses of technology
CHAPTER 2 • ROCK ON!			
4. "Question: How Old Is Earth?" (university Web site)	• Directed reading • Read a diagram	• Complete a chart • Cite evidence to support position	• Write dramatically
5. "Locked up in Crystals" and "Doubting Andy" (scientist's eulogy)	• Make a sketch • Read for details	• Present opposing opinions	• Generate questions • Propose solutions
6. "Pebbles" (poem)	• Read a poem	• Hands-on activity • Descriptive writing	• Write a poem

THE CHAPTERS IN THIS UNIT ARE...

CHAPTER 1:
What Earth Looks Like
Find out: How can we show lumpy, bumpy Earth on a flat map?

CHAPTER 2:
Rock On!
Find out: What do geologists have in common with detectives?

CHAPTER 3:
Energy Resources
Find out: How can hot magma deep below Earth's surface be used to generate electricity?

CHAPTER 4:
Fossil Hunters
Find out: How did a poor, self-educated woman living in the 1800s help scientists learn about Earth's history?

Did You Know?
Certain geologists, called "forensic geologists," use their knowledge of Earth's surface to help solve crimes. Mud or bits of rock stuck in a tire or on the bottom of someone's shoe can show that the person was at the scene of a crime. In some cases, suspects can be identified with no other clues.

Answers to *Find Out* Questions

CHAPTER 1
The height of Earth's land features can be shown on a topographic map. (p. 10)

CHAPTER 2
Like detectives looking for clues at a crime scene, geologists look for clues in rocks as evidence of Earth's history. (pp. 20–21, 23, 25–27)

CHAPTER 3
Water heated by the magma becomes extremely hot or turns to steam. The hot water or steam can be used to power a generator that produces electricity. (p. 35)

CHAPTER 4
She discovered, examined, and preserved fossils and shared her work with other scientists. (pp. 41, 45)

SCILINKS
THE WORLD'S A CLICK AWAY

www.scilinks.org
Keyword: Gender Equity
Code: GSSD01

SELECTION	READING	WRITING	APPLICATION
CHAPTER 3 • ENERGY RESOURCES			
7. "Into the Coal Mine" (autobiographical children's book)	• Make a sketch • Read a table	• Interpret a map • Explain your answer	• Create a journal entry
8. "Energy From the Earth" (California Energy Commission Web site)	• Use prior knowledge • Read for details	• Interpret a map • Make inferences	• Brainstorm uses for geothermal energy
9.	• Make a concept map • Read a table	• Compare and contrast	• Generate questions for an interview
CHAPTER 4 • FOSSIL HUNTERS			
10. "A Family Business" (museum Web site)	• Brainstorm ideas • Identify descriptive words	• Make inferences • Classify characteristics	• Conduct an interview • Write a report
11. "An Extraordinary Young Woman" (museum Web site)	• Use prior knowledge • Directed reading	• Make inferences • State an opinion	• Complete a graphic organizer
12. "Dinosaur Dig" (cable TV program)	• Read for understanding	• Make inferences	• Write a brochure

UNIT 1 EARTH'S SURFACE   9

CHAPTER 1
Overview

What Earth Looks Like

LESSON 1
Paradise Island!
Point of Lesson: *Topographic maps can be used to describe Earth's surface.*

This lesson describes how topographic maps are constructed using contour lines to indicate elevation. Students then construct their own topographic maps of an imaginary island.

Materials
Activity (p.11), for each student:
- drawing paper
- colored pencils
- clay (optional)

Enrichment (p. 11), for the class:
- topographic maps of your area

LESSON 2
The View From There
Point of Lesson: *Pictures from space help us map Earth.*

This lesson describes a technology called imaging radar, which is deployed on the Space Shuttle. Imaging radar allows accurate topographic maps of Earth's surface to be made much more quickly than through traditional methods. In the lesson, students interpret diagrams that explain how imaging radar works, then consider ways in which imaging radar maps are helpful to different people.

Materials
Before You Read (p. 12), for each student:
- ruler

Enrichment (p. 13), to make one model:
- clay
- shoebox
- markers, 10–12 colors
- 30-cm wooden dowel
- metric ruler

LESSON 3
Viewing Earth With Two "Eyes"
Point of Lesson: *New technologies can lead to maps that reveal new kinds of information about Earth.*

The reading in this lesson describes how scientists have combined imaging radar with another technology called interferometry to make three-dimensional images of Earth's surface. In the lesson, students relate their own binocular vision to the dual-antenna technique used in interferometry and generate ideas about how the images created using this technique can be used.

Materials
Science Scope Activity (p. 17), for the class:
- world map with longitude and latitude lines
- articles about earth science events (collected by students)

Science Scope Activity
Mapping Earth Events

NSTA has chosen a Science Scope *activity related to the content in this chapter. You'll find the activity in Lesson 3, page 17.*

In this activity, students gather information about current geological, environmental, and meteorological events occurring worldwide and find the locations of these events on a world map. Students also discuss how the events affect people in the immediate area, the region, and distant locations. In this way, students are encouraged to regard our planet as a global community.

(continued on page 17)

Background Information

Lesson 3

Interferometry improves the resolution of an image—that is, it makes it possible to distinguish clearly between land features that are close together. The distance between the two points where data are collected is called the baseline. The longer the baseline, the better the resolution of the image. The baseline of the Shuttle Radar Topography mission setup is 60 meters—the distance between the two antennas that receive the radar signals.

Interferometry is used in optical and radio astronomy as well as in mapmaking. Most major optical telescopes built in the past 20 years have taken advantage of interferometry to improve resolution. Perhaps the best-known example is the twin Keck telescopes on top of Mauna Loa in Hawaii.

UNIT 1 Earth's Surface

CHAPTER 1 / LESSON 1

Point of Lesson
Topographic maps can be used to describe Earth's surface.

Focus
▶ Structure of the earth system

Skills and Strategies
▶ Measuring
▶ Using space/time relationships
▶ Making and using models
▶ Interpreting data

Advance Preparation

Vocabulary
Make sure students understand these terms. Definitions can be found in the glossary at the end of the student book.
▶ map
▶ map scale

Materials
Gather the materials needed for *Activity* (p. 11) and *Enrichment* (p. 11).

CHAPTER 1 / LESSON 1
What Earth Looks Like

Paradise Island!

How can you show the height of land features on a map?

A topographic map shows the elevations of surface features such as mountains and valleys. The elevation of a feature is its height above or below sea level. Topographic maps also include other natural features such as marshes, forests, and rivers. Structures such as roads, bridges, and buildings are also shown.

▶ Explore

WHAT ARE CONTOUR LINES?
Topographic maps use contour lines to show the elevations of land features. A contour line connects points at the same elevation. All the lines have the same difference in elevation. That difference is called the *contour interval*.

Suppose you wanted to draw a topographic map of a mountain. First, you'd decide on a contour interval. Next you would measure to find points all around the mountain at the elevation of each contour interval. Then you'd draw a bird's-eye view of the mountain. Using your measurements, you'd draw one contour line to connect all the points at the elevation of one contour interval. Then you'd draw another contour line to connect all the points at the elevation of the next contour interval. You'd continue drawing contour lines like this until you had mapped the entire mountain.

▶ What is the contour interval of the topographic map shown above?
   20 meters

In some places on this map, the contour lines are closer together. In other places, the lines are farther apart.

▶ What do you think a mountain looks like where the contour lines are closer together?
   The slope of the mountain is steep.

▶ What do you think a mountain looks like where the contour lines are farther apart?
   The slope is more gentle.

FIND OUT MORE
SCIENCESAURUS
Showing Earth on Maps	166
Map Basics	167
Topographic Maps	172
Contour Lines	173
Topographic Map Symbols	174

TEACHING PLAN pp. 10–11

INTRODUCING THE LESSON
This lesson describes how topographic maps are constructed, then gives students an opportunity to create their own topographic map. Students may believe that maps are useful only for transportation purposes. To explain the broad range of uses of maps, bring in examples of different sorts: sailing maps, subway maps, or prospecting maps. Let students examine the different ways information is shown. Ask: *How could you make a flat map that shows elevation and the shape of landforms?* (Students might suggest that a map could use symbols.)

▶ Explore

WHAT ARE CONTOUR LINES? Explain that contour lines are like horizontal slices through Earth's surface. A mapmaker selects a contour interval suited to the terrain and the scale of the map. Discuss why the perspective of a topographic map is called a bird's-eye view. (It is made from above looking down.) Ask: *If the contour interval for a map is 20 meters and the altitude of the highest point of land is 100 meters, what contour lines would be drawn?* (20, 40, 60, 80, and 100)

Discuss how features in the terrain can be imagined from the map's contour lines. Using the board, explain to students how connecting all the points at one elevation would form a closed loop indicating the top of a mountain or hill. Ask students to look at the graphic and determine what the spacing between contour lines represents. (Closely spaced lines mean the slope is steep. Widely spaced lines mean the slope is gradual.)

Activity

DRAW A MAP

What's your idea of the perfect island? Is it big or small? Does it have steep hills or flat beaches? Draw a topographic map of your island.

What You Need:
- drawing paper
- colored pencils

What to Do:
1. Sketch an outline of your island. Color the area around the island blue (for water).
2. Decide on a contour interval. If your island has steep hills, use a larger contour interval, such as 3 meters. If your island is not steep, use a smaller contour interval, such as 1 meter. Write the contour interval below your map.
3. Add contour lines to show elevations.
4. Add symbols to your map to show the location of each of the following:

map scale: ___cm = ___m	stream
North arrow	house
woods (shade in green)	unpaved road
pond	sandy area

   Think about where these features would belong in relation to the elevation of your land. (For example, streams would flow downhill, not sideways along ridges.)
5. Give your island a name.

What Do You Think?
▶ If you were going for a hike, why would it be helpful to have a map with contour lines?

The lines show how steep or level the land is.

▶ Trade maps with a classmate. Try to figure out what your classmate's island would look like. On a separate sheet of paper, describe your classmate's island.

Answers will vary with students' maps.

More Resources
The following resources are also available from Great Source.

SCIENCESAURUS
Topographic Maps   172
Contour Lines   173
Topographic Map Symbols   174

READER'S HANDBOOK
Elements of Graphics: Map 555

Enrichment
Time: 20 minutes
Materials: topographic maps of your area

Display some topographic maps of your area. Have students locate places they are familiar with by focusing on roads and other surface features that can be easily identified from above. Have them use the contour lines to describe the terrain.

Assessment
Skill: Making and using models

Use the following questions to assess each student's progress:

How is elevation shown on topographic maps? (Contour lines show elevation.) *How are water, vegetation, roads, and buildings shown?* (Symbols are used for different features: blue for water, green for vegetation, black for buildings, and another color for roads.)

Activity

Time: 45 minutes
Materials: drawing paper, colored pencils, clay (optional)

▶ Have students work alone or with a partner to draw a topographic map.
▶ Instead of having students imagine an island, you could have them make a small model out of clay and map the model.
▶ Ask: *If your island has high mountains and hills, should you use a large or small interval?* (large) *If your island is fairly flat, should you use a large or small interval?* (small)
▶ Remind students to number the contour lines to indicate elevations.
▶ You may need to help some students determine a map scale. First, ask students to write down the dimensions of their islands. Using ratios set up as fractions, they can start by looking at meters and centimeters in a one-to-one ratio and decide from there how many meters one centimeter represents. Students may want to convert centimeters to kilometers.

CHECK UNDERSTANDING
Skill: Interpreting scientific illustrations

Ask students: *How can you determine the shape of landforms from a topographic map?* (Figure out the contour interval, then see how the contour lines are spaced and shaped.)

CHAPTER 1 / LESSON 1   11

UNIT 1 Earth's Surface

CHAPTER 1 / LESSON 2

Point of Lesson
Pictures from space help us map Earth.

Focus
- Earth in the solar system
- Understanding about science and technology

Skills and Strategies
- Using space/time relationships
- Organizing information
- Interpreting scientific illustrations
- Making and using models
- Evaluating source material
- Generating ideas

Advance Preparation

Vocabulary
Make sure students understand these terms. Definitions can be found in the glossary at the end of the student book.

- glacier
- lava
- map
- radar
- topographic map
- volcano

Materials
Gather the materials needed for *Before You Read* (p. 12) and *Enrichment* (p. 13).

TEACHING PLAN pp. 12–13

INTRODUCING THE LESSON
This lesson focuses on how NASA scientists used the Space Shuttle to produce accurate images of Earth's surface and even more detailed topographic maps.

Ask students to describe what they know about the various uses of the Space Shuttle. Some students may not understand that traveling through space is not just exciting but useful; missions often collect information that is used by scientists.

CHAPTER 1 / LESSON 2

What Earth Looks Like

THE VIEW FROM THERE

Where can we get a bird's-eye view of our entire planet? From space!

The best way to make a map of an area is to have a bird's-eye view of it. Mapmakers and NASA space engineers have teamed up to make new topographic maps of Earth's surface.

People have drawn topographic maps for a long time. In 1879 U.S. Geologic Survey (USGS) mapmakers traveled on foot with pack mules to collect the data needed to draw maps. Today newer technologies are used to produce maps. Over the years, USGS has produced very detailed topographic maps of the entire United States. But even in the year 2000, such maps did not exist for most of the rest of the world. The solution? Use Space Shuttle data to map the rest of the world.

▲ Space Shuttle *Endeavour*

▶ Before You Read

DRAW A MAP Use your memory to create a bird's-eye view of your neighborhood, school grounds, or another area you know well. Show the features and structures that would be seen from above. Use shading or patterns to show different kinds of surfaces, such as grass, trees, roofs, and roads.

Drawings will vary. An example is shown.

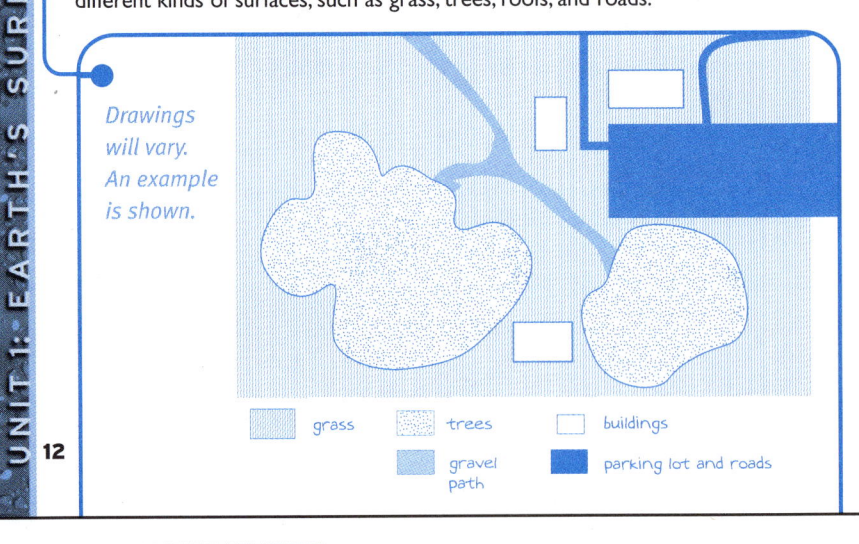

Key: grass, trees, buildings, gravel path, parking lot and roads

▶ Before You Read

Materials: ruler

DRAW A MAP Making a small map of a familiar area will enable students to focus on the various types of surfaces that might be represented on a map. Encourage them to choose an area that includes a variety of surfaces. Remind them to include a key that identifies the different types of surfaces coded on the map.

> **Read**

Making Maps From Space

Here's how the team collected the data they needed to show the surface details of nearly every place on Earth.

The National Imagery and Mapping Agency of the U.S. Department of Defense, along with NASA,...are making the most detailed and accurate topographic map ever of almost the whole world. And they... gathered all the information for it in only 10 days!

The Shuttle Radar Topography Mission flew on the Space Shuttle Endeavour in February 2000. It used a technology called imaging radar. Imaging radar bounces a radar signal off the ground, then measures how long the signal takes to come back and how strong it is. From this information, we can make very accurate pictures of the surface, its bumps (like mountains, hills, and valleys), [and] its textures (like forests, lakes, and cities).... And imaging radar can see all this day or night, cloudy or clear.

Telescopes use [visible] light. Imaging radar uses a different kind of light, at a much longer, lazier wavelength that our eyes do not see. Radar can penetrate clouds. It passes right through them.

NASA: National Aeronautics and Space Administration, the U.S. agency in charge of spacecraft
texture: appearance of the surface—for example, smooth or bumpy
wavelength: the length of a wave from one high point to the next high point; different forms of light have different wavelengths
penetrate: go through

From: "Building a 3-D Map of Earth From Space!." *The Space Place.* California Institute of Technology/NASA. (spaceplace.jpl.nasa.gov/srtmmak2.htm)

▲ View of the Great Lakes from the Space Shuttle

NOTEZONE
Underline the words that describe the advantages of imaging radar over visible light telescopes.

FIND OUT MORE
SCIENCESAURUS
Showing Earth on Maps 166
Topographic Maps 172
Contour Lines 173
Topographic Map Symbols 174

SCiLINKS
THE WORLD'S A CLICK AWAY
www.scilinks.org
Keyword: Map Making
Code: GSED01

13

Enrichment

Time: 20 minutes for teacher preparation; 35–40 minutes for student activity
Materials: clay; shoebox; markers, 10–12 colors; 30-cm wooden dowel; metric ruler

Use this activity to model how radar imaging technology makes a picture of a hidden surface.

1. Have one student build a clay terrain model in a shoebox. Do not show the surface to anyone else.
2. Before the next class period, trace the top of the box on a piece of paper. Use a ruler to make a grid of squares over the tracing. Label the grid with letters across the top and numbers down the left side, as shown below. Tape the grid over the box. Make a similar grid on another sheet of paper to use as a map.

	A	B	C	D	E
1					
2					
3					
4					
5					
6					
7					
8					
9					
10					
11					
12					
13					
14					

3. Mark the dowel with 10–12 colored bands, each 1 cm wide, to use as a probe. Use a pencil to poke a hole in each square of the grid.

(continued on page 15)

> **Read**

Ask: *How is a map that is produced by imaging radar similar to a topographic map?* (Both maps show land features from a bird's-eye view.) Encourage students to compare this sophisticated mapping technology with their own mapping efforts: *What surface details do both methods include?* (hills, trees, open spaces) *What is different about the way the two maps are made?* (One is made using direct measurements of the land; the other uses bounced signals to determine elevation.)

Encourage students to evaluate the advantages the new technology offers over earlier mapping methods.

CHECK UNDERSTANDING
Skill: Organizing information
Ask students to summarize the advantages of imaging radar over light telescopes. (Imaging radar can be used at night or when it is cloudy.)

CHAPTER 1/ LESSON 2 13

CHAPTER 1 / LESSON 2

More Resources
The following resources are also available from Great Source and NSTA.

ScienceSaurus
Showing Earth on Maps	166
Topographic Maps	172
Contour Lines	173
Topographic Map Symbols	174

Reader's Handbook
Elements of Graphics: Map	555

SCILINKS
THE WORLD'S A CLICK AWAY

www.scilinks.org
Keyword: Map Making
Code: GSED01

Teaching Plan pp. 14–15

▶ Explore

ANALYZING ADVANTAGES Encourage students to review the words they underlined in the NoteZone activity. Ask them to consider how difficult it might be to send survey teams into remote wilderness areas: *What problems might they encounter?* (They would not know the location of fuel or water sources and might encounter physical hazards or hostile people.) Then ask: *How would using imaging radar help avoid these problems?* (Mapmakers on the ground would not be needed if images could be made from space.)

INTERPRETING DIAGRAMS Explain that the information bounced back from Earth is transmitted to a computer, which may enhance the images to reveal hidden details. Encourage students to examine each image and try to determine what happened to the radar signals when they hit the surface.

You might compare the bounced-back signals to echoes. Depending on the time it takes for a sound to return, it is possible to judge distance or the type of surface that a sound is striking.

▶ Explore

ANALYZING ADVANTAGES For many places on Earth, topographic maps are incorrect or do not exist. Some of these places are very hard to get to by land.

▶ **How does using the Space Shuttle to carry mapping equipment help solve this problem?**
The Space Shuttle collects the map data from space, so mapmakers do not have to travel to hard-to-reach locations.

▶ **What makes imaging radar a good way to collect mapping data from space?**
Imaging radar works through clouds and in the dark.

INTERPRETING DIAGRAMS Like visible light hitting a mirror, radar signals move in straight lines. When they hit different Earth surfaces, the signals bounce—or reflect. If the surface is at a right angle to the signals, the signals will bounce back to the radar receiver. Signals that hit a surface at less than or greater than a right angle bounce away at the same angle and do not return to the radar receiver.

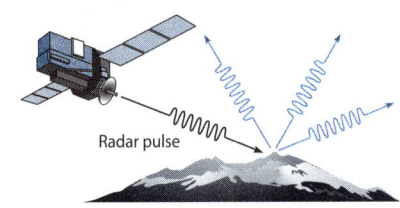

Radar pulse

This is the diagram that the team of mapmakers and space engineers uses to explain how they make topographic images from space.

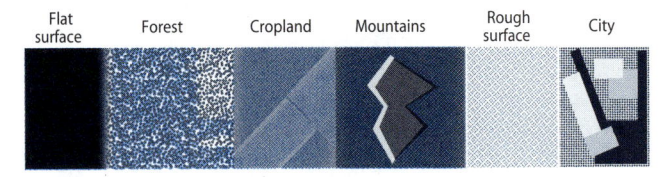

| Flat surface | Forest | Cropland | Mountains | Rough surface | City |

Each radar image shows the pattern that was formed by the radar signals. Dark areas show places that bounced back few signals. Bright areas show places that bounced back many signals.

▶ **Why would the image of a smooth road look dark?**
Most signals would bounce off the road in the same direction, away from the receiver.

▶ **Why would the image of a leafy forest look like a pattern of light and dark spots?**

The leaf surfaces of the trees are all at different angles, so some signals bounce away but others bounce back to the radar receiver.

Look at the radar image of the mountains. One edge of the image is very bright.

▶ **What does this tell you about the surface at that part of the mountain?**

That part of the mountain was at a right angle to the radar signal so most of the signals were reflected back.

▶ Propose Explanations

GENERATING IDEAS With practice, scientists can interpret radar images and tell one kind of land surface from another. For example, imaging radar can show the difference between old lava flows and fresh lava.

▶ **How would this information be useful in describing a volcano?**

The information could be used to show how lava flowed out of the volcano during different eruptions.

Imagine you are a scientist studying Earth's arctic regions. For several months of the year, these areas receive very little sunlight. The radar images show where ice on the ocean is thin and where it is thick.

▶ **How could these images be useful to ship owners?**

The ship owners can use the images to decide if their ships can find a path through the areas of thin ice.

Imaging radar maps can show the boundaries of glaciers. The maps can also detect the thickness of the ice.

▶ **How might this information be useful to scientists studying changes in Earth's climate?**

Scientists could use it to tell if a glacier is growing or shrinking.

A melting glacier might mean Earth's atmosphere is warming.

Enrichment
(continued from page 13)

4. Tell students to insert the probe in the first hole, labeled A1, until it hits the clay surface. The deeper the probe, the lower the surface feature.
5. Note the color on the probe that is even with the grid. Color the A1 square on the map with that color. Have students continue until the entire surface is mapped.

Ask two or three volunteers to draw their versions of the clay terrain's side view on the board before the box is opened for the class.

Assessment
Skill: Interpreting diagrams

Use the following task to assess each student's progress:

Ask students to draw diagrams with lines showing radar signals sent out from the Space Shuttle and other lines showing what happens when the signals strike the following surfaces: a calm sea, city streets and buildings, and an area with thick vegetation. Tell students to add labels to their diagrams to explain why each image looks the way it does. (Student diagrams should show that the sea would reflect most of the signals away; the city would show multiple reflections; and vegetation would scatter the signals.)

▶ Propose Explanations

GENERATING IDEAS Explain that the brightness or dullness of images indicates different densities of material within a radar image—for example, the difference between old and new lava flows or between thin and thick ice.

Ask students: *What concerns boat captains the most when traveling in arctic regions?* (finding shipping routes and avoiding hazards such as icebergs) Then ask students to consider how the thickness and boundaries of glaciers might provide information about climate changes. (If glaciers are becoming thinner and smaller, the climate may be getting warmer.)

UNIT 1 Earth's Surface
CHAPTER 1 / LESSON 3

Point of Lesson
New technologies can lead to maps that reveal new kinds of information about Earth.

Focus
- Earth in the solar system
- Understanding about science and technology

Skills and Strategies
- Using space/time relationships
- Interpreting scientific illustrations
- Making inferences
- Generating ideas
- Creating and using tables

Advance Preparation
Vocabulary
Make sure students understand these terms. Definitions can be found in the glossary at the end of the student book.

- elevation
- topographic map
- map
- volcano
- radar

Materials
Gather the materials needed for *Science Scope Activity* (p. 17) and *Connections* (p. 18).

TEACHING PLAN pp. 16–17

INTRODUCING THE LESSON
This lesson explores how a type of radar-imaging technology called interferometry can be used to make better three-dimensional (3-D) maps of Earth's surface. Ask students to recall from Lesson 2 how radar images are used to create topographic maps of Earth's surface. Then ask them to predict how scientists might use radar technology to produce 3-D images.

CHAPTER 1 / LESSON 3
What Earth Looks Like

Viewing Earth With Two "Eyes"

What does it take to make a map showing the ups and downs of Earth's surface?

Using radar from space allows scientists to "see" and map Earth's surface through clouds and in the dark of night. But it is not so easy to see the elevations of the land on radar images. What scientists needed was a 3-D (three-dimensional) view of surface features such as volcanoes, valleys, and canyons. A 3-D view shows height as well as length and width. To get a 3-D image, you need two different views of the same thing. Your two eyes produce the 3-D images you see. NASA engineers had to come up with a way of collecting and using data from two different viewpoints in order to make a 3-D image.

▲ Interferometry image of Mt. Cotopaxi, an active volcano in Ecuador

▶ Before You Read

TEST YOUR 3-D VISION Hold this book at arm's length. With both eyes open, center your nose over the small photo of Mt. Cotopaxi. Next, close one eye. Hold one arm out straight in front of you. Hold the thumb up so it completely hides the volcano. Now close that eye and open the other one. What do you notice? Why do you think that happens?

▼ Mt. Cotopaxi

My thumb seemed to move to the side, and it didn't completely cover the volcano anymore. My eyes are spaced apart, so each sees the volcano from a different position.

▶ Before You Read

TEST YOUR 3-D VISION If students have trouble with this activity, tell them to pay close attention to where they are focusing their eyes, which should be on the small picture of Mt. Cotopaxi. If they wear glasses, tell them to try the test without them. Ask: *What is the advantage of having two eyes instead of one?* (Each eye sees the same area from a slightly different viewpoint. The two views have much in common, but each eye picks up visual information that the other doesn't.) *Where are the two views from our eyes combined?* (The two views arrive in the brain at the same time. The brain combines them into one image.) *What are the advantages of having two points of view?* (The combined image provides depth perception.)

▶ Read

The NASA team solved the problem of how to get 3-D images of Earth's surface. Here's how they explain it.

Making Better Maps

We have flown imaging radar missions before and made radar images of different parts of the world.... But what was really new and special about the Shuttle Radar Topography Mission is that it combined imaging radar with another wonderful technology called interferometry....

The Shuttle Radar Topography Mission used interferometry by flying two separate radar antennas placed 60 meters apart! The mast that [held] the two radar antennas apart [was] the largest "unfolding" structure to ever fly in space.... When the mast [was] folded up inside the Space Shuttle bay for launch, it [was] only 3 meters long. That's like squashing basketball star Shaquille O'Neal from his normal 7-feet 1-inch down to only about 4 inches tall!

The "images" received by the two antennas [are] very carefully combined to give precise information about the height of the terrain below—in other words, to give a 3-D image! We end up with the best topographical map of the world ever made.

interferometry: using the interaction of waves to measure distances
antenna: a metal device used to send or receive signals
mast: a long pole that holds an object
precise: exact
terrain: ground

From: "Building a 3-D Map of Earth From Space!" *The Space Place*. California Institute of Technology/NASA. (spaceplace.jpl.nasa.gov/srtmmak2.htm)

▲ Space Shuttle Endeavour maps topography of Earth

NOTEZONE
Underline the words that tell how a 3-D image is made.

FIND OUT MORE
SCIENCESAURUS
Showing Earth on Maps 166
Topographic Maps 172
Contour Lines 173
Topographic Map Symbols 174

Science Scope Activity

Mapping Earth Events
Time: ongoing
Materials: world map with longitude and latitude lines, articles about earth science events

Procedure:
1. Review how to use lines of latitude and longitude on a map to pinpoint locations.
2. Read the coordinates for major cities, and have students find them on the map.
3. Ask students to bring in clippings about earth science events taking place around the world, such as droughts, hurricanes, mudslides, deforestation, and tornado sightings.
4. Have students share their clippings and discuss each event. Bring up science concepts involved in the events.
5. Ask students to predict how the event might affect the lives of people living nearby, in neighboring regions, or on the other side of the globe. Encourage them to check their predictions by reading any follow-up articles that are available.
6. Students can use reference sources to find the coordinates of the locations mentioned in the articles. They can then mark those locations on the map with a reference number. Post the article alongside the map.

▶ Read

Encourage students to recall the test they did in Before You Read. Ask them to compare the two views produced by their eyes with the two different antennas receiving signals on the Shuttle. Ask: *How is the test you did similar to the way 3-D images are created with two antennas?* (In both, visual information is collected from two different viewpoints and then combined.)

Tell students that in addition to making 3-D images of Earth, interferometry technology is being used in ground telescopes and in StarLight space telescopes. The Keck telescope in Hawaii uses two 10m mirrors that are spaced 85 meters apart. The StarLight mission spacecraft consists of two telescope mirrors placed about 1 km apart. The mirrors are held in place with laser beams and are both focused at the same star. Astronomers use both the ground telescopes and the StarLight spacecraft to look for planets around other stars.

CHECK UNDERSTANDING
Skill: Communicating
Ask students to describe how the technology of interferometry is used to create 3-D maps of surface features such as volcanoes, valleys, and canyons. (Two separate radar antennas on the Space Shuttle are positioned about 60 meters apart. The images received by the antennas are combined to produce a 3-D image.)

CHAPTER 1 / LESSON 3

CHAPTER 1 / LESSON 3

More Resources
The following resource is also available from Great Source.

ScienceSaurus
Showing Earth on Maps	166
Topographic Maps	172
Contour Lines	173
Topographic Map Symbols	174

Connections
Time: 30 minutes
Materials: map of Ecuador

GEOGRAPHY/SOCIAL STUDIES
Have students find Mt. Cotopaxi on a map of Ecuador. Tell students that it is the tallest active volcano in the world. To learn about the history of Mt. Cotopaxi's eruptions, students can access the following Web site: kilburn.keene.edu/Courses/GEOL498/cotopaxi/Table1.html

Have students create a brief time line showing the history of the major eruptions, starting with its first recorded eruption in 1532. Point out that most of Mt. Cotopaxi's violent eruptions occurred in the 18th century. Ask students how the eruptions might have affected the surrounding areas. (Towns may have been destroyed, people and animals may have been injured or killed, and plant life may have been destroyed.)

TEACHING PLAN pp. 18–19

▶ **Explore**

UNDERSTANDING SPACE AND TIME Here's a diagram that the NASA team uses to show how radar signals are transmitted and received aboard the Space Shuttle.

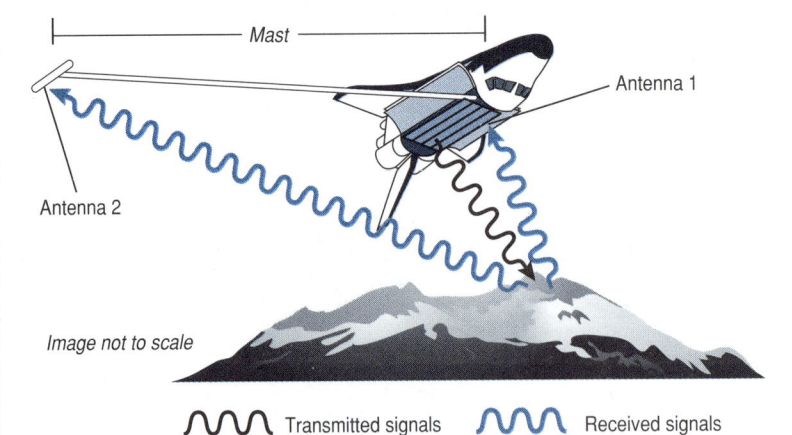

Image not to scale

〰️ Transmitted signals   〰️ Received signals

▶ From what are radar signals transmitted toward Earth's surface?
   from a transmitter on the Space Shuttle

▶ In what two places are the reflected radar signals received?
   The signals are received on the Shuttle and at the end of the mast.

MAKE INFERENCES
▶ Based on what you see in the diagram, does the signal arrive at each antenna at the same time? If not, which antenna receives the signal first?
   The signal is received at the Shuttle before it is received at the end of the mast.

▶ How will the data from the two antennas be used to determine land height? (Hint: Think about what happened when you looked at the volcano picture with one eye at a time.)
   The data of the signals, with the time difference, will be used to create one 3-D image.

18

▶ **Explore**

UNDERSTANDING SPACE AND TIME
Emphasize that the diagram in this section is not drawn to scale. The spacecraft is shown much larger and closer to Earth's surface than it actually would be. Have students identify the source of the original signals (on the body of the Shuttle) and the two places where the bounced-back signals are received (on the body and at the end of the antenna).

MAKE INFERENCES To answer the questions correctly, students need to recall what they learned about reflected radar signals in the previous lesson. If students need help determining which signal will arrive first, have them use a ruler to measure and compare the distances traveled by the signal returning to Antenna 1 and the signal returning to Antenna 2. Ask students to recall the Before You Read activity.

Ask them how their eyes and the two antennas are alike. (Both their eyes and the antennas are separated by a space.) Point out how the positions of their eyes and of the antennas provide the two points of view needed to make a detailed topographical map of surface features. Explain that the computer will make calculations and process the data from the two signals.

18   CHAPTER 1 / LESSON 3

▶ Propose Explanations

UNDERSTANDING THE SCIENCE-TECHNOLOGY CONNECTION Sometimes the challenges scientists face can result in the invention of a new technology. At other times a new technology will give scientists ideas for new investigations.

▶ What challenge did the mapmakers have?

The mapmakers needed to figure out how to make detailed 3-D topographic maps of Earth.

▶ How did NASA engineers use technology to meet that need?

They came up with a plan to put two antennas 60 m apart on the Space Shuttle and use interferometry to make 3-D images.

GENERATE IDEAS

▶ Briefly explain how people in the following situations might use 3-D images from space.

3-D Image Users	How They Could Use the Images
Pilots of small planes	To navigate a flight path
Backpackers	To decide on a safe route over a mountain
Hang gliders	To pick a suitable place to launch a glider
Rescue workers	To figure out where a lost person might have taken shelter
Flood control engineers	To determine where floodwater is likely to collect
Scientists studying volcanoes	To see changes in the shape of the volcanoes and to track lava flows

Assessment
Skill: Sequencing

Use the following task to assess each student's progress:

Have students create a flowchart that shows the sequence used by interferometry to create 3-D images. (Flowcharts may include the following: Antenna 2 is unfolded from the Space Shuttle; signals from the Shuttle's body are transmitted to Earth; signals bounce back and are received by Antenna 1 on the Shuttle and by Antenna 2 at the end of the mast; images are combined to produce a 3-D image.)

▶ Propose Explanations

UNDERSTANDING THE SCIENCE-TECHNOLOGY CONNECTION Ask students to make a list of the science skills NASA technicians may have used to develop the new technology of interferometry. (measuring, using numbers, communicating, using space/time relationships, sequencing, collecting and recording data, organizing information)

Explain to students that the need for something is often a prerequisite to the development of a new technology. For example, the need for efficient methods to preserve food preceded the invention of the refrigerator. Ask students to think of other examples of how need leads to the development of new technologies.

GENERATE IDEAS Have students discuss what they know about each profession. Let them write their responses independently. Then call on volunteers to briefly explain their ideas about how people in each group are likely to use the more detailed topographic maps. Ask students to suggest other jobs or situations that might make use of 3-D images from space. (town planners, watershed protection, resort planning, road construction)

CHAPTER 2
Overview

Rock On!

LESSON 4
Rock Clocks
Point of Lesson: *Scientists' understanding of the rock cycle helps them investigate the age of planet Earth.*

A student's question to a scientist—"How old is Earth?"—and the scientist's response introduce an exploration into the rock cycle and the nature of geologic dating. Students examine a diagram of the rock cycle and identify sequences of geologic processes in order to understand why scientists must look beyond Earth to the moon and meteorites in order to find rocks that are old enough to radiometrically date the solar system.

Materials
Science Scope Activity (pp. 20B and 21), for each station:
- packages of common household items such as deodorant, toothpaste, dishwasher and laundry detergent, antacid, cleanser, and artificial sweetener
- samples of sandstone and limestone

for each group:
- Periodic Table of Elements (copymaster page 226)

Connections (p. 23), for each group:
- map showing the entire length of the Grand Canyon and the Colorado River

Laboratory Safety
Only empty packages and not the products they contained are necessary for the Science Scope Activity in this lesson. However, as there may be residue present, review these safety guidelines with students before they do the activity.
- Be careful not to inhale any powdered material or get it in your eyes.
- Do not taste any substances.
- Wash your hands thoroughly after the activity.

LESSON 5
Crystal Conclusions
Point of Lesson: *Experimenting can lead to exciting new evidence when a scientist has the right "attitude."*

New scientific theories are accepted only through the work of many scientists, testing and examining the evidence from many sources. In this lesson, students read about the experiments of a young geologist, Andy Gratz, whose investigations into microscopic mineral structures supported the meteorite impact theory for the mass extinction at the end of the Cretaceous Era. Students identify the scientist's observations and describe how he tested his hypothesis in the laboratory. They then consider the importance of skepticism in the advancement of scientific ideas.

Materials
Before You Read (p. 24), for the class:
- geodes
- magnifiers
- salt
- sugar

Enrichment (p. 25), for each group:
- table salt or granulated sugar
- glass
- hot water
- spoon
- dental floss
- magnifier

Connections (p. 26), for each student:
- colored construction paper
- scissors

Laboratory Safety
Review these safety guidelines with students before they do the Before You Read and Enrichment activities in this lesson.
- Be careful not to inhale any powdered material or get it in your eyes.
- Do not taste any substances.
- Wash your hands thoroughly after handling the powdery substances.

LESSON 6
Pebble Poetry
Point of Lesson: *The physical properties of a pebble can be used to write a poem.*

In this lesson, a poem about pebbles leads students into examining a pebble and making inferences about its history. The activity encourages students to observe closely, using their senses of touch and sight, in order to unravel the riddle of their pebble.

Materials
Activity (p. 29), for each student:
- pebble
- magnifier
- water
- Field Hardness Scale (optional)

Enrichment (p. 29)
- egg cartons (at least one per student)

Laboratory Safety
Review these safety guidelines with students before they do the Enrichment activity in this lesson.
- Always go with an adult when collecting in the field.
- Obtain permission to collect from the landowner.
- Check the weather forecast and plan your trip and equipment accordingly.
- Stay away from difficult or dangerous terrain.

Science Scope Activity

What's the Connection?

NSTA has chosen a Science Scope activity related to the content in this chapter. The activity begins here and continues in Lesson 4, page 21.

Time: 40 minutes
Materials: see page 20A

This activity should help students realize that silicates and carbonates—common components of rocks—are found in many household products.

Procedure

1. Set up identical stations with the household items and several pieces of sandstone and limestone.
2. Divide the class into small groups. Give each group a copy of the periodic table.

(continued on page 21)

Background Information

Lesson 4

The use of a particular radioactive isotope depends on the age of the material being dated. Carbon-14 is probably the best-known isotope used in radiometric dating; however, its relatively short half-life (5,730 years) limits its use to dating objects less than about 50,000 years old. Isotopes with longer half-lives, such as Uranium-235 (700 million years) and Potassium-40 (1.25 billion years), are used to date igneous rocks.

Lesson 6

The shape and surface of a pebble tell a great deal about how it was formed. Smooth, round pebbles were shaped by moving water, either in a stream or on a beach. Smooth surfaces that meet at sharp angles can be formed when a pebble sits exposed to the wind for many years. A rough surface suggests that the pebble was not exposed to wind or water for very long (geologically speaking) since the time it broke off its parent rock.

UNIT 1 Earth's Surface

CHAPTER 2 / LESSON 4

Point of Lesson
Scientists' understanding of the rock cycle helps them investigate the age of planet Earth.

Focus
- Structure of the earth system
- Earth's history
- Evidence, models, and explanation

Skills and Strategies
- Interpreting scientific illustrations
- Sequencing
- Interpreting data
- Creating and using tables
- Communicating
- Generating questions

Advance Preparation
Vocabulary
Make sure students understand these terms. Definitions can be found in the glossary at the end of the student book.

- erosion
- igneous rock
- magma
- metamorphic rock
- pressure
- radioactive
- rock
- rock cycle
- sedimentary rock
- solar system
- weathering

(continued on page 21)

TEACHING PLAN pp. 20–21

INTRODUCING THE LESSON
This lesson introduces the concept that geologists use evidence from the rock cycle and processes like radiometric dating to figure out Earth's age. Ask students how old Earth is. Many students may think Earth is only a few million years old. Explain that organisms were alive on Earth many millions of years ago, so Earth must be much older. Then ask students what evidence they think scientists use to estimate Earth's age. Lead students to suggest that objects such as rocks and fossils give scientists the clues they need to determine Earth's age.

CHAPTER 2 / LESSON 4

Rock On!

Rock Clocks

How old is Earth? Ask a geologist!

Where do you go if you're a middle school student who wants to know the age of Earth? One idea is to go to an "ask-a-scientist" Web site. The question about Earth's age was sent to a geologist who studies rocks and the origin, history, and structure of Earth.

▶ **Read**

Here's the answer the geologist posted on the Web.

Question: How Old Is Earth?

Answer: According to geologists, Earth is about 4.5 billion years old. But the oldest rocks ever found on Earth are "only" about 3.8 billion years old. How did scientists arrive at 4.5 billion years as Earth's age? The process of plate tectonics "recycles" Earth's crust, so rocks as old as 4.5 billion years no longer exist. Since Earth formed at the same time as the rest of the solar system, scientists look at rocks that aren't from Earth. They study rocks taken from the moon by the Apollo missions, meteorites that fell to Earth, and very old igneous rocks present in Earth's crust.

Unlike Earth, the moon doesn't have plate tectonics. Rocks on its surface formed when the moon formed or arrived as meteorites from outer space. The oldest moon rocks and meteorites have been dated at about 4.5 billion years old.

Moon rock ▲

Scientists date the rocks by radiometric dating. They know that certain radioactive isotopes in rocks decay at a constant rate over time. They measure the amount of an

---

▶ **Read**

Point out that the reading is a message that a geologist posted on a Web site in answer to a student's question. Remind students about the importance of examining the credentials of authors of Internet material.

Suggest to students that a good way to evaluate the reading would be to make a critical reading chart to help organize their thoughts. Tell them to identify the main idea, summarize the evidence presented, evaluate how reliable the source is, and decide whether they think the evidence is convincing.

Sample Chart:

CRITICAL READING CHART	
Main idea	Earth is 4.5 billion years old.
Summary of evidence	The solar system was created all at once. The oldest rocks, though not from Earth, were formed at the same time as Earth. Scientists are able to date rocks from the moon. Earth is as old as these moon rocks and meteorites.
Reliability of source	The source is a geologist, a trained scientist who studies rocks and Earth's history.
Is the evidence convincing?	yes

isotope in a rock to get the rock's age. Igneous rocks form when molten magma solidifies. As the magma solidifies, certain radioactive isotopes become trapped. Scientists know the decay rate of the isotopes, so they can measure how much is left in the rock and determine its age.

Geologists and other scientists are still searching for rocks that may be older and could perhaps tell us more about the early solar system.

plate tectonics: the theory that Earth's crust is made of large sections that move on top of a softer, fluid layer
crust: outermost, rocky, solid layer of Earth
meteorite: a piece of rock that has fallen to Earth from space
igneous: rock formed from hot melted material that cooled
radioactive: giving off particles from its nucleus
isotope: an atom of a certain element with the same number of protons as other atoms of that element but a different number of neutrons

From: MadSci Network. Washington University Medical School. (www.madsci.org)

NOTEZONE
Circle the objects that scientists use to tell how old Earth is.

▶ Explore

IDENTIFY SEQUENCES Geologists find most of the isotopes needed to do radiometric dating in igneous rocks. So they test igneous rocks from around the world, looking for the oldest rocks. To find out how igneous rocks form, look at this diagram of the rock cycle.

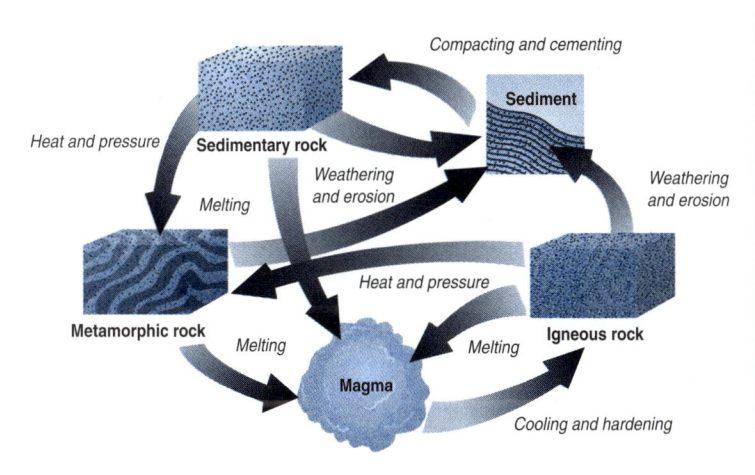

FIND OUT MORE
SCIENCESAURUS
Rocks 180
Plate Tectonics and Mountain Building 181
Continental Drift 182
Lithospheric Plates 183
Relative and Absolute Age Dating 197
Atomic Structure 256

SCLINKS
THE WORLD'S A CLICK AWAY
www.scilinks.org
Keyword: Rock Cycle
Code: GSED02

(continued from page 20)

Materials
Gather the materials needed for *Science Scope Activity* (p. 20B and p. 21) and *Connections* (p. 23).

Science Scope Activity
(continued from page 20B)

3. Each group should visit a station to study the items, decide how they are related, and discuss possible connections among them.
4. Encourage each group to share its ideas with the class. Ask students to describe how the rocks fit in with the household items.
5. Write the terms *silica* and *carbonate* on the board. Explain that sandstone is a compound of silicon and oxygen and is called a *silicate*. Limestone is a compound of calcium, carbon, and oxygen and is called *calcium carbonate*.
6. Have students find the chemical symbols for silicon, carbon, oxygen, and calcium on the periodic table. Encourage them to reexamine the ingredients of the household items at the stations.
7. Have students organize the data in chart form and classify each item as a silicate, a carbonate, or a combination of both.
8. Students can extend their charts by adding a column labeled *Use* and listing household items containing silicates, calcium carbonates, or both.

▶ Explore

IDENTIFY SEQUENCES In this section, students use a diagram of the rock cycle to identify sequences that result in the formation of magma. As needed, review the processes by which rock changes from one form to another: weathering; erosion; heat and pressure; melting, cooling, and hardening; and compacting and cementing of sediments.

Ask: *What happens to a rock's radioactivity when magma solidifies?* (Certain radioactive isotopes become trapped.) *Why is this important to scientists?* (They know the isotopes' decay rate, so they can measure how much is left and calculate the rock's age.) Point out that for a rock to melt, the temperature must be extremely high—about 1,000°C, compared with 0°C to melt ice.

CHECK UNDERSTANDING
Skill: Classifying
Ask students to identify each type of rock that is being described:
a. This type of rock forms when layers of sand particles and the remains of living things settle out of water and are cemented together and compacted. (sedimentary)
b. This type of rock forms when another type of rock is exposed to heat and pressure. (metamorphic)
c. This type of rock forms when melted rock cools and hardens. (igneous)

CHAPTER 2 / LESSON 4

CHAPTER 2 / LESSON 4

More Resources
The following resources are also available from Great Source and NSTA.

ScienceSaurus
Rocks	180
Plate Tectonics and Mountain Building	181
Continental Drift	182
Lithospheric Plates	183
Relative and Absolute Age Dating	197
Atomic Structure	256
Evaluating Sources	424

Reader's Handbook
Elements of Graphics: Diagram	552
How to Read a Chart or Table	600

Write Source 2000
Using Strong, Colorful Words	135

SciLinks — THE WORLD'S A CLICK AWAY

www.scilinks.org
Keyword: Rock Cycle
Code: GSED02

Teaching Plan pp. 22–23

▶ Explore

(continued from page 21)
The first question on this page asks students to identify how igneous rocks form. If they cannot answer the question from memory, tell them to go back to the rock cycle diagram on page 21, find the igneous rock, and work backward to its origin (magma). Students may also need to refer to the diagram to complete the chart on this page. Remind them of the importance of reading the labels and following the arrows in the diagram to identify the steps in each sequence.

22   CHAPTER 2 / LESSON 4

Examine the diagram on the previous page.
▶ *In what way can igneous rock form?*
from the cooling and hardening of magma

A rock's radioactive clock is reset each time rock changes to magma. Examine the diagram again.
▶ *Find six different sequences that result in the formation of magma. A sequence may have more than one change before it melts into magma. Fill in the table to organize your ideas. One example is shown.*

	ROCK TYPE AT START	HOW THE ROCK CHANGES	ROCK TYPE AFTER CHANGE	HOW THE ROCK CHANGES	CLOCK IS RESET
1	Sedimentary	melts			magma
2	Sedimentary	heat and pressure	metamorphic	melts	magma
3	Metamorphic	melts			magma
4	Metamorphic	weathers and erodes; compacts and cements	sedimentary	melts	magma
5	Igneous	melts			magma
6	Igneous	weathers and erodes; compacts and cements	sedimentary	melts	magma
7	Igneous	heat and pressure	metamorphic	melts	magma

▼ Granite mountains

▶ Propose Explanations

SUPPORTING EVIDENCE Geologists often use evidence from one place to support conclusions about rocks they observe in other places. For example, observing layers in beach sand gives evidence to support how layers may have formed in a piece of sandstone found in a river canyon.

▶ *The actions of plate tectonics make rocks on Earth younger than Earth itself. According to the reading, what evidence do geologists use to support their conclusion? Where does that evidence come from?*

The moon rocks and meteorites are like those found on Earth when it first formed. Rocks on Earth are changed by plate tectonics and other forces of nature. Rocks on the moon and in space are not being changed by these forces. As a result, those unchanged rocks can be compared with Earth rocks. They are evidence of how Earth processes have changed rocks on Earth from their original state.

▶ Take Action

WRITE DRAMATICALLY On a separate piece of paper, create a story that describes one of the rock sequences you identified in the chart. Use vivid language to describe how the rock was changed at each stage and the forces that changed it. When you are finished, write a sentence below explaining how your choice of words would be different if you were writing a scientific description rather than a dramatic one.

Student stories will vary. Students should note that a scientific description uses science terms instead of vivid language.

Connections

Time: 10–15 minutes
Materials: map showing the entire length of the Grand Canyon and the Colorado River

GEOGRAPHY Have students locate the Grand Canyon on the map. Tell them to use the scale in the map key to calculate the approximate length of the canyon. (about 482 km, 300 mi) Tell students that the Grand Canyon was carved by the Colorado River. Have them locate the Colorado River and trace its path from the Rocky Mountains through the Grand Canyon. Point out that the layers of rocks visible in the canyon walls show over a billion years of Earth's history.

Assessment

Skill: Sequencing

Use the following task to assess each student's progress:

Have each student draw a flowchart to illustrate the process by which sedimentary rock changes to metamorphic rock, then to igneous rock, and then back to sedimentary rock. (Sedimentary rock → heat and pressure → metamorphic rock → heat → magma → cools and hardens → igneous rock → weathered and eroded to create sediments → compaction and cementation → sedimentary rock)

▶ Propose Explanations

SUPPORTING EVIDENCE Explain to students that now that they are more familiar with the processes involved in the rock cycle, they are in a better position to evaluate the supporting evidence that the geologist referred to in the reading on pages 20–21. Tell them to go back to the reading to locate that evidence and explain how it supports geologists' conclusions about the age of planet Earth.

▶ Take Action

WRITE DRAMATICALLY Encourage students to use their imagination to tell the "life story of rock." Tell them to include dramatic events such as being thrust out of an erupting volcano, being crushed during the building of the Rocky Mountains, or being changed back into magma at an ocean trench. Ask students to use vivid verbs to describe the action. Allow them to do library or Internet research to strengthen their stories with facts about the forces that cause such events. Remind them to write a sentence telling how the story differs from a strictly scientific account of the same events.

UNIT 1 Earth's Surface

CHAPTER 2 / LESSON 5

Point of Lesson
Experimenting can lead to exciting new evidence when a scientist has the right "attitude."

Focus
- Structure of the earth system
- Earth's history
- Science as a human endeavor
- Nature of science

Skills and Strategies
- Recognizing cause and effect
- Drawing conclusions
- Understanding that scientists change their ideas in the face of experimental evidence that does not support existing hypotheses
- Understanding that scientists share their results to form a common core of knowledge
- Generating questions

Advance Preparation

Vocabulary
Make sure students understand these terms. Definitions can be found in the glossary at the end of the student book.

- climate
- comet
- crater
- crystal
- crystal structure
- meteor/meteorite
- microscopic
- mineral

TEACHING PLAN pp. 24–25

INTRODUCING THE LESSON
This lesson presents shocked crystals as evidence of a meteorite impact that caused the extinction of dinosaurs. Ask students to define *extinction* in their own words. Some students may not realize that extinction means the complete disappearance of an entire species from Earth. Make two lists on the board, one with examples of animals that are extinct (including different sorts of dinosaurs) and the other with animals that have hovered on the verge of extinction.

CHAPTER 2 / LESSON 5
Rock On!

Crystal Conclusions

What clues to Earth's history are in the crystals that make up rocks?

For many years, scientists have debated how the dinosaurs were wiped out 65 million years ago. At one time, the theory was that volcanic activity caused climate changes that killed the dinosaurs. In the past 25 years, scientists have gathered new evidence. This evidence supports the theory that dinosaurs died when a comet or meteor struck Earth, throwing dust particles into the air and blocking sunlight. Without sunlight, plants could not grow. Plant-eating dinosaurs starved, and then so did meat-eating dinosaurs. It takes the work of many scientists to investigate a new theory. Some of the evidence they find is as large as a crater. Some is as small as a microscopic crystal hidden inside a rock.

▲ Geologists inside a huge underground crystal cluster

▶ Before You Read

SEEING PATTERNS Minerals are natural materials that make up Earth's rocks. Minerals have a crystal structure. Crystals are solids that show regular, repeating patterns of the same shape. Draw or describe other objects in nature that show regular, repeating patterns.

Answers will vary. Examples: snowflakes, seashells, ocean waves, flower petals, fish scales

▶ Before You Read

Time: 20 minutes
Materials: geodes, magnifiers, salt, sugar

SEEING PATTERNS Refer students to the photograph on this page. Make sure they understand that the photo does not show a single crystal. Allow students to examine the geode and the salt and sugar crystals with a magnifier. You might explain that crystals of the same substance always have the same general shape. Table salt crystals are shaped like cubes. Crystals of other substances have different shapes.

▶ Read

Andy Gratz was a geologist who studied crystals. He wondered whether any crystals might hold evidence about the impact theory of dinosaur extinction. Here's what Andy's college geology professor had to say about Andy.

Locked Up in Crystals

Andy's scientific passion was the secret life of crystals.... He took an interest in the [tiny] chips of quartz that are found around the world, in that centimeter-thick layer of clay that divides the Mesozoic world of dinosaurs from the Tertiary world of mammals. Specifically, he studied the strange textures called *lamellae* (which is Latin for "weird little streaky things") found only in these chips. At extreme magnification...he proved that these are tiny layers of glass, which...formed when the crystals were violently pulled apart by shocks. Then he [used] big machines to [shock some rocks and make more lamellae in the laboratory]. In this way, he put to rest the proposal that the crystals, and the catastrophe, were volcanic. From the intensity of the shock, he showed that they could result from nothing less than a major meteorite impact.... This result has been discussed around the world....This is truly fine detective work.

quartz: a hard, glassy mineral
Mesozoic: the time period in Earth's history from 230 million to 65 million years ago
Tertiary: the time period in Earth's history from 65 million to 2 million years ago
shock: in this case, a sudden shaking from something being hit very hard (not an electrical shock)
catastrophe: a terrible event

From: Bird, Dr. Peter. "Andy Gratz, a Scientist's Eulogy." Unpublished.

NOTEZONE

Underline the words that refer to the laboratory equipment that Andy used in his crystal research.

▼ Copper sulfate crystal

FIND OUT MORE
SCIENCESAURUS
Extinction 128
Minerals 179

25

Materials
Gather the materials needed for *Before You Read* (p. 24), *Enrichment* (p. 25), and *Connections: Art* (p. 26).

Enrichment
Time: 15 minutes for initial setup
Materials: table salt or granulated sugar, glass, hot water, spoon, dental floss, magnifier

Students can use this procedure to grow crystals from a saturated solution. Dissolve about 25 grams of salt or sugar into a glass filled with 200 mL of hot water. Hang a piece of dental floss in the solution, letting it drape over the edge of the glass. Within a week, cystals will begin to form on the dental floss. Have students observe the crystals with a magnifier and sketch their shape.

Connections
Time: 30 minutes for class presentations

GEOGRAPHY Tell students that the meteorite impact theory received additional support when a crater of the appropriate age was found in the ocean near Mexico's Yucatan Peninsula. Suggest that students use the Internet to research evidence of other impact craters on Earth, such as Barringer Crater, Arizona; Clearwater Lakes, Quebec, Canada; Kara-Kul, Afghanistan; Roter Kamm, Namibia; and Wolfe Creek, Australia. Have them share what they learn in a class presentation.

▶ Read

Point out that Andy Gratz was a young man when he did this research. He had completed his PhD at UCLA and had published 12 scientific papers on his work with crystals, including the research described in this excerpt, when he died of cancer at the age of 31. Andy's experiments with shocked quartz supported the impact theory of Luis and Walter Alverez, which is still being debated today. You may want to discuss this theory: In 1980, the Alverezes discovered high levels of a mineral called iridium in the layer of clay that marks the Cretaceous/Tertiary boundary, when the dinosaurs became extinct. This mineral is rare on Earth but common in meteorites. The Alverezes proposed that extinction was caused by the impact of an asteroid 10 km (6 mi) in diameter that blasted tons of dust and rock into the sky, causing a global environmental crisis.

Tell students to highlight words and phrases that describe the way the strange quartz crystals looked and how this evidence supported the theory that dinosaur extinction was the result of a meteorite impact.

CHECK UNDERSTANDING
Skill: Organizing information
Ask students to write a paragraph explaining the evidence Andy Gratz found that supported the theory of dinosaur extinction. Have students explain how he found this evidence. (Gratz found lamellae in crystals and tested the crystals by shocking them to show that the lamellae could only have been formed by a huge impact.)

CHAPTER 2 / LESSON 5

CHAPTER 2 / LESSON 5

More Resources
The following resources are also available from Great Source.

SCIENCESAURUS
Extinction	128
Minerals	179

READER'S HANDBOOK
Elements of Nonfiction: Cause and Effect	275
Elements of Poetry: Metaphor	455
Cause-Effect Organizer	667

MATH ON CALL
Prisms	394

Connections
Time: 30 minutes
Materials: colored construction paper, scissors

ART Explain that *tessellation* means fitting together repeating shapes to form a design or picture. Have students draw and cut out shapes from colored construction paper. Tell them to use different colors for different shapes: squares, triangles, hexagons, and so on. Have students put shapes together to create their own designs with all the shapes touching and no space between them.

TEACHING PLAN pp. 26–27

▶ Explore

THINK ABOUT IT
▶ When Andy examined the crystals, what evidence did he find that they had been violently pulled apart by shocks?
He found strange textures called lamellae.

▶ What did Andy do to model how the crystals formed?
He shocked some rocks using big machines.

▶ How did his results support the theory that it was a meteorite impact that caused the extinction of dinosaurs?
The crystals formed by his experiment happened from shocks that were too intense to be from a volcano.

NOTEZONE
Andy's professor used a metaphor to describe how Andy thought about what he read. Underline the words that describe the metaphor.

His professor had more to say about Andy's attitude as a research scientist.

Doubting Andy

[Andy] was skeptical, in the best way. When he would read what others had done, he would remember their experimental data, and file that in one part of his mind. In quite another place, he would file their conclusions, more as interesting gossip about the authors than as facts. He always maintained the firmest division between what we really know, and what we only like to pretend we know.

skeptical: doubting or questioning

From: Bird, Dr. Peter. "Andy Gratz, a Scientist's Eulogy." Unpublished.

26

▶ Explore

THINK ABOUT IT These questions require students to refer back to the reading and draw conclusions about the evidence presented. Have students focus on the words they highlighted earlier (see Read, p. 25).

▶ Read

Explain to students that Andy Gratz was a graduate student in geology when he was diagnosed with cancer. His thesis advisor, Dr. Bill Bird, wrote the eulogy from which this reading and the previous one were taken. Point out that scientific knowledge advances through the work of many contributors. Andy's story is an example of how even a young scientist who is experiencing personal adversity can contribute to the advancement of a new theory.

Explain that a metaphor describes something that is unfamiliar as being like something we know well. It compares two things without using the connective word "like" or "as." A metaphor is used to create a memorable picture. In this case, the author compares Andy's thinking process to a file cabinet. Ask students why Andy's skeptical attitude is a good habit for scientists to develop. (Scientists often disagree about the interpretation of evidence. Maintaining a skeptical attitude allows them to keep an open mind about new ideas but remain realistic about interpreting the supporting evidence.)

▶ Propose Explanations

PRACTICING SKEPTICISM Being skeptical is an important part of thinking like a scientist. A simple example from everyday life can help you understand why. Suppose you and your sister come home from school and find the kitchen table on its side. (Think of this as your data.)

▶ **Think of two different reasons (or conclusions) why the table got that way.**

Answers will vary. Examples: The table was turned on its side by an earthquake, by someone who is fixing it, by a child using it as a play fort, and so on.

▶ **Why do you think Andy was skeptical of the conclusions drawn by scientists?**

He knew that scientists can interpret the same data in different ways and reach different conclusions.

▶ Take Action

GENERATE QUESTIONS Andy Gratz was curious about crystals. All successful scientists have a great interest in the topics they investigate. Imagine that you will become a geologist.

▶ **Make a list of questions about Earth's surface, and processes that form it, that might interest you. Then describe how you think you might find the answers to those questions.**

Answers will vary. Students should list questions that can be explored scientifically and describe scientific methods for answering them.

Connections

LANGUAGE ARTS Present the following example of a metaphor. Then have students write a brief paragraph using metaphors of their own.

The fiction was draped over the bones of fact, but in places the bones showed through.

Assessment

Skill: Testing hypotheses

Use the following question to assess each student's progress:

Ask students to explain how scientists test new hypotheses. Ask them to give an example from the lesson showing how scientists use evidence to support their hypotheses. (Scientists generally reach conclusions about the validity of a hypothesis based on how well it fits the known facts. They will discard it if enough evidence or test results do not support it. Students should mention the lamellae Andy found in the quartz crystals and the results of subjecting rocks to shocks. This evidence supported the theory that dinosaurs died as a result of a meteorite or comet striking Earth.)

▶ Propose Explanations

PRACTICING SKEPTICISM Discuss the variety of conclusions that students suggested in answer to the first question. Ask what evidence they would look for to support their conclusions. (For example, if they concluded there was an earthquake, they would check news reports. If they concluded that a child was playing with the table, they would ask other people in the house who had been in the kitchen. If they concluded that the table was being fixed, they would look for tools or evidence of some problem with the table.) Also ask them why it is important to be skeptical about their own conclusions as well as those of others when they look for evidence. (They may want to change their conclusions in the face of evidence that does not support their original hypothesis.)

▶ Take Action

GENERATE QUESTIONS Before students begin writing their questions, write a list of earth science processes on the board: mountain building, volcanism, plate tectonics, weathering and erosion, and so on. Then have students list questions that interest them and describe how they might find the answers using scientific methods.

UNIT 1 Earth's Surface
CHAPTER 2 / LESSON 6

Point of Lesson
The physical properties of a pebble can be used to write a poem.

Focus
- Structure of the earth system
- Earth's history

Skills and Strategies
- Observing
- Communicating
- Recognizing cause and effect
- Making inferences

Advance Preparation

Vocabulary
Make sure students understand this term. The definition can be found in the glossary at the end of the student book.
- hardness

Materials
Gather the materials needed for *Activity* (p. 29) and *Enrichment* (p. 29).

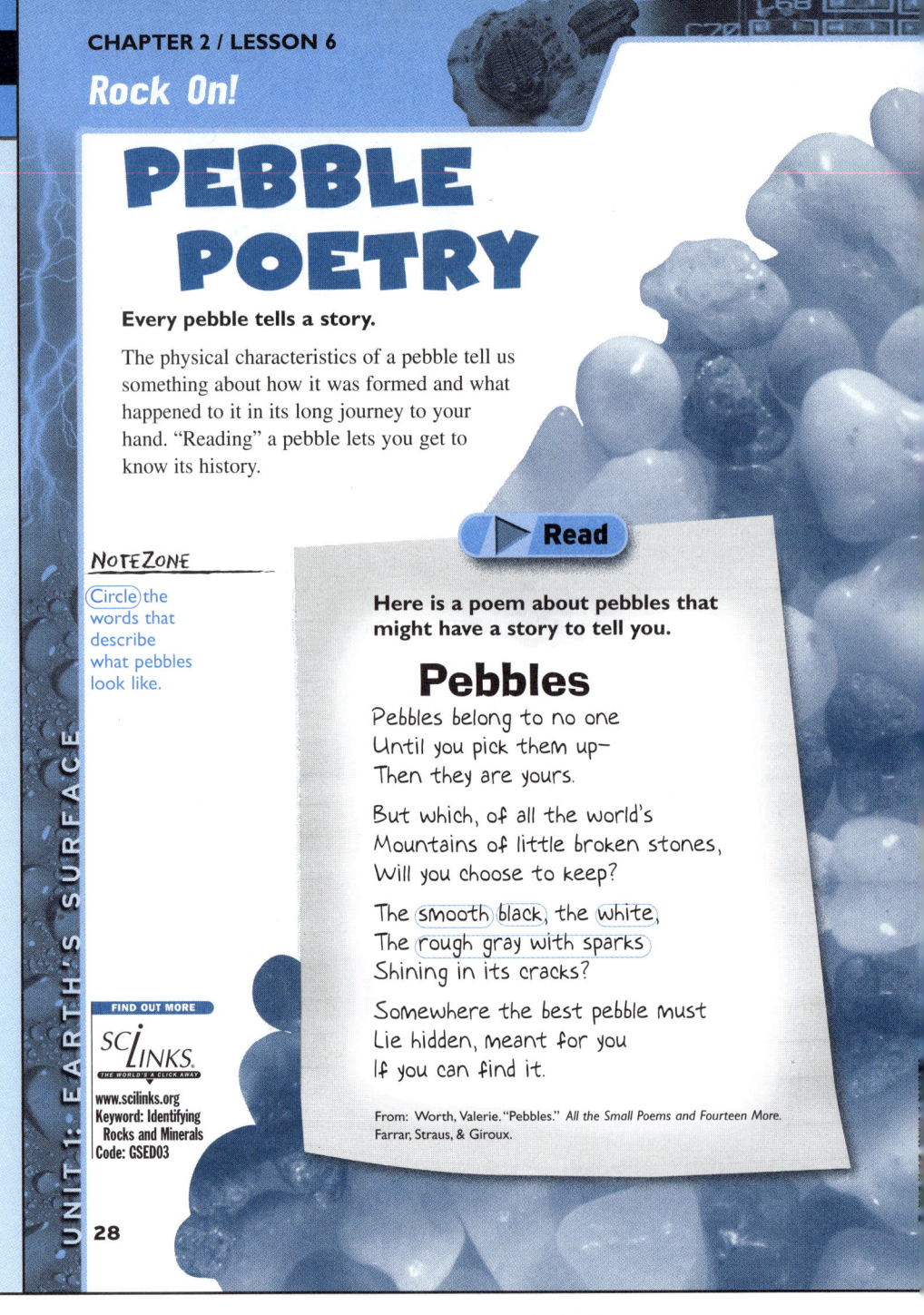

CHAPTER 2 / LESSON 6
Rock On!

PEBBLE POETRY

Every pebble tells a story.

The physical characteristics of a pebble tell us something about how it was formed and what happened to it in its long journey to your hand. "Reading" a pebble lets you get to know its history.

NOTEZONE
Circle the words that describe what pebbles look like.

▶ **Read**

Here is a poem about pebbles that might have a story to tell you.

Pebbles

Pebbles belong to no one
Until you pick them up—
Then they are yours.

But which, of all the world's
Mountains of little broken stones,
Will you choose to keep?

The smooth black, the white,
The rough gray with sparks
Shining in its cracks?

Somewhere the best pebble must
Lie hidden, meant for you
If you can find it.

From: Worth, Valerie. "Pebbles." *All the Small Poems and Fourteen More.* Farrar, Straus, & Giroux.

FIND OUT MORE
SCiLINKS
THE WORLD'S A CLICK AWAY
www.scilinks.org
Keyword: Identifying Rocks and Minerals
Code: GSED03

UNIT 1: EARTH'S SURFACE
28

TEACHING PLAN pp. 28–29

INTRODUCING THE LESSON
In this lesson, students examine a pebble and make inferences about its history. Many students may not realize that scientists can learn much about the history of Earth by observing rocks. For example, a rock that contains a fossilized shell might reveal that the rock formed under water.

Ask students if they have ever collected anything. Students will probably name a wide assortment of collectibles, from shells to trading cards to stamps. Encourage volunteers to describe an object in their collections that is a personal favorite and tell why it is important or special to them.

▶ **Read**

Tell students to read the poem several times, each time with a different purpose:

1. Read to feel how the author uses words. Look for words that bring visual images to mind.
2. Read again for meaning.
3. Study the poem's structure and see if it has a rhyme scheme.
4. Read once more to make personal connections with the message.

Ask students to evaluate what they did or did not like about the poem.

28   CHAPTER 2 / LESSON 6

Activity

GET TO KNOW A PEBBLE

Look closely at a pebble. What can you infer about its history?

What You Need:
- pebble
- magnifier
- water

What To Do:
1. Find a pebble that you would like to "make your own."
2. Use the magnifier to look closely at your pebble. Rub a little water on the surface to bring out any patterns that might be there.
3. In the chart, record the physical characteristics of your pebble—its shape, color, surface texture (rough or smooth), hardness, layers or bands, whether it contains crystals or has marks on the surface, and any other things you notice.
4. Think about the characteristics that might tell you about the pebble's history. For example, how did its "mother" rock form? How long ago was your pebble separated from the "mother" rock? How has it changed? Where has it traveled? Has it been in water? Write your inferences in the chart.

What Do You See?

Pebble Characteristic	Inferences About the Pebble's History
smooth edges	It broke off the "mother" rock a while ago and has been weathered by wind or water.
dirt on it	It's been on or under the ground.
light brownish color	It formed from sand, mud, or soil.
gritty texture	It formed from sand.
stripes visible	It formed as layers of sand were compacted.

Take Action

WRITE YOUR PEBBLE'S STORY On a separate sheet of paper, write a poem that describes your pebble's history from its beginning as part of the "mother" rock to your hand. Include the characteristics you observed. Don't forget to give your poem a title.

Students' poems will vary.

More Resources
The following resources are also available from Great Source and NSTA.

WRITE SOURCE 2000
Writing Poetry   193

SCILINKS
THE WORLD'S A CLICK AWAY

www.scilinks.org
Keyword: Identifying Rocks and Minerals
Code: GSED03

Enrichment
Time: will vary
Materials: egg cartons

Invite students to collect rocks near their homes or school, or plan a class collecting trip. Students can use egg cartons to organize and label their collections. For each rock, students should record where and when the rock was found and its appearance.

Assessment
Skill: Inferring

Use the following task to assess each student's progress:

Read through students' poems to see which ones provide the clearest descriptions of the pebbles. Give students several pebbles and three or four poems written by their classmates. Ask them to match each poem description with the correct pebble.

Activity
Time: 20 minutes
Materials: pebble, magnifier, water, Field Hardness Scale (optional)

- Students can work alone or with a partner.
- Tell students to bring in a pebble.
- Ask students to think about which part of the rock cycle produces pebbles. (weathering and erosion)
- You might want to provide students with a copy of the Field Hardness Scale to check their samples for relative hardness.

Take Action
WRITE YOUR PEBBLE'S STORY Prior to this creative writing exercise, you may want to review different verse forms with your class, such as haiku and free verse. Discuss ways to organize the poems and the use of rhythm and repeated words or sounds. Tell students that the important thing is to paint a clear picture of the pebble's characteristics. Collect students' pebbles and poems for use in the Assessment activity.

CHECK UNDERSTANDING
Skill: Drawing conclusions
Ask students what properties proved most useful in making inferences about the pebble's history. (Students should mention some of the properties identified in step 3 of the Activity.)

CHAPTER 2 / LESSON 6

CHAPTER 3
Overview

Energy Resources

LESSON 7
Digging Up Energy
Point of Lesson: *Coal and other fossil fuels are nonrenewable energy resources.*

This lesson focuses on what has been one of our most valuable energy resources for over 150 years—coal. Students read a description from the book *Rocket Boys,* in which Homer Hickam describes his experience going into a coal mine for the first time as a teenager. Students then observe the location of coal deposits in the United States on a map and compare the location of coal deposits to the reliance of various states on coal as a means of generating electricity.

Materials
Explore (p. 31), for the class:
- large map of the United States

Science Scope Activity (p. 30B and p. 31), for each pair:
- piece of coal
- dried plant materials (leaves, lettuce, grass, newspaper)
- ice cube tray or other cube-shaped plastic mold
- water
- mortar and pestle
- graduated cylinder
- balance
- metric ruler
- lamp, radiator, or other heat source

Laboratory Safety
Review the following safety guidelines with students before they do the Science Scope Activity in this lesson.
- Use extreme caution with the lamp. Never allow an electrical appliance to come in contact with water. Never pick up an electrical appliance with wet hands.
- Do not taste any substances.
- Immediately report any broken glass to your teacher. Stay out of the area until it has been cleaned up.
- Wipe up spills immediately to avoid risk of slips and falls.

LESSON 8
The Heat Is On
Point of Lesson: *Geothermal energy is a renewable energy source.*

This lesson describes how heat within Earth can be used to heat buildings and to generate electricity. The reading describes two uses of geothermal energy in California. Students examine a map showing the best locations in the United States for the development of geothermal energy and identify ways in which geothermal energy is both renewable and inexhaustible.

Materials
Enrichment (p. 35), for teacher demonstration:
- ring stand with metal ring
- hot plate
- plastic food container with hole in bottom for tubing
- boiling water
- Erlenmeyer flask
- one-hole rubber stopper with 0.5–1 m of tubing inserted
- plumber's putty
- cool water
- stopwatch or clock with second hand

Connections (p. 36), for the class:
- map showing the Ring of Fire (see *ScienceSaurus* section 185)

Laboratory Safety
Observe the following guidelines when you do the Enrichment demonstration.
- Wear safety goggles.
- Have students observe from a safe distance.
- Emphasize to students that they should not try this activity at home.

LESSON 9
Energy Choices
Point of Lesson: *Each energy source has its advantages and disadvantages.*

In this lesson, students learn about the factors that must be considered when making decisions about energy sources. They compare data related to the cost and use of both coal and geothermal energy, then consider these data to make an informed choice about an imaginary new power plant.

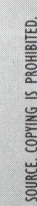

Science Scope Activity

How Is Coal Formed?

NSTA has chosen a Science Scope *activity related to the content in this chapter. The activity begins here and continues in Lesson 7, page 31.*

Time: 40 minutes

Materials: piece of coal; dried plant materials (leaves, lettuce, grass, newspaper); ice cube tray or other cube-shaped plastic mold; water; mortar and pestle; graduated cylinder; balance; metric ruler; lamp, radiator, or other heat source

Have students work in pairs, and give them the instructions on page 31. **Note:** You may need to help students with step 4, as follows:

4. **To calculate the densities of the coal and the compressed pulp:**
   a. First use a balance to find the mass of each object.
   b. Next, find the volume of each object.
      ▸ To find the coal's volume, measure the volume of water displaced by the coal when you place it in a measured amount of water in a graduated cylinder.
      ▸ To find the volume of the compressed pulp, measure the sides of the block and use this equation:
      volume = length × width × height
   c. To find the density of each object, use this equation:
   $$density = \frac{mass}{volume}$$

(continued on page 31)

Background Information

Lesson 7
Homer Hickam's career has spanned four decades. After graduating from the Virginia Polytechnical Institute, he served as an officer in the United States Army during the Vietnam war, followed by 10 years as an engineer with the U.S. Army Missile Command before joining NASA in 1981 as an aerospace engineer. At NASA, he specialized in training astronaut crews. His writing career was launched in 1989 with the publication of *Torpedo Junction,* a military history bestseller.

Lesson 8
The map on page 36 shows that the western states have the most potential to benefit from the use of geothermal energy. The U.S. Department of Energy sponsors a program called "Geopowering the West" that works with businesses, industries, private citizens, and state and local officials to promote the development and use of geothermal energy in those states and reduce barriers to its use.

UNIT 1 Earth's Surface
CHAPTER 3 / LESSON 7

Point of Lesson
Coal and other fossil fuels are nonrenewable energy resources.

Focus
- Structure of the earth system
- Populations, resources, and environments

Skills and Strategies
- Interpreting scientific illustrations
- Making inferences
- Communicating

Advance Preparation

Vocabulary
Make sure students understand these terms. Definitions can be found in the glossary at the end of the student book.
- coal
- electrical energy
- electricity
- energy
- natural gas
- organism

Materials
Gather the materials needed for *Science Scope Activity* (p. 30B and p. 31) and *Explore* (p. 31).

TEACHING PLAN pp. 30–31

INTRODUCING THE LESSON
This lesson focuses on what has been one of our most valuable energy resources for over 150 years—coal. Ask: *Where does our electrical energy come from?* (Much comes from the burning of fossil fuels.) Students may not realize that electricity is produced by converting other types of energy to electrical energy. You may want to review different types of energy and then explain that all types of energy can be converted to other forms. For example, wood and coal have *chemical energy*, which can be converted to heat and light through burning. Explain that other sources of energy are converted to electrical energy to produce the electricity we use.

CHAPTER 3 / LESSON 7
Energy Resources

DIGGING UP ENERGY

What lies hidden in the dark, deep below Earth's surface? A source of light!

Much of our electricity comes from burning fossil fuels—coal, oil, and natural gas. Fossil fuels form over millions of years from the remains of dead organisms. Because they take such a long time to form, these fuels are called *nonrenewable resources*.

▶ Read

NOTEZONE
In the box, sketch a diagram showing the coal seam, draw rock, and jack rock.

In the mid-1800s, American coal miners began to work in deep underground mines. Homer Hickam grew up during the 1950s in a West Virginia coal mining town. He made his first trip into a coal mine at the age of 15. Homer described his trip like this.

Into the Coal Mine

I was almost shaking with excitement. I'd lived in Coalwood my whole life, but had never been where Dad was going to take me. I was going into the mine!

"Come over here," he beckoned, spreading a map of the mine on the table. He pointed at a winding black streak that ran across it. "That's the Number Four Pocahontas Seam, the finest and purest soft coal in the world. These lines I've drawn represent the tunnels we've driven through it since the mine has been operational."

He...brought out another drawing. "This is the side view of a typical seam. The coal is overlaid by a hard shale called draw rock. Underneath is what we call jack rock. Engineers have to know how to hold up the draw rock to keep it from falling and how to move the jack rock out of the way...."

The attendant swung the gate aside, and for the first time in my life I stepped onto the wooden-plank

▶ Read

If students have difficulty drawing the sketch for the NoteZone activity, suggest that they first highlight the sentences in the reading that describe a typical coal seam. Have them use the description in the reading to explain what they think a coal mine looks like. Ask: *How do the miners get down to the coal?* (They ride a lift down a shaft.) *What role do engineers play in coal mining?* (Engineers develop ways to hold up the draw rock and move the jack rock out of the way so the coal seam can be mined.)

30 CHAPTER 3 / LESSON 7

platform of the lift.... The boards in the floor were set apart enough that I could see between them. There was nothing beneath us but a dark chasm.... The man-hoist winch began to creak and the lift dropped quickly, my stomach lifting up around my throat. I grabbed Dad's arm, then quickly let go in embarrassment.... I watched the solid rock of the shaft slip by.... We were being swallowed by the earth, and I hadn't decided yet whether I liked that.

beckoned: signaled
operational: in use
shale: fine-grained rock formed from mud or clay
attendant: a helper in charge of something (in this case, a gate)
chasm: a deep opening in the ground
man-hoist: a device to lower and raise workers in a narrow space
winch: a crank used to move the hoist
shaft: a long, vertical passage

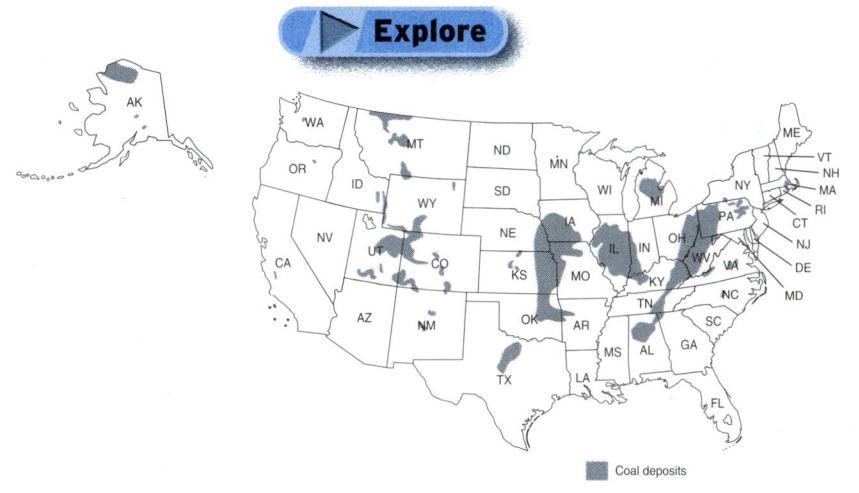

From: Hickam, Homer H., Jr. *Rocket Boys*. Delacorte Press Books for Younger Readers, a division of Random House, Inc.

FIND OUT MORE
SCIENCESAURUS
Fossil Fuels 325

Explore

FIND THE COAL The map shows where coal deposits are located in the United States.

▶ *Where are the largest coal deposits?*

in Pennsylvania, Ohio, West Virginia, Kentucky, Indiana, Illinois, Iowa, Nebraska, Kansas, Missouri, and Oklahoma

31

Science Scope Activity
(continued from page 30B)

Procedure
1. Examine a lump of coal and record your observations.
2. Using the mortar and pestle, add a little water to the plant materials and grind them to a pulp.
3. Compress the pulp into a mold, using as much pressure as you can without breaking the mold. When the pulp is firmly molded into a block, carefully remove it from the mold.
4. Compare the densities of the coal and the compressed pulp.
5. Store the compressed pulp near a heat source. Compare the densities of the coal and the pulp after one week and again after one month.

In general, the piece of coal will be more dense than the block of compressed pulp, since the pulp was not subjected to the extreme heat and pressure that formed the coal. In addition, as water evaporates from the pulp, the block will most likely become even less dense over time. However, results can vary depending on the humidity of the air in the room, the specific plant materials chosen to form the pulp, and the intensity of the heat applied to the pulp block.

Point out that this reading is taken from Homer Hickam's book *Rocket Boys,* one of a three-book series called *The Coalwood Trilogy.* Students may have seen the movie *October Sky,* which is based on this book. Tell students that Homer became a NASA engineer and is now a famous writer and lecturer. Encourage interested students to read the book *Rocket Boys.* (**Note:** The official Homer Hickam Web site at www.homerhickam.com has a teacher's guide and discussion topics for the book as well as information about Coalville and Homer's life.)

Explore

Time: 15 minutes
Materials: large map of the United States

FIND THE COAL Review with students how to read thematic maps. Have students locate West Virginia on the map (where Homer Hickam grew up). Then have them find their home state on the map and identify whether the state has any coal deposits. Ask: *Which state is not included on this map? Why not?* (Hawaii; students may conclude that there are no coal deposits in Hawaii.)

CHECK UNDERSTANDING
Skill: Classifying
Ask students to name three fossil fuels and explain why they are classified as nonrenewable resources. (Coal, oil, and natural gas; fossil fuels are considered nonrenewable energy resources because they take such a long time to form.)

CHAPTER 3 / LESSON 7 31

CHAPTER 3 / LESSON 7

More Resources
The following resources are also available from Great Source.

ScienceSaurus
Fossil Fuels   325

Reader's Handbook
Elements of Graphics:
   Map   555
   Table   559

Math on Call
Understanding Percent   442

Write Source 2000
Journal Writing   145
Autobiographical Writing   153

Connections

MUSIC The Appalachian region of the United States—which includes Homer Hickam's home state of West Virginia—is famous for its music, much of which is influenced by coal mines and the lives of miners. Students may be familiar with songs such as "Coal Miner's Daughter," "Working in a Coal Mine," or "Sixteen Tons." Have students sing or listen to recordings of coal mining music, then discuss what the songs reveal about coal mining.

(continued on page 33)

Teaching Plan pp. 32–33

▶ **How important do you think coal mining was to the economy of West Virginia (WV), where the Hickam family lived? Explain.**

Since coal is found in most of the state, it was probably a source of income to many people of West Virginia.

The coal mined by Homer's dad and other men in the 1950s was sold to steel-making companies in Pennsylvania, Ohio, and Indiana. The coal was needed as fuel for furnaces used in steel manufacturing.

▶ **How can you explain the choice to build steel plants in these three states?**

These states have large coal deposits. It was probably cheaper for steel factories to be built close to the suppliers of their raw materials.

One hundred years ago, coal was used mainly to heat homes and to power railroads and factories. Today, almost all the coal mined in the United States is burned to produce electricity. The table shows what percentage of electric power is generated from each fossil fuel in 14 states.

Percent of Electricity from Fossil Fuels

State	% from Coal	% from Oil	% from Gas
Alabama	62	0	4
Alaska	10	8	68
California	1	1	51
Idaho	0	0	2
Illinois	47	0	3
Kentucky	97	0	0.5
Missouri	82	0	4
Montana	74	1	0
North Carolina	32	1	1
Oklahoma	64	0	32
Pennsylvania	59	2	2
Texas	36	1	52
Vermont	0	1	1
West Virginia	98.8	0.2	0.2

Adapted and edited from "State by State: Percentage of Total Electricity Generation" (2000) by the Nuclear Energy Institute

---

▶ Explore *(continued)*

To help students answer the last question, explain that it takes two tons of coal to process one ton of iron ore to make steel. Also explain that most of the iron ore in the United States is mined in Minnesota, Michigan, and Wisconsin. Ask how those facts might have figured into the decision to build steel plants near large coal deposits. (It is cheaper to move one ton of iron ore than two tons of coal.) Have students find Pennsylvania, Ohio, and Indiana on a large map of the United States. Ask: How could iron ore be transported to these states? (on rivers and across the Great Lakes)

▶ Propose Explanations

WHAT DO YOU THINK? If students have difficulty answering the last question in this section, discuss other energy sources. Point out that in the table on page 32, the three percentages for each state do not total 100 percent. Ask students why they think this is. (The states use sources of energy other than coal, oil, and gas.) Ask students what other sources of energy they know of besides fossil fuels. (Examples: solar energy, wind, geothermal energy, hydroelectric power, nuclear power) In a class discussion, have students use the map on page 31 and the table on page 32 to predict where they think those other sources are probably used in the United States. (Example: Solar energy, geothermal sources, and wind are probably used in the Southwest and West.)

▶ Propose Explanations

WHAT DO YOU THINK? Look at the table on the opposite page and the map on page 31 to answer the following questions.

▶ Notice that only 1 percent of California's electrical energy comes from coal. Why do you think this percentage is so small?

There are almost no coal deposits in California.

▶ Notice that 98.8 percent of West Virginia's electrical energy comes from coal. Why do you think this percentage is so large?

Coal deposits occur throughout most of West Virginia.

▶ Which state in the table depends most on fossil fuels for electric power? (Hint: Add up the percentages for all three fuels.)

West Virginia (99.2% from fossil fuels)

▶ Notice that none of the states depend entirely on fossil fuels to generate electricity. What are some other energy sources these states might use?

Answers will vary. Examples: geothermal energy, hydroelectric energy, nuclear energy, windmills

▶ Take Action

WRITE HOMER'S JOURNAL ENTRY Imagine what 15-year-old Homer Hickam, Jr., wrote in his journal the night after entering a coal mine with his father for the first time. How did he feel about being underground? Do you think he wants to go back underground for a visit or to work?

Students' journal entries will vary.

(continued from page 32)

Two collections of coal mining songs are available from the Library of Congress Sales Shop at: www.locstore.com/folrec.html.

The Archives of Appalachia have a videotape called "Come All Ye Coal Miners" available for loan at: cass.etsu.edu/archives/outreach.htm. This program features songs performed by coal miners and their families.

Assessment
Skill: Comparing and contrasting

Use the following question to assess each student's progress:

How was coal used in the United States 100 years ago, and how is it used today? (One hundred years ago, coal was used mostly to heat homes and to power railroads and factories. Today almost all coal is burned to produce electricity.)

▶ Take Action

WRITE HOMER'S JOURNAL ENTRY
Remind students that journals are usually written in the first person; encourage them to describe Homer's visit to the mine as if they had experienced it themselves. Prompt students to consider not only what Homer felt and thought but also what he must have seen, heard, touched, or even smelled in the coal mine. Point out that people were probably working in the mine during Homer's visit, and encourage students to include descriptions of the people and activities he might have seen in the mine.

CHAPTER 3 / LESSON 7

UNIT 1 Earth's Surface
CHAPTER 3 / LESSON 8

Point of Lesson
Geothermal energy is a renewable energy source.

Focus
- Structure of the earth system
- Populations, resources, and environments
- Transfer of energy
- Understanding about science and technology

Skills and Strategies
- Making inferences
- Interpreting scientific illustrations
- Forming operational definitions
- Comparing and contrasting
- Generating ideas

Advance Preparation
Vocabulary
Make sure students understand these terms. Definitions can be found in the glossary at the end of the student book.
- electricity
- energy
- fossil fuel
- heat energy
- magma

Materials
Gather the materials needed for *Enrichment* (p. 35) and *Connections* (p. 36).

TEACHING PLAN pp. 34–35

CHAPTER 3 / LESSON 8
Energy Resources

THE HEAT IS ON

Hot water is good for more than just taking baths!

Scientists are always looking for sources of energy that we can use without using them up. Energy sources that cannot be used up are called *renewable resources*. Hot springs and geysers like Yellowstone's Old Faithful are one clue that there is heat energy within Earth's crust. In some places, that energy can be used to produce electricity. One of those places is California.

▶ **Before You Read**

HEAT ON THE MOVE Heat energy is energy related to the temperature of a substance. Heat energy is transferred between materials at different temperatures. Heat energy always moves from a warmer material to a cooler one. Within Earth, heat energy moves from warmer rock to cooler water, heating the water.

▶ *Describe three situations in your home or school in which heat energy is transferred from one material to another.*

  Answers will vary. Examples: Heat energy transfers from the
  burner of an electric stove to a pot, from a light bulb to the
  air around it, and from your hand to an ice cube.
  _____
  _____
  _____

▲ Old Faithful

INTRODUCING THE LESSON
This lesson describes how heat within Earth can be used to generate electricity. Ask students if they have ever seen a natural hot spring or a geyser. Have students who have seen these describe them to the class.

Students may think that heat and temperature are the same thing; a common belief related to this misconception is the idea that cold can be transferred from one object to another. Explain that while heat is the total amount of energy in a material, temperature is a *measure* of the energy in the material. Thinking of heat as a form of energy may help students understand that temperature changes occur when heat is transferred from a warmer object to a cooler one.

▶ **Before You Read**

HEAT ON THE MOVE Have students share their examples, and use them in a class discussion. Make sure students' examples describe heat energy moving from an object or material at a higher temperature to one at a lower temperature. If students give examples of heat energy moving from cooler to warmer objects, coach them to rephrase the example.

Explain that in a closed system, heat energy continues to move from warmer objects to cooler objects until all objects in the system are at the same temperature.

▶ Read

NOTEZONE
Underline each substance mentioned in the reading that contains heat energy.

Here's what you can learn about geothermal energy on California's energy Web site.

Energy From the Earth

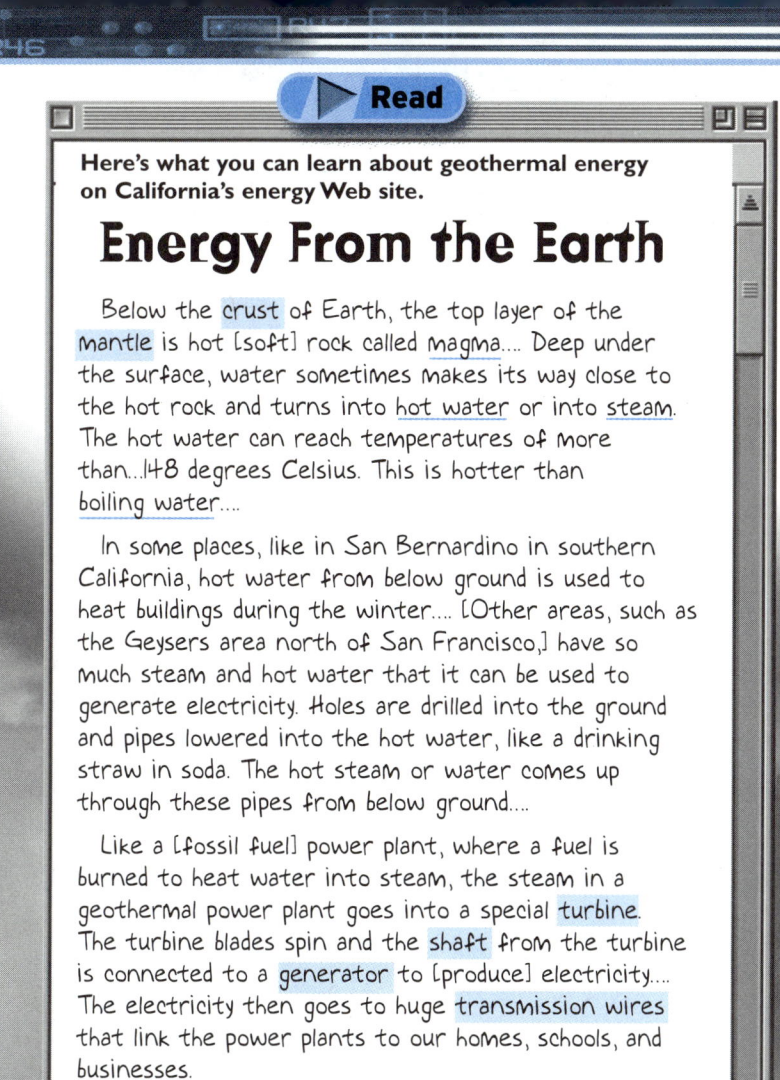

Below the crust of Earth, the top layer of the mantle is hot [soft] rock called magma.... Deep under the surface, water sometimes makes its way close to the hot rock and turns into hot water or into steam. The hot water can reach temperatures of more than...148 degrees Celsius. This is hotter than boiling water....

In some places, like in San Bernardino in southern California, hot water from below ground is used to heat buildings during the winter.... [Other areas, such as the Geysers area north of San Francisco,] have so much steam and hot water that it can be used to generate electricity. Holes are drilled into the ground and pipes lowered into the hot water, like a drinking straw in soda. The hot steam or water comes up through these pipes from below ground....

Like a [fossil fuel] power plant, where a fuel is burned to heat water into steam, the steam in a geothermal power plant goes into a special turbine. The turbine blades spin and the shaft from the turbine is connected to a generator to [produce] electricity.... The electricity then goes to huge transmission wires that link the power plants to our homes, schools, and businesses.

crust: Earth's surface layer
mantle: the layer of Earth below the crust
turbine: a machine that converts heat energy to mechanical energy
shaft: a rotating bar that connects two objects
generator: a machine that converts mechanical energy to electrical energy
transmission wires: wires that carry electrical energy from one place to another

From: "Energy Story: Geothermal Energy." *Energy Quest*. California Energy Commission. (www.energyquest.ca.gov/story/chapter11.html)

FIND OUT MORE
SCIENCESAURUS
Geothermal Energy 326

SCILINKS
THE WORLD'S A CLICK AWAY
www.scilinks.org
Keyword: Renewable and Nonrenewable Energy
Code: GSED04

35

Enrichment
Time: 25 minutes
Materials: ring stand with metal ring; hot plate; plastic food container with hole in bottom for tubing; boiling water; Erlenmeyer flask; one-hole rubber stopper with 0.5–1 m of tubing inserted; plumber's putty; cool water; stopwatch or clock with second hand

Demonstration
This demonstration shows how geysers erupt and how hot water is forced up from beneath Earth's surface.
Caution: Wear appropriate safety gear, and have students observe from a safe distance. Also emphasize that students should not try this activity at home.

1. Set a ring stand next to an unplugged hot plate. Carefully place a flask filled with boiling water on the hot plate. Use the stopper to close the flask.
2. Place the metal ring on the ring stand and over the tubing. Insert the tubing through the hole in the bottom of the plastic container. The top of the tubing should be in the middle of the container.
3. Seal any gaps between the tubing and container with the putty.
4. Tighten the ring securely to hold the plastic container over the flask. Fill the container with cool water so that the top of the tubing is 1–2 cm below the water.
5. Plug in and turn on the hot plate and move away. Tell students to watch for cycles and to use the stopwatch

(continued below)

▶ Read

Ask volunteers to share their answers to the NoteZone task. Discuss the transfer of energy from one substance to another in the production of electricity from geothermal energy. To help students keep track of the various energy transfers described in the reading, have them use a graphic organizer such as the Process Notes shown here.

Ask students to identify each energy transfer in the process, such as heat energy in steam causing the turbine's blades to spin (kinetic energy).

Electricity from Geothermal Energy

Magma heats underground water.
↓
Water becomes very hot or turns into steam.
↓
Holes are drilled into the ground.
↓
Pipes are lowered into the hot water.
↓
Hot water or steam comes up through the pipes.
↓
Steam goes into a turbine.
↓
Turbine blades spin and turn shaft.
↓
Shaft causes a generator to produce electricity.

(Demonstration continued)
to time them. The hot water will rise through the tubing and create a "geyser" in the plastic container. After several cycles, turn off the hot plate. Have students describe how this demonstration models the process described in the excerpt.

CHECK UNDERSTANDING
Skill: Organizing information
Ask: *How is geothermal energy used in California?* (to heat buildings during the winter and to generate electricity)

CHAPTER 3 / LESSON 8

CHAPTER 3 / LESSON 8

More Resources
The following resources are also available from Great Source and NSTA.

ScienceSaurus
Geothermal Energy 326

Reader's Handbook
Elements of Graphics: Map 555
Process Notes 677

Write Source 2000
Brainstorming for Ideas 10

SCILINKS
THE WORLD'S A CLICK AWAY

www.scilinks.org
Keyword: Renewable and Nonrenewable Energy
Code: GSED04

Connections
Time: 15–20 minutes
Materials: map showing the Ring of Fire (see *ScienceSaurus* section 185)

GEOGRAPHY Point out that parts of the western United States are very active geologically. Let students examine a map showing the string of volcanoes known as the Ring of Fire and compare it with the map on this page. Ask: *What relationship do you*

(continued on page 37)

TEACHING PLAN pp. 36–37

▶ Explore

INTERPRETING A MAP Geothermal energy sources are found only in certain areas of the United States. The map below shows those areas.

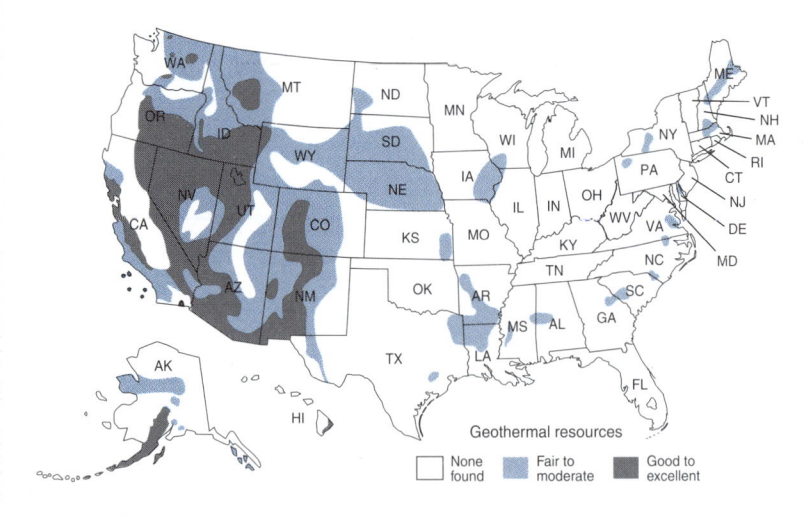

▶ In what area of the U.S. are most geothermal energy sources located?
in the western U.S.

▶ Why do you think geothermal energy sources occur in some places but not in others?
Geothermal energy sources are found only where magma is close to the surface and underground water is heated by magma. The places that do not have geothermal energy sources must not have magma close to underground water.

36

▶ Explore

INTERPRETING A MAP Orient students to the map by having them first locate your state and local area and then use the legend to determine whether there are geothermal resources in the area. If there are, discuss how those resources are used in your area. If not, have students find the nearest source of geothermal energy.

Encourage students to refer back to the reading on page 35 if they need help answering the second question. Ask:

What do the areas with good to excellent geothermal resources have in common? (They are in the western United States and near mountains.) Lead students to understand that the presence of magma near the surface indicates a geologically active area—an area where earthquakes are fairly common and volcanic eruptions are possible.

▶ Propose Explanations

DEFINING RESOURCES Students may be alarmed by the idea that geothermal energy comes from the radioactive decay of elements inside Earth. They may think that the hot water and steam are radioactive or that areas with high levels of geothermal energy are dangerous. Explain that radioactive decay is constantly occurring inside Earth and that some everyday objects, such as certain rocks, are slightly radioactive. This type of radiation is known as *background radiation* because it is always

36 **CHAPTER 3 / LESSON 8**

▶ Propose Explanations

DEFINING RESOURCES Some of the heat inside Earth is left over from the formation of our planet over 4 billion years ago. Most heat inside Earth comes from the radioactive decay of elements in rocks. In some places, water moves through Earth's crust, deep enough to be heated. Geothermal power plants are built where the hot water is near enough to the surface to reach by drilling wells. Once the heat energy is removed, the water can be pumped back down into the ground where it is reheated. The heat energy used in this way is more than replaced by Earth's crust.

Renewable resources are those that can be replaced. Inexhaustible resources are those that people cannot use up, no matter how much they use.

▶ **In what way is geothermal energy an inexhaustible resource?**

Magma constantly heats the water.

▶ **In what way is geothermal energy a renewable resource?**

The water is used as it is taken out of the ground but is replaced when it is pumped back down into the ground.

▶ Take Action

THINK CREATIVELY Only underground water heated above 150°C is hot enough to be used for generating electrical energy. But water heated to between 20°C and 150°C can also be used as an energy source. Water in this temperature range can be piped to homes and greenhouses to heat them.

▶ **List your ideas for more ways to use geothermal energy. Keep in mind what both city dwellers and people who live in the country might need. Also think about things that might limit the distance that geothermal energy could be transported.**

Answers will vary. Examples: warm water for washing clothes and for bathing; heating barns and other animal shelters; thawing frozen ground or melting ice off roads. The cost of insulating pipes, and the fact that water would cool as it traveled through pipes, would limit the distance it could be shipped.

(continued from page 36)
see between the Ring of Fire and the states where geothermal energy sources are found? (The Ring of Fire includes areas along the California coast and the peninsula of Alaska that have geothermal energy sources.) *What does this tell you about those areas?* (Magma must be close to Earth's surface there.)

Assessment
Skill: Sequencing

Use the following task to assess each student's progress:

Ask students to make a series of drawings to show the sequence of steps by which geothermal energy is used to generate electricity. Tell students to label each drawing to explain what is happening at each step. (Students' drawings should include the steps listed in the Process Notes graphic organizer on page 35.)

---

present and is not dangerous. Make sure students understand that exposure to high levels of radiation is dangerous.

To help students classify different types of energy, write the words *Nonrenewable, Renewable,* and *Inexhaustible* on the board. Have students identify different energy sources, and ask the class which heading each source belongs under. (Examples: Nonrenewable: coal, oil, gas; Renewable: wood, hot water or steam; Inexhaustible: geothermal energy, wind energy, solar energy)

▶ Take Action

THINK CREATIVELY To encourage creative thinking, you may want to have students work in small groups to brainstorm uses for geothermal energy. Encourage students to consider practical uses as well as luxurious or artistic uses. Prompt students to consider a wide range of possibilities by asking them to imagine the needs of a family home, a working farm, a large business, a hotel, and a city.

If geothermal energy is used in your area, you may want to invite an energy consultant or a business owner who uses geothermal energy to come talk to your class. Have students prepare a list of questions before the visit.

CHAPTER 3 / LESSON 8   37

UNIT 1 Earth's Surface
CHAPTER 3 / LESSON 9

Point of Lesson
Each energy source has its advantages and disadvantages.

Focus
- Structure of the earth system
- Populations, resources, and environments
- Understanding about science and technology
- Science and technology in society

Skills and Strategies
- Creating and using tables
- Concept mapping
- Comparing and contrasting
- Generating questions

Advance Preparation

Vocabulary
Make sure students understand these terms. Definitions can be found in the glossary at the end of the student book.
- coal
- electricity
- geothermal energy
- nonrenewable resources
- pollution
- renewable resources

TEACHING PLAN pp. 38–39

INTRODUCING THE LESSON
This lesson discusses the choices involved in determining which energy resources to use. Ask: *When you have a difficult decision, do you flip a coin, or do you try to evaluate the alternatives?* Make a list of the ways students approach the decision-making process. Ask students if the process they use depends on whether they are making an important decision that will have significant effects. Students may not know how the electricity in your area is generated. If possible, provide information about this from the local power company.

CHAPTER 3 / LESSON 9
Energy Resources

Energy Choices

Is there a best way to produce electricity? You decide.

Electrical energy can be generated from either nonrenewable energy sources such as coal or from renewable energy sources such as geothermal energy. Each source has its benefits and its drawbacks. It's up to citizens to weigh the pros and cons of each source and make the best decision.

▶ Explore

ELECTRICITY NEEDS Most communities rely on a dependable supply of electricity. Make a concept map to show the uses of electricity in your home or in your school.

Answers will vary. Examples: In a home—lamps, heat, computers, television, kitchen appliances, and so on. In school—lighting, computers, projectors, copy machines

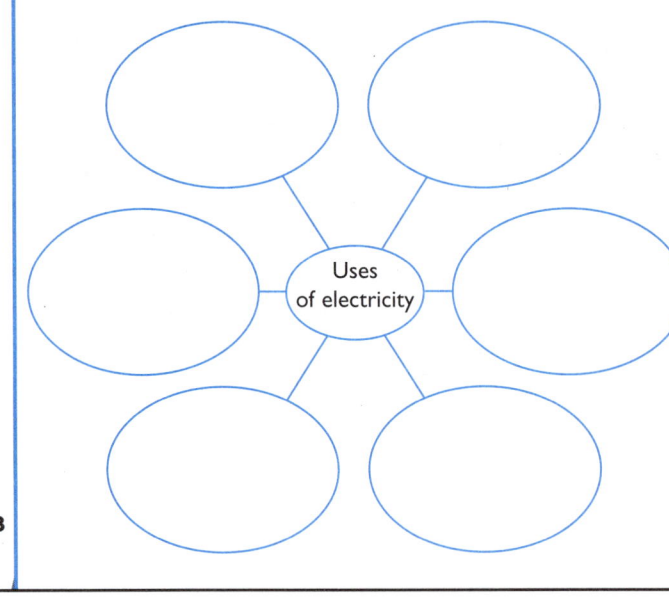

(Concept map: Uses of electricity)

▶ Explore

ELECTRICITY NEEDS Emphasize that graphic organizers are useful tools to visualize all the details about a concept. They can help sort out the key facts and evaluate evidence. When students have completed their organizers, invite volunteers to share their ideas.

Activity

CONSIDER YOUR OPTIONS This chart compares two ways of producing electricity—from coal and from geothermal energy.

	Electricity from Coal	Electricity from Geothermal Energy
Energy source	Burn coal to produce steam	Steam and hot water from heat in Earth's crust
Availability of fuel source	Coal is plentiful and cheap.	Mostly limited to parts of western states, Alaska, and Hawaii
Location of plant	Can be built just about anywhere that coal can be delivered by ship or railroad	Needs to be near a geothermal source that can be reached by drilling wells
Pollution	Large amounts of carbon dioxide and sulfur dioxide	Steam and tiny amounts of carbon dioxide and sulfur dioxide; poisonous heavy metals in water; noise pollution
Space	Large facility required	Small facility required
Cost to customer	$0.035–$0.04 per kilowatt-hour	$0.05–$0.08 per kilowatt-hour
Disruption to land	Most coal mining today requires stripping away land surface.	Wells drilled into ground for steam to rise up through
Transportation and storage of fuel	Need to ship in and store large amounts of coal	No transportation or storage needed
Power plant maintenance	High cost to obtain and transport coal	Low cost (Steam and hot water are free.) Maintenance can be high due to corrosiveness of water.
Reliability	Generating electrical energy 60–70% of the time	Generating 95% of the time
Long-term sustainability	There is a limited amount of coal on Earth.	Earth's heat is unlimited.

Imagine that you live in a western state where there are good geothermal energy sources. Your region needs a new power plant. One citizens' group proposes a coal-fired plant. Another group proposes a geothermal plant.

▶ You've been asked to interview both groups for a report in the newspaper. Using the table for ideas, list questions that you would ask both groups. Your goal is to report on the plans for both types of plants without trying to influence the readers about which plant is a better choice.

Answers will vary. Questions may include the cost to build and operate

the plant, how much space the plant will take up, how much pollution

can be expected, the cost of electricity, and so on.

More Resources

The following resources are also available from Great Source and NSTA.

READER'S HANDBOOK
Elements of Graphics: Table   559
Using Graphic Organizers   662
Reading Tools: Concept Map   670

WRITE SOURCE 2000
Writing News Stories   167

SciLINKS
THE WORLD'S A CLICK AWAY

www.scilinks.org
Keyword: Renewable and Nonrenewable Resources
Code: GSED05

Assessment
Skill: Comparing and contrasting

Use the following questions to assess each student's progress:

To prompt students to compare the benefits and drawbacks associated with generating electricity from geothermal energy and from coal, ask: *Which energy source costs the customer less?* (coal) *Which energy source causes less air pollution?* (geothermal energy) *Which source can be used only in certain areas?* (geothermal energy)

Activity

CONSIDER YOUR OPTIONS When students list their questions, remind them that interviewers often use the five W's—*Who, What, Where, When,* and *Why*—to guide their questioning. To this list of question starters, suggest that they add the word *How*. Encourage students to generate questions that begin with those words.

After students have written their questions, have them conduct a debate about the two energy alternatives. Divide the class into three groups: two to represent the citizen groups and one to represent the press. Have members of the press group pose their questions to the group in favor of geothermal power and to the group in favor of coal. As an extension, have students write a newspaper article about the issue and the debate.

CHECK UNDERSTANDING
Skill: Recognizing cause and effect
Ask: *What do you think are the most important factors in choosing an energy source?* (Answers will vary but may include cost to customers, disruption to land, reliability, and long-term sustainability.)

CHAPTER 4
Overview

Fossil Hunters

LESSON 10
She Sells Seashells

Point of Lesson: *A successful fossil hunter has to be in the right place at the right time.*

This lesson uses the example of fossil hunter Mary Anning to show students that nonscientists can make significant contributions to scientific knowledge. Mary Anning lived on the southern shores of Great Britain in the 1800s. She came from a very poor family and never enjoyed the benefit of formal education. Despite these disadvantages, she made remarkable discoveries in paleontology that were important in reconstructing the history of life on this planet.

Materials
Science Scope Activity (p. 41), for each group:
- fossils or pictures of fossils of various ages
- newspapers (14 days' worth)

Laboratory Safety
Review this safety guideline with students before they do the Science Scope Activity in this lesson.
- Handle fossils carefully. Not only are fossils delicate, but they often have sharp edges.

LESSON 11
Markers of Time

Point of Lesson: *A fossil hunter who thinks scientifically about Earth's past is more than a collector.*

From data Mary Anning and other fossil hunters collected, scientists have made inferences about how Earth has changed over time. For example, oceans once covered what is now dry land. Layers of organic material that settled to the ancient ocean bottom can be read as a timetable of periods in Earth's history.

Materials
Enrichment (p. 45), for each student:
- clay
- plaster of Paris

Connections (p. 46), for each student:
- colored pencils
- drawing paper

Laboratory Safety
Review these safety guidelines with students before they do the Enrichment activity in this lesson.
- Avoid inhaling plaster of Paris.
- Wash your hands thoroughly after the activity.

LESSON 12
Against All Odds

Point of Lesson: *Amateur fossil hunters can make important scientific contributions.*

Lou Tremblay volunteered to work at a fossil dig run by paleontologists. By carefully observing, collecting, and recording data and communicating with the paleontologists on the dig, he became a major contributor to an astounding discovery—one of the largest tyrannosaur specimens ever found.

Materials
None

Science Scope Activity

Pages of History

NSTA has chosen a Science Scope *activity related to the content in this chapter. You'll find the activity in Lesson 10, page 41.*

This activity is a fossil collection simulation that has students digging through strata of newspaper. Students work in teams as paleontologists and geoscientists to search for fossil evidence, document the fossil record, and create a stratigraphic record.

Background Information

Lesson 10

Mary Anning continued to comb the beach for fossils throughout her life. Her collection was unrivalled, though she continued to sell and give away many of her specimens. She is credited with finding the first almost complete plesiosaur; the first British pterodactyl; and the first squaloraja, a transitional fish somewhere between sharks and rays.

Her method for staying ahead of the competition was to dash out in the midst of a storm and collect what she could before the waves washed the fossils away. The limestone cliffs of Lyme Regis are very delicate, and a powerful storm is enough to start a minor landslide, exposing new fossils.

Lesson 11

The town of Lyme Regis was at the bottom of the ocean 200 million years ago. In this ocean lived ammonites, relatives of the modern nautilus; belemnites, similar to modern squid; ichthyosaurs, "fish lizards" that superficially resembled a cross between a dolphin and a crocodile; plesiosaurs, long-necked marine animals; and dozens of species of fish. The area remained an ocean throughout the Jurassic period.

Lesson 12

Scientists have estimated that 0.1 percent of all living things undergo the fossilization process. Although this percentage is only an estimate, it clearly illustrates that the Jurassic period was teeming with life.

UNIT 1 Earth's Surface

CHAPTER 4 / LESSON 10

Point of Lesson
A successful fossil hunter has to be in the right place at the right time.

Focus
- Abilities necessary to do scientific inquiry
- Earth's history
- Nature of science

Skills and Strategies
- Organizing information
- Making inferences
- Understanding that scientists share their results to form a common core of knowledge
- Generating questions
- Using space/time relationships

Advance Preparation

Vocabulary
Make sure students understand this term. The definition can be found in the glossary at the end of the student book.
- organism

Materials
Gather the materials needed for *Science Scope Activity* (p. 41).

CHAPTER 4 / LESSON 10
Fossil Hunters

SHE SELLS SEASHELLS

Can a self-taught person do *real* science? Mary Anning did.

Back in the 1800s, few girls went to school—especially those who came from poor families. Despite the disadvantages she faced, young Mary Anning of Lyme Regis, England, learned to think scientifically. As a result, she made a valuable contribution to paleontology, the study of fossils. Fossils are the remains or traces of organisms that lived on Earth thousands or millions of years ago.

▲ Mary Anning

▶ Before You Read

ORGANIZE YOUR IDEAS What kinds of things can become fossils? How does something become "fossilized"?
▶ Record your ideas below. Draw a picture of a fossil you might have seen.

Answers will vary. Example: The hard parts of once-living things and the impressions they leave, such as footprints, can become fossils. Things become "fossilized" when they get buried by sediment that later turns to rock, caught inside sap, or buried in layers of ice.

TEACHING PLAN pp. 40–41

INTRODUCING THE LESSON
This lesson introduces the characteristics of a scientific mind through a brief biography of an untrained fossil hunter.

Ask the class: *What is a fossil?* Students will most likely refer to the bones or skeleton of an ancient animal. Point out that other remains can be fossilized as well, including tracks, leaf imprints, shells, and the like.

▶ Before You Read

ORGANIZE YOUR IDEAS Explain that fossils are formed from the remains of an organism or traces (such as footprints) that it has left behind. Tell students that fossil skeletons are not the actual bones of an animal but minerals that have replaced the bones over time and hardened inside layers of sediment, sap, or ice. Point out that only the hard parts of organisms become fossilized.

> **Read**

Fossil collecting was the Anning family's business.

A Family Business

Mary Anning was born in 1799 to Richard and Mary Anning of Lyme Regis...on the southern shores of Great Britain. The cliffs at Lyme Regis were—and still are—rich in spectacular fossils from the seas of the Jurassic period.... Richard was a cabinetmaker and occasional fossil collector. Unfortunately, Richard died in 1810, leaving his family in debt [and] without a provider. He did, however, pass on his fossil hunting skills to his wife and children....

The Anning family lived in poverty and anonymity, selling fossils from Lyme Regis.... By the middle of the 1820s, daughter Mary had established herself as the keen eye and accomplished anatomist of the family, and began taking charge of the family fossil business....

Mary Anning...help[ed] to discover the first specimen of *Ichthyosaurus* to be known by the scientific community of London. This specimen was probably discovered sometime between 1809 and 1811, when Mary was only 10 to 12 years old.... Mary's skill and dedication produced many remarkable finds and thus provided the fatherless family with a means of income. It is clear...that Anning was not only a collector, but was well-versed in the scientific understanding of what she collected, and won the respect of the scientists of her time. Her discoveries were important in reconstructing the world's past and the history of its life.

▼ Ichthyosaurus fossil

NoteZone
Underline the words that tell what made Mary Anning a successful fossil hunter.

spectacular: unusually good or impressive
Jurassic: the time period from 208 million to 144 million years ago
anonymity: not being known or recognized by others
anatomist: a person who studies the structure of organisms
specimen: an individual that is thought to be typical of its kind
Ichthyosaurus: an extinct ocean reptile with a fishlike body and paddlelike limbs
dedication: commitment

From: "Mary Anning (1799-1847)." University of California Museum of Paleontology. The University of California Museum of Paleontology, Berkeley, and the Regents of the University of California. (www.ucmp.berkeley.edu/history/anning.html)

FIND OUT MORE
SCIENCESAURUS
Rocks 180
Fossils 198

SCILINKS
THE WORLD'S A CLICK AWAY
www.scilinks.org
Keyword: Fossils
Code: GSED06

41

Science Scope Activity

Pages of History
Time: 40 minutes
Materials: (for each group) fossils or pictures of fossils of various ages; newspapers (14 days' worth)

Preparation: Stack the newspapers in chronological order with the oldest on the bottom. Conceal fossils between the newspaper layers. Label each fossil with its age, and insert the fossils into the stack in the correct geological order. Make one stack per group.

Procedure
Create a Data Collection Sheet (see sample below) with days numbered 1–14. Divide the class into small groups, and give each group a copy. Explain that the pages of newspaper represent layers of rock. Give students the following instructions:

1. Search for fossils from the top of the stack to the bottom—as geologists would search for them in a dig.
2. When you find a fossil, record the type, and the date and page number of the newspaper layer in which the fossil was found.

Ask: Why is the fossil record important? (It provides evidence about the history of life on Earth.)

Day	Fossil type	Newspaper date and p. number	Approximate age of fossil
1			
2			

> **Read**

Ask students to expand the list of characteristics that someone would need in order to be a successful paleontologist. (Examples: patience, determination, good observational skills, and knowledge of the organisms for which he or she is searching)

Ask students to define the term *oral history*. (traditions passed from generation to generation by word of mouth) Explain that much of what is known about Mary Anning is through oral histories of those who knew of her and of her work with fossils.

CHECK UNDERSTANDING
Skill: Making inferences
Pose the following question: *Suppose a scientist found several layers of fossils from seashells and other marine organisms several kilometers inland from a shoreline. What might the scientist conclude about the area where the fossils were found?* (The area was most likely under water at the time the organisms lived.)

CHAPTER 4 / LESSON 10   41

CHAPTER 4 / LESSON 10

More Resources

The following resources are also available from Great Source and NSTA.

ScienceSaurus
Rocks 180
Fossils 198

Reader's Handbook
Making Inferences 40

Write Source 2000
Interviewing 170

SCILINKS
THE WORLD'S A CLICK AWAY

www.scilinks.org
Keyword: Fossils
Code: GSED06

Connections

LANGUAGE ARTS Have students use a dictionary to look up the root word *ichthyo-* and the suffix *-saurus*. (*Ichthyo* is a Greek word meaning "fish," and *saurus* is a Greek word meaning "lizard.") Explain that the suffix *-saurus* is used to form the scientific name of many reptiles and dinosaurs that lived millions of years

(continued on page 43)

Teaching Plan pp. 42–43

Explore

MAKING INFERENCES Students should be able to infer that the cliffs in which Mary Anning found fossils were once under water. Point out that in many parts of the world, shorelines and the land just inland from the shorelines were once under water. That explains why fossils of marine organisms are often found far from present-day shorelines.

Ask students if they would expect to find older fossils in the top or bottom layers of the cliffs. (The bottom layers would hold the oldest specimens, since those layers would have been deposited first.)

42   CHAPTER 4 / LESSON 10

Explore

MAKING INFERENCES In the 1820s, Mary Anning walked the beaches and climbed the cliffs of Lyme Regis. But 200 million years earlier, the rock of Lyme Regis was located at the bottom of the ocean.

The ocean then was full of many types of organisms. Today we know many of these ancient organisms only as fossils. *Ichthyosaurs*, like the fossilized one Mary Anning found, were plentiful. When the organisms died, their remains sank to the ocean floor. In that part of the ocean, the water was calm and shallow, and the remains stayed where they were. Some remains became trapped in sand and mud. Over millions of years, pressure, compacting, and cementing turned the sand and mud to stone. The organisms' remains were fossilized in the stone.

▶ **Why were there so many fossils in the cliffs of Lyme Regis?**
  The area used to be under an ocean that was full of organisms.
  The water was calm enough for the remains to stay in place and
  become fossils.

▶ **Think about conditions on the ocean shore. Why do you think there were more fossils to be found along the beaches at the base of the cliffs in Lyme Regis than in other places around town?**
  The pounding of the waves wore away the cliffs, exposing the fossils.
  In other areas of town, the fossils might have remained hidden.

▶ **Scientific discoveries are often made when a person with the right knowledge is in the right place at the right time. In what ways was Mary Anning in the right place at the right time? In what ways was she the right person?**
  She lived in an area where many fossils could be found. People at the
  time were interested in buying fossils, and she needed to support her
  family. She understood a lot of what she saw and taught herself more.

THINKING LIKE A SCIENTIST
▶ Based on what you read, what do you think was one reason Mary Anning started collecting fossils?

Answers will vary. Example: She wanted to make money to support her family.

▶ In what ways was Mary Anning like a scientist today?

She was a keen observer and studied anatomy.

▶ In what ways was Mary Anning not like most scientists today?

She had no formal schooling.

▶ **Take Action**

CONDUCT AN INTERVIEW Imagine that you are a reporter from a scientific magazine who will interview Mary Anning. What questions would you ask about her life and fossil hunting? List the questions below. What do you think her responses might be? On a separate sheet of paper, write your report of the interview.

Interviews will vary. Sample questions: What do you like best about fossil hunting? What were some of the best fossils you found? How old were you when you found your first fossil?

(continued from page 42)
ago. Ask students to use dictionaries and other sources to find the meanings of the names of some ancient organisms they know of—for example, *brachiosaurus*, *plesiosaurus*, and *tyrannosaurus*.

Assessment
Skill: Inferring

Use the following questions to assess each student's progress:

What science skills did Mary Anning use in her hunt for fossils? (Mary Anning used the skills of observing, making inferences, drawing conclusions, and classifying.) *How are these skills similar to those practiced by trained scientists today?* (Scientists today also use these skills when they discover new kinds of fossils, record data, and draw conclusions about how an organism must have looked when it was alive.)

THINKING LIKE A SCIENTIST Have students refer back to the list of words they made of the characteristics of a scientist and the words that tell what made Mary Anning a successful fossil hunter. Ask students if they would like to revise, change, or add to their lists. Ask students how scientists today differ from those who lived in Mary Anning's time. (Today's scientists have the advantage of modern technology, and they have access to information that was not yet known in Mary Anning's time.)

▶ **Take Action**

CONDUCT AN INTERVIEW Point out to students that a good article includes questions that ask who, what, when, where, why, and how. Tell them that their questions could cover both personal and professional information about Mary Anning. Have volunteers role-play interviews.

UNIT 1 Earth's Surface
CHAPTER 4 / LESSON 11

Point of Lesson
A fossil hunter who thinks scientifically about Earth's past is more than a collector.

Focus
- Earth's history
- Science as a human endeavor
- Nature of science

Skills and Strategies
- Comparing and contrasting
- Making inferences
- Understanding that scientists share their results to form a common core of knowledge
- Using space/time relationships
- Creating and using tables

Advance Preparation

Vocabulary
Make sure students understand these terms. Definitions can be found in the glossary at the end of the student book.

- continent
- coral reef
- fossil
- inference
- rock

Materials
Gather the materials needed for *Enrichment* (p. 45) and *Connections* (p. 46).

TEACHING PLAN pp. 44–45

INTRODUCING THE LESSON
This lesson discusses how scientists gather and share information and how fossils provide us with evidence about Earth's history. Ask students to describe various kinds of fossils they have seen and what these fossils can tell us about the history of Earth. Many students will not understand that the surface of Earth has changed over many millions of years. Explain that fossil evidence helps scientists determine how Earth has changed.

CHAPTER 4 / LESSON 11
Fossil Hunters

Markers of Time

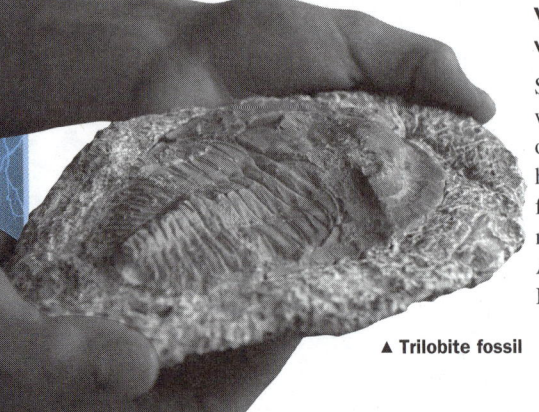

What makes a scientist's work extraordinary?

Scientists of Mary Anning's time were shocked when they heard of the work of the young fossil hunter. In the early 1800s, a person from a poor family did not think of being a scientist. And a female scientist? Next to impossible!

▲ Trilobite fossil

▶ Before You Read

THINK ABOUT IT Every fossil is like one piece of the puzzle of Earth's history.

▶ What do fossil hunters need to do to make their fossils count as pieces of this puzzle?

Answers will vary. Examples: They need to record what rock the fossils were in, make sure all the parts stay together, share their finds with scientists, and spend time reading what others have written about the subject.

▶ Before You Read

THINK ABOUT IT Direct students' attention to the photographs of fossils on these two pages. Explain that a trilobite is a segmented marine organism that lived from 225 million to 600 million years ago. An ammonite is a marine mollusk that lived as long as 325 million years ago. Ask: *What inferences could scientists make based on these fossils?* (The land on which these fossils were found was most likely covered by water at the time the organisms lived.)

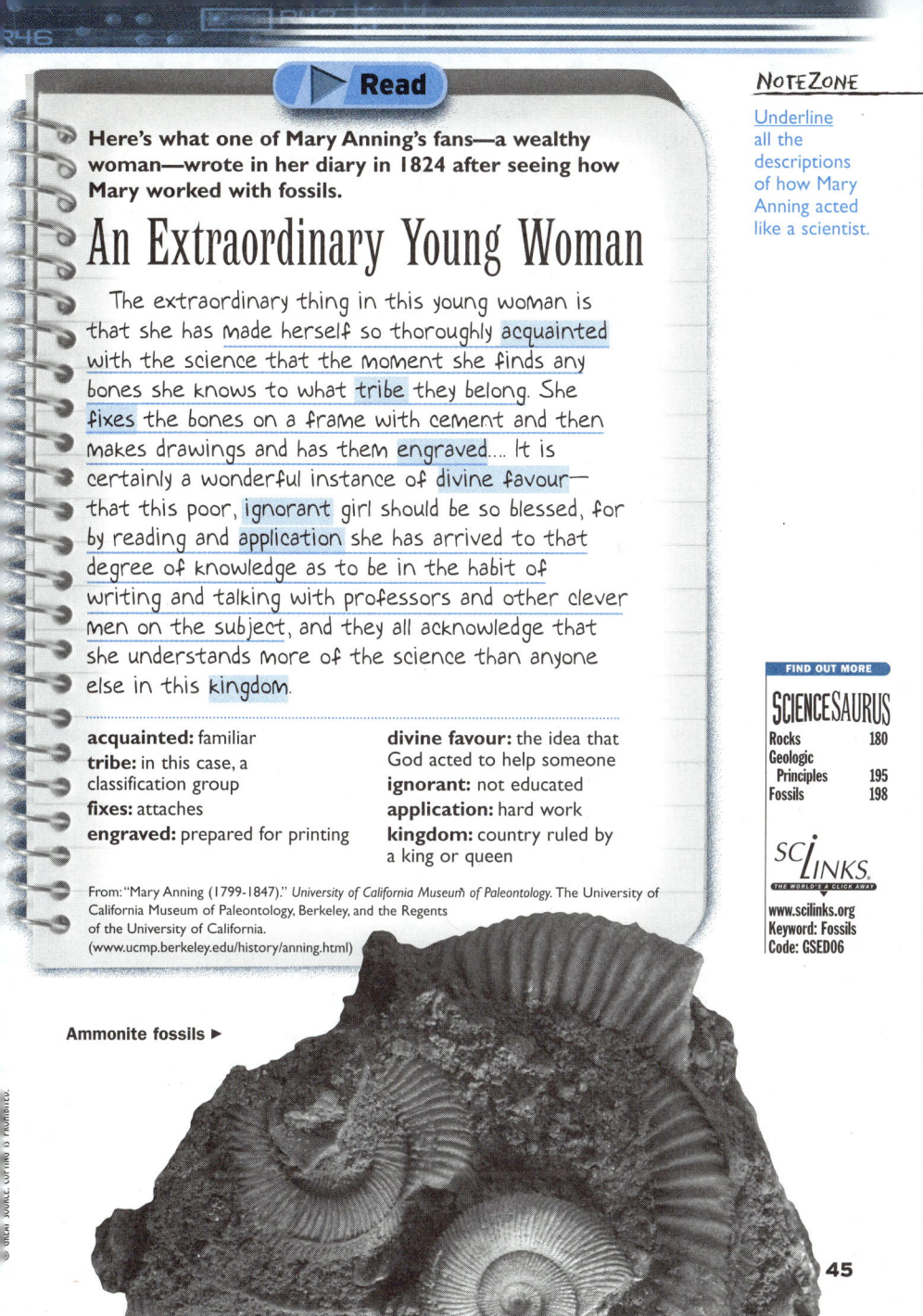

Read

Here's what one of Mary Anning's fans—a wealthy woman—wrote in her diary in 1824 after seeing how Mary worked with fossils.

An Extraordinary Young Woman

The extraordinary thing in this young woman is that she has made herself so thoroughly acquainted with the science that the moment she finds any bones she knows to what tribe they belong. She fixes the bones on a frame with cement and then makes drawings and has them engraved.... It is certainly a wonderful instance of divine favour—that this poor, ignorant girl should be so blessed, for by reading and application she has arrived to that degree of knowledge as to be in the habit of writing and talking with professors and other clever men on the subject, and they all acknowledge that she understands more of the science than anyone else in this kingdom.

acquainted: familiar
tribe: in this case, a classification group
fixes: attaches
engraved: prepared for printing
divine favour: the idea that God acted to help someone
ignorant: not educated
application: hard work
kingdom: country ruled by a king or queen

From: "Mary Anning (1799-1847)." *University of California Museum of Paleontology.* The University of California Museum of Paleontology, Berkeley, and the Regents of the University of California.
(www.ucmp.berkeley.edu/history/anning.html)

◄ Ammonite fossils

NoteZone

Underline all the descriptions of how Mary Anning acted like a scientist.

FIND OUT MORE

SCIENCESAURUS
Rocks 180
Geologic Principles 195
Fossils 198

SCILINKS
www.scilinks.org
Keyword: Fossils
Code: GSED06

45

Enrichment

Time: 40–45 minutes
Materials: clay, plaster of Paris

Have students prepare "fossils" from clay or plaster of Paris. Students can make imprints of objects and share their fossils with classmates. Students should make a list of questions they would like to know about each fossil, then examine the fossils to note similarities and differences between them. Encourage students to make inferences about the fossils as they make their observations.

Read

After students have completed the reading, ask them: *What was the writer's opinion of Mary Anning?* (The writer seems to have a good opinion of Mary Anning and to admire her work.)

Then refer students to the descriptions they underlined. Ask them how Mary Anning used the science skill of classification in her work. (She was able to determine which group of organisms a fossil belonged to.)

Finally, ask students how Mary's presentation of the fossils would have been helpful to other scientists interested in learning more about them. (The fossil presentations provided evidence and examples of Earth's history.)

CHECK UNDERSTANDING

Skill: Recognizing cause and effect
Ask students how Mary Anning won the respect of the scientists of her time. (She was a collector who was also well-versed in the scientific knowledge of what she collected. Her discoveries helped reconstruct Earth's history.)

CHAPTER 4 / LESSON 11   45

CHAPTER 4 / LESSON 11

More Resources
The following resources are also available from Great Source and NSTA.

ScienceSaurus
Rocks	180
Geologic Principles	195
Fossils	198

Reader's Handbook
Reading Science	100

SciLinks
THE WORLD'S A CLICK AWAY

www.scilinks.org
Keyword: Fossils
Code: GSED06

Connections
Time: 40 minutes
Materials: colored pencils, drawing paper

ART/WRITING Have students create drawings of one or two sets of fossilized footprints, then exchange drawings with classmates to interpret. Students could research animal tracks so they have some models to follow as they create the footprints. As students develop their drawings, have them keep the following questions in mind: How many animals made the

(continued on page 47)

Teaching Plan pp. 46–47

▶ Explore

UNDERSTANDING THE WORK OF SCIENTISTS Have students make a list of the science skills Mary Anning used in her study of fossils and give examples of how she practiced these skills. (For example, she made *observations* by preparing drawings and engravings of the fossils. She might have made observations of features such as fins, webbed feet, sharp teeth, or molars. She was able to *classify* the fossils by comparing their features. She might have looked at the location of fossils to help in classification.)

Extend the concept by asking students what other science skills they might apply to the study of fossils. (measuring the size of fossils, sequencing the ages of a group of fossils, organizing information to draw conclusions about how Earth has changed)

WHAT DO YOU THINK? Invite students to share their experiences with any fossil collections they might have seen in museums or in other science exhibits. Ask students what they learned by examining the fossils.

46 CHAPTER 4 / LESSON 11

▶ Explore

UNDERSTANDING THE WORK OF SCIENTISTS Mary Anning did not go to school to learn to be a scientist. Yet she acted like one in the field.

▶ **According to the reading, how did Mary Anning develop her skills as a scientist?**
through reading and application (hard work) and by communicating with other scientists

▶ **How did Mary Anning record her findings?**
by making drawings

▶ **How did Mary Anning display the fossils for scientists to study?**
by attaching them to frames with cement

▶ **How did Mary Anning make her discoveries available to scientists?**
by having her drawings engraved so they could be printed and distributed

Over the years, Mary Anning's knowledge grew as she saw more fossils.
▶ **How do you think seeing so many fossils helped her understand them?**
Answers will vary. Examples: She could compare new fossils with fossils she'd already found and learn which organisms lived at the same time in the past. She shared information with others and learned about their discoveries as well.

WHAT DO YOU THINK? Some people collect natural objects just to have a collection or to sell. Other collectors do more. They keep detailed records of their finds, learn about their collections, and share what they learn. By doing so, they may add to scientific knowledge.

▶ **Which type of collector was Mary Anning? Why do you think so?**
Mary Anning was both types. She collected to sell so she could support her family. She also added to scientific knowledge. She made drawings of her fossils and talked with professors to learn and share information about fossils.

46

Propose Explanations

MAKING INFERENCES Earth's surface has constantly changed over billions of years. Continents that were once joined have been separated and then joined again. Rocks that were once under the ocean have been pushed up and today are dry land. New layers of rock have formed on top of older layers and then have been covered by even newer layers. Rocks on land have been pushed under the ocean. By studying fossils, scientists can make inferences about Earth's history.

▶ *Imagine that you are studying the fossil data described below. For each piece of evidence, write an inference you can make about Earth's history or the age of a rock layer.*

Evidence	Inference
Fossils of the same kind of land animals are found on different continents.	*The continents were once connected.*
Fossils of organisms that lived on coral reefs are found on the plains of Iowa.	*A sea once covered the land that is now dry.*
Coral-reef fossils are found in rocks on a mountaintop in Canada.	*The land was pushed high above sea level.*
Fossil A is found in a lower layer of rock than Fossil B.	*The rock that holds Fossil A is probably older than the rock that holds Fossil B.*
Fossils of a kind of organism that lived for only a short time 400 million years ago are found at different locations around the world.	*The rocks that the fossils were found in are about 400 million years old.*

(continued from page 46)
footprints? How many legs was each animal walking on? In what direction were the animals traveling? How large were the animals that made the prints? Each student should write a paragraph explaining his or her inferences about the classmate's fossilized footprints and identifying the evidence on which the inferences are based.

Assessment
Skill: Making inferences

Use the following question to assess each student's progress:
How are fossils used as evidence that Earth has changed over time? (Fossils of marine organisms often appear on dry land or in mountainous regions. Many fossils of the same kind are found on different continents, indicating that the continents were once joined. Fossils are buried in layers of sediment; their position indicates their relative age.)

Propose Explanations

MAKING INFERENCES Emphasize to students that their inferences must be made based on the given evidence and what they already know about the formation of fossils. Remind students to refrain from making inferences that are overly broad or from making generalizations that are not related to the evidence.

Direct attention to the fourth example. Explain to students that, normally, younger rock lies on top of older rock. In geology this is known as the Law of Superposition. Point out that, in some cases, rock layers may be overturned so that younger rock lies underneath older rock.

UNIT 1 Earth's Surface

CHAPTER 4 / LESSON 12

Point of Lesson
Amateur fossil hunters can make important scientific contributions.

Focus
- Understanding about scientific inquiry
- Science as a human endeavor
- Nature of science

Skills and Strategies
- Making inferences

Advance Preparation

Vocabulary
Make sure students understand this term. The definition can be found in the glossary at the end of the student book.
- fossil

Enrichment
Encourage students to use the Internet to research some well-known fossil digs. Some examples are the La Brea Tar Pits in California, known for their large variety of ice age animals, and Dinosaur National Monument in Utah, the largest quarry of Jurassic dinosaur bones ever discovered. Tell students to describe the events that led to the discoveries and the types of fossil remains that were found. Let students share their findings.

TEACHING PLAN pp. 48–49

INTRODUCING THE LESSON
This lesson describes the ways in which an amateur paleontologist can contribute to scientific knowledge. Ask students what they know about dinosaur digs, particularly the kinds of tools that paleontologists might use to uncover and study fossil remains. Many students may believe that it is easy to discover dinosaurs. Point out that paleontologists must work long, hard hours and that in many cases, it may take years to make an important discovery.

CHAPTER 4 / LESSON 12

Fossil Hunters

Against All Odds

Even a retired science teacher on vacation can make a contribution to science.

Mary Anning became a respected fossil hunter. Can someone living today do the same thing? Lou Tremblay did. He's a retired earth science teacher who volunteers to help scientists looking for fossils.

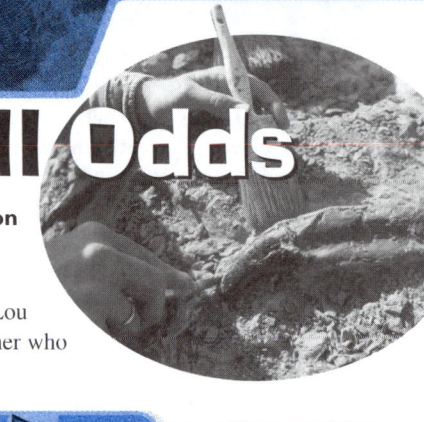

NOTEZONE
Circle the tools the volunteers used to dig and record what they found.

FIND OUT MORE

SCIENCESAURUS
Fossils 198

SCILINKS
THE WORLD'S A CLICK AWAY
www.scilinks.org
Keyword: Fossils
Code: GSED06

▶ **Read**

On a field trip in Montana, Mr. Tremblay made quite a discovery.

Dinosaur Dig

Lou Tremblay, a dinosaur dig volunteer, noticed nothing but the ground two feet [60 cm] in front of him. "I was determined to make a find," he recalls…. So Tremblay, with head hung low and eyes fixed downward, paced over baked brown clay until finally he stopped, stooped, and scooped up what looked like a bone fragment….

But that was just the beginning. Using [soft] paintbrushes, he and [a] fellow volunteer…cleared away surface dirt to discover that this knob was the weathered tip of a long, slender bone. As they had been taught in field school, they snapped some photos, noted their location in a logbook, and loosened some surrounding soil with a scratch awl. "At this point we knew it was something big," Tremblay says….

Some weeks later…Keith Rigby, a paleontologist at the University of Notre Dame, told Tremblay that the rib he found, along with a pelvis, claw, and toe bone found nearby, clearly belonged to a large carnivorous dinosaur. Tremblay's find may even be the largest tyrannosaur specimen ever found.

scratch awl: a hand tool with a sharp point
paleontologist: a scientist who studies fossils to learn about organisms of the past
pelvis: the bones at the base of the spine where the legs are attached to the body
carnivorous: meat-eating

From: "Join a Dig." *Dinosaur Digs.* Travel Channel. (travel.discovery.com/ideas/outdoors_parks/dinodigs/join.html)

48

▶ **Read**

After students have completed the reading and the NoteZone task, ask: *Why is it important for a paleontologist to know how to use these tools?* (The tools help unearth the fossil remains and record their position in the rock.)

Ask students if they think that finding a dinosaur in a dig is an easy chore. Stress that many paleontologists often search for weeks, months, or even years before making a small or minor discovery.

Explore

MAKING INFERENCES Mr. Tremblay volunteers to work at fossil digs run by paleontologists. The scientists run a field school before allowing the volunteers to dig.

▶ **Why do you think the volunteers need to go to the field school before digging for fossils?**
If the volunteers weren't trained first, they could damage fossils or miss important data.

▶ **What do you think scientists teach the volunteers at the field school?**
how to recognize fossils sticking out of the ground, how to record the location and position of the fossils, how to get the fossils out of the ground without damaging them

▶ **Volunteers are not allowed to take fossils home. Why do you think that is the case?**
If the fossils were taken home, then they would not be studied and shared with other scientists and would not contribute to scientific knowledge.

▶ **How did Mr. Tremblay, who was not a paleontologist, contribute to scientific knowledge?**
By working with paleontologists, he helped uncover an unusual skeleton that the scientists could study and share with other scientists.

Take Action

LEAVE THE BONES ALONE! Imagine that you are a park ranger in an area where fossilized bones are often found. On a separate sheet of paper, write a paragraph for the park brochure telling visitors what they should do if they find a fossil. Explain why they should not take the fossil.

Answers will vary. Example: If you find a fossil in the park, do not touch it. Tell a park ranger about your find. Fossils are important clues about Earth's history. Digging up a fossil can damage it or destroy important information about Earth's history.

49

More Resources
The following resources are also available from Great Source and NSTA.

SCIENCESAURUS
Fossils   198

SCILINKS
THE WORLD'S A CLICK AWAY

www.scilinks.org
Keyword: Fossils
Code: GSED06

Assessment
Skill: Organizing information

Use the following question to assess each student's progress:
What tools and knowledge are necessary for paleontologists to look for fossils? (Tools: notebook, camera, paintbrushes, scratch awl; Knowledge: how to look for and recognize fossils, how to extract fossils from the earth without damaging them)

Explore

MAKING INFERENCES Ask students to identify the science skills that Mr. Tremblay may have used on the dig. (observing, classifying, inferring, measuring, using numbers, communicating, collecting and recording data) Discuss examples of how each skill was practiced. For example, Mr. Tremblay might have used measuring and numbers when he recorded the location of the bone. Taking photos is one method of collecting and recording data. Make sure students understand that anyone can use and apply these science skills.

Take Action

LEAVE THE BONES ALONE! Explain that all fossils, no matter how large or small, are part of a larger puzzle about the history of Earth. Ask students to give examples of fossil collections they know about and discuss what an observer may learn from these collections. Then ask students to share the brochures they have made with classmates.

CHECK UNDERSTANDING
Skill: Collecting and recording data
Tell students to imagine that they are going on a fossil dig similar to the one that Mr. Tremblay went on during his vacation. Ask students to make a list of tools they would take with them and to write a sentence describing what they might expect to find on the dig. (Tools: paintbrushes, camera, notebook, scratch awl; Find: bones, imprints, footprints)

CHAPTER 4 / LESSON 12   49

UNIT 2 Dynamic Earth

About the Photo
In the large photo, lava from Aloi Crater in Hawaii creeps across a parking lot. The man in the small photo is watching one of the most active volcanoes in the world: Mount Bromo in Java, Indonesia. Students undoubtedly know that volcanic eruptions can cause destruction and death. In many cases, however, minerals contained in erupted material help build fertile soil in the area.

About the Charts
A major goal of the *Science Daybooks* is to promote reading, writing, and critical thinking skills in the context of science. The charts below describe the types of reading selections included in this unit and identify the skills and strategies used in each lesson.

UNIT 2 Dynamic Earth

There's never a dull moment here on Earth! Earth's surface is continuously changing. Things shift, wash away, scatter in the wind, and sometimes explode. Things we take for granted—even major things like the position of Earth's continents—haven't always been the way they are now. And they won't be the same hundreds, thousands, or millions of years from now, either!

In this unit you'll explore some ways that Earth's surface changes. You'll see how wind and water move soil and sand from one place to another. You'll learn about the evidence that scientists used to determine that Earth's continents move over time. And you'll find out what makes some volcanoes explode in a violent eruption.

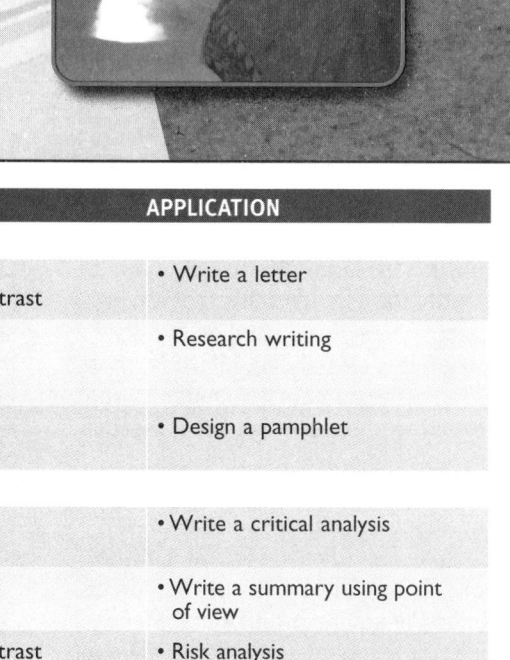

SELECTION	READING	WRITING	APPLICATION
CHAPTER 5 • CONSERVING SOIL			
13. "Farming the Great Plains" (historical novels)	• Quickwrite • Directed reading	• Interpret a map • Compare and contrast	• Write a letter
14. "Dust Storm Disaster" (folk song)	• Quickwrite • Directed reading	• Read a time line • Make inferences • Supporting details	• Research writing
15.	• Interpret a table	• Critical thinking • Cause and effect	• Design a pamphlet
CHAPTER 6 • CHANGING SHORELINES			
16. "Beach Erosion" (university Web site)	• Concept map • Cause and effect	• Label a diagram • Point of view	• Write a critical analysis
17. "A Lighthouse on the Move" (university Web site)	• Use prior knowledge • Critical thinking	• Make a list • Point of view	• Write a summary using point of view
18. "Eye-Popping Erosion" (USGS press release)	• Directed reading • Critical thinking	• Compare and contrast • Draw conclusions	• Risk analysis

THE CHAPTERS IN THIS UNIT ARE ...

CHAPTER 5:
Conserving Soil
Find out: Why did farmers in the Great Plains suddenly abandon their farms and move west?

CHAPTER 6:
Changing Shorelines
Find out: When waves remove sand from a beach, where does the sand go?

CHAPTER 7:
The Puzzle of Earth's Crust
Find out: How do scientists know that California and Japan are moving closer to each other?

CHAPTER 8:
Volcanoes
Find out: What does a volcano have in common with a can of soda?

Did You Know?
In 1883, the most powerful volcanic eruption in recorded history blew away most of the island of Krakatoa in Indonesia. Waves 37 meters (120 feet) high killed 36,000 Indonesians. People in Australia over 3,200 kilometers (2,000 miles) away reported hearing the explosions. A huge dust cloud rose 80 kilometers (50 miles) into the atmosphere, blocking sunlight worldwide and lowering temperatures by one degree.

Answers to *Find Out* Questions

CHAPTER 5
The Great Plains suffered a prolonged drought (the Dust Bowl) in the 1930s, and farmers were unable to grow crops or raise livestock. (pp. 53, 54, 56–57)

CHAPTER 6
It is deposited somewhere else, enlarging existing beaches or creating new ones. (p. 64)

CHAPTER 7
Scientists use the Global Positioning System (GPS) satellites to measure the distances between points on Earth's crust. (p. 80)

CHAPTER 8
Both the soda in a can and the molten rock inside a volcano contain gases under pressure. When the pressure is suddenly released, the gases escape. (p. 82)

SCILINKS
THE WORLD'S A CLICK AWAY

www.scilinks.org
Keyword: New Teacher Resources
Code: GSSD02

SELECTION	READING	WRITING	APPLICATION
CHAPTER 7 • THE PUZZLE OF EARTH'S CRUST			
19. "A Revolutionary Idea" (biography)	• Quickwrite • Directed reading	• Compare and contrast • Descriptive writing	• Analyze a cartoon
20. "Underwater Clues" (nonfiction science book)	• Build background information	• Interpret a diagram • Descriptive writing	• Use supporting evidence
21. "A Moveable Crust" (nonfiction science book)	• Build background information • Generate questions	• Descriptive writing	• Plan an expedition
CHAPTER 8 • VOLCANOES			
22. "How Do Volcanoes Erupt?" (USGS document)	• Use prior knowledge • Directed reading	• Hands-on activity • Record observations	• Analyze observations • Defend your answer
23. "St. Pierre Entirely Wiped Out" (university Web site)	• Critical thinking • Questioning	• Interpret a table	• Propose explanations
24. "Ask a Volcano-logist" (interview)	• Quickwrite • Predict	• Explore predictions • Compare data	• Generate questions

UNIT 2 DYNAMIC EARTH

CHAPTER 5 Overview

Conserving Soil

LESSON 13

Blown Away

Point of Lesson: *Wind, drought, and people's actions can cause soil erosion.*

The drought of the 1930s in the Great Plains, combined with the farming techniques of that era, created the Dust Bowl. In this lesson, students use passages from well-known literature to compare and contrast soil conditions in the Great Plains in the early 1900s and in the 1930s. They interpret a map showing the severity and extent of Dust Bowl conditions in 1937 and relate the disaster to the farming practices that allowed it to happen.

Materials

Before You Read (p. 52), for the class:
- map of the United States

Science Scope Activity (p. 53), for each group:
- local soil survey map (aerial view)
- soil samples (collected by students)
- crayons or markers
- paper
- glue stick

Connections (p. 55), for the class:
- research sources about farming technology

Laboratory Safety

Review the following safety guidelines with students before they do the Science Scope Activity in this lesson.
- Always go with an adult to collect samples in the field.
- Check with the landowner for permission, and ask about the safety of the soil you plan to collect. For example, some lawns and gardens are treated with chemicals. Pet cats often leave waste in soil near houses rather than using a litter box. Soil near old buildings can contain high levels of lead compounds. Avoid any unsafe areas.
- Dispose of any excess soil in an appropriate area outside. Do not put it in the sink drain.
- Wash your hands thoroughly after the activity.

LESSON 14

Dust in the Wind

Point of Lesson: *The Dust Bowl of the 1930s was a natural disaster that affected farmers and farmland.*

In this lesson, students consider the impact on people who lived through the Dust Bowl. Using the words to Woody Guthrie's song, "Dust Storm Disaster," which describes a particularly severe dust storm in April 1935 and a time line describing events on that day, students infer conditions that led up to the storm and the actions families took after it had ended.

Materials

Enrichment (p. 57), for each pair or small group:
- safety goggles (for each student)
- newspaper
- cardboard or paper bag
- shallow tray or box
- soil, sand, and pebbles
- drinking straw (one for each student)

Laboratory Safety

Review the following safety guidelines with students before they do the Enrichment activity in this lesson.
- Use only the straw assigned to you. Do not share straws.
- Avoid blowing the sand anywhere but in the tray.
- Avoid breathing in any soil.
- Dispose of soil, sand, and pebbles in an appropriate area outside.
- Wash your hands thoroughly after the activity.

LESSON 15

Saving the Land

Point of Lesson: *Soil conservation helps prevent soil erosion.*

Farming practices that were encouraged in the late 1800s and early 1900s directly contributed to the Dust Bowl disaster. In this lesson, students evaluate farming methods that can reduce soil erosion and write an updated government pamphlet encouraging soil-conserving farming practices.

Materials

Enrichment (p. 61), for each group:
- safety goggles (for each student)
- newspaper
- cardboard or paper bag
- shallow tray or box
- soil, sand, and pebbles
- drinking straws (one for each student)
- seed for small cover plants such as grass, rye, or oats
- plastic mesh
- leafy twigs

Laboratory Safety

Review the following safety guidelines with students before they do the Enrichment activity in this lesson.
- Use only the straw assigned to you. Do not share straws.
- Avoid blowing the sand anywhere but in the tray.
- Avoid breathing in any soil.
- Handle plants with care. Do not handle plants that irritate your skin.
- Dispose of soil, sand, and pebbles in an appropriate area outside.
- Wash your hands thoroughly after the activity.

Science Scope Activity

Making a Local Soil Map

NSTA has chosen a *Science Scope activity related to the content in this chapter. The activity begins here and continues in Lesson 13, page 53.*

Students may not understand the nature of many geological processes, but most are quite familiar with the dirt in their own backyards. During this activity, students not only work with the actual soils of their area, but they also gain an understanding of what a soil's characteristics reveal about its origins.

Two or three days before the activity, assign students to collect and bring in soil samples from their neighborhoods. Review the safety guidelines on page 52A with students before sending them to collect.

(continued on page 53)

Background Information

The Dust Bowl

The dust storms began in the summer of 1931 and grew progressively larger and more frequent each year. Some storms blew continuously for days on end. People became lost when they could not see to walk or to drive home. Farm animals suffocated in the fields. Dry air and blowing dust generated static electricity that burned any crops still standing.

The fine dust carried by the storms got into everything—buildings, cars, clothing, food, water. It was difficult to avoid breathing it. The dust clogged the lungs, causing "dust pneumonia," which claimed the lives of many people, especially children.

It was not immediately clear what was happening, and farmers continued to plant each year, confident that rains would soon come. But the drought continued. Close to a billion tons of topsoil was blown off the land in one year alone. The loss of topsoil made millions of hectares of farmland useless. Hundreds of thousands of people gave up their farms and left their homes, many heading for California.

During the worst years of the Dust Bowl, congress declared soil erosion "a national menace." Extensive soil conservation programs were begun, in some cases paying farmers to try new methods that would help protect the soil.

UNIT 2 Dynamic Earth
CHAPTER 5 / LESSON 13

Point of Lesson
Wind, drought, and people's actions can cause soil erosion.

Focus
- Structure of the earth system
- Populations, resources, and environments
- Natural hazards

Skills and Strategies
- Comparing and contrasting
- Making inferences
- Interpreting scientific illustrations
- Recognizing cause and effect
- Communicating
- Predicting

Advance Preparation

Vocabulary
Make sure students understand these terms. Definitions can be found in the glossary at the end of the student book.

- erosion
- grassland
- nutrient
- soil
- topsoil

Materials
Gather the materials needed for *Science Scope Activity* (p. 53).

TEACHING PLAN pp. 52–53

INTRODUCING THE LESSON
This lesson introduces the history of farming practices in the Great Plains that led to the Dust Bowl.

Find out what students already know about erosion by asking them to describe how human activities contribute to soil erosion.

Students may believe that soil consists simply of "dirt." Explain that soil is composed of both nonliving elements, such as rock particles and decomposing plant and animal matter, and living organisms, including bacteria and fungi.

CHAPTER 5 / LESSON 13
Conserving Soil

Blown Away

To most of us, soil is just the material that covers the ground. But to farmers, it's the source of their livelihood.

Farmers who settled much of the Great Plains in the late 1800s were amazed by the soil they found. It was deep, dark, rich, and almost free of rocks. Unlike the eastern United States, where farms were on hilly, rocky ground surrounded by forest, the level land had only a few trees to cut down.

After farmers had plowed through the thick tangle of wild grasses, they planted wheat and corn in the bare soil. After the harvest, the fields were left unplanted. The farmers thought that giving the soil a rest promised a good crop next year, too. They also believed this wonderful topsoil would be there forever. But they were wrong.

▶ Before You Read

THINK ABOUT IT The rich soil of the Great Plains took thousands of years to form. As the wild grasses died, nutrients from the rotting plants became part of the soil. Each year young grasses sprouted up through the decaying stems and roots. Plowing did two things. It broke up the tangled plants and roots that held the surface soil together. It also cut deeply into the land, loosening packed soil and bringing it to the surface.

▶ *What can happen to soil after it is plowed? How might weather conditions such as rain, drought, and wind affect the plowed soil?*

Plowing the soil exposes it to the sun, so it could dry out. Plowed soil

is also exposed to the wind, which could lift the dry, loosened soil

particles and carry them away.

▶ Before You Read

Time: 10 minutes
Materials: map of the United States

THINK ABOUT IT Explain that the Great Plains is a flat, treeless grassland in the central United States. Help students locate the Great Plains states on a U.S. map. (See page 54 for a list of the states.)

Ask students to describe what the action of plowing land is like and why land must be plowed before planting. *What purpose does plowing serve?* (It turns and loosens soil enough for seed to be buried.)

Ask students: *What do living things add to soil?* (Decaying leaves, branches, bark, and roots from plants and waste products from animals add nutrients that help support plant growth.) *How do plant roots help protect the soil?* (Plant roots hold the soil in place.) Emphasize how slowly soil develops—as long as 500 years for 2.5 centimeters (1 inch) of soil.

Farming the Great Plains

> Read

Willa Cather wrote about farming on the Great Plains of Nebraska in the early 1900s. Here's what she said.

> There are few scenes more [pleasing] than a spring plowing...where the furrows of a single field often lie a mile in length, and the brown earth, with such a strong, clean smell, and such a power of growth and fertility in it, yields itself eagerly to the plow.... The wheat-cutting sometimes goes on all night as well as all day, and in good seasons there are [hardly enough] men and horses...to do the harvesting. The grain is so heavy that it bends toward the blade and cuts like velvet.

In the 1930s, disaster struck. It did not rain, and the soil dried in the hot sun. Winds picked up the dry soil and blew it into the air. Here's how writer John Steinbeck described the dust storms.

> Now the wind grew strong and hard and it worked at the rain crust in the corn fields. Little by little, the sky was darkened by the mixing dust, and the wind felt over the earth, loosened the dust, and carried it away. The wind grew stronger. The rain crust broke and the dust lifted up out of the fields and drove gray plumes into the air like sluggish smoke. The corn threshed the wind and made a dry, rushing sound. The finest dust did not settle back to earth now, but disappeared into the darkening sky.

furrow: a shallow trench left by a plow
fertility: the ability to support much plant life
yields: gives in
rain crust: the thin top layer of soil that hardened after light rain
plume: resembling a feather
sluggish: slow, lazy
threshed: struck over and over again

top: From: Cather, Willa. *O Pioneers!* Houghton Mifflin.
bottom: From: Steinbeck, John. *The Grapes of Wrath.* Penguin Putnam.

NoteZone

This reading tells about planting and harvesting crops. (Circle) the sentences that describe planting. Underline the sentences that describe harvesting.

What happened to the finest dust?
It was carried off.

FIND OUT MORE

SCIENCESAURUS
Weathering, Soil, and Erosion ... 188
Soil ... 191
Erosion and Deposition ... 192

SCILINKS
www.scilinks.org
Keyword: Wind Erosion
Code: GSED07

53

Science Scope Activity

Making a Local Soil Map
Time: 45 minutes
Materials: local soil survey map (aerial view), soil samples (collected by students), crayons or markers, paper, glue stick

Procedure
Give students the following instructions:

1. Sort the soil samples, putting similar samples together. Base the classification on criteria such as particle size and color. Write a description of each kind of soil.
2. On one sheet of paper, draw or trace the area where you collected samples. Label the general areas where each soil type was collected.
3. On the map, label and color landmarks, natural features, and waterways.
4. Carefully spread a thin layer of glue on the paper where the first type of soil was found. Sprinkle a small sample of that soil on the paper until it completely covers the glue. Allow the glue to dry.
5. Repeat step 4 for each of the other soil types.

Have each group explain its classifications and show its maps.

> Read

Remind students that one of the ways writers interest readers in their subject is by painting a vivid picture with words. Suggest that students highlight any descriptive words in the readings that stimulate the senses. Ask students which words help them visualize what the authors were describing.

Point out that the two readings are taken from novels set 30 years apart. Tell students to study the readings for key words and specific details about how the soil changed during that period. Ask them to recall the inferences they made in Before You Read about plowing and the effects of rain, drought, and wind on plowed soil. Suggest that they create a Venn diagram as a graphic organizer to record what happened to the land and the environment between the two periods.

CHECK UNDERSTANDING

Skill: Recognizing cause and effect
Ask: *What factors caused the dramatic changes in the soil between the time Willa Cather wrote and the time John Steinbeck wrote?* (Plowing broke up the plant roots that held the soil together. It also exposed the loosened soil to wind and sun.)

CHAPTER 5 / LESSON 13   53

CHAPTER 5 / LESSON 13

More Resources
The following resources are also available from Great Source and NSTA.

SCIENCESAURUS
Weathering, Soil, and Erosion	188
Soil	191
Erosion and Deposition	192

READER'S HANDBOOK
Focus on Comparing and Contrasting	383
Elements of Graphics: Map	555

WRITE SOURCE 2000
Writing Friendly Letters	149
Autobiographical Writing	153

SCILINKS
THE WORLD'S A CLICK AWAY

www.scilinks.org
Keyword: Wind Erosion
Code: GSED07

▶ Explore

COMPARE AND CONTRAST
▶ Willa Cather and John Steinbeck describe the soil of the Great Plains very differently. Compare their descriptions. How did soil conditions change from 1900 to the 1930s?

The soil that used to be brown and fertile with a strong clean smell dried out, turned to dust, and was eroded by wind.

INTERPRET A MAP

1937 Drought Conditions

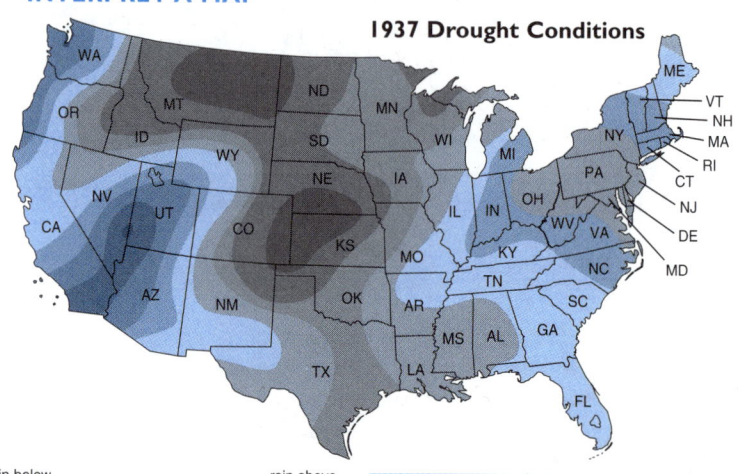

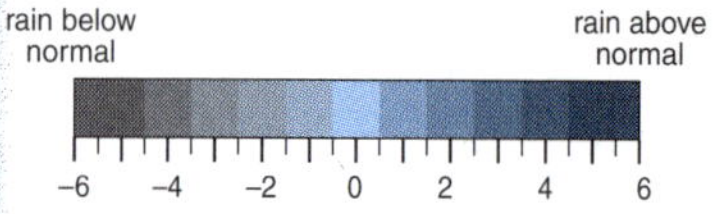

rain below normal — rain above normal
−6 −4 −2 0 2 4 6

Great Plains States
Colorado (CO)	Nebraska (NE)	South Dakota (SD)
Kansas (KS)	New Mexico (NM)	Texas (TX)
Minnesota (MN)	North Dakota (ND)	Wyoming (WY)
Montana (MT)	Oklahoma (OK)	

Farmers and crops suffered across the Great Plains in the 1930s. During a drought—a long period of time with little or no rain—crops cannot grow well. The map shows how bad the drought was in 1937. The key shows drought conditions on a scale from −6 to 6. A −6 stands for the driest conditions. A 6 stands for very wet conditions. Use the key to match the numbers to the shading on the map.

▶ What were conditions like in Willa Cather's home state of Nebraska?
About one third of Nebraska had −6 drought conditions. Most of the rest of the state had −4.5 conditions.

54

TEACHING PLAN pp. 54–55

▶ Explore

COMPARE AND CONTRAST Encourage students to refer to the Venn diagrams they created during the Read activity for details. If students did not make organizers, tell them to review the readings and look for descriptive words and phrases that describe the soil.

INTERPRET A MAP Review with students how to read thematic maps. Remind them that maps use a variety of symbols and colors or shading to show distributions and patterns. Review the map key to make sure students understand that 0 represents normal rainfall for a particular area and that the numbers above and below 0 do not refer to any particular amount of rain. (For example, 3 does not stand for 3 inches or centimeters of rain.) Emphasize that negative numbers mean rainfall was below normal, and numbers higher than 0 mean rainfall was above normal. To answer the last question on this page, students may need to refer to the list of states to find the abbreviation for Nebraska (NE).

54   CHAPTER 5 / LESSON 13

▶ **How did conditions in the Great Plains compare with conditions in other parts of the country?**

The entire Great Plains had severe droughts. Montana, North Dakota, Nebraska, Kansas, and eastern Colorado were driest.

▶ Propose Explanations

THINK ABOUT SOIL EROSION Each area has an amount of rainfall that is average, or typical, for that area. Some years bring heavier than average rainfall, while others are drier than average. Droughts are natural. The grasslands of the Great Plains had droughts before the settlers arrived from the east. And high winds are common in this mainly flat, treeless area. But these winds did not carry away soil until after the land was farmed.

Farmers replaced the thick tangles of native grasses with crops such as corn and wheat. After harvesting the crops, farmers left the fields unplanted. The few trees that did exist were removed so that farm equipment could move easily through the fields.

▶ **How did these farming practices contribute to soil erosion?**

Crops such as corn and wheat did not hold soil in place as well as tangles of native grasses did. When farmers left fields unplanted, there were no plant roots to hold the soil in place and protect it from erosion. Cutting down trees exposed the soil to wind erosion, since trees block the wind and slow it down. Faster-moving wind erodes more soil.

▶ Take Action

WRITE A LETTER Imagine that your family moved to a farm on the Great Plains in 1928 when there was plenty of rain. It is now 1934 and three years into the drought.

▶ **On a separate sheet of paper, write a letter to a cousin on the East Coast. Describe how the land and farming has changed since your family arrived. Explain what you think your family will do next.**

Students' letters will vary.

55

Connections

Time: will vary
Materials: research sources about farming technology

SOCIAL STUDIES Encourage students to research the technology that made it possible to develop the grasslands of the Great Plains region and make the land available for ranching and farming. Possible research topics include the John Deere steel plow; railroads; barbed wire; mechanical steam plows; cultivators; threshing machines; harvesters; windmills; dams; and irrigation. Have students share what they learned with their classmates in oral presentations.

Assessment

Skill: Making inferences

Use the following question to assess each student's progress:

Why didn't the winds erode the soil during droughts before the settlers arrived? (The land had not been farmed, so the soil was not loosened and the roots of native grasses held it in place.)

▶ Propose Explanations

THINK ABOUT SOIL EROSION Student explanations should be based on information provided in the Think About It section on page 52 and in the introductory paragraphs for this section. They already know that plowing changes the structure of the soil by making it looser. Point out that corn and wheat plants do not have the extensive, deep root systems of native grasses.

▶ Take Action

WRITE A LETTER Review the placement of the following five parts of a letter: heading, salutation, body, closing, and signature. Point out that letter writing is an excellent way to share personal thoughts and feelings. Encourage students to think of the cousin as someone about their age. Tell them to include descriptive details that will enable the cousin to visualize the conditions in 1928 compared with those in 1934.

CHAPTER 5 / LESSON 13   55

UNIT 2 Dynamic Earth
CHAPTER 5 / LESSON 14

Point of Lesson
The Dust Bowl of the 1930s was a natural disaster that affected farmers and farmland.

Focus
- Structure of the earth system
- Populations, resources, and environments
- Natural hazards

Skills and Strategies
- Drawing conclusions
- Making inferences

Advance Preparation

Vocabulary
Make sure students understand this term. The definition can be found in the glossary at the end of the student book.
- topsoil

Materials
Gather the materials needed for *Enrichment* (p. 57).

CHAPTER 5 / LESSON 14
Conserving Soil

Dust in the Wind

Dust storms blew many farmers out of town.

The drought of the 1930s was a disaster for many Great Plains farmers. The dry topsoil blew away in great dust storms. This dust gave the region and the disaster their unwelcome name—the Dust Bowl. As the drought wore on, many farm families packed up their belongings and left. About 350,000 people moved from the Great Plains to California between 1935 and 1939.

Woody Guthrie was a popular songwriter and folksinger of that time. He wrote several songs about the Dust Bowl.

▲ Dust Bowl refugees

▶ Before You Read

USE YOUR IMAGINATION Imagine yourself outdoors as a dust storm approaches. It may help to think of a heavy, windy snowstorm, then imagine the snow as sand and dust. How would the sky look? How would farm animals react? How would you react? Write your ideas.

Possible answers: The sky would get dark from the dust. The dust would feel gritty in my eyes and on my skin. Animals would go inside or turn their backs to the wind. People would go indoors and close all the windows and doors. They would probably be worried and frightened.

TEACHING PLAN pp. 56–57

INTRODUCING THE LESSON
This lesson focuses on the ecological consequences of the misuse of the land and the human face of the Dust Bowl disaster.

Ask students to consider that 350,000 people left the area, and see if they can give an example of a location with a population of about that size. Then point out that it would be as if the entire population of Minneapolis today picked up and moved. Students may believe that the entire population of the Great Plains packed up and left. While it was the largest exodus in U.S. history, three out of four farmers stayed on their land. Explain that the dispossessed probably moved west because they believed there were more opportunities there for agricultural workers. In reality, things were not much better for them in California.

▶ Before You Read

USE YOUR IMAGINATION As students write their impressions of what a dust storm might be like, encourage them to focus on sensory images and personal reactions. Tell them to make comparisons with unusual weather they may have experienced. Remind them to consider how the dust would affect people's health. Suggest that students make drawings to supplement their verbal accounts. These images could be made into two-sided postcards or displayed on a bulletin board.

Ask students whether they think the lack of rainfall alone was responsible for what happened. *Why didn't dust storms occur before the region was intensively farmed?* (Agricultural practices loosened the soil and exposed it to sun and wind. The crops that were planted did not have the deep root systems of the native plants they replaced.)

▶ **Read**

In this song, Woody Guthrie describes "Black Sunday," the worst storm of the Dust Bowl.

DUST STORM DISASTER

On the fourteenth day of April of nineteen thirty five
There struck the (worst) of dust storms that ever filled the sky.
You could see that dust storm coming the cloud looked (death-like black)
And through our mighty nation It left a (dreadful) track....

The storm took place at sundown. It lasted through the night.
When we looked out next morning We saw a (terrible) sight.
We saw outside our window Where wheatfields they had grown,
Was now a rippling ocean Of dust the wind had blown.

It covered up our fences, it covered up our barns,
It covered up our tractors In this (wild) and (dusty) storm.
We loaded our jalopies And piled our families in,
We rattled down the highway To never come back again.

jalopies: old, beat-up cars

From: Guthrie, Woody. "Dust Storm Disaster." Ludlow Music, Inc.

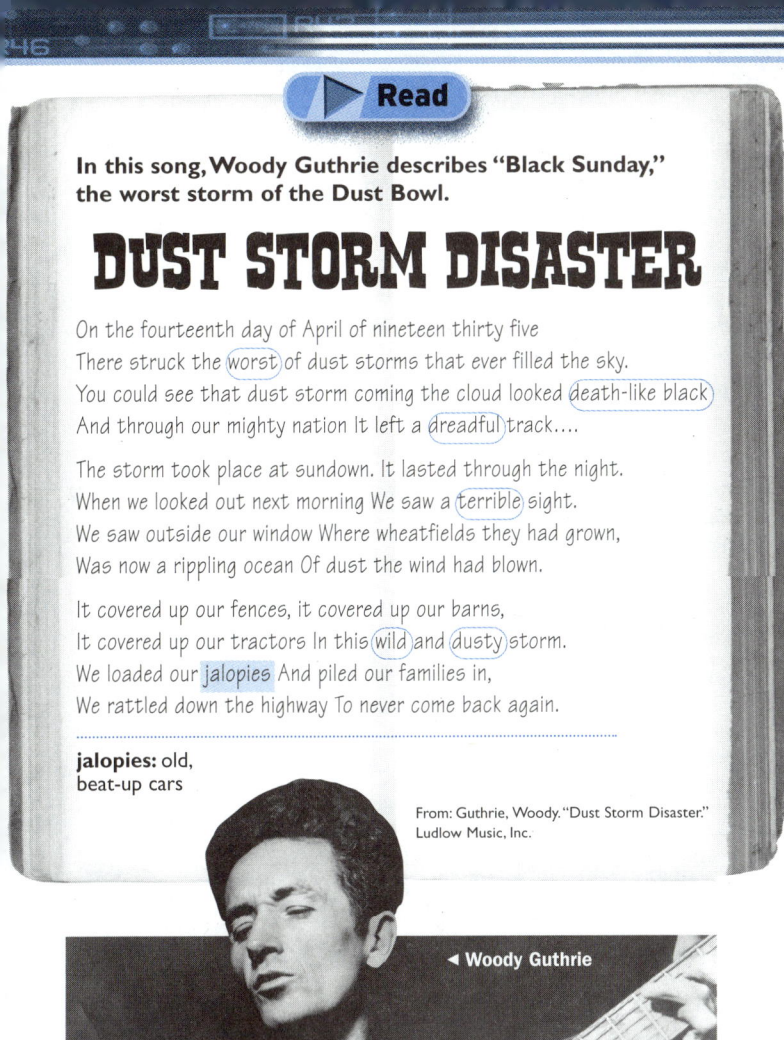

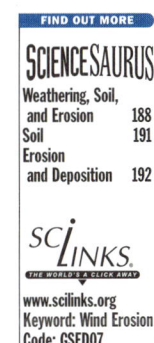

◀ Woody Guthrie

NoteZone
(Circle) all the adjectives that describe how bad the dust storm was.

FIND OUT MORE
SCIENCESAURUS
Weathering, Soil,
  and Erosion   188
Soil   191
Erosion
  and Deposition   192

SCiLINKS
THE WORLD'S A CLICK AWAY
www.scilinks.org
Keyword: Wind Erosion
Code: GSED07

57

Enrichment

Time: 30–40 minutes
Materials: safety goggles; newspaper; cardboard or paper bag; shallow tray or box; soil, sand, and pebbles; drinking straw

Have students work with partners or in small groups. Give them the following instructions. **Caution:** Tell students to avoid blowing the sand and soil into someone's face.

1. Cover the work area with newspaper.
2. With cardboard or a paper bag, build a three-sided shield around a shallow tray or box. Leave one end open.
3. Mix soil, sand, and pebbles at the front of the tray. Shape the mixture into a mound.
4. Stand in front of the open end of the shield. Hold a drinking straw near the hill and blow through the other end.
5. Gradually increase the amount of force. Which material scatters most easily? (the soil)
6. Draw a picture of the setup and label it to show what happened.

▶ **Read**

Explain that Woody Guthrie, who was born in 1912 in Okemah, Oklahoma, headed west with the mass migration of Dust Bowl refugees known as "Okies." Woody crisscrossed the country, listening to the plight of farmers, migrant workers, the homeless, and others affected by the Great Depression. He became the voice of the people.

Introduce deposition by asking whether students have ever seen sand dunes. Elicit a description from a student who has. Ask: *What happens to snow or sand and soil when the wind encounters a barrier?* (The wind slows down, and this causes the material to be deposited.) Draw a simple diagram on the board to help students visualize the process.

As students read the lyrics, have them highlight and number the events in the order in which they occurred. Then have them highlight in another color any words or phrases that confirm some of the inferences they made in the Before You Read activity. Have students focus on the song as a literary form. Encourage them to analyze the use of sounds, rhyming pattern, and structure.

CHECK UNDERSTANDING
Skill: Organizing information
Ask students to describe some of the immediate effects of the 1930s dust storms and people's response. (Answers will vary but should include the following: The fields were covered in a layer of dust. The eroded soil covered fences, barns, and farm equipment. People left their homes and farms and headed west.)

CHAPTER 5 / LESSON 14   57

CHAPTER 5 / LESSON 14

More Resources
The following resources are also available from Great Source and NSTA.

ScienceSaurus
Weathering, Soil, and Erosion	188
Soil	191
Erosion and Deposition	192

Reader's Handbook
Focus on Sound and Structure	439
Search Engine	533
Timeline	561

SciLinks — THE WORLD'S A CLICK AWAY

www.scilinks.org
Keyword: Wind Erosion
Code: GSED07

Connections

HEALTH In their imaginary descriptions of a dust storm, students may have commented about breathing difficulties, coughing, and throat irritation due to exposure to airborne particles. Point out that respiratory diseases such as asthma and bronchitis remain important health issues for people working in agriculture. Sources of particles affecting these workers include dust, mold, pollen,

(continued on page 59)

Teaching Plan pp. 58–59

▶ Explore

MAKING INFERENCES

▶ Where did the dust described in Woody Guthrie's song come from?
from dried-up topsoil in fields

▶ What produced the "deathlike black cloud" Woody describes? (Hint: Look for clues later in the song.)
Wind lifted the dusty soil into the air, forming a dark cloud.

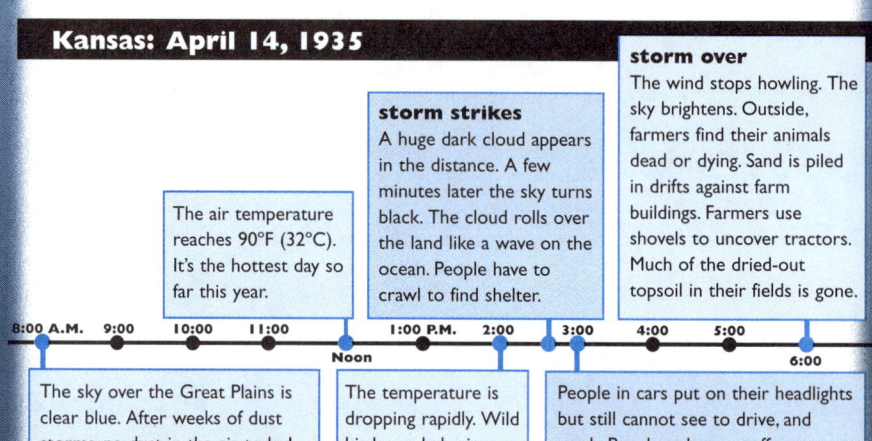

Kansas: April 14, 1935

storm strikes — A huge dark cloud appears in the distance. A few minutes later the sky turns black. The cloud rolls over the land like a wave on the ocean. People have to crawl to find shelter.

storm over — The wind stops howling. The sky brightens. Outside, farmers find their animals dead or dying. Sand is piled in drifts against farm buildings. Farmers use shovels to uncover tractors. Much of the dried-out topsoil in their fields is gone.

The air temperature reaches 90°F (32°C). It's the hottest day so far this year.

Timeline: 8:00 A.M., 9:00, 10:00, 11:00, Noon, 1:00 P.M., 2:00, 3:00, 4:00, 5:00, 6:00

The sky over the Great Plains is clear blue. After weeks of dust storms, no dust in the air today! Farm families hang their wash on clotheslines, expecting it will still be clean when it is dry.

The temperature is dropping rapidly. Wild birds are behaving strangely.

People in cars put on their headlights but still cannot see to drive, and crash. People at home stuff rags around their doors and windows to keep the dust out. It gets in anyway—in their noses, their mouths, and in their food.

▶ Some people called this day "the day of the black blizzard." How was the dust storm like a severe snowstorm? How was it different?
Both involve strong winds that blow material into drifts, make it difficult to see and to drive, and can kill animals. The material blown in a blizzard is snow; the material blown in a dust storm is soil, dust, and sand. Snow will melt but dust will not. There are often weather clues to predict a snowstorm, but not for a dust storm.

58

▶ Explore

MAKING INFERENCES Encourage students to combine the information they learned in Lesson 13 about the connection between farming practices and soil erosion with Guthrie's description of Black Sunday. Students should be able to figure out that the source of the dust is loose, dry topsoil. They should also understand that the smallest soil particles would be lifted up by the wind and become suspended in the air to form dark clouds of dust.

KANSAS: APRIL 14, 1935 Point out that the time line events and Guthrie's song lyrics differ on the timing of events. For example, the time line says the storm struck in midafternoon and was over by nightfall. In the song lyrics, the storm struck at sundown and lasted through the night. Explain that the song and the time line were written in two different locations.

Before students compare a dust storm with a snowstorm, have them review the time line and jot down examples of the effects of dust.

▶ Propose Explanations

THINK ABOUT IT Suggest that students reread the song lyrics and time line and make notes that will help them answer the questions. Clues include the use of the adjective "worst" and the fact that the time line mentions earlier storms.

58 CHAPTER 5 / LESSON 14

Propose Explanations

THINK ABOUT IT Woody Guthrie wrote his song "Dust Bowl Disaster" about April 14, 1935.

► What clues do the song and time line give that the dust storm on this day was only one of many?

The song says it was "the worst of dust storms," and the time line says "after weeks of dust storms."

► In what ways was this dust storm a disaster for the people who experienced it?

Cars crashed, farm animals died, farm machinery was damaged by dust, and topsoil was blown away.

► According to the song, what did many farm families do after the "Black Sunday" dust storm? Why would they do this?

They packed up their belongings and moved away. They did this because they could no longer make a living from their farms.

Take Action

RESEARCH FOLK SONGS Woody Guthrie was one of many folksingers who wrote songs about the hardships of ordinary working people in the United States. Folk songs were one way that the stories of struggling people could be heard. Research songs by Guthrie and other songwriters of the 1930s. Find and listen to their recordings. What do their lyrics tell you about how most people lived? Give some examples of the songs and lyrics.

Answers will vary. Example: I listened to "Boomtown Bill" by Woody Guthrie ("I've worked in wind and weather of rain and sleet and snow / Yes, I done all the work, folks, but John D. got the dough"); the lyrics talk about how important workers are and how there is a lot of suffering and unequal rights in the world.

(continued from page 58)

and pesticides. Ask: *What are some common signs of respiratory disease?* (coughing without a cold, whistling or wheezing sounds, shortness of breath, tightness in the chest, and feeling tired)

Assessment

Skill: Recognizing cause and effect

Use the following question to assess each student's progress:

How did the Dust Bowl affect the farming communities of the Great Plains? (Property was destroyed, the topsoil dried out and blew away, and farming families moved away.)

Connections

LITERATURE Encourage students to extend their research to include literature such as *The Grapes of Wrath* by John Steinbeck or *Cat Running* by Zilpha Keatley Snyder. As a starting point for this research, direct students to the following Web site: www.weru.ksu.edu/DustBowl/

Have students share the information they learned in oral presentations.

Take Action

RESEARCH FOLK SONGS To begin their research with Guthrie's album "Dust Bowl Ballads" (reissued as "Woody Guthrie: A Legendary Performer," CD: Camden 1995), direct students to the following Web site: www.geocities.com/Nashville/3448/dbball.html

Another useful Web site is the Archive of American Folk Songs of the American Folklife Center, of the Library of Congress at: lcweb.loc.gov/folklife/

Other songwriters students might research include Dave Macon, Sarah Ogan Gunning, Dorsey Murdock Dixon, Jim Garland, and Bob Miller. Once they locate the artist and song titles, students can listen to sound recordings found in library collections or online. Often lyrics can also be found on the Internet. The written song lyrics can be analyzed for clues about people's lifestyles. If students use Web sites for their research, remind them to look at them just as critically as they would evaluate any written source. If possible, take time for students to share the recordings they found.

CHECK UNDERSTANDING
Skill: Drawing conclusions
Ask students to imagine that they are soil scientists with the Department of Agriculture in the 1930s who predict the disaster represented by the Black Sunday dust storm. As scientists, what suggestions might they have presented to the farmers before it was too late? (Answers will vary, but soil scientists might have suggested planting different crops with deeper and wider-spreading roots or keeping fields planted so the soil would not dry up and blow away.)

CHAPTER 5 / LESSON 14

UNIT 2 Dynamic Earth

CHAPTER 5 / LESSON 15

Point of Lesson
Soil conservation helps prevent soil erosion.

Focus
- Structure of the earth system
- Science and technology in society
- Natural hazards

Skills and Strategies
- Creating and using tables
- Recognizing cause and effect
- Communicating

Advance Preparation

Vocabulary
Make sure students understand these terms. Definitions can be found in the glossary at the end of the student book.

- conservation
- erosion
- grassland
- soil
- topsoil

Materials
Gather the materials needed for *Enrichment* (p. 61).

More Resources
The following resource is also available from Great Source.

READER'S HANDBOOK
Elements of Graphics: Table   559

TEACHING PLAN pp. 60–61

INTRODUCING THE LESSON
This lesson focuses on methods that farmers can use to prevent soil erosion.

To find out what students know about soil conservation, ask: *What are some methods currently used to conserve soil in agricultural areas?*

Students may think that the 1930s Dust Bowl was an isolated case. Explain that droughts and soil erosion in grassland areas occurred repeatedly before the Dust Bowl and continue to occur today throughout the world. As recently as April 15, 2001, dust clouds arrived in California as a result of drought along the border between Mongolia and China across the Pacific Ocean. Dust storms often occur in the Sahel, the grassland that lies south of the Sahara Desert in North Africa. Ask students if they think a severe drought in the Great Plains could trigger another Dust Bowl today.

CHAPTER 5 / LESSON 15

Conserving Soil

Saving the Land

North Americans learned many lessons from the Dust Bowl.

In 1900 the United States Bureau of Soils published a pamphlet about soil. It described soil as a resource that would always be available. At first, the hopeful farmers of the Great Plains agreed. But in the 1930s, wind eroded the soil from their sun-baked fields into giant dust clouds. It didn't take long for farmers to see that to save the Great Plains topsoil, they had to change their farming methods so they would conserve soil.

▲ Dust Bowl farm in Texas

▶ Explore

READING A TABLE In the 1930s, U.S. government officials started to announce ways to keep the rich soil of the Great Plains from being eroded by wind. Today wind is still a problem on the flat, dry Great Plains. Farmers use several methods to prevent soil erosion. Read about their methods in the table.

GREAT PLAINS SOIL CONSERVATION	
Method	**Description**
Conservation tillage	plowing less deeply into the soil
Stubble mulching	leaving the stems (stubble) and roots of crop plants in the soil after harvest
Cover crops	growing low, grass-like plants in harvested fields until it is time to plant the next crop
Strip cropping	planting strips of wind-resistant crops next to crops that do not resist the wind
Windbreaks	planting trees or hedges along the edges of fields
Restoring wild grasslands	stop planting crops on land that erodes; instead, replant it with wild grasses that grow in thick tangles

60

▶ Explore

READING A TABLE Tell students that the first step in using a table is to read the title to find out what it is about. Explain that the table identifies farming methods introduced to conserve soil resources. Many methods are simple, such as finding a different way to plow the soil. Other methods require planning, such as determining which crops could protect others. Point out that cover crops are sometimes called "green manure" because they add nutrients when they are plowed into the soil.

60   CHAPTER 5 / LESSON 15

Propose Explanations

RECOGNIZING CAUSE AND EFFECT Using the information in the table, explain how each of the six methods could prevent soil erosion by wind.

- **Conservation tillage**

  loosens and exposes less soil to drying by the sun and erosion by wind

- **Stubble mulching**

  holds moisture in the soil; holds the soil together so the wind does not erode it, even when the soil is dry

- **Cover crops**

  hold the soil in place and shade it from the sun

- **Strip cropping**

  Wind-resistant crops slow down the wind; slower wind erodes less soil under crops that do not resist the wind.

- **Windbreaks**

  Trees and hedges slow down the wind before it reaches farm fields; the slower the wind, the less soil it can erode.

- **Restoring wild grasslands**

  Wild grasses' roots hold soil in place; unplowed soil is not loosened to be exposed to wind.

Take Action

DESIGN A PAMPHLET You have a chance to update the 1900 pamphlet from the Bureau of Soils. On a separate sheet of paper, design a new pamphlet for farmers. Stress the importance of soil conservation. Use both words and pictures to communicate your message. Design an eye-catching cover that communicates the main message of the pamphlet.

Students' pamphlets will vary.

Enrichment

Time: 30–40 minutes
Materials: materials from Enrichment, page 57, plus seed for small cover plants such as grass, rye, or oats; plastic mesh; leafy twigs

Invite students to devise models of the soil conservation methods described in the table to see how well the methods reduce or prevent erosion. For example, they might seed the soil with quick-growing plants such as grass or use pebbles, leafy twigs, and plastic mesh to create a windbreak.

Assessment

Skill: Making inferences

Use the following questions to assess each student's progress:

Imagine a cornfield in the spring right after planting and the same field late in the summer when the stalks are heavy with ripe corn. During which season is the soil more in danger of erosion? Why? (during early spring just after plowing when the soil is loose and the plant roots haven't spread as far as they eventually will) *What can farmers do to protect their fields and soil during that season?* (As a long-term solution, farmers could plant trees or shrubs at the edge of their fields to slow down the wind. However, it might take several years for trees and shrubs to mature enough to block the wind.)

Propose Explanations

RECOGNIZING CAUSE AND EFFECT Tell students that in order to answer the question, they need to refer back to the table and focus on how each method reduces the effects of wind on the soil. Students can then draw on previously learned facts about the effects of earlier farming methods.

Take Action

DESIGN A PAMPHLET Provide students with examples of effective pamphlets designed to promote a cause or communicate information. Allow them to use a word processing program or graphic design tools to give their work a polished look. Remind them to review their answers to Before You Read and Propose Explanations in Lesson 13 and Explore in Lesson 14 so they can organize their arguments and use what they learned about soil erosion and conservation practices. Invite interested students to construct dioramas of the Great Plains in three eras: 1900, 1930s, and now. They could display the completed pamphlets alongside the dioramas.

CHECK UNDERSTANDING

Skill: Recognizing cause and effect
Have students make a cause-and-effect organizer that relates to soil conservation. Tell them to include information about the causes and effects of soil erosion as well as what they have learned about good soil management practices.

CHAPTER 5 / LESSON 15

CHAPTER 6
Overview

Changing Shorelines

LESSON 16
Shifting Sands
Point of Lesson: *Shorelines and beaches are constantly changing.*

An article explaining the processes of beach erosion and deposition leads students into considering the impact of beach dynamics on oceanfront buildings. Students identify barrier beaches and islands and recognize rivers as the source of sediment. Given the risks from beach erosion to houses and other properties, students consider the different points of view people might have on whether tax money should be spent to protect these structures.

Materials
Enrichment (p. 63), for each group:
- stream table or rectangular tank
- water
- sand
- metric ruler
- wood block or plastic lid

Laboratory Safety
Review the following safety guidelines with students before they do the Enrichment activity in this lesson.
- Avoid getting sand in your eyes.
- Do not put any sand in the sink drain.
- Wash your hands thoroughly after the activity.

LESSON 17
Saving a Lighthouse
Point of Lesson: *Structures built along shorelines are at risk of destruction.*

The existing Cape Hatteras Lighthouse was built in 1870 on a barrier island to warn ships of shallow water. Unfortunately, the beach between the lighthouse and the ocean has been eroding since that time, putting the historic lighthouse in danger of collapse. This lesson describes what was done over the years to protect the Cape Hatteras Lighthouse.

Materials
Enrichment (p. 67), for each group:
- stream table or rectangular tank
- water
- metric ruler
- sand
- wood block or plastic lid
- rocks
- pebbles
- clay
- cardboard tube
- small plastic bags

Connections (p. 68), for the class:
The Lighthouse Keeper by James Michael Pratt (St. Martins, 2001)

Laboratory Safety
Review the following safety guidelines with students before they do the Enrichment activity in this lesson.
- Avoid getting sand in your eyes.
- Do not put any sand in the sink drain.
- Wash your hands thoroughly after finishing the activity.

LESSON 18
Investigating Erosion
Point of Lesson: *Scientists gather data to inform the public about the dangers of building on coastlines.*

In 1999, Hurricane Dennis caused massive erosion to North Carolina's beaches. Scientists made measurements and used photographs and video taken from airplanes to assess the damage. This information is used to evaluate the kinds of shoreline changes that can be expected with any major storm and to help people make decisions about whether and where to build along coastlines.

Materials:
none

UNIT 2: DYNAMIC EARTH

62A

Background Information

Beach erosion occurs on the East, West, and Gulf coasts of the United States, but the nature of the erosion varies with the topography of the coastline.

Barrier beaches and islands are common on the East and Gulf coasts, where a long, gently sloping continental shelf keeps sediment nearer to shore. These natural barriers help to shield on-shore areas from the brunt of major storms, chiefly hurricanes. However, the barriers themselves change location, size, and shape continually, most dramatically during storms.

A popular method for protecting barrier beaches—and the inland areas they in turn protect—is beach nourishment. Beach nourishment consists of dumping sand in a location where it will be carried onto the eroding beach by natural currents. The idea is to replenish the sand that is being lost due to erosion. This method is effective but must be repeated frequently because the sand is constantly removed by the natural forces causing erosion. Other methods of beach protection include sea walls and jetties. These methods trap traveling sand, keeping it near the structure rather than allowing it to continue down the coastline. These methods tend to protect one area of beach at the expense of another.

The West coast has a much narrower continental shelf, but the main issue for beaches in places such as California is cliff erosion. Winter storms associated with El Niño events are the main cause of erosion. Because these events do not occur annually, a West coast beach cliff can be stable for many years, then suffer many meters of loss in just one or two storms. Efforts for dealing with cliff erosion center on moving structures. Beach nourishment has been practiced in southern California since the early 1900s, in part because residents wanted the beaches, which are naturally narrow, to match beaches they were familiar with on the East coast. Nourishment, however, faces the same challenges on the West coast as it does in other areas.

UNIT 2 Dynamic Earth
CHAPTER 6 / LESSON 16

Point of Lesson
Shorelines and beaches are constantly changing.

Focus
- Structure of the earth system
- Populations, resources, and environments
- Change, constancy, and measurement
- Motion and forces
- Evolution and equilibrium

Skills and Strategies
- Concept mapping
- Making inferences
- Classifying
- Recognizing cause and effect
- Generating ideas

Advance Preparation

Vocabulary
Make sure students understand these terms. Definitions can be found in the glossary at the end of the student book.

- deposition
- dune
- erosion
- hurricane
- sediment
- wave

Materials
Gather the materials needed for *Enrichment* (p. 63).

CHAPTER 6 / LESSON 16
Changing Shorelines

Shifting Sands

What's attacking our beaches? The elements, my dear Watson.

If you've ever visited the ocean, you know that waves constantly pound the shore. On stormy days the waves are bigger and strike with greater force. On calm days the waves are smaller and strike with lesser force. But the pounding is constant. Erosion takes place when blowing wind or moving water carries away sediments such as sand and soil particles. Deposition takes place when wind and water drop those sediments in a new place. Erosion and deposition are constantly at work along our nation's shorelines. Some areas are built up while other areas are worn down.

▶ **Before You Read**

MAP YOUR IDEAS Shorelines make up less than 10 percent of Earth's land surface. Yet about 66 percent of the world's population lives along a coast.

▶ *Why do you think people want to live, work, and vacation close to the ocean? Organize your ideas by completing the idea map.*

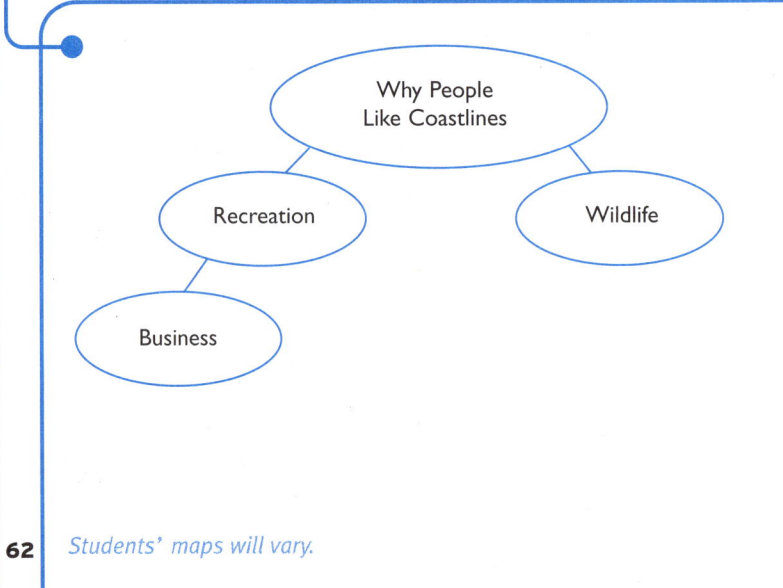

```
        Why People
        Like Coastlines
       /              \
  Recreation         Wildlife
      |
  Business
```

Students' maps will vary.

TEACHING PLAN pp. 62–63

INTRODUCING THE LESSON
In this lesson, students learn about the effects of erosion and deposition on beaches and shorelines. To determine what students already know, ask questions such as: *How do beaches form or get larger?* (Wind and water deposit sediments such as soil particles and sand.) *What could cause a beach to erode and eventually disappear?* (Wind and water move sediments away.) *How are these two processes related?* (Material that is eroded from one place is deposited somewhere else.)

Students may believe that erosion is always destructive. Tell them that erosion sometimes has positive effects. *What happens to material that is eroded?* (Eventually it is deposited someplace else.) *How could that be a positive effect?* (Deposition could create or enlarge a beach, might bring more fertile soil to an area, and the like.)

▶ **Before You Read**

MAP YOUR IDEAS Ask students to think about their own experiences— times they might have gone to the beach on a family trip, at camp, on field trips, or on group outings. If your community is not near a seacoast, remind students that the processes of erosion and deposition also occur on the shorelines of lakes and rivers.

When students start their idea maps, tell them to focus on how people interact with the ocean's coastal features. Invite volunteers to share what they wrote.

62   CHAPTER 6 / LESSON 16

Read

Here's how erosion affects shorelines.

Beach Erosion

Erosion is...plaguing [America's shorelines]. Coastal residents up and down the United States are worrying about undermined cliffs, disappearing beaches, and the occasional dwelling diving into the briny.

Beaches are constantly moving, building up here and eroding there, in response to waves, winds, storms and relative sea level rise.... Hurricanes or [storms called] northeasters...cause the most dramatic damage to beaches.

...Barrier beaches...protect land from the sea [and are] vulnerable to obliteration by the very factor that makes [them] so glamorous: the sea.... And the problem is increasing because the sea is rising [at a faster rate] after centuries of relatively slow rise, and scientists anticipate that the rate of rise will continue to increase...[during this] century.

Still, erosion cuts in two directions, says Jim O'Connell, a coastal processes specialist with the Sea Grant program at Woods Hole Oceanographic Institution [in Massachusetts]. "Without the process of erosion, we would not have the beaches, dunes, barrier beaches, and the highly productive bays and estuaries that owe their very existence to the presence of barrier beaches."

undermined: gradually worn away from below
dwelling: house
briny: the ocean
barrier beach: a long, low, sandy beach attached to the mainland; the shallow water between a barrier beach and the mainland is called a lagoon

obliteration: total destruction
processes: actions and changes
estuary: an area where a river empties into the ocean and there is mixing of fresh water and salt water (See diagram on page 64.)

From: "Beach Erosion." *The Why Files*. University of Wisconsin. (whyfiles.org/091beach/)

NOTEZONE

Underline the factors that cause beach erosion.

FIND OUT MORE

SCIENCESAURUS
Erosion and Deposition   192

SCiLINKS
THE WORLD'S A CLICK AWAY
www.scilinks.org
Keyword: Wave Erosion
Code: GSED08

63

Enrichment

Time: 10–15 minutes per group
Materials: stream table or rectangular tank, water, sand, metric ruler, wood block or plastic lid

The best way for students to visualize the processes involved in beach erosion is to set up a small stream table or rectangular tank in your classroom. Place some clean sand at one end and create a gentle slope to simulate a beach. Pour water into the container until it is 5 cm (2 in.) deep.

Invite small groups of students to model the effects of beach erosion by creating waves with a plastic lid or wood block. Tell them to first draw the way the beach looks at the start, then create gentle waves for one or two minutes and redraw the beach afterward. Students can leave the new beach in place, create larger waves for the same period of time, and again draw the resulting beach.

Ask students to describe the differences between the beach created by the small waves and the beach that resulted from the larger waves. Encourage students to design and carry out their own tests of beach erosion and ways to prevent it.

Read

BEACH EROSION In addition to underlining the causes of erosion, students could highlight the coastal features mentioned in the reading.

Explain that sea levels rise as the polar ice caps melt due to a general increase in Earth's temperature.

Suggest that students use a cause-effect organizer to clarify the processes described in the reading. Ask them to recall the ideas they listed on their idea maps and to consider how human actions might contribute to beach erosion. Have them add to their organizers any human-related causes and effects they identify. You might point out that many things people do to prevent or slow down erosion, such as building breakwaters, may actually make things worse—if not at the spot where they occur, then farther downstream on the beach.

CHECK UNDERSTANDING

Skill: Recognizing cause and effect
Ask: *What is one problem that beach erosion can cause?* (Erosion can destroy beaches, wash away buildings, and so on.) *What is one positive effect of beach erosion?* (When the materials are deposited, they can enlarge a beach or create a new one.)

CHAPTER 6 / LESSON 16   63

CHAPTER 6 / LESSON 16

More Resources

The following resources are also available from Great Source and NSTA.

ScienceSaurus

Erosion and Deposition   192

Reader's Handbook

Reading Science:
 Cause-Effect Order   111
Concept Map   670

Write Source 2000

Thinking Through an Argument 121
Adding Support   122

www.scilinks.org
Keyword: Wave Erosion
Code: GSED08

Connections

LANGUAGE ARTS Students who conducted their own tests of beach erosion and ways to prevent it during the Enrichment activity can write a pamphlet, newspaper article, or a letter to the editor discussing what beach communities can do to prevent or reduce erosion.

Teaching Plan pp. 64–65

► Explore

CUTTING IN TWO DIRECTIONS
▶ Find and label the barrier beaches in the diagram. Use the definition on page 63 to help you identify them.

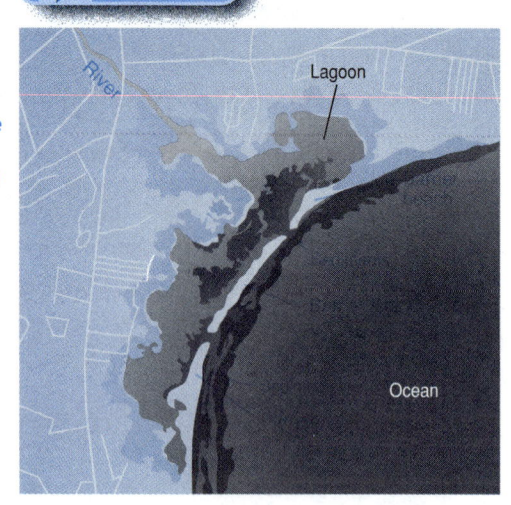

Jim O'Connell points out that while erosion *does* cut away at beaches, it is also the *source* of beach sand in the first place. Beaches are made up of sediments such as sand. Most beach sediments are carried to coastlines by rivers. The rivers deposit the sediments at the shore and on the ocean floor beyond the shore. Then wave action pushes most of the sediments onto the shoreline to build beaches. Waves also push sand along the shore.

▶ Label the river in the diagram. Label where sediments are deposited by the river and by wave action. Draw arrows to show in which direction forces move the sediments.

Jim O'Connell says without erosion there would be no beaches at all.

▶ How does erosion contribute to making beaches?
Erosion of mainland sediments is the source of beach sand.

RECOGNIZING CAUSE AND EFFECT

▶ What is it about beaches that makes them erode so easily? Think about both what they are made of and the forces they are exposed to.
Beaches are exposed to crashing waves, currents, and strong winds.
Because beaches are made of small, loose particles of sand, wind and water can easily erode them.

64

► Explore

CUTTING IN TWO DIRECTIONS Have students review the definition of *barrier beach* on page 63, then ask: *How are barrier beaches different from other beaches?* (A regular beach is part of the mainland, but only part of a barrier beach is connected to the mainland; the rest is separated from the mainland by a shallow body of water called a lagoon.)

Next, ask students to describe how they think barrier beaches form. If necessary, point out that some barrier beaches are formed when a rising sea level isolates dunes from the shoreline. Others are formed when waves move toward the coast at an angle and move sand along the beach—a process called *longshore drift*. On the east coast of North America, the net movement of sand is north to south.

Point out the statement in the reading that barrier beaches protect land from the sea. Ask students to explain how a barrier beach could protect the land. (A barrier beach shelters the land from strong ocean waves.)

RECOGNIZING CAUSE AND EFFECT

If students have difficulty answering this question, ask: *What materials are beaches made from?* (sand, pebbles, rock fragments, shells, boulders) *What might cause an area made of these materials to be so fragile?* (Small pieces of material can be washed or blown away easily.)

64   CHAPTER 6 / LESSON 16

▶ Propose Explanations

COMINGS AND GOINGS OF ISLAND PEOPLE Barrier beaches and barrier islands stretch along much of the eastern and Gulf coastlines of the U.S. A barrier island is like a barrier beach except it is not attached to the mainland. Many of these beaches and islands are covered with vacation homes, hotels, restaurants, and other buildings. Both beaches and islands are made mostly of loose sand. Wind, waves, and water currents move the sand. The sand is deposited on other parts of the island or dragged out to sea.

▶ Label the barrier island in the diagram on page 64.

How have people who live and work on these beaches and islands coped with erosion? One hundred years ago, when these areas had small populations, whole towns moved and rebuilt on the mainland. People who owned property along the ocean sometimes moved their houses and other structures back from the water. Over time, however, the number of people living in these places has grown. There are fewer places that people can move to when their houses are threatened by erosion.

▶ Why might people today not want to move?

People today spend a lot of money on their homes and cannot afford to move or give up what they have. Since the population has grown, there may not be open space farther inland to move a whole town.

▶ Take Action

ANALYZE THE ISSUE In 2000 the U.S. Congress asked scientists to report on erosion hazards. Their report said that 25 percent of homes and other structures within 500 feet (152 meters) of the U.S. coastline might be lost to erosion in the next 60 years. Should the government use taxes collected from everyone to help save homes built along the shoreline?

▶ How might people who own beach houses answer the question?

They might think that the government should help pay for them to move or protect their houses.

▶ How might people who don't own beach houses answer?

They might feel that it's not fair to spend taxpayer dollars to help those who own beach homes, especially if having the homes there means that the beach is closed to the public. Also, the people knew the risks of building on the coast, so they should not expect others to pay for their losses.

Assessment
Skill: Organizing information

Use the following task to assess each student's progress:

Have students sketch a section of ocean coastline. Ask them to draw and label at least one barrier beach, one barrier island, and a lagoon. (Students' drawings should resemble the illustration on page 64.)

▶ Propose Explanations

COMINGS AND GOINGS OF ISLAND PEOPLE You may want to give students the following examples of barrier islands: Fire Island on Long Island, New York; Padre Island in Texas; and Plum Island in Massachusetts.

Have students highlight the words and phrases in the first paragraph that identify the factors that cause beach erosion. (wind, waves, water currents) Then ask: *How do you think people's activities could contribute to beach erosion?* (Human activities such as walking, digging holes, playing games such as volleyball, and driving on the beach make the sand even looser so it will erode more easily.) You may also want to explain that such activities kill the plants that anchor sand in place.

In the second paragraph, students could highlight the methods that people used in the past to cope with beach erosion, then circle the reason these methods no longer work. Ask: *What might happen to the buildings if people could not move them farther away from the water?* (The buildings eventually could be damaged or destroyed by ocean waves.)

▶ Take Action

ANALYZE THE ISSUE Have each student choose one viewpoint and then list at least two or three reasons to support that viewpoint. If time allows, you could have students prepare and conduct a debate on the question.

If students do not live near a coast, help them relate to the question by guiding them to identify and discuss local issues that are similar.

CHAPTER 6 / LESSON 16

UNIT 2 Dynamic Earth

CHAPTER 6 / LESSON 17

Point of Lesson
Structures built along shorelines are at risk of destruction.

Focus
- Structure of the earth system
- Science and technology in society
- Change, constancy, and measurement
- Motion and forces

Skills and Strategies
- Using space/time relationships
- Recognizing cause and effect
- Sequencing
- Making inferences
- Communicating

Advance Preparation

Vocabulary
Make sure students understand this term. The definition can be found in the glossary at the end of the student book.
- erosion

Materials
Gather the materials needed for *Enrichment* (p. 67) and *Connections* (p. 68).

CHAPTER 6 / LESSON 17
Changing Shorelines

Saving a Lighthouse

Sometimes, retreating is the best option.

For 200 years the Cape Hatteras Lighthouse stood on a North Carolina barrier island, warning ships away from dangerous waters. But over the years, erosion carried away much of the sand between the lighthouse and the Atlantic Ocean. By 1999 something had to be done if people wanted to save the lighthouse. The local community had to make some hard decisions. Scientists analyzed the patterns of erosion. Engineers proposed ways to protect the lighthouse.

▶ **Before You Read**

WHY WE NEED LIGHTHOUSES What is the purpose of a lighthouse? Explain what you know about lighthouses. You can use a drawing in your explanation.

Lighthouses shine a bright light that warns of dangers along the coastline so ships can find their way safely.

FIND OUT MORE
SCIENCESAURUS
Erosion and Deposition 192

TEACHING PLAN pp. 66–67

INTRODUCING THE LESSON
This lesson further explores the effects of beach erosion through the example of the Cape Hatteras Lighthouse. The lighthouse was moved inland in 1999 because coastal erosion had brought the ocean dangerously close to the spot where the lighthouse had stood for almost 130 years.

If any students have visited a lighthouse, ask them to describe the structure and its setting. Some students may be under the impression that lighthouses are a thing of the past. Explain that lighthouses are still used today to warn ships of dangerous shoals and other navigation hazards.

▶ **Before You Read**

WHY WE NEED LIGHTHOUSES
Encourage students to draw on their own experiences in explaining the function of a lighthouse as a navigation aid. Explain that lighthouse signal lamps project light through a lens that focuses the lamp's light into a strong beam. Ask: *What conditions might affect the visibility of the light beam from a distance?* (the strength of the light; its height above sea level; weather conditions such as rain, fog, or snow)

Explain that most modern lighthouses are automated and do not require a lighthouse keeper. Many are now equipped with a radio beacon to send out radio signals.

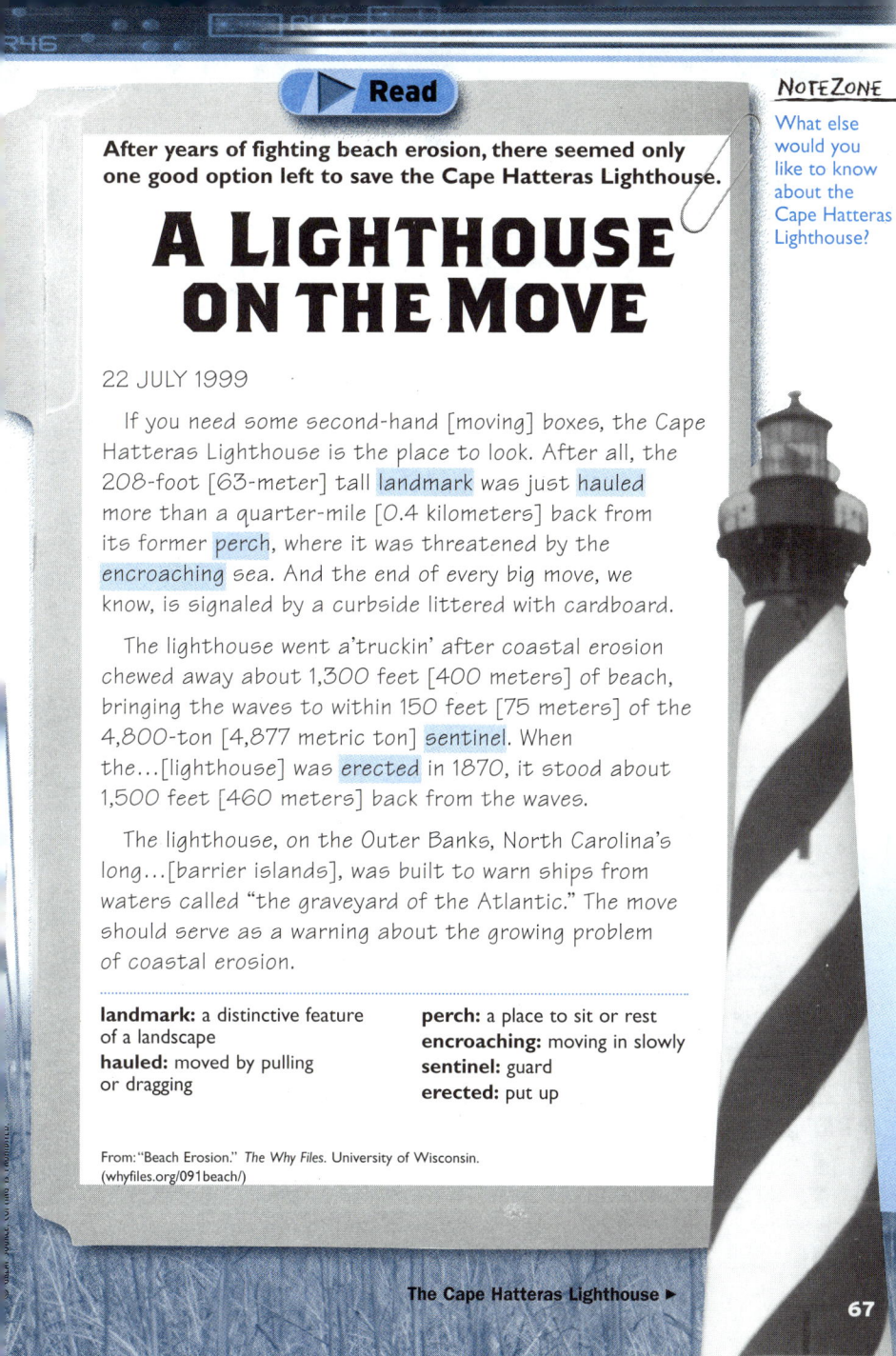

Read

After years of fighting beach erosion, there seemed only one good option left to save the Cape Hatteras Lighthouse.

A LIGHTHOUSE ON THE MOVE

22 JULY 1999

If you need some second-hand [moving] boxes, the Cape Hatteras Lighthouse is the place to look. After all, the 208-foot [63-meter] tall landmark was just hauled more than a quarter-mile [0.4 kilometers] back from its former perch, where it was threatened by the encroaching sea. And the end of every big move, we know, is signaled by a curbside littered with cardboard.

The lighthouse went a'truckin' after coastal erosion chewed away about 1,300 feet [400 meters] of beach, bringing the waves to within 150 feet [75 meters] of the 4,800-ton [4,877 metric ton] sentinel. When the…[lighthouse] was erected in 1870, it stood about 1,500 feet [460 meters] back from the waves.

The lighthouse, on the Outer Banks, North Carolina's long…[barrier islands], was built to warn ships from waters called "the graveyard of the Atlantic." The move should serve as a warning about the growing problem of coastal erosion.

landmark: a distinctive feature of a landscape
hauled: moved by pulling or dragging
perch: a place to sit or rest
encroaching: moving in slowly
sentinel: guard
erected: put up

From: "Beach Erosion." *The Why Files.* University of Wisconsin. (whyfiles.org/091beach/)

NOTE ZONE
What else would you like to know about the Cape Hatteras Lighthouse?

The Cape Hatteras Lighthouse ▶

67

Enrichment

Time: 45 minutes
Materials: stream table or rectangular tank, water, metric ruler, sand, wood block or plastic lid, rocks, pebbles, clay, cardboard tube, small plastic bags

After students read about the methods that were tried in an attempt to prevent erosion at the Cape Hatteras Lighthouse (see time line, next page), suggest that they use the stream table or tank from the Enrichment activity on page 63 to model the methods, as follows: Pile a slope of sand along one side of the container and use clay to make an elevated "rocky" area at one edge. Use a cardboard tube to build a tall structure on the rock. Add water until the level is just below the rocky area. Use a plastic lid or wood block to make diagonal waves along the shore.

Instruct students to review the methods described in the time line and devise ways to model them. For example, they could use pebbles and rocks or small bags of sand to build up a barrier. Have them test to see which methods work best.

Read

A LIGHTHOUSE ON THE MOVE Point out that a K-W-L chart is a good tool for keeping track of what you already know, what you have learned, and questions that you are interested in having answered about a new topic. Encourage students to use this type of organizer to sort out the details presented in the reading about the Cape Hatteras Lighthouse preservation project. The format for a K-W-L chart is shown to the right.

Explain why the area of North Carolina's Outer Banks is known as the "graveyard of the Atlantic." Because of rough conditions, frequent storms, and shallow water, this area has one of the highest incidences of shipwrecks in the world. Throughout maritime history, thousands of ships have wrecked in the area.

What I **K**now	What I **W**ant to Know	What I **L**earned

CHECK UNDERSTANDING
Skill: Predicting
Ask: *What might have happened to the lighthouse if it had not been moved?* (It might have been damaged or destroyed in a storm.)

CHAPTER 6 / LESSON 17   67

CHAPTER 6 / LESSON 17

More Resources
The following resources are also available from Great Source.

ScienceSaurus
Erosion and Deposition   192

Reader's Handbook
Elements of Graphics: Timeline   561

Connections
Time: will vary
Materials: *The Lighthouse Keeper* by James Michael Pratt (St. Martins, 2001)

LANGUAGE ARTS Encourage students to read about the lives of people who tended lighthouses. Provide a copy of Pratt's book. Written as a light-keeper's log, the book records the fictional saga of the O'Banyon family, when Uncle Billie O'Banyon became Port Hope's first lighthouse keeper after WWI. After students have read the book, tell them to imagine that they were lighthouse keepers during a period in American history and to write a log entry describing an experience.

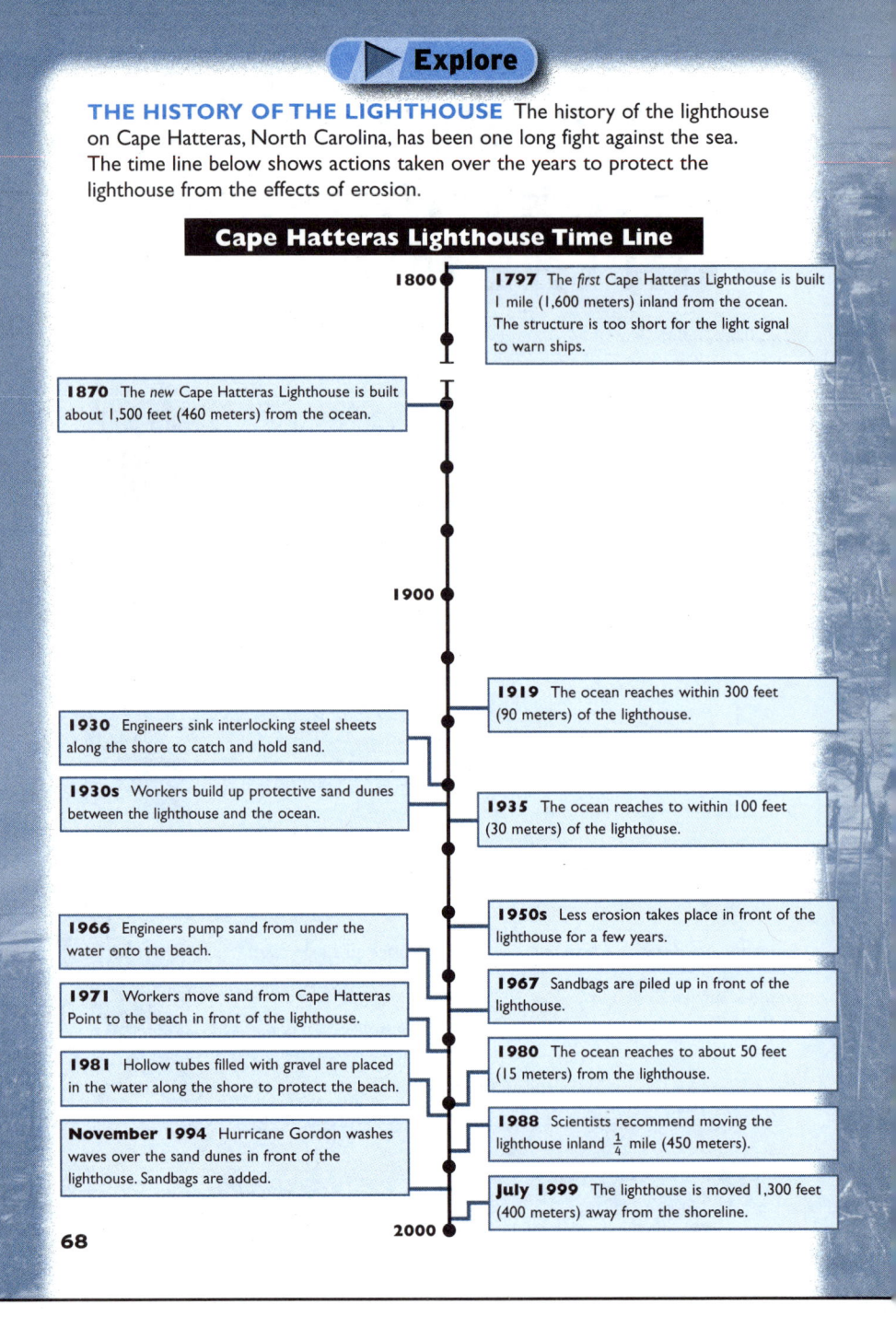

Teaching Plan pp. 68–69

▶ Explore

THE HISTORY OF THE LIGHTHOUSE The history of the lighthouse on Cape Hatteras, North Carolina, has been one long fight against the sea. The time line below shows actions taken over the years to protect the lighthouse from the effects of erosion.

Cape Hatteras Lighthouse Time Line

1797 The *first* Cape Hatteras Lighthouse is built 1 mile (1,600 meters) inland from the ocean. The structure is too short for the light signal to warn ships.

1870 The *new* Cape Hatteras Lighthouse is built about 1,500 feet (460 meters) from the ocean.

1919 The ocean reaches within 300 feet (90 meters) of the lighthouse.

1930 Engineers sink interlocking steel sheets along the shore to catch and hold sand.

1930s Workers build up protective sand dunes between the lighthouse and the ocean.

1935 The ocean reaches to within 100 feet (30 meters) of the lighthouse.

1950s Less erosion takes place in front of the lighthouse for a few years.

1966 Engineers pump sand from under the water onto the beach.

1967 Sandbags are piled up in front of the lighthouse.

1971 Workers move sand from Cape Hatteras Point to the beach in front of the lighthouse.

1980 The ocean reaches to about 50 feet (15 meters) from the lighthouse.

1981 Hollow tubes filled with gravel are placed in the water along the shore to protect the beach.

1988 Scientists recommend moving the lighthouse inland $\frac{1}{4}$ mile (450 meters).

November 1994 Hurricane Gordon washes waves over the sand dunes in front of the lighthouse. Sandbags are added.

July 1999 The lighthouse is moved 1,300 feet (400 meters) away from the shoreline.

68

▶ Explore

THE HISTORY OF THE LIGHTHOUSE
Review how to read a time line. Point out that this time line should be read from top to bottom. Caution students to pay close attention to the years labeled in the boxes so they read the events in their correct order, not down the left column and then down the right column.

For more information about the Cape Hatteras Lighthouse, students can visit the Cape Hatteras restoration project Web site at:
www.nps.gov/caha/lighthousereports

THINK ABOUT IT To answer the first question in this section, students could first highlight the time line labels that describe the actions taken to prevent erosion. After students have completed their answers to the remaining questions, discuss their ideas.

You might point out that moving a lighthouse is not a new practice. Lighthouses that have been moved include Block Island's Southeast Lighthouse, Rhode Island; Cape San Blas Lighthouse, Florida; Tybee Lighthouse, Georgia; and Nauset Lighthouse on Cape Cod, Massachusetts.

In the 1800s, some lighthouses were even built on tracks on the assumption that they would have to be moved farther inland at some time in the future.

68   **CHAPTER 6 / LESSON 17**

THINK ABOUT IT

▶ List the ways that people tried to prevent erosion of the beach around the lighthouse.

by placing interlocking steel sheets along the beach, building sand dunes, pumping sand from the ocean onto the beach, piling sandbags in front of the lighthouse, moving sand from offshore to the beach, placing gravel-filled tubes in the water, adding more sandbags

▶ Why do you think the first lighthouse was built so far from the ocean?

Answers will vary. Examples: The people who built it were afraid that erosion could destroy it or they did not have the ability to build a tall lighthouse on sand.

▶ Why do you think so many other solutions were tried before the lighthouse was moved in 1999?

Answers will vary. Examples: The people who lived nearby liked the idea of keeping the lighthouse where it had been for so many years. The cost of moving the lighthouse might have been too high, or engineers may not have known how to move the lighthouse without damaging it.

▶ **Take Action**

EXPLORING PROS AND CONS Think about all the ways engineers tried to reduce or repair the effects of erosion on Cape Hatteras. None of the methods worked for long. What would you say to a community trying to save its beach? List the arguments for and against fighting beach erosion. List the arguments for and against letting erosion take place. On a separate sheet of paper, summarize your ideas in a chart that presents both sides of the issue.

Answers will vary.

Assessment
Skill: Interpreting data

Use the following question to assess each student's progress:

Why did engineers move the lighthouse away from the shoreline in 1999 instead of trying other ways to protect the lighthouse where it was? (Many different ways to protect the lighthouse where it was had been tried, but none of them had worked for very long. Moving the lighthouse was the best long-term solution.)

▶ **Take Action**

EXPLORING PROS AND CONS After students complete their charts, discuss the ideas they identified. In the discussion, check to make sure students have considered the following arguments.

For fighting erosion: could preserve the beach, at least temporarily

Against fighting erosion: very expensive; looks less natural; none of the methods used to prevent erosion works for very long

For letting erosion take place: more natural environment for people to visit; less expensive

Against letting erosion take place: beach may lose much of its sand; eroded sand may be deposited where it interferes with boat traffic

UNIT 2 Dynamic Earth
CHAPTER 6 / LESSON 18

Point of Lesson
Scientists gather data to inform the public about the dangers of building on coastlines.

Focus
- Structure of the earth system
- Science and technology in society
- Change, constancy, and measurement
- Natural hazards

Skills and Strategies
- Making inferences
- Recognizing cause and effect
- Predicting
- Using space/time relationships

Advance Preparation
Vocabulary
Make sure students understand these terms. Definitions can be found in the glossary at the end of the student book.
- data
- erosion
- hurricane

More Resources
The following resource is also available from Great Source.

ScienceSaurus
Erosion and Deposition   192

TEACHING PLAN pp. 70–71

CHAPTER 6 / LESSON 18
Changing Shorelines

Investigating Erosion

Hurricanes cause the most beach erosion.

When Hurricane Dennis struck the east coast of the U.S. in September 1999, it did a lot of damage. A hurricane's strong winds and powerful waves can change shorelines dramatically in a short period of time. Scientists are interested in what kinds of erosion damage are done by hurricanes. They hope to use the information to save properties and lives in future storms.

▶ **Read**

NoteZone

When did Hurricane Dennis strike North Carolina's coast?

September 1999

When was the Cape Hatteras Lighthouse moved?

July 1999

What do you notice about these dates?

The lighthouse was moved only two months before the hurricane struck.

When a hurricane strikes, erosion scientists move in to check the damage.

EYE-POPPING EROSION

10 September 1999

[Hurricane] Dennis...teased the Atlantic coast with whipping winds and battering waves before finally making landfall on Saturday.... [Dennis] caused "eye-popping erosion" and...the worst scouring of North Carolina's coast in 20 years. This week, teams of USGS scientists are on the ground, making measurements of the eroded beaches.... [The scientists are also] flying over the coastline to take video and still photographs of the damage caused by Dennis....

The data collected this week will be compared with data collected before and after other hurricanes and coastal storms.... [This will help scientists] track long-term changes to the coastline.... [It will also help them understand] the effects of storms on beaches, protective dunes, and the topography of the region. These changes... reflect the hazards to life and property during a major coastal storm.

"Ultimately, we want to be able to provide sound, scientific data to local officials and builders.... [They] can then decide how far back structures should be set or

---

INTRODUCING THE LESSON
This lesson explores the erosion of North Carolina's coast caused by 1999's Hurricane Dennis and the methods that scientists use to evaluate coastline changes. Ask students to relate any experiences they may have had with hurricanes—particularly Hurricane Dennis, if they live on the East Coast. Students who have not experienced a hurricane may have seen news reports on television.

Students who do not live in a coastal area may think that a hurricane is simply a violent wind- and rainstorm. Explain that powerful waves, storm surges, and flooding cause severe damage along the coastline.

▶ **Read**

To answer the second NoteZone question, students may need to refer back to the last box of the time line on page 68.

Then ask: *Why was it so fortunate that the lighthouse had already been moved when Dennis struck?* (After Hurricane Gordon in 1994, sandbags had to be added to secure the dunes in front of the lighthouse. During Hurricane Dennis, the water likely would have reached the lighthouse if it hadn't been moved.)

After students have completed the reading, have them highlight the sentences that explain how scientists plan to use the information they have collected.

where they shouldn't be set at all," said [USGS oceanographer and coastal erosion expert Abby] Sallenger.

making landfall: reaching land
scouring: forceful scrubbing
USGS: United States Geological Survey, a government life and earth science agency
topography: features of the land surface
oceanographer: a scientist who studies the ocean

From: "Dennis Dissipates, Work Just Begins for USGS Scientists." *United States Geological Survey.* U.S. Department of the Interior. (www.usgs.gov/public/press/public_affairs/press_releases/pr979m.html)

FIND OUT MORE
SCIENCESAURUS
Erosion and Deposition 192

Enrichment
Erosion can change things dramatically in a short period of time, but it can also change features slowly over a long period of time. Ask students to approach their surroundings with an eye for "erosion," or things wearing down over time. Have each student list at least three examples. They might cite carpet becoming worn in the center of a staircase, the plastic of a keyboard losing its texture from use, knives becoming dull, and teeth wearing down.

Assessment
Skill: Recognizing cause and effect

Use the following question to assess each student's progress:

Why did the scientists from the United States Geological Survey study the damage caused by Hurricane Dennis and other storms? (They wanted to provide scientific data so local officials and builders could decide where future structures should or should not be built.)

▶ **Explore**

BEFORE AND AFTER This photo was taken by the USGS team after Hurricane Dennis. The X marks the position of the lighthouse before it was moved. You can see the lighthouse's straight pathway through the sand dunes when it was moved.

▶ What might have happened if the lighthouse had not been moved before the hurricane? What details in the photo support your answer?

The photo shows water in the lighthouse's pathway and behind its old position. If the lighthouse had not been moved, waves would have washed over it and might have damaged or even destroyed it.

▶ How can people use what the scientists learned about coastline erosion during storms? Think about risks to both life and property.

People can use the information to decide where it is safe to build structures along the coastline and whether to move structures that have already been built there.

71

▶ **Explore**

BEFORE AND AFTER When students answer the first question, encourage them to examine the picture carefully and look for evidence to support their ideas. If necessary, point out the flooded sections around the lighthouse's previous position. Guide them to understand that even though buildings can be constructed to withstand hurricane winds, waves and flooding can still damage or destroy the buildings.

CHECK UNDERSTANDING
Skill: Making inferences
Ask: *The data collected by scientists can help people decide where and where not to build homes and other structures on the coast. What other decisions might this information help people make?* (deciding whether existing structures should be moved)

CHAPTER 6 / LESSON 18   71

CHAPTER 7 Overview

The Puzzle of Earth's Crust

LESSON 19
Fitting the Continents Together
Point of Lesson: *Wegener's theory of continental drift was not accepted by other scientists at first.*

In the early 1900s, most geologists thought it was impossible for continents to move. Astronomer and meteorologist Alfred Wegener shocked the scientific community when he proposed the theory of continental drift. Geologists initially rejected Wegener's idea, for several reasons: it contradicted their own theories; Wegener was not a trained geologist; and Wegener's theory did not explain *how* continents could move.

Materials
Read (p. 73), for each student:
- photocopy of world map
- scissors
- tape

Enrichment (p. 73), for each student:
- 2 photocopies of world map
- photocopy depicting Pangaea
- sheets of 11-by-14-inch paper
- tape
- *for the class:* research sources showing scientists' predictions of the continents' future positions

Explore (p. 74), for each student
- sheet of newspaper

Take Action (p. 75), for each student
- paper
- colored pencils

LESSON 20
Explaining How Continents Move
Point of Lesson: *New information convinced scientists that continents could move.*

By the mid-1900s, data collected by echo sounders allowed geologists to map the ocean floor. Geologist Harry Hess used this map to develop his theory of seafloor spreading. Hess hypothesized that magma flowing from mountain ridges on the ocean floor caused Earth's crust to move, carrying the continents with it.

Materials
Introducing the Lesson (p. 76), for the class:
- maps of ocean floor

Explore (p. 77), for the class:
- table tennis ball

Enrichment (p. 77), for each student:
- paper
- colored pencils

Propose Explanations (p. 78), for teacher demonstration:
- bar magnet
- string

Connections (p. 78), for each student:
- graph paper

LESSON 21
Using New Technology
Point of Lesson: *The newest technologies help confirm the theories of Wegener and Hess.*

New technologies have made it possible for scientists to further explore and confirm the ideas of Alfred Wegener and Harry Hess. The Global Positioning System (GPS) uses space satellites to identify the exact location of points on Earth's surface. By using GPS to measure and track the relative positions of various points, scientists can determine the direction and pace of continental movement.

Materials
Read (p. 80), for the class:
- world map showing diverging and converging plate boundaries (see *ScienceSaurus* section 185)

Take Action (p.81), for each student or group:
- map of the ocean floor (see *ScienceSaurus* section 185)

Enrichment (p. 81), for each group:
- clay

Laboratory Safety
Review these safety guidelines with students before they do the Enrichment activity in this lesson.
- If your skin is irritated by clay, let your lab partner handle it. Do not handle it yourself.
- Wash your hands thoroughly after the activity.

Background Information

Lesson 19

One of the main problems with Alfred Wegener's theory of continental drift was his failure to explain how and why the continents moved. Wegener incorrectly theorized that the continents plowed through Earth's seemingly static crust as the result of centrifugal and tidal forces. But as Wegener's opponents pointed out, moving through oceanic crust would have distorted the continents beyond recognition, and centrifugal and tidal forces are not strong enough to move continents.

Today, the term *continental drift* is outdated. We now know that it is not just the continents themselves that drift but the continents along with the oceanic crust beneath them that move together in plates.

Lesson 20

In 1953, physicists discovered the Great Global Rift, a deep volcanic canyon running through the mid-ocean ridges. The rift seeemed to be caused by breaks in Earth's crust—but perfectly matched breaks, like joints made by a carpenter. (The word "tectonic" in the term *plate tectonics* comes from a Greek word meaning "carpenter.")

The discovery of the Great Global Rift caused Harry Hess to look back at the echo-sounding and other ocean-floor studies he had done during World War II. In the early 1960s, Hess (along with scientists Frederick Vine, Drummond Matthews, Lawrence Morley, Allan Cox, and Richard Doell and Robert S. Deitz) proposed the theory of seafloor spreading, which stated that hot magma was oozing up from vents in the Rift. As the magma cooled and expanded, it pushed the existing sea floor away from the Rift on either side.

The theory of seafloor spreading not only supported Wegener's theory of continental drift but explained and linked several other puzzles in marine geology, including the relative youth of the ocean floor, the existence of deep sea trenches, and the formation of the mid-ocean ridges.

Lesson 21

The Global Positioning System (GPS) is a satellite navigation system controlled and funded by the United States Department of Defense. Although designed for and operated by the U.S. military, GPS has many civilian uses, including those described in this lesson.

UNIT 2 Dynamic Earth
CHAPTER 7 / LESSON 19

Point of Lesson
Wegener's theory of continental drift was not accepted by other scientists at first.

Focus
- Structure of the earth system
- Earth's history
- Evidence, models, and explanation
- History of science
- Science as a human endeavor

Skills and Strategies
- Understanding that scientific findings undergo peer review
- Understanding that scientists may disagree about interpretation of the evidence and even arrive at conflicting conclusions
- Understanding that scientists share their results to form a common core of knowledge
- Making inferences

Advance Preparation
Vocabulary
Make sure students understand these terms. Definitions can be found in the glossary at the end of the student book.

- continent
- fossil
- hypothesis
- rock
- theory

(continued on page 73)

TEACHING PLAN pp. 72–73

CHAPTER 7 / LESSON 19
The Puzzle of Earth's Crust
Fitting the Continents Together

In science, new ideas are accepted only when there is evidence to support them.

Alfred Wegener was trained as an astronomer and worked as a meteorologist. A meteorologist is a scientist who studies weather. But what made Wegener famous were his ideas about geology. Geology is the study of Earth's processes, structure, composition, and history. In the early 1900s, geologists thought that the continents had always been where they are today. Wegener studied reports of similar fossils and rocks found on continents separated by the ocean. He hypothesized that today's continents were at one time joined as one giant continent. He explained that slowly, the giant continent had broken apart. Over 200 million years, the pieces drifted to where they are found today. Wegener's idea—called *continental drift*—was revolutionary. And it was not very popular with other scientists.

▶ Before You Read

WHAT WOULD YOU DO? Imagine you are at a scientific meeting of geologists. Someone stands up and says, "My name is Alfred Wegener and I am a meteorologist. Let me tell you my great new idea about Earth's history. It's based on evidence from fossils and rocks found on different continents."
▶ Would you be willing to listen to Wegener? Explain your answer.

Answers will vary. Examples: No, I probably wouldn't listen because I'd think that a meteorologist wouldn't know enough about geology. Yes, I would listen because Wegener said he had evidence and because scientists should be willing to listen to new ideas.

INTRODUCING THE LESSON
This lesson introduces students to Alfred Wegener's theory of *continental drift,* which states that the continents were once one great landmass that broke apart and slowly drifted to their present positions. You may want to point out that Wegener named the once-giant land mass *Pangaea* (pan-JEE-ah), a Greek word that means "all Earth."

Ask students if they think the continents were always positioned as they are today. Many students will think that the continents are in a fixed position and that this position has always been as it is now. Tell students that the continents have been drifting for millions of years and even now are changing position.

▶ Before You Read

WHAT WOULD YOU DO? Explain to students that Alfred Wegener earned his Ph.D. in astronomy in 1904 but chose to do research in the then-new field of meteorology. He was always interested in geophysics as well. Ask students if they think that someone who does not have a background in geology can form believable explanations for scientific questions in the field of geology.

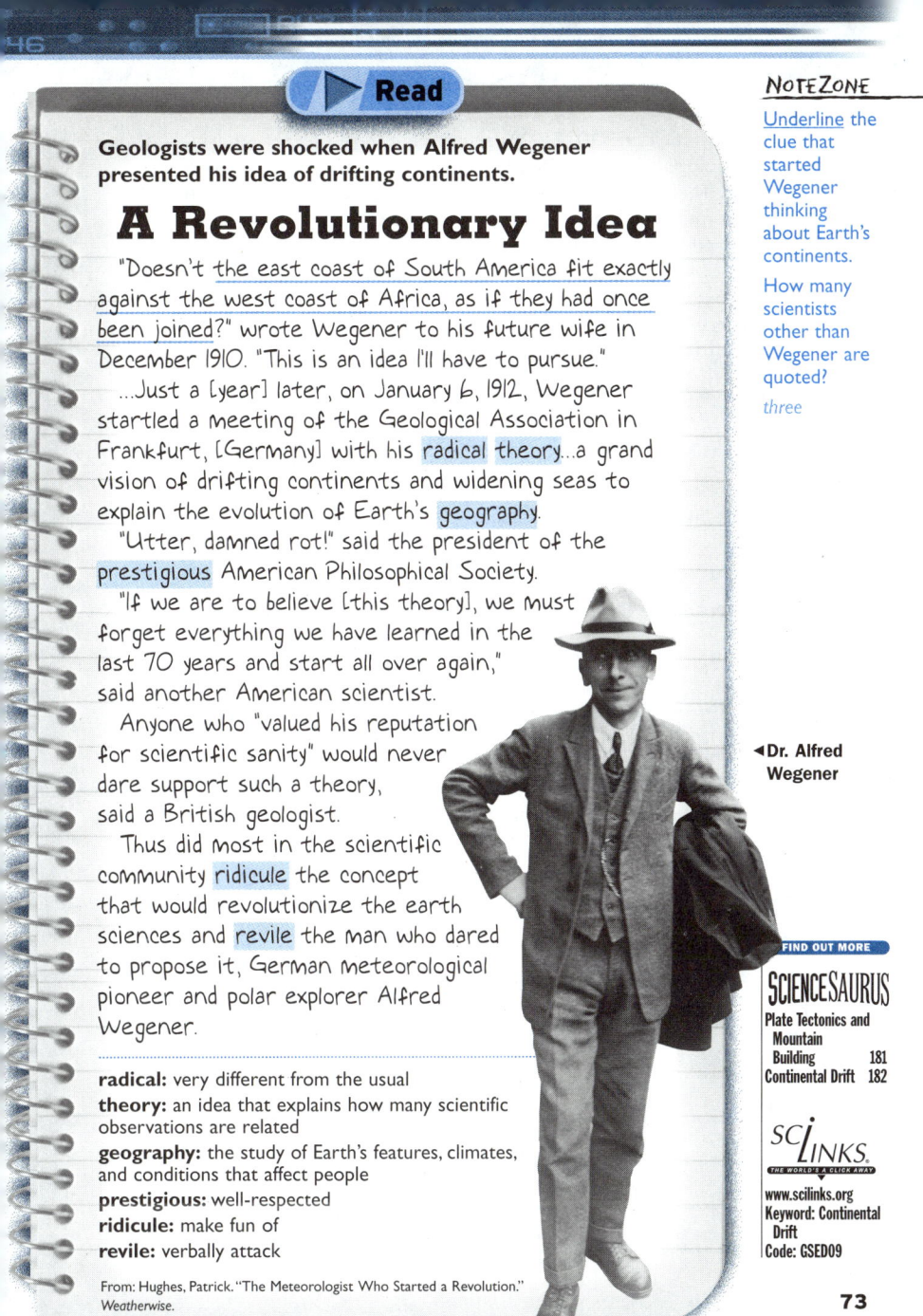

▶ Read

Geologists were shocked when Alfred Wegener presented his idea of drifting continents.

A Revolutionary Idea

"Doesn't the east coast of South America fit exactly against the west coast of Africa, as if they had once been joined?" wrote Wegener to his future wife in December 1910. "This is an idea I'll have to pursue."

...Just a [year] later, on January 6, 1912, Wegener startled a meeting of the Geological Association in Frankfurt, [Germany] with his radical theory...a grand vision of drifting continents and widening seas to explain the evolution of Earth's geography.

"Utter, damned rot!" said the president of the prestigious American Philosophical Society.

"If we are to believe [this theory], we must forget everything we have learned in the last 70 years and start all over again," said another American scientist.

Anyone who "valued his reputation for scientific sanity" would never dare support such a theory, said a British geologist.

Thus did most in the scientific community ridicule the concept that would revolutionize the earth sciences and revile the man who dared to propose it, German meteorological pioneer and polar explorer Alfred Wegener.

radical: very different from the usual
theory: an idea that explains how many scientific observations are related
geography: the study of Earth's features, climates, and conditions that affect people
prestigious: well-respected
ridicule: make fun of
revile: verbally attack

From: Hughes, Patrick. "The Meteorologist Who Started a Revolution." *Weatherwise.*

NOTEZONE

Underline the clue that started Wegener thinking about Earth's continents.

How many scientists other than Wegener are quoted?

three

◀ Dr. Alfred Wegener

FIND OUT MORE
SCIENCESAURUS
Plate Tectonics and Mountain Building 181
Continental Drift 182

SCILINKS
www.scilinks.org
Keyword: Continental Drift
Code: GSED09

73

(continued from page 72)

Materials
Gather the materials needed for *Read* (p. 73), *Enrichment* (p. 73), *Explore* (p. 74), and *Take Action* (p. 75).

Enrichment
Time: 45 minutes
Materials: world map (two photocopies per student), photocopy depicting Pangaea (one per student), sheets of 11-by-14-inch paper, tape, research sources showing scientists' predictions of the continents' future positions

Provide each student with two photocopies of a world map and a drawing of Pangaea. Have students trace around each continent on the two world maps and cut them out of one of the maps. Have them arrange the continents to form Pangaea, then figure out how they must have drifted to be in the positions they are in today. Ask students to predict what the world map might look like millions of years from now if the continents keep moving apart. Have students tape the continents on a large sheet of paper to show their predictions. They can use the remaining map to reference the current positions of the continents. Then have them check their predictions against a map that shows scientists' predictions of what the world may look like in the far-distant future.

▶ Read
Time: 15 minutes
Materials: photocopies of world map, scissors, tape

Have students highlight the quotes in the reading that show how the scientists felt about Wegener's theory. Ask them if they think scientists today would be so opposed to new, radical ideas. (Students might say that scientists need evidence before they will accept a new theory. Challenging a scientist's own work might provoke the same sort of negative response as Wegener received.)

Provide each student with a copy of a world map. Tell students to cut apart the continents, leaving Asia and Europe as one piece. Then have them place the continents of North and South America next to those of Europe and Africa. Students should note how closely the continents fit together.

CHECK UNDERSTANDING
Skill: Making inferences
Ask: *Why didn't scientists accept Wegener's theory of continental drift?* (Wegener was a meteorologist, not a geologist. Scientists felt that they would have to disregard everything they had learned in the previous 70 years about how Earth moved.)

CHAPTER 7 / LESSON 19   73

CHAPTER 7 / LESSON 19

More Resources
The following resources are also available from Great Source and NSTA.

SCIENCESAURUS
Plate Tectonics and Mountain Building	181
Continental Drift	182
History of Science Time Line	446
Famous Scientists	461

READER'S HANDBOOK
Reading Geography	84
Elements of Graphics: Cartoon	550

WRITE SOURCE 2000
Editorial Cartoons	173

SCILINKS
THE WORLD'S A CLICK AWAY
www.scilinks.org
Keyword: Continental Drift
Code: GSED09

▶ Explore

COMPARING THEORIES Wegener spent most of 1911 studying the work of geologists. He read about identical fossils found in South America and Africa. The fossils showed that the same kinds of animals lived on the two continents at the same time. Most geologists thought it was impossible for continents to move. Even Wegener could not explain how it happened. Some geologists hypothesized that long land bridges must have connected the two continents. They believed that over time, these bridges had sunk into the ocean so they could no longer be seen.

▶ **How did Wegener explain why the fossils matched?**
   He said that the continents were once joined together.

Wegener researched the work of other geologists. He read that rock formations on the east coast of South America and the west coast of Africa matched.

▶ **How did Wegener's theory explain these matching rock formations?**
   His theory said that the two continents were joined at one time, so the rock formations along the two coasts had been joined, too.

▶ **How might the land bridge hypothesis explain the same fossils and rock formations?**
   The matching fossils and rock formations could have been part of the land bridges.

▶ **Why do you think the scientists at the Geological Association meeting rejected Wegener's theory of continental drift?**
   Wegener could not explain how continents could move, and they had another theory to explain Wegener's observations. Also, if Wegener's theory were true, it would mean they were wrong and would have to give up their own ideas.

74

TEACHING PLAN pp. 74–75

▶ Explore

Time: 15 minutes
Materials: sheet of newspaper

COMPARING THEORIES Remind students that all scientific theories must be supported with evidence. Ask students what Wegener might have taken from his studies as an astronomer and his work as a meteorologist that would have helped him develop theories in geology. Identify evidence as a key to the development of all scientific theories.

Point out that many geologists thought it was impossible for the continents to move. Scientists also thought that the distances between continents was so great that it would be impossible to support a land bridge from one continent to the other.

Present students with this model: Tear up a sheet of newspaper into several pieces. Have students work in small groups to put the newspaper pieces back together. Ask: *What evidence did you use to put the pieces back together?* (the type and pictures on the page) Then ask: *How does this serve as a model for the theory of continental drift?* (The matching print is much like the matching fossils and landforms found on different continents.)

74   CHAPTER 7 / LESSON 19

▶ Propose Explanations

AN ADVENTUROUS SCIENTIST As a boy, Wegener dreamed of exploring the Arctic. He was excited by the challenge of exploring and making new discoveries. As an adult scientist he was also adventurous. He tested a new weather instrument in a long hot-air balloon flight. He survived the longest crossing of an ice sheet ever made. (An ice sheet is a huge, thick glacier covering a large land area.) In fact, Wegener died on the Arctic ice after trying to save other men.

▶ Someone who is adventurous is willing to take chances. What kinds of chances did Wegener take as an explorer?

He risked freezing to death in the Arctic or crashing on the balloon flight.

▶ What kinds of chances did Wegener take as a thinker?

He was not afraid to take a chance on new ideas and give up old ideas.

Wegener did not give up on his theory of continental drift. He continued to work on it for the rest of his life. It was another 50 years before other scientists accepted the idea that continents could be moving.

▶ Take Action

IT'S FUNNY—BUT IS IT SCIENCE?

▶ This cartoon is funny because it doesn't represent continental drift accurately. Explain why the cartoon and caption are not accurate.

Continents drift much too slowly to be noticed in one person's lifetime.

Continental drift would eventually force Og to raise his rates.

75

Connections

SOCIAL STUDIES Ask students to create a time line that shows the events in Alfred Wegener's life that are discussed in this chapter. Students should note his specific accomplishments, including when he proposed his theory of continental drift. To put Wegener's life into historical perspective, include a few other important historical events after his death—for example, the invention of the automobile, the beginning of World Wars I and II, the sinking of the *Titanic*, and the first successful launch of a spaceship.

Assessment
Skill: Organizing information

Use the following question to assess each student's progress:

What evidence did Alfred Wegener use to develop his theory of continental drift? (Identical fossils and rock formations on separate continents today showed that the continents were once joined together but moved apart.)

▶ Propose Explanations

AN ADVENTUROUS SCIENTIST Tell students that Wegener died in his sleeping bag on the return of a trip to rescue members of his exploration party. It has been proposed that he died of a heart attack. Ask students if they think it is important for scientists to take chances in their thoughts and actions. Have them give reasons for their answers.

▶ Take Action

Time: 30 minutes
Materials: paper, colored pencils

IT'S FUNNY—BUT IS IT SCIENCE?
Invite students to create their own cartoons about continental drift. Allow students class time to share their cartoons with classmates.

CHAPTER 7 / LESSON 19   75

UNIT 2 Dynamic Earth
CHAPTER 7 / LESSON 20

Point of Lesson
New information convinced scientists that continents could move.

Focus
- Structure of the earth system
- Earth's history
- Evidence, models, and explanation
- History of science
- Science as a human endeavor

Skills and Strategies
- Interpreting scientific illustrations
- Recognizing cause and effect
- Understanding that scientists change their ideas in the face of experimental evidence that does not support existing hypotheses

Advance Preparation
Vocabulary
Make sure students understand these terms. Definitions can be found in the glossary at the end of the student book.

- continent
- continental drift
- crust
- data
- echo
- magma
- map
- mineral
- theory

(continued on page 77)

TEACHING PLAN pp. 76–77

INTRODUCING THE LESSON

Materials: maps of the ocean floor

This lesson introduces Henry Hess's theory of seafloor spreading. Ask students to describe what they think the ocean floor's features are, such as terrain and rock formations.

Many students will think that the ocean floor is flat. Provide maps of the ocean floor for students to observe. (Many science textbooks and atlases contain this type of map.) Point out that the ocean floor has many mountainous regions.

CHAPTER 7 / LESSON 20
The Puzzle of Earth's Crust

EXPLAINING HOW CONTINENTS MOVE

While at sea with the U.S. Navy, Harry Hess found time to do scientific research.

Harry Hess was a geologist at Princeton University. He was also a ship commander in the United States Navy. During World War II, Hess was at sea on a navy ship. Crossing back and forth across the oceans gave Hess the chance to collect data about the ocean floor.

After the war, geologists continued to collect data. During the late 1940s and 1950s, the first complete map of the ocean floor was put together. Hess studied the map and had an idea that could explain how continents move.

▶ **Read**

NOTEZONE
Underline the words that describe the kind of scientist Harry Hess was.

Here's how Harry Hess came up with his idea.

Underwater Clues

Between military missions, Hess's thoughts often turned to geology. Like most ships of its class, the *Cape Johnson* was equipped with an echo sounder.... [The echo sounder sent] out pulses of sound that bounced off the ocean floor. [Then it] measured the time for [the pulses] to return,...calculating the water's depth. As Hess voyaged around the globe in this ship,...the steady ping of the echo sounder generated a profile of the ocean floor....

In 1960 [Hess] attempted to explain...[these] observations of the ocean floor [and his theory about seafloor spreading].... A brilliant scientist, Hess was... perhaps tentative about the new ideas he was presenting. In his introduction [to a scientific report] he adopted a cautious tone. "I shall consider this paper an essay in geopoetry," he wrote, hinting that his colleagues should keep an open mind about his conclusions.

FIND OUT MORE
SCIENCESAURUS
Plate Tectonics and Mountain Building 181
Lithospheric Plates 183
Plate Boundaries 184
Map of Plate Boundaries 185
Ocean Floor 207

76 UNIT 2: DYNAMIC EARTH

▶ **Read**

Ask students to recall the reaction of scientists to Wegener's theory of continental drift. (They rejected the idea as ridiculous.) Then ask students if scientists reacted in a similar way to Hess's ideas about seafloor spreading. (They viewed Hess's ideas with skepticism and disdain, so the reaction was similar.)

The International Geophysical Year, 1957–1958, was an 18-month period of scientific exploration of the physical aspects of Earth. Scientists from 67 nations worked together on experiments and shared the resulting data. The timing of this study had a great impact on Hess's work.

...More than geopoetry, Hess's theory of seafloor spreading was the key to the earth's behavior. But most of his contemporaries didn't see it that way. At the time, the geological community, particularly in the United States, still believed strongly in an earth with an immovable crust. They greeted Hess's ideas with skepticism or outright disdain.

generated: produced
profile: a view from the side
tentative: unsure
geopoetry: poetry about geology
colleague: a member of the same profession
contemporary: a person living at the same time
skepticism: disbelief
disdain: dislike, scorn

▲ Harry Hess

From: Vogel, Shawna. *Naked Earth: The New Geophysics.* Dutton, a division of Penguin Putnam, Inc.

▶ Explore

INTERPRETING A DIAGRAM The diagram below shows how an echo sounder works. As the ship moves forward, the transmitter sends sound signals down to the ocean floor. The signals bounce back to the receiver. The length of time it takes for a signal to bounce back shows how deep the ocean floor is at that point. Where the ocean floor is deeper, the signal takes longer to bounce back. Where the ocean floor is shallower, the signal bounces back more quickly. All the "bounce-back" times are plotted on a graph. Connecting the points with a line creates a profile of the ocean floor.

▶ If the line on the graph suddenly went up and then down again, what would that tell you about that area of the ocean floor?

The area suddenly became shallower and then deeper again.

▶ What kind of feature would you expect to see there on the ocean floor?

a steep hill or mountain

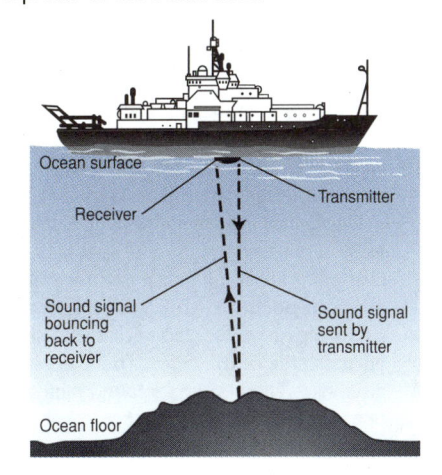

(continued from page 76)

Materials
Gather the materials needed for *Introducing the Lesson* (p. 76), *Explore* (p. 77), *Enrichment* (p. 77), *Propose Explanations* (p. 78), and *Connections* (p. 78).

Enrichment

Time: 45 minutes
Materials: paper, colored pencils

Tell students that scientists have developed many tools that are used in underwater research. Among these are the JIM suit, a deep-sea diving suit named for its inventor, Jim Jarret. Another is the benthoscope, an underwater vehicle used to explore ocean depths. The Remote Underwater Manipulator (RUM), controlled by a computer, collects samples and takes photos without the aid of an on-board crew. Ask students to find pictures of these and other underwater technologies. Then ask them to draw a design for a vehicle that would be appropriate for exploring the ocean floor. Tell them to consider whether the vehicle is designed for humans or as a robot and to consider the following factors: water pressure, temperatures, the need for windows, and the types of sensors that would be needed.

77

▶ Explore

INTERPRETING A DIAGRAM As students examine the diagram, remind them that sound waves are able to travel through different substances besides air. Call attention to the dashed lines. Have students draw a solid line from the ship to the lowest point on the ocean floor. Ask them if it would take longer for the return signal to reach the ship along the dashed line or the line they drew and explain why. (It would take longer from the lowest point on the ocean floor because the bounced signal would travel a longer distance.)

Time: 10 minutes
Materials: table tennis ball

Use the following activity to model echo-sounding. Choose a wall in a hallway or the gymnasium. Have a volunteer bounce the ball against the wall. Tell the other students to count slowly to time how long it takes the ball to return to the student who threw it. Repeat the activity several times with other volunteers standing at different distances from the wall.

CHECK UNDERSTANDING
Skill: Sequencing

Have students draw a simple diagram showing how an echo sounder measures the depth of the ocean floor. Then have them draw the profile that might result from several minutes of echo-sounding. (Students' diagrams should show these steps: 1. A sound signal is sent to the ocean floor. 2. The signal bounces back to the receiver. 3. The length of time for the signal to bounce back is measured. 4. The "bounce back" times are plotted on a graph.)

CHAPTER 7 / LESSON 20   77

CHAPTER 7 / LESSON 20

More Resources
The following resources are also available from Great Source.

ScienceSaurus
Plate Tectonics and Mountain Building	181
Lithospheric Plates	183
Plate Boundaries	184
Map of Plate Boundaries	185
Ocean Floor	207

Math on Call
Single-Line Graphs	298

Connections
Time: 20 minutes
Materials: graph paper

MATH The graphs that oceanographers use to plot terrain show the outline of the ocean floor based on the data they receive. Have each student create a graph with the vertical axis labeled *Depth (km)* and numbered from 0 to 5, using two squares per kilometer. Have them label the horizontal axis *Time (seconds)* and use four squares per second from 0 to 5. Then tell students to imagine that the following data were collected by an echo sounder. Have students plot the coordinates on the graph and then

(continued on page 79)

Teaching Plan pp. 78–79

HESS'S NEW THEORY The echo sounding profiles collected by Hess and others showed at least one mountain ridge in every ocean. New magma, hot melted rock, flowed out of each ridge. The profiles also showed deep trenches along the edges of the oceans. Hess hypothesized that new crust formed from the magma flowing out of the ridge. He also hypothesized that older crust was destroyed at the trenches. In this way Earth's crust was always moving. Hess's theory was called *seafloor spreading*.

▶ Label the diagram to show where new crust forms. Label where old crust is destroyed.

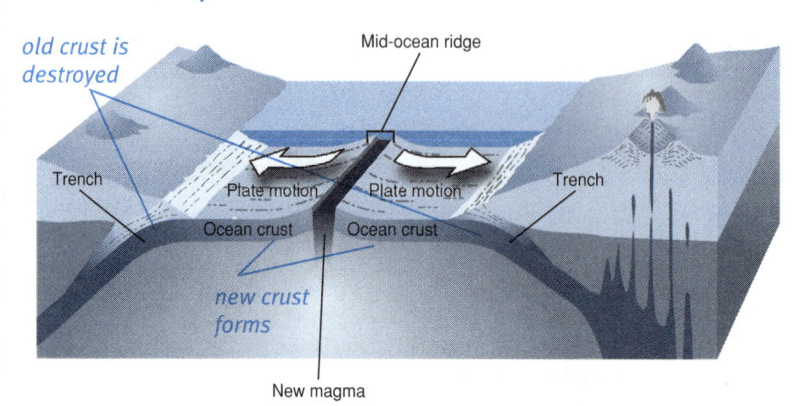

old crust is destroyed — Mid-ocean ridge — Trench — Plate motion — Plate motion — Trench — Ocean crust — Ocean crust — *new crust forms* — New magma

▶ Propose Explanations

MAGNETIC EVIDENCE Hess developed a theory to explain how Earth's crust could move. A few years later, geologists discovered new evidence that supported Hess's theory. They found that the crust on both sides of a ridge has a pattern of magnetized bands. The magnetized minerals in the bands line up with Earth's magnetic poles, just like a compass needle does. In some bands, the magnetic pole in the minerals that should point north, does point north. In other bands, that same magnetic pole in the minerals points south.

Geologists already knew that Earth's magnetic poles have switched places many times over millions of years. They concluded that as bands of new crust formed at an ocean ridge, the minerals in the bands lined up with Earth's magnetic poles. When Earth's magnetic poles reversed, the magnetic poles in new bands of crust also reversed. This produced alternating magnetized bands on each side of the ridge. Then came the most important part of the new discovery. The geologists found *matching pairs* of magnetized bands on opposite sides of the ridge!

78

▶ Explore

HESS'S NEW THEORY Call attention to the diagram, and have students note the direction of plate movement. (They appear to be moving apart.) Make sure students understand that much of Earth's volcanic activity takes place on the ocean floor. Point out that it is upwelling of magma, not necessarily explosive volcanic eruptions, that causes seafloor spreading. As the crust of the ocean floor moves, continental crust moves as well.

▶ Propose Explanations

Time: 10 minutes
Materials: bar magnet, string

MAGNETIC EVIDENCE To help students understand the concept of shifting magnetic poles, do this simple demonstration. Tie a piece of string around the center of another piece of string. Tie the ends of the second piece of string around both ends of a bar magnet. Hold the free end of the first string, and let the magnet hang freely. (Make sure the magnet is balanced.) The north pole of the magnet will point to the north. Remind students that opposites attract, which means that Earth's south magnetic pole is located near its north geographic pole. Explain that Earth's magnetic poles will reverse themselves in time and the north magnetic pole will once again line up with the geographic North Pole.

Now call attention to the diagram and have students locate the pattern of magnetic bands. Ask students how the matching bands are evidence of seafloor spreading. (As the magma hardens on both sides of the ridgeline, the rock on one side of the ridge moves in one direction, and the rock on the other side moves in the opposite direction.)

78 CHAPTER 7 / LESSON 20

Ridge

Magma

Matching bands

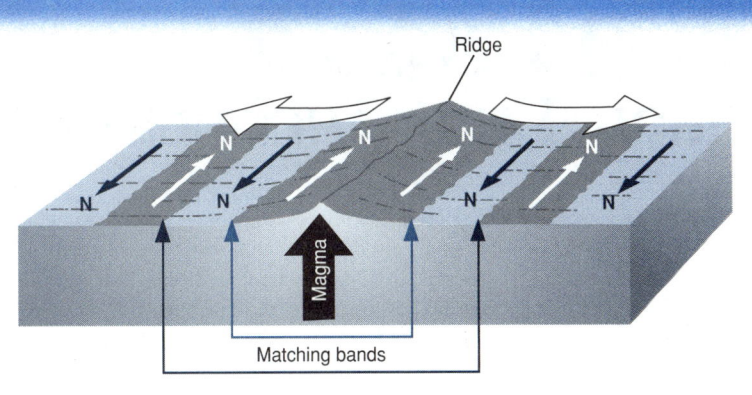

▶ **How did this new evidence support Hess's theory of seafloor spreading?**

It showed that new crust formed at the ridge and then spread apart on both sides as more magma flowed out of the ridge.

LINKING TWO THEORIES As you learned in Lesson 19, Alfred Wegener presented his theory of continental drift in 1912. Wegener said that over millions of years, the continents had slowly drifted to their present locations. But Wegener could not explain *how* continents could move. In the 1960s, Harry Hess's theory of seafloor spreading explained how Earth's crust moved. Because the continents sit on pieces of crust, they are carried along, too.

▶ **How did Hess's theory of seafloor spreading support Wegener's earlier ideas? How did this new evidence make it easier for scientists to accept the idea that continents are moving?**

Hess's theory explained how the continents could have moved.

Scientists will accept a new theory when there is evidence to support it.

▶ **What would have happened to Wegener's theory if no one had found evidence that helped explain how continents could move?**

Scientists would not have reconsidered Wegener's theory, and it would have been rejected.

(continued from page 78)

describe the profile of the ocean floor. (The graph shows two sharp peaks and one deep valley.)

▶ at 1 second, 1 km
▶ at 3 seconds, 2 km
▶ at 5 seconds, 2 km
▶ at 7 seconds, 4 km
▶ at 8 seconds, 0.5 km
▶ at 10 seconds, 5 km
▶ at 12 seconds, 3 km
▶ at 14 seconds, 2 km
▶ at 15 seconds, 1 km

Assessment
Skill: Draw conclusions

Use the following activity to assess each student's progress:

Ask students to identify the reasons why Hess's theory of seafloor spreading supported Wegener's theory of continental drift. (Magma flows out of ocean ridges. Matching pairs of magnetized bands on both sides of an ocean ridge show that new crust was formed at the ridge. The continents sit on Earth's crust, so the continents must also be moving.)

▶ **Take Action**

LINKING TWO THEORIES Point out that several other scientists worked on the magnetic evidence for seafloor spreading. These included Frederick Vine, Drummond Matthews, Lawrence Morley, Allan Cox, and Richard Doell. It was actually Robert S. Deitz, working on the same problem as Hess, who coined the term "seafloor spreading."

Have pairs of students write an imaginary dialogue between Wegener and Hess in which Wegener expresses frustration at not being able to explain how continental drift occurs and Hess explains the process and evidence. Encourage students to make the dialogue lively and realistic. Emphasize, however, that Wegener and Hess were not contemporaries, so it was impossible for them to talk with each other.

UNIT 2 Dynamic Earth

CHAPTER 7 / LESSON 21

Point of Lesson
The newest technologies help confirm the theories of Wegener and Hess.

Focus
- Structure of the earth system
- Earth's history
- Evidence, models, and explanation
- Change, constancy, and measurement
- Science and technology in society

Skills and Strategies
- Making inferences
- Generating ideas
- Interpreting data
- Predicting

Advance Preparation

Vocabulary
Make sure students understand these terms. Definitions can be found in the glossary at the end of the student book.

- crust
- satellite
- technology
- theory

Materials
Gather the materials needed for *Read* (p. 80), *Take Action* (p. 81), and *Enrichment* (p. 81).

TEACHING PLAN pp. 80–81

INTRODUCING THE LESSON
This lesson explains how the Global Positioning System is used to make observations of Earth. Ask students if they have ever ridden in a car equipped with a tracking system to locate it in case of a breakdown. Explain that this type of tracking system is also being used to show movement of the continents.

▶ Read
Time: 10 minutes
Materials: world map showing diverging and converging plate boundaries (See *ScienceSaurus* section 185.)

CHAPTER 7 / LESSON 21

The Puzzle of Earth's Crust

Using New Technology

With satellites, we can watch Earth move.

Both Alfred Wegener and Harry Hess made inferences about events they could not see. In recent years, scientists have used new technologies to gather evidence to test Wegener's and Hess's theories. One such technology is the Global Positioning System (GPS). GPS uses space satellites to identify the exact locations of points on Earth's surface.

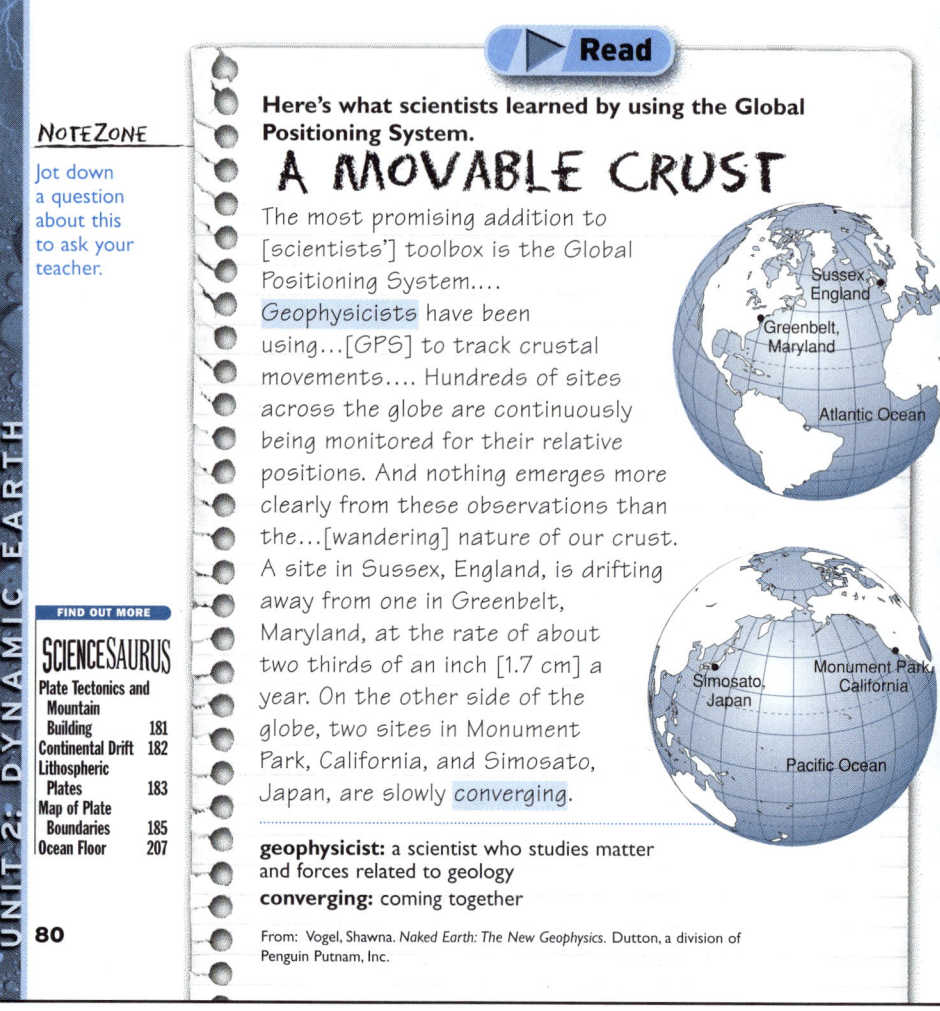

▶ Read

NOTEZONE
Jot down a question about this to ask your teacher.

FIND OUT MORE
SCIENCESAURUS
Plate Tectonics and Mountain Building 181
Continental Drift 182
Lithospheric Plates 183
Map of Plate Boundaries 185
Ocean Floor 207

Here's what scientists learned by using the Global Positioning System.

A MOVABLE CRUST

The most promising addition to [scientists'] toolbox is the Global Positioning System.... Geophysicists have been using...[GPS] to track crustal movements.... Hundreds of sites across the globe are continuously being monitored for their relative positions. And nothing emerges more clearly from these observations than the...[wandering] nature of our crust. A site in Sussex, England, is drifting away from one in Greenbelt, Maryland, at the rate of about two thirds of an inch [1.7 cm] a year. On the other side of the globe, two sites in Monument Park, California, and Simosato, Japan, are slowly converging.

geophysicist: a scientist who studies matter and forces related to geology
converging: coming together

From: Vogel, Shawna. *Naked Earth: The New Geophysics.* Dutton, a division of Penguin Putnam, Inc.

After students have completed the NoteZone task, list their questions on the board. Assign groups of students to investigate answers to selected questions.

Have students review the reading to find pairs of specific points that are drifting apart or converging. Call attention to the two maps on this page. Ask students to make inferences about the movement of the continents based on the information in the reading. (North America is drifting away from Europe and toward Asia.) Point out that even with new technologies, there are still many things that scientists cannot observe directly.

Finally, to help students visualize Earth's moving crust, display a world map showing diverging and converging plate boundaries. Students could also construct a "Tectonic Globe" using a tennis ball and a map and instructions available at: www.usgs.gov/education (Click on Paper Models, scroll down to Make Your Own Earth and Tectonic Globes.)

▶ Explore

NEW EVIDENCE
▶ What do geophysicists measure with GPS technology? What can they figure out from these measurements?

They measure the exact location of certain points on Earth's crust.
They can figure out changes in the distance between those points
on different continents.

▶ How do the data from GPS measurements support the theories of Wegener and Hess?

The measurements show that the continents are moving.

Recently scientists measured the age of rocks near ridges and trenches. Hess said crust is made along a ridge and destroyed at the trenches.

▶ Where does Hess's theory predict that the youngest rocks would be found?

near a ridge

▶ Take Action

PLAN AN EXPEDITION You have been awarded the use of the deep-sea submersible *Alvin* for a scientific expedition. *Alvin* has a camera for taking pictures, robotic arms that can be used to pick up objects, and a sled to hold equipment for experiments.

▼ *Alvin*

You have eight hours to explore an ocean ridge or trench. It takes about two hours to reach the ocean floor and another two hours to return to the surface. On a separate sheet of paper, describe how you will use the remaining time for exploring, collecting, and experimenting. Be sure to tell whether you'll explore a ridge or a trench.

Answers will vary.

81

More Resources
The following resource is also available from Great Source.

SCIENCESAURUS
Plate Tectonics and Mountain Building	181
Continental Drift	182
Lithospheric Plates	183
Plate Boundaries	184
Map of Plate Boundaries	185
Ocean Floor	207

Enrichment
Time: will vary
Materials: clay

Have small groups of students develop clay models of converging and diverging plate boundaries. Ask students to present their models to the class and explain what happens at each type of boundary.

Assessment
Skill: Interpreting data

Use the following task to assess each student's progress:

Ask students to describe the evidence gathered from the GPS system that supports Wegener's theory of continental drift and Hess's theory of sea-floor spreading. (Measurements show that England and the eastern United States have moved farther apart, while the western United States and Japan have moved closer together.)

▶ Explore

NEW EVIDENCE Ask: *Suppose the GPS technology of today had been available in Wegener's lifetime. Do you think scientists still would have rejected his theory of continental drift?* (Students may say that the technology would have supported Wegener's theory so scientists might have been more open to it.) Stress that often many years of experimentation and data collection are necessary to either support or disprove a theory.

▶ Take Action

Time: will vary
Materials: map of the ocean floor (See *ScienceSaurus* section 185.)

PLAN AN EXPEDITION Let students use a map of the ocean floor to plan their expeditions. Encourage them to note specific sites they would like to explore. Allow students class time to share their expedition plans.

CHECK UNDERSTANDING
Skill: Predicting

Tell students that millions of years ago, India was a separate continent that slowly moved against the Asia continent, forming the Himalayas. Ask them to predict what might happen at that plate boundary during the next 10 million years. (India will continue to move into the landmass that makes up Eurasia. The Himalayas may get taller. New mountains may be created.)

CHAPTER 7 / LESSON 21   81

CHAPTER 8
Overview

Volcanoes

LESSON 22
The Pressure Builds
Point of Lesson: *Volcanoes erupt when gases and magma trapped below Earth's surface are released.*

The force with which a volcano erupts depends on the properties of the magma inside it. If the magma is thin and runny, gases pass through it easily and the eruption is not as explosive. If the magma is thick and sticky, pressure builds until the trapped gases escape violently and explosively.

Materials
Enrichment (p. 83), for each student or group:
- drawing materials such as poster board and colored markers
- modeling materials such as clay or papier-mâché
- reference books about volcanoes

Activity (p. 84), for each student or pair:
- two paper cups, 6-oz or larger
- two drinking straws for each student
- 50 mL water
- 50 mL thick sugar syrup, such as corn syrup

Connections (p. 84), for the class:
- world map

Laboratory Safety
Review these safety guidelines with students before they do the activities in this lesson.
- *Enrichment:* If your skin is irritated by clay or papier-mâché, let your lab partner handle it. Do not handle it yourself.
- *Activity:* Do not share the straws with your partner or use any straws other than those assigned to you.

- Dispose of the sugar syrup by pouring it back into the bottle, capping the bottle tightly, and placing it in the classroom wastebasket. Do not pour the syrup into a sink drain.
- Wash your hands thoroughly after both activities.

LESSON 23
Rivers of Fire
Point of Lesson: *A lava flow and a pyroclastic flow have different properties.*

A lava flow may destroy property but moves slowly enough for people to escape its path. A pyroclastic flow occurs when the gas-rock mixture from an explosive eruption behaves more like a liquid and flows downhill. A pyroclastic flow can be extremely deadly because it moves too fast for people to escape it and is low enough in density to flow over the surface of water.

Materials
Connections (p. 87), for the class:
- world map

LESSON 24
Can Eruptions Be Predicted?
Point of Lesson: *Scientists are improving their methods of predicting volcanic eruptions.*

To predict when a volcano will erupt, scientists study its history and monitor the volcano for factors such as changes in seismic activity, tilt, and the amount and type of gases being released. Although volcanic eruptions cannot be predicted with a high degree of accuracy, methods are improving. Eventually, scientists hope to predict not only when an eruption will occur but how violent the eruption will be.

Materials
Enrichment (p. 89), for the class:
- research sources about predicting volcanic eruptions

Explore (p. 90), for the class:
- map of the Caribbean, including Montserrat

Connections (p. 90), for the class:
- map of Pacific Ocean area

Take Action (p. 91), for the class:
- research sources about specific volcanoes

Background Information

Lesson 22

Mount St. Helens, pictured on page 82 in the student book, is located in Washington State. On May 18, 1980, an earthquake measuring 5.1 on the Richter scale rocked Mount St. Helens, causing its north face to collapse in a massive avalanche of rock and ice. The avalanche released pressurized gases inside the volcano, and a violently explosive eruption resulted. The force of the explosion flattened 150 acres (60 hectares) of forest. Pyroclastic flows of gas, ash, and pumice poured down the mountain's north flank at speeds of up to 100 miles (160 km) per hour.

The landscape surrounding Mount St. Helens was dramatically changed within seconds of the eruption in 1980. The area, which is now the 110,000-acre National Volcanic Monument, has been left to respond naturally to the disaster.

Lesson 23

Mount Nyiragongo, described on page 86 of the student book, demonstrates that eruptions can vary for the same volcano at different times. The speed of Nyiragongo's January 2002 lava flow was less than 2 km (1.2 mi) per hour. However, when a lava lake near the volcano's summit suddenly drained in 1977, the flow was estimated at up to 60 km (36 mi) per hour.

Lesson 24

A volcano's history is learned through the same techniques used to unravel geologic history in other areas. Although Mt. Pinatubo was considered dormant before its 1991 eruption, scientists have identified previous periods when it was active: about 400–500 years ago, 3,000 years ago, 9,000 years ago, 17,000 years ago, and 35,000 years ago. These dates, all of which are considered recent in geologic terms, were arrived at by examining layers of ash deposits and using carbon-14 dating of wood and charcoal buried by the eruptions. Although data are scarce, scientists have tentatively concluded that Pinatubo goes through long periods of dormancy followed by brief, violent periods of activity. The most recent event is the least violent so far in the past 35,000 years.

UNIT 2 Dynamic Earth
CHAPTER 8 / LESSON 22

Point of Lesson
Volcanoes erupt when gases and magma trapped below Earth's surface are released.

Focus
- Structure of the earth system
- Properties and changes of properties in matter
- Natural hazards

Skills and Strategies
- Recognizing cause and effect
- Observing
- Making and using models
- Comparing and contrasting
- Drawing conclusions
- Making inferences

Advance Preparation
Vocabulary
Make sure students understand these terms. Definitions can be found in the glossary at the end of the student book.

- gas
- lava
- liquid
- magma
- mineral
- pressure
- volcano

Materials
Gather the materials needed for *Enrichment* (p. 83), *Activity* (p. 84), and *Connections* (p. 84).

TEACHING PLAN pp. 82–83

INTRODUCING THE LESSON
This lesson explains how pressure builds up inside a volcano to cause an eruption. It also explores different types of volcanic eruptions and what causes those differences.

Ask students what they know about volcanoes. Some questions you might ask are: *Where are volcanoes located? What makes a volcano erupt? What kinds of materials come out of a volcano when it erupts?*

Ask: *Where does lava come from?* Many students will be under the impression that lava comes from deep inside Earth (from the core). Explain that molten rock comes from the mantle, the layer just beneath Earth's crust. Show students a diagram of the layers of Earth to reinforce your explanation.

CHAPTER 8 / LESSON 22
Volcanoes

The Pressure Builds

A volcano such as Mount St. Helens contains extremely hot gases and thick, sticky magma—an explosive combination.

Think about what happens when you shake a can of soda and then pop the top. Believe it or not, soda and magma—the molten rock inside a volcano—have something in common. Both liquids are full of gases. And when a gas under pressure is released, it can pack a lot of power.

▲ Mount St. Helens after its 1980 eruption

▶ Before You Read

BURSTING FORTH If you shake a can of soda, gas escapes from the liquid into the space at the top of the can. When you open the top, the pressure is suddenly released and the gas escapes. This is one example of pressure building and then releasing.

▶ *Describe other common examples of pressure building up and then being released. What happens when the pressure is released?*

   Answers will vary. Examples: water pressure building in a garden hose
   before spraying out with force, squeezing a tube of toothpaste,
   a sealed container bursting open in a microwave oven, an overinflated
   balloon popping, an egg breaking open while being boiled

▶ Before You Read

BURSTING FORTH Before students write their answers, remind them that liquids and gases are two different states of matter. The molecules of a liquid are more closely packed together than those of a gas. Both states take on the shapes of their containers if capped, but gases expand to fill all the available space.

Read

Beneath a volcano's surface, pressure is mounting.

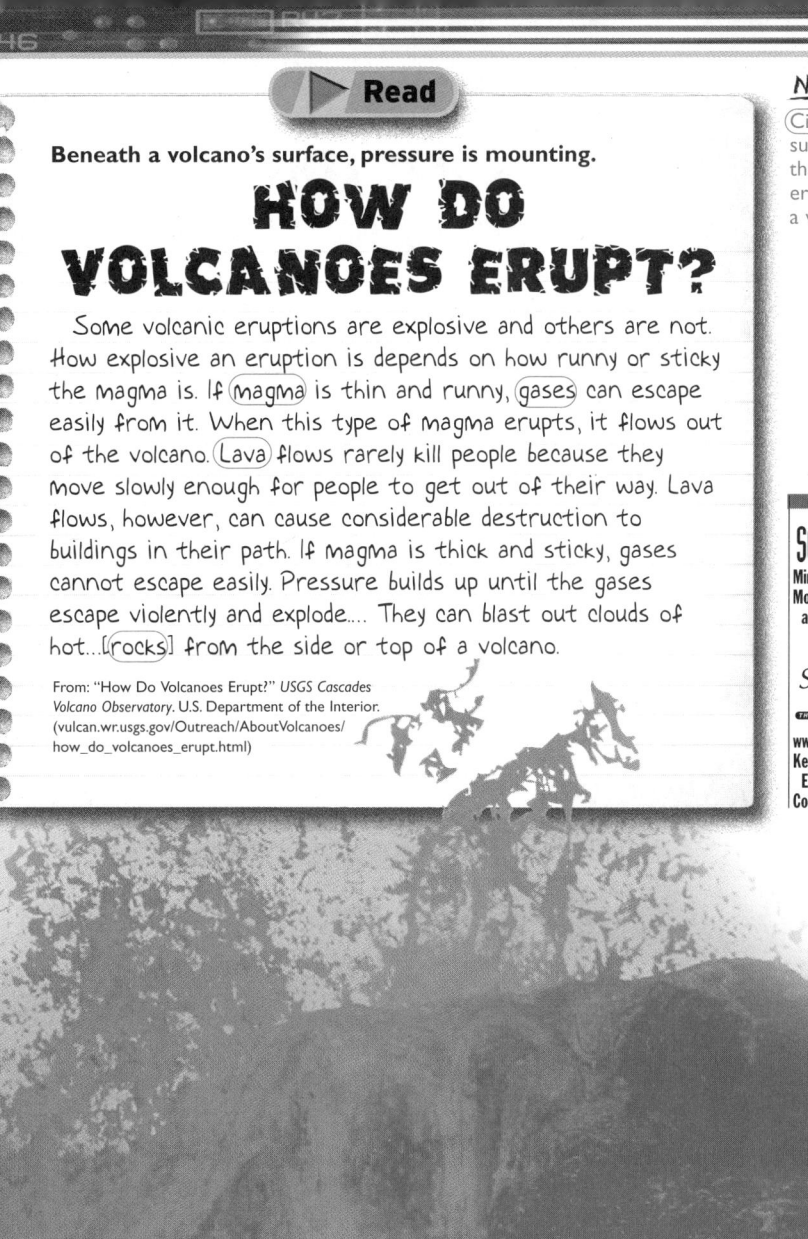

HOW DO VOLCANOES ERUPT?

Some volcanic eruptions are explosive and others are not. How explosive an eruption is depends on how runny or sticky the magma is. If (magma) is thin and runny, (gases) can escape easily from it. When this type of magma erupts, it flows out of the volcano. (Lava) flows rarely kill people because they move slowly enough for people to get out of their way. Lava flows, however, can cause considerable destruction to buildings in their path. If magma is thick and sticky, gases cannot escape easily. Pressure builds up until the gases escape violently and explode.... They can blast out clouds of hot...[rocks] from the side or top of a volcano.

From: "How Do Volcanoes Erupt?" *USGS Cascades Volcano Observatory*. U.S. Department of the Interior. (vulcan.wr.usgs.gov/Outreach/AboutVolcanoes/how_do_volcanoes_erupt.html)

NOTEZONE
(Circle) each substance that can erupt from a volcano.

FIND OUT MORE
SCIENCESAURUS
Minerals 179
Mountain Building and Volcanoes 187

SCiLINKS
THE WORLD'S A CLICK AWAY
www.scilinks.org
Keyword: Volcanic Eruptions
Code: GSED10

▲ Mauna Ely in Hawaii

Enrichment

- Invite students to find out about the island of Surtsey, which was created by a volcanic eruption in 1963. This offshore island near Iceland lies atop the mid-Atlantic ridge, an area of volcanic activity on the ocean floor. Then ask students to write a descriptive paragraph summarizing how the island was formed.

- **Time:** will vary
  Materials: drawing materials such as poster board and colored markers; modeling materials such as clay or papier-mâché; reference books about volcanoes

  Invite interested students to draw a diagram or build a 3-D model showing a cross-section of a volcano. Students should label the magma chambers, lava flows, vents, and craters on their models. Students could also obtain a 3-D model of a volcano from the following USGS Web site:
  www.usgs.gov/education
  Click on Paper Models, then scroll down to Make Your Own Paper Model of a Volcano.

Read

Ask volunteers to identify which substances in the reading they circled. Point out the difference between magma and lava: Magma is molten rock that is found beneath Earth's surface, and lava is magma that reaches Earth's surface. Emphasize that both substances are made of the same materials.

Have students compare the two types of volcanic eruptions. Ask them to find words and phrases in the reading that describe each type. Point out that some volcanoes are built from quiet lava flows, while others are built from violent eruptions.

Ask students to give examples of famous volcanoes they know about. Prompt them by mentioning Mount Vesuvius and Mount St. Helen's.

CHECK UNDERSTANDING
Skill: Predicting
Pose the following question: *Suppose the magma inside a particular volcano is very thick and sticky. What kind of eruption might that volcano have, and why?* (The eruption would most likely be explosive. Thick magma traps gases, and the pressure builds up until the gases are finally released in a violent eruption.)

CHAPTER 8 / LESSON 22

CHAPTER 8 / LESSON 22

More Resources
The following resources are also available from Great Source and NSTA.

ScienceSaurus
Minerals 179
Mountain Building
  and Volcanoes 187

Reader's Handbook
Comparing and Contrasting ... 42

Math on Call
The Metric System 535

SCiLINKS
THE WORLD'S A CLICK AWAY

www.scilinks.org
Keyword: Volcanic Eruptions
Code: GSED10

Connections
Time: 10 minutes
Materials: world map
GEOGRAPHY Tell students that the eruption of Krakatoa in 1883 resulted in the most violent volcanic explosion on Earth in modern times. Krakatoa is located in the Sunda Strait, south of Sumatra and west of Java, Indonesia. Tell students that the explosion was heard as far away as Rodrigues

(continued on page 85)

Teaching Plan pp. 84–85

▶ **Activity**

STUCK INSIDE

Have you ever tried blowing bubbles into thick syrup?

What You Need:
- two small paper cups (6-ounce or larger)
- two straws
- 50 mL water
- 50 mL thick sugar syrup, such as corn syrup

What to Do:
1. Pour the water into one cup and the syrup into the other cup.
2. Put a straw in each cup.
3. Blow into each straw with one short breath.

What Do You See?
▶ Describe what happened when you blew into each straw.

When I blew into the straw in the water...	When I blew into the straw in the syrup...
It was easy to make many small gas bubbles that rose very quickly to the surface and popped.	I had to blow harder just to make one large bubble that rose above the surface before it slowly broke.

84

▶ **Activity**

Time: 15 minutes
Materials: two small paper cups (6-oz or larger); two drinking straws; 50 mL water; 50 mL thick sugar syrup, such as corn syrup

▶ Students may work individually or in pairs. Make sure each student gets his or her own set of straws.

▶ In step 3, emphasize to students that they should blow with *one short* breath, to represent the sudden release of gases.

▶ Ask students to relate the consistency of the water and syrup to the consistency of magma. Remind students that magma can be either thick or runny.

84   CHAPTER 8 / LESSON 22

▶ **Propose Explanations**

WHAT'S THE DIFFERENCE? Think about your observations with the water and syrup.

▶ **What can you conclude about the difference between how a gas moves through thinner liquids and how it moves through thicker liquids?**

Gas moves more easily through thinner liquids than thicker liquids. The thicker the liquid that the gas is moving through, the more pressure that builds up before the gas is released.

▶ **What do your observations tell you about why thicker magma makes an eruption more explosive than thinner magma does?**

Gas gets trapped in thicker and stickier substances like magma. It is harder for the gas to escape, and pressure builds up. The pressure causes a more explosive eruption.

The thickness of the magma inside a volcano depends on two things. The first is temperature. All magma is extremely hot (about 1,000°C). But hotter magma is thinner and runnier than slightly cooler magma. The mineral ingredients in the magma also affect its thickness. Different mineral ingredients have different properties. For example, silica—an important part of many solid minerals—makes magma syrupy thick when it is a liquid. As a result, magma that contains a lot of silica is very thick and sticky.

▶ **Would you expect the lava from an explosive eruption to have more silica or less silica than the lava from a quieter eruption? Explain.**

More silica; magma with more silica is thicker and stickier than magma with less silica, so it traps more gas.

(continued from page 84)

Island, near Mauritius, about 4,800 km (3,000 mi) away in the Indian Ocean. Have students locate these places on a world map. Point out that the explosion blew away the northern two-thirds of the island.

Assessment
Skill: Comparing and contrasting

Use the following task to assess each student's progress:

Ask students to create a compare-and-contrast chart describing the two types of volcanic eruptions. Remind them to mention magma, lava, rock, and gas in their charts.

EXPLOSIVE ERUPTIONS	QUIET ERUPTIONS
hot, thick magma with high silica content	thin, runny magma with low silica content
gas and rocks blasting from the volcano	quiet lava flows

▶ **Propose Explanations**

WHAT'S THE DIFFERENCE? For the first question, students should conclude that gas moving through thick magma acts much like the gas moving through the syrup. For the second question, students should realize that with thicker magma, gas does not escape, so pressure builds and can produce a violent explosion.

Tell students that scientists use other words to describe the thickness of a liquid. Write the following terms and definitions on the board:

viscous—thick and sticky
viscosity—the thickness of a liquid

Give an example of a viscous liquid, such as motor oil, and then ask students to supply additional examples. (maple syrup, salad oil, molasses, hand lotion, shampoo, and the like)

UNIT 2 Dynamic Earth

CHAPTER 8 / LESSON 23

Point of Lesson
A lava flow and a pyroclastic flow have different properties.

Focus
- Properties and changes of properties in matter
- Structure of the earth system
- Natural hazards

Skills and Strategies
- Comparing and contrasting
- Creating and using tables
- Recognizing cause and effect
- Making inferences

Advance Preparation

Vocabulary
Make sure students understand these terms. Definitions can be found in the glossary at the end of the student book.

- density
- gas
- lava
- liquid
- speed
- temperature
- volcano

Materials
Gather the materials needed for **Connections** (p. 87).

TEACHING PLAN pp. 86–87

INTRODUCING THE LESSON
This lesson presents pyroclastic flows and compares them with lava flows.

After students have read the first paragraph of the lesson introduction, tell them that 300,000 people fled the city of Goma. There were reports that 45 people died as a result of the volcanic activity.

Ask students to identify the most dangerous thing in a volcanic eruption. Students are likely to say erupting lava. Explain that another type of eruption is generally even more dangerous. Draw students' attention to the second paragraph of the lesson introduction.

CHAPTER 8 / LESSON 23

Volcanoes

▼ Goma resident watching lava flowing after Mount Nyiragongo erupted

Rivers of Fire

The most dangerous kind of volcanic eruption quickly destroys everything in its path.

Volcanoes erupt in different ways at different times. Some eruptions produce a lava flow. This happened in January 2002, when Mount Nyiragongo in the Democratic Republic of Congo erupted. Red-hot lava flowed through the city of Goma. The homes of more than 12,000 families were destroyed.

Other eruptions are explosive, throwing a mixture of hot ash, rocks, and gases high into the air. Sometimes a gas-rock mixture behaves more like a liquid and flows downhill. This is called a *pyroclastic flow*.

NOTEZONE
What questions do you have after reading this?

FIND OUT MORE
SCIENCESAURUS
Mountain Building and Volcanoes 187

SCLINKS
www.scilinks.org
Keyword: Volcanic Eruptions
Code: GSED10

▶ Read

A pyroclastic flow took place when Mount Pelée on the island of Martinique erupted in 1902.

St. Pierre Entirely Wiped Out

At about 7:50 A.M. on May 8, the volcano erupted with a deafening roar. A large black cloud composed of **superheated** gas, ash and rock rolled headlong down the south **flank** of Mt. Pelée at more than 100 miles [160 km] per hour.... In less than one minute it struck St. Pierre with hurricane force. The blast was powerful enough to carry a three-ton statue sixteen meters from its mount....The searing heat of the cloud **ignited** huge bonfires....The cloud continued to advance over the harbor where it destroyed at least twenty ships anchored offshore. The...blast **capsized** the steamship *Grappler*, and its scorching heat set ablaze the American sailing ship *Roraima*, killing most of her passengers and crew.... Of the...[almost] 28,000 people in St. Pierre, there were only two known survivors.

superheated: heated excessively
flank: side or slope
ignited: caught fire
capsized: turned over

From: Camp, Dr. Vic. "Mt. Pelée Eruption (1902)." *How Volcanoes Work*. Department of Geological Sciences, San Diego State University. (www.geology.sdsu.edu/how_volcanoes_work/Pelee.html)

▶ Read
Have students highlight words and phrases in the reading that describe what a pyroclastic flow is made of. (superheated gas, ash, and rock)

When students have finished the NoteZone activity, have them share their questions with classmates. Encourage students to find answers to their questions through research and additional reading.

Point out that one of the two known survivors in the city of St. Pierre was a man named Auguste Ciparis, who was a prisoner kept in a deep dungeon. Ask students to speculate why Ciparis might have survived. (He was deep enough underground not to be in the path of the pyroclastic flow.)

86 CHAPTER 8 / LESSON 23

Explore

DIFFERENT FLOWS This table compares some properties of lava and pyroclastic flows. Use the information to answer the questions below.

	LAVA FLOW	PYROCLASTIC FLOW
Materials	molten rock with small gas bubbles	a cloud of gases containing rock particles
Density	quite dense	low density but dense enough to flow along the ground
Speed of flow	1–30 kilometers per hour	160–260 kilometers per hour
Temperature	700°–1,200°C	600°–700°C
Effect on ocean	sinks below ocean water while heating it	flows over ocean's surface

▶ What do a pyroclastic flow and a lava flow have in common?
  Both result from a volcanic eruption and contain very hot materials.

▶ Why does a pyroclastic flow travel more quickly than a lava flow?
  A cloud of gases can move more quickly than liquid rock.

▶ Do you think people can escape from a lava flow? Explain.
  Yes. Lava moves fairly slowly.

▶ Do you think people can escape from a pyroclastic flow? Explain.
  No. A pyroclastic flow moves too fast.

▶ How could the pyroclastic flow from Mt. Pelée capsize and burn boats in the harbor? Could a lava flow cause the same destruction?
  A pyroclastic flow moves over the surface of water, so the heat and gases were able to reach boats in the harbor. A lava flow could not cause the same destruction because lava sinks when it reaches the ocean.

87

More Resources
The following resources are also available from Great Source and NSTA.

ScienceSaurus
Mountain Building and Volcanoes   187

SciLinks — THE WORLD'S A CLICK AWAY
www.scilinks.org
Keyword: Volcanic Eruptions
Code: GSED10

Connections
Time: will vary
Materials: world map

GEOGRAPHY Have students find out about recent volcanic activity at the Smithsonian Institution's Global Volcanism Network Web site: www.volcano.si.edu/gvp Ask students to locate the volcanoes on a world map.

Assessment
Skill: Classifying

Use the following question to assess each student's progress:

What are the characteristics of a pyroclastic flow? (a cloud of gases, hot ash, and rocks; low density but dense enough to flow along the ground; high speeds; temperatures not as high as a lava flow; flows over ocean surface instead of sinking)

Explore

DIFFERENT FLOWS Review the meaning of the term *density* with students. (the amount of matter contained in a certain volume of a substance) Ask: *Which would contain more matter, a certain volume of lava or the same volume of pyroclastic matter?* (lava) *Why?* (Pyroclastic matter is mostly gases; lava is molten rock with only small gas bubbles. Liquids are denser than gases.)

Call attention to the chart and ask students questions such as the following: *Which of the flows is made up of materials with a low density?* (pyroclastic) *Which of the flows has a higher temperature?* (lava) Then ask: *Why would a lava flow sink below ocean water but a pyroclastic flow would not?* (A lava flow is denser than a pyroclastic flow. Dense materials tend to sink in water.)

CHECK UNDERSTANDING
Skill: Making inferences
Ask students why the speed and density of a pyroclastic flow make it more dangerous than a lava flow. (Because a pyroclastic flow is less dense than a lava flow, it travels at greater speeds, which gives people less time to escape its path.)

CHAPTER 8 / LESSON 23   87

UNIT 2 Dynamic Earth

CHAPTER 8 / LESSON 24

Point of Lesson
Scientists are improving their methods of predicting volcanic eruptions.

Focus
- Structure of the earth system
- Change, constancy, and measurement
- Science as a human endeavor
- Natural hazards
- Risks and benefits

Skills and Strategies
- Comparing and contrasting
- Making inferences
- Predicting
- Generating questions

Advance Preparation

Vocabulary
Make sure students understand these terms. Definitions can be found in the glossary at the end of the student book.

- atmosphere
- earthquake
- gas
- lava
- magma
- prediction
- pyroclastic flow
- volcano

Materials
Gather the materials needed for *Enrichment* (p. 89), *Explore* (p. 90), *Connections* (p. 90), and *Take Action* (p. 91).

TEACHING PLAN pp. 88–89

INTRODUCING THE LESSON
This lesson introduces students to the methods that volcanologists use to predict volcanic eruptions and the accuracy of these predictions. Ask students whether they think a volcanic eruption can be predicted and, if so, how accurate those predictions are. Students are likely to believe that science and technology have advanced to the point that it is possible and commonplace to successfully predict a volcanic eruption. Ask students to think about your question again when they complete this lesson.

CHAPTER 8: LESSON 24

Volcanoes

Can Eruptions Be Predicted?

Volcanologists are working on the answer.

A volcanologist is a scientist who studies volcanoes. Volcanologists investigate the structure of volcanoes. They also study how volcanoes form rocks and change the atmosphere. Some volcanologists investigate ways to predict eruptions. Making accurate predictions is difficult. All the changes leading to an eruption take place below Earth's surface. Yet all the tests that scientists do take place on or above Earth's surface. Predictions about volcanoes are not yet reliable, but scientists keep observing and improving their techniques.

▶ **Before You Read**

WHAT DO YOU THINK? Volcanic eruptions release molten lava, gases, rock particles, and ash onto Earth's surface and into the atmosphere.
▶ *What signs might there be that a volcano is about to erupt? Draw a diagram and write your ideas.*

> *Drawings will vary. Students may draw Earth's crust and show an opening with gases and magma trapped below the surface. Students may mention earthquakes, changes in the shape of the volcanic mountain, and escaping gases.*

▶ **Before You Read**

WHAT DO YOU THINK? As students complete the activity, have them think back to what they know about magma and its movement below Earth's surface. Provide students with an opportunity to share their diagrams and ideas with classmates. Discuss the fact that some dormant (inactive) volcanoes still give off steam, other gases, and hot ash for many years after an eruption.

▶ Read

Here's how Chuck Wood, a volcanologist, answered a question about predicting volcanoes.

ASK A VOLCANOLOGIST

Question: Which method of predicting a volcanic eruption is the most useful and reliable?

Answer: Meaningful prediction requires careful monitoring of a volcano's vital signs. Seismometers can be used to pinpoint earthquakes which [follow] the rise of magma and its movement along fissures. Measurements of the tilt of the entire mountain provide additional information about the "breathing" of the volcano as magma moves inside it. Instruments that sniff...[sulfur dioxide, carbon dioxide] and other gases also can signal changes in the volcano. At some volcanoes the seismic information seems most reliable, at others the tilt tells the story. But the best predictions come from the combination of all of these methods into a volcano monitoring and prediction system.

And you must remember that each volcano is unique. The pattern of events that signifies an eruption at one volcano may not occur before an eruption at a different volcano. And the same volcano may change its eruptive behavior at any time! The good news is that general trends...are being observed at a variety of volcanoes around the world so that volcanologists are getting better at predicting eruptions.

monitoring: watching
vital signs: signs of life
seismometer: a device that senses earthquake motion
fissure: a fracture or crack in Earth's crust
seismic: related to an earthquake
signifies: is a sign of
trend: a change over time

From: Wood, Chuck. "Which Method Of Volcano Prediction Is The Most Useful And Reliable?." *Volcano World*. University of North Dakota. (volcano.und.nodak.edu/vwdocs/frequent_questions/grp3/question229.html)

NOTEZONE

Circle all the clues used to predict volcano eruptions.

FIND OUT MORE

SCIENCESAURUS
Earthquakes 186
Mountain Building and Volcanoes 187

SCILINKS
www.scilinks.org
Keyword: Volcanic Eruptions
Code: GSED10

89

▶ Read

After students complete the reading, have them identify the instrument that volcanologists use to predict volcanic eruptions and the types of activity the instrument detects. (seismometer, detects earthquakes) Ask: *Why might the seismometer be useful in predicting volcanic eruptions?* (A volcanic eruption is often preceded by earthquake activity.)

Ask students to identify the science skills that volcanologists use when they monitor volcanic activity. (measurement when taking seismic readings and determining the tilt of the volcano; observational skills as they note the types of gases that are emitted from the volcano; drawing conclusions based on the data they gather)

Enrichment

Time: will vary
Materials: research sources about predicting volcanic eruptions

Ask students to find out more about the technologies that are used to predict volcanic eruptions. Have them describe the instruments volcanologists use, provide drawings or photos of the instruments, and describe the kind of data the instruments measure. Allow students to display their research results.

CHECK UNDERSTANDING

Skill: Generating ideas

Ask students to identify the advantages of having permanent monitoring stations located on or near high-risk volcanoes. Have students give reasons for their answers. (Scientists could be more accurate in their measurements of volcanic activity and might be better able to predict an eruption. People could be warned in time to evacuate an area.)

CHAPTER 8 / LESSON 24   89

CHAPTER 8 / LESSON 24

More Resources
The following resources are also available from Great Source and NSTA.

ScienceSaurus
Earthquakes 186
Mountain Building
  and Volcanoes 187

Reader's Handbook
Interview 282

SciLinks
THE WORLD'S A CLICK AWAY

www.scilinks.org
Keyword: Volcanic Eruptions
Code: GSED10

Connections
Time: 10 minutes
Materials: map of Pacific Ocean area

GEOGRAPHY Have students locate Mt. Pinatubo in the Philippine Islands on a map. Explain to students that the Philippines lie in a region known as the Ring of Fire, a zone of earthquake and volcanic activity that surrounds the Pacific Ocean. (A map of the Ring of Fire is available in *ScienceSaurus* section 185.) Have students name the continents that lie near the Ring of Fire. (Asia, Australia, North America, South America)

Teaching Plan pp. 90–91

▶ Explore

PREDICTING ON PINATUBO Explain to students that sulfur dioxide is a colorless gas with a strong odor. Tell students that in addition to increased emissions of sulfur dioxide, indications that an eruption may take place also include small-scale earthquakes as magma rises up through the volcano and an actual physical expansion of the mountain slopes. Have students recall that scientists can detect earthquakes using a seismometer and can measure the tilt of the volcano.

Time: 5 minutes
Materials: map of the Caribbean, including Montserrat

PREDICTING RISK Have students locate the island of Montserrat on a map. Begin a discussion with this question: *Would it be in the best interests of the island's residents if they were forbidden to live on the island?* Ask students if they would want to live in an area with an active, erupting volcano.

▶ Explore

PREDICTING ON PINATUBO On May 13, 1991, scientists measured 500 tons of sulfur dioxide coming out of Mt. Pinatubo in the Philippines. Two weeks later, scientists measured 5,000 tons. On June 12, 1991, Pinatubo erupted.

▶ How many times greater than the May 13 release was the release measured two weeks later?
   10 times

An increase in the release of sulfur dioxide gas is evidence that magma is moving toward the surface.

▶ What could scientists predict about Pinatubo when they took the second measurement?
   Pinatubo could erupt soon if magma reached the surface.

The first sign of activity on Pinatubo had been a cloud of steam on April 2, 1991. A team of scientists from the United States recommended that people living nearby be evacuated. In all, 100,000 people moved away from their homes. If they hadn't, thousands of lives would have been lost in the eruption on June 12.
  Two factors help volcanologists predict eruptions more successfully. The first is knowing the volcano's history of eruptions. The second is establishing a permanent station on the volcano. These stations make observations 24 hours a day, year-round.

▶ How can each of these factors make scientists' predictions more accurate?
   Knowing how often the volcano erupted in the past could help them predict when it will erupt again. When observations are being made all the time, it is easier to notice changes that might signal an eruption.

PREDICTING RISK Volcanologists are getting better at predicting when an eruption will take place. But they also want to predict how bad the eruption will be. They want to be able to predict the risk to people, crops, livestock, and structures. For example, there is an active volcano on Montserrat Island in the Caribbean Sea. Volcanologists have been monitoring the eruptions that began there in 1995. Since then, there have been lava flows, pyroclastic flows, and ash clouds.

Volcanologists recommended creating an exclusion zone on Montserrat where only scientists and others with government permission may go.

▶ **Why would most people be kept out of an exclusion zone? What risk might there be in that area?**

People who aren't studying the volcano shouldn't risk their lives.

There is a high risk of an eruption harming or killing people very quickly.

Volcanologists compared their data from Montserrat with data from similar volcanoes around the world. They found that if an eruption has been going on for 80 months or longer, then it can be expected to last at least 20 years.

▶ **If Monseratt erupted from July 1995 to March 2002, should scientists predict it will erupt for 20 years? Explain.**

Yes; from July 1995 to March 2002 was exactly 80 months.

▶ Take Action

ASKING QUESTIONS There are 1,300 active volcanoes around the world. Half a billion people live close to them.

▶ **Make a list of questions you'd want scientists to answer in order to decide how dangerous it is to be near a particular volcano.**

Answers will vary. Examples: When did the volcano last erupt? Have most eruptions been explosive or lava flows? How far did the effects of the last eruption reach? Were people killed? Were structures destroyed? In what direction does the lava usually flow? What methods are used to keep track of the volcano's activity? How much warning time would people probably have to escape?

Assessment
Skill: Predicting

Use the following question to assess each student's progress:

What are some of the signs that volcanologists look for to determine if a volcano might erupt? (an increase in gas emissions such as sulfur dioxide and carbon dioxide; earthquake activity; measurements that indicate changes in the tilt of the volcano's slope)

▶ Take Action

Time: will vary
Materials: research sources about specific volcanoes

ASKING QUESTIONS After students have composed their lists of questions, have them form small groups and choose several questions to investigate with regard to a specific volcano. Tell students to organize their information into a presentation that they can share with other groups. Encourage students to use illustrations, data charts, and other graphics in their presentations.

UNIT 3 Water on Earth

About the Photo
The Iguassu Falls, shown here, are one of several waterfalls on the Iguasso River separating Argentina and Brazil. Students might like to know that the name *Iguasso* comes from the Guarani Indian word for "Great Water." Also tell them that the river's largest and loudest falls, called "The Devil's Throat," sends out a roar that can be heard miles away.

About the Charts
A major goal of the *Science Daybooks* is to promote reading, writing, and critical thinking skills in the context of science. The charts below describe the types of reading selections included in this unit and identify the skills and strategies used in each lesson.

UNIT 3 Water on Earth

Earth has its own water recycling system.

If you've ever been caught in a downpour, you might have wondered where so much water could come from. Rain doesn't fall from outer space. All water on Earth is found on or below Earth's surface or in the air above us. Water molecules simply move from one place to another.

In this unit you'll learn about Earth's water. You'll examine the water cycle—the continuous movement of water between Earth's surface and the atmosphere. You'll find out what was done to a river in western Massachusetts to provide a water supply for the city of Boston. You'll explore creative ways to obtain water in dry areas—catching fog, removing the salt from ocean water, and towing icebergs. And you'll find out how ocean water can be used to generate electricity.

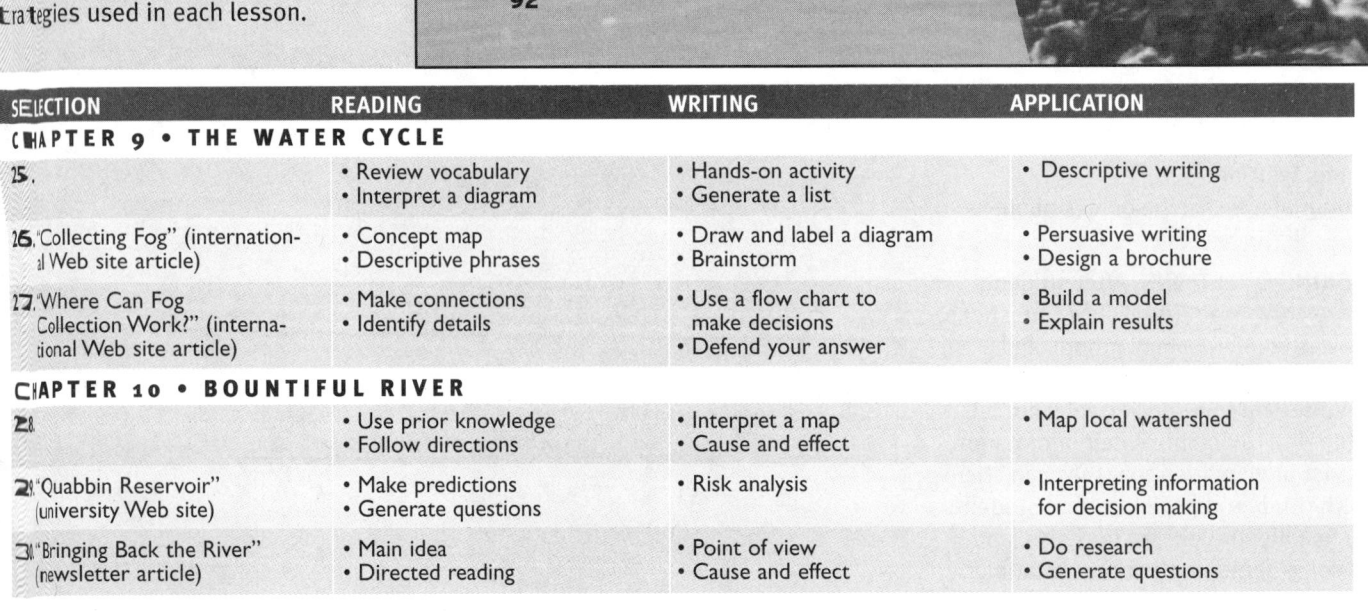

SELECTION	READING	WRITING	APPLICATION
CHAPTER 9 • THE WATER CYCLE			
25.	• Review vocabulary • Interpret a diagram	• Hands-on activity • Generate a list	• Descriptive writing
26. "Collecting Fog" (international Web site article)	• Concept map • Descriptive phrases	• Draw and label a diagram • Brainstorm	• Persuasive writing • Design a brochure
27. "Where Can Fog Collection Work?" (international Web site article)	• Make connections • Identify details	• Use a flow chart to make decisions • Defend your answer	• Build a model • Explain results
CHAPTER 10 • BOUNTIFUL RIVER			
28.	• Use prior knowledge • Follow directions	• Interpret a map • Cause and effect	• Map local watershed
29. "Quabbin Reservoir" (university Web site)	• Make predictions • Generate questions	• Risk analysis	• Interpreting information for decision making
30. "Bringing Back the River" (newsletter article)	• Main idea • Directed reading	• Point of view • Cause and effect	• Do research • Generate questions

UNIT 3 WATER ON EARTH

THE CHAPTERS IN THIS UNIT ARE...

CHAPTER 9:
The Water Cycle
Find out: How can people "catch" fog?

CHAPTER 10:
Bountiful River
Find out: Why did four towns in western Massachusetts disappear in the 1930s?

CHAPTER 11:
Water Watch
Find out: What would it be like to live in Africa during a drought?

CHAPTER 12:
Current Events
Find out: How can sneakers be used to learn about the ocean?

Answers to *Find Out* Questions

CHAPTER 9
People can erect large mesh nets. When fog passes through the mesh, it leaves behind water droplets that can be collected. (p. 97)

CHAPTER 10
The towns disappeared because all the people and businesses were relocated and the buildings were destroyed so the Swift River Valley could be flooded to create a reservoir. (p. 107–108)

CHAPTER 11
During a drought, people might have to walk long distances to find fresh water or boil water from ponds to kill microbes. They might not have enough water to grow crops. (pp 115–116)

CHAPTER 12
When a ship's cargo of sneakers spilled into the Pacific Ocean, oceanographers were able to track ocean currents from reports of where the sneakers washed ashore. (pp. 125–126, 129)

SCILINKS
THE WORLD'S A CLICK AWAY

www.scilinks.org
Keyword: Science Fair
Code: GSSD03

? Did You Know?
The Iguassu Falls in Brazil are made up of 275 waterfalls and are about as wide as 36 football fields! An average of 1.2 million cubic meters (42.4 million cubic feet) of water falls every second.

SELECTION	READING	WRITING	APPLICATION
CHAPTER 11 • WATER WATCH			
31. "Too Little, Too Much" (United Nations Web site)	• Make connections • Directed reading	• Compare and contrast • Interpret circle graphs	• Brainstorm solutions • Draw a diagram
32. "Fresh Water From Salt Water" (science magazine article)	• Generate questions	• Use a chart to analyze two sides of an issue	• Build a model • Write observations • Draw conclusions
33. "Icebergs to Africa" (Australian TV news report)	• Directed reading	• Analyze and interpret a map	• Explain events
CHAPTER 12 • CURRENT EVENTS			
34. "These Shoes Just Did It" (Smithsonian Institution exhibition)	• Use prior knowledge and experiences • Retell	• Make a list • Interpret a map • Make inferences	• Generate questions • Design a poster
35. "Tracking Currents With Sneakers" (newspaper article)	• Reflect on experiences • Directed reading	• Identify scientific habits	• Analyze and interpret events
36. "Water Mills at the Bottom of the Sea" (Norwegian research article)	• Graphic organizer • Main Idea	• Make inferences • Cause and effect	• Write a script • Give a news report

UNIT 3 WATER ON EARTH

CHAPTER 9 Overview

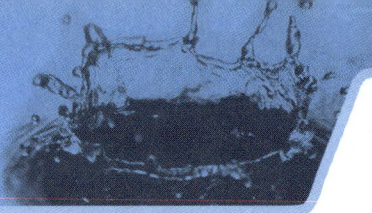

The Water Cycle

LESSON 25
Round and Round It Goes
Point of Lesson: *You can trace water's movement from any point in the water cycle to any other point.*

Water on Earth's surface and in the atmosphere exists in three states: solid, liquid, and gas. Water is constantly cycled between states through the processes of precipitation, evaporation, transpiration, and condensation. The lesson includes a simple activity in which students identify and explain these processes.

Materials
Activity (p. 95), for each pair or group:
- copy of full-size cube diagram (copymaster page 227)
- sheet of paper
- pencil
- scissors
- clear tape

LESSON 26
Fog Catchers
Point of Lesson: *Fresh water can be collected from fog.*

Very little rain falls in Chungungo, a small town on Chile's dry northern coast, and not enough fresh water was available. A team of scientists helped the town set up a system of nets in the mountains above the village where fog rolls in from the ocean. The nets capture fresh water from the fog. The water runs down a trough and is collected in a storage tank.

Materials
Science Scope Activity (p. 97 and p. 101), for each student:
- copy of the story "The Life of a Drop of Water" (available at waves.marine.usf.edu/disaster_menu/disaster_menu_article.htm)
- research sources about tornadoes, floods, and other natural disasters

Connections (p. 98), for the class:
- topographic map of Chile

Enrichment (p. 99), for each group:
- water faucet
- bucket
- large beaker (calibrated)

LESSON 27
To Fog or Not to Fog
Point of Lesson: *Fog collection does not work everywhere.*

Fog collection worked well for the village of Chungungo because of its location, terrain, and weather. Before fog collection systems are built in other locations, scientists must evaluate conditions and build a test collector to see whether a system will work. The lesson concludes with an activity in which students build a small distillation system to purify water.

Materials
Read (p. 101), for the class:
- rain gauge and anemometer (or photographs of these instruments)

Activity (p. 102), for each group:
- large plastic bowl
- water
- dust and soil
- dark food coloring
- small, heavy drinking glass
- clear plastic wrap
- tape
- pebble

Enrichment (p. 103), for the class:
- research sources about the Namib Desert
- posterboard
- colored markers

Laboratory Safety
Review these safety guidelines with students before they do the activities in this lesson.
- Handle the dust carefully to keep it out of the air. Avoid breathing in any of the dust or dirt particles.
- Do not put any dust, dirt, or dirty water into the sink drain.
- Wash your hands thoroughly after the activity.

Science Scope Activity

Journeys in the Water Cycle

NSTA has chosen a *Science Scope* activity related to the content in this chapter. You'll find the activity in Lesson 26, page 97, and Lesson 27, page 101.

This activity allows students to incorporate their knowledge of the water cycle into a creative writing activity. The activity provides an opportunity to involve teachers from different subject areas.

Background Information

Lesson 25

The water cycle does not allow natural access to groundwater, but humans have dug and drilled wells to reach groundwater since ancient times. Groundwater use has increased greatly since the mid-20th century, allowing people to farm and live in areas that are naturally arid. However, in many areas that rely on groundwater, use has outstripped recharge. For example, a survey in Kansas suggests that unless groundwater use is reduced drastically, the High Plain aquifer may run out in the 2020s.

Lesson 26

For a short period after 1914, the village of Chungungo was supplied with water and electricity by the U.S. Bethlehem Steel Company. At that time, the company was operating the largest iron-ore mine in the world close to the village. After the company left, Chungungo relied on twice-weekly water deliveries by truck. Now, although Chungungo is experiencing a 20-year drought, the villagers have a constant supply of fresh water from the fog collectors and are not dependent on any outside sources for water.

Lesson 27

In other dry parts of the world, tests have been done to determine whether fog collection can work as well as it did in Chungungo, Chile. A long series of experiments were carried out near Cape Town, South Africa. One scientist determined that the annual precipitation collected from fog would equal close to 170 percent of the area's annual rainfall.

UNIT 3 Water on Earth
CHAPTER 9 / LESSON 25

Point of Lesson
You can trace water's movement from any point in the water cycle to any other point.

Focus
- Structure of the earth system
- Change, constancy, and measurement
- Properties and changes of properties in matter

Skills and Strategies
- Interpreting scientific illustrations
- Sequencing

Advance Preparation

Vocabulary
Make sure students understand these terms. Definitions can be found in the glossary at the end of the student book.

- atmosphere
- cloud
- mineral
- organism
- water cycle

Materials
Gather the materials needed for *Activity* (p. 95).

TEACHING PLAN pp. 94–95

INTRODUCING THE LESSON
This lesson introduces students to the water cycle. Some prior knowledge of evaporation, condensation, precipitation, and transpiration is assumed. Review these concepts as needed before the lesson.

Students may not realize that some of the water in clouds comes from evaporated ocean water. Ask students what clouds consist of and how they are formed. Make note of any questions or inaccurate ideas, and ask students to look for the correct information as they proceed through the chapter.

CHAPTER 9 / LESSON 25
The Water Cycle

Round and Round It Goes

Like a merry-go-round, water is always on the move.

Water to drink, to cook our food, to shower in, to grow plants to eat, to keep cool—it's necessary for life. How often do you think about where your water comes from?

▶ Explore

FOLLOW THE WATER There's only so much water on Earth. It just gets recycled—naturally. Trace the movement of water on the diagram.

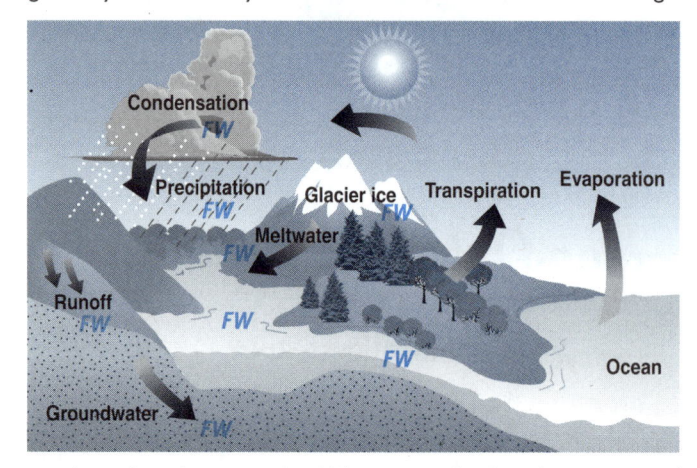

condensation: the process in which a gas changes to a liquid
precipitation: liquid or frozen water falling from clouds
runoff: water that flows over the ground surface
groundwater: water that collects below the ground surface

transpiration: the process in which plants give off water vapor through their leaves
evaporation: the process in which a liquid changes to a gas
glacier: a large mass of ice
meltwater: water melting from a glacier

Ocean water contains many dissolved minerals. This makes the ocean salty. Land organisms cannot use salty water. They need fresh water—water with much less dissolved salts.

▶ Find all the places on the water cycle diagram that have fresh water. Mark these parts of the diagram "FW."

▶ Explore

FOLLOW THE WATER Point out that water is an unusual substance in that it can be found in three states—solid (ice, snow, sleet, hail), liquid, and gas (water vapor)—within a relatively narrow temperature range. The continuous change of water from one state to another makes life on Earth possible.

As necessary, guide students through the diagram and text on this page. Choose a starting place on the diagram, and help students follow the arrows from one part of the cycle to the next. Pause briefly to explain each labeled item on the diagram and to answer any questions students may have about that part of the cycle.

Activity

WATER, WATER, EVERYWHERE

A particle of water can end up anywhere in the water cycle. Toss a water cycle cube and see for yourself.

What You Need:
- full-size cube diagram
- sheet of paper
- pencil
- scissors
- clear tape

What To Do:
1. Your teacher will give you a full-size copy of the cube diagram on this page. DO NOT CUT THIS BOOK.
2. Cut along the solid lines.
3. Fold on the dotted lines.
4. Tape the squares together to make a cube.
5. Toss the cube four times. Read the label shown on the top side of the cube each time. On the sheet of paper, list the labels in the order they appear. If you get any label twice, toss again.

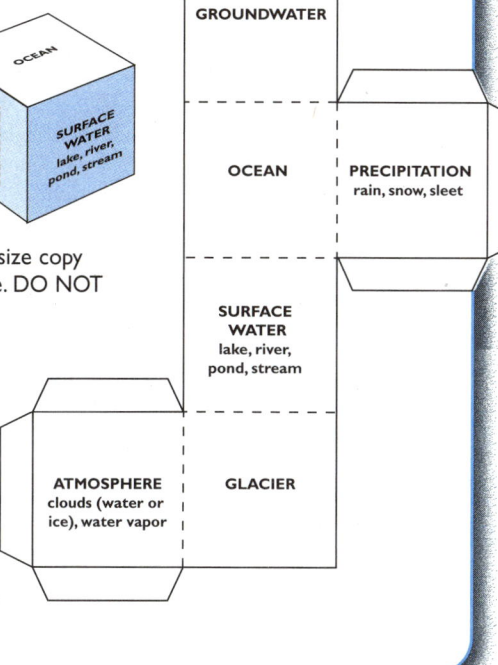

Cube faces: OCEAN; ATMOSPHERE clouds (water or ice), water vapor; SURFACE WATER lake, river, pond, stream

Diagram labels: GROUNDWATER; OCEAN; PRECIPITATION rain, snow, sleet; SURFACE WATER lake, river, pond, stream; ATMOSPHERE clouds (water or ice), water vapor; GLACIER

WHAT DO YOU SEE? Describe how water moves from the first place on your list to the second. Identify the changes that the water goes through to get there and what makes those changes happen. (The water may go through more than one step to get from the first place to the second.) Then explain how the water gets from the second place to the third and from the third to the fourth.

Lists will vary. Beginning at any point, a particle of water could, through several steps, end up at any other point in the water cycle.

FIND OUT MORE

SCIENCESAURUS
Water Cycle 216
Clouds 223
States of Matter 253
Changing States of Matter 255

www.scilinks.org
Keyword: Water Cycle
Code: GSED11

95

Activity

Time: 20–25 minutes
Materials: (for each pair or group) copy of full-size cube diagram (see page 227), sheet of paper, pencil, scissors, clear tape

Have students work with a partner or in small groups.

WHAT DO YOU SEE? Students should be able to describe what happens to water as it moves from place to place on their lists. Suggest that they use the diagram on page 94 to help them track the steps in the process. Emphasize that they should supply intermediate steps if needed. For example, if the list includes the sequence ATMOSPHERE . . . GLACIER, students should insert PRECIPITATION between the two. After students have completed their written responses, ask volunteers to read their sequences aloud.

More Resources

The following resources are also available from Great Source and NSTA.

ScienceSaurus
Water Cycle 216
Clouds 223
States of Matter 253
Changing States of Matter 254

SCILINKS
THE WORLD'S A CLICK AWAY

www.scilinks.org
Keyword: Water Cycle
Code: GSED11

Assessment
Skill: Making inferences

Use the following questions to assess each student's progress:

▶ *What happens to rainwater when the ground has absorbed as much as it can?* (The water collects in puddles or flows into streams, lakes, and other bodies of water.)

▶ *Why does dew appear in the early morning and then disappear later in the day?* (Dew appears because the air is cooler than the land and water vapor in the air condenses and forms water droplets. As the air becomes warmer, the dew evaporates.)

▶ *What happens to minerals dissolved in ocean water when it evaporates?* (The minerals remain behind in the ocean.)

CHECK UNDERSTANDING
Skill: Making and using models
Ask students to draw their own diagrams of the water cycle and label the parts without referring to the diagram on page 94. Then have them write a few sentences describing what is happening at each point in the cycle.

CHAPTER 9 / LESSON 25   95

UNIT 3 Water on Earth

CHAPTER 9 / LESSON 26

Point of the Lesson
Fresh water can be collected from fog.

Focus
- Structure of the earth system
- Science and technology in society
- Science as a human endeavor
- Populations, resources, and environments

Skills and Strategies
- Concept mapping
- Making inferences
- Organizing information
- Understanding that scientists share their results to form a common core of knowledge
- Communicating

Advance Preparation

Vocabulary
Make sure students understand this term. The definition can be found in the glossary at the end of the student book.
- water cycle

Materials
Gather the materials needed for *Science Scope Activity* (p. 97 and p. 101), *Connections* (p. 98), and *Enrichment* (p. 99).

TEACHING PLAN pp. 96–97

INTRODUCING THE LESSON
This lesson describes a system that uses the condensation of water vapor from fog to collect fresh water.

Ask students to tell what they already know about fog. Briefly review what students learned about the water cycle in Lesson 25, and ask them to explain how and at what stage of the water cycle they think fog is formed.

CHAPTER 9 / LESSON 26
The Water Cycle

Fog Catchers

How do you collect fresh water from fog?

The fishing village of Chungungo sits on Chile's dry northern coast. Although the seacoast is often foggy, the area gets little rain. The villagers were always in need of fresh water. A team of scientists from Chile and Canada thought about the problem. They knew that for thousands of years, people around the world collected fog water that got caught in trees and ran down the trunks. The scientists planned a new twist on this old idea to obtain fresh water for the village.

Professor Pilar Cereceda is a member of the team. She has visited Chungungo many times to work with the villagers on the water project.

▶ **Before You Read**

MAKE A CONCEPT WEB Have you ever been in fog or seen a picture of it? What time of day was it? How did it look? How far could you see? How did it feel? What did it remind you of? Complete this concept web to organize your ideas.

Concept web: FOG — damp, cloud, looks like steam, morning, hard to see through it

---

Ask students: *Why does fog form near the ground instead of high in the sky like other clouds?* Students may be unaware of the conditions that cause fog to form. Before they begin reading, tell them to look for information about the conditions under which fog forms.

▶ **Before You Read**

MAKE A CONCEPT WEB Ask questions to stimulate student interest in the upcoming reading, such as: *How do the ocean and the mountain slope contribute to fog formation? How do you think you could trap the water contained in foggy air?*

Brazil

> **Read**

Here's how Professor Cereceda helped make a big difference for a small village.

Collecting Fog

Returning to the tiny seaside village of Chungungo (population 330) in northern Chile is quite often an emotional experience for Pilar Cereceda, researcher and geography professor at the University of Chile in Santiago.

Fourteen years ago, when Cereceda first arrived to begin her research project, Chungungo was just one of hundreds of villages in the region that had no local source of fresh water.... The "miracle" of clean fresh water...came about through the introduction of large fog collectors: "a kind of volleyball net, which captures the fog (called camanchaca), typical of northern Chile," explains Cereceda....

The process involves the installation of polypropylene mesh nets, 12 meters [39 feet] long and 4 meters [13 feet] high, situated high in the mountains above the village. Fog, which is a regular phenomenon in the area, passes through the mesh and leaves behind droplets that trickle down to a trough that carries the water to a storage tank in the village.

"I still remember the day the village of Chungungo inaugurated the water system. This is something they never, ever thought would come to their village," recalls Cereceda.

fog: a cloud close to the ground
installation: setting up
polypropylene: a type of plastic
phenomenon: an event that can be observed
trough: a long, shallow channel
inaugurated: formally began

From: de Luigi, Maria. "Pilar Cereceda (Chile)." *In Person.* International Development Research Centre. (www.idrc.ca/library/document/102386/cereceda.html))

NOTEZONE

Underline the words or phrases that describe the fog catchers.

▼ Fog collectors

FIND OUT MORE

SCIENCESAURUS
Water Cycle 216
Clouds 223
Steps in Technology Design 357

SCILINKS
THE WORLD'S A CLICK AWAY
www.scilinks.org
Keyword: Clouds and Fog
Code: GSED12

Science Scope Activity

Journeys in the Water Cycle

Time: 2–3 class sessions
Materials: copy of the story "The Life of a Drop of Water" (see **Note** below); research sources about tornadoes, floods, and other natural disasters

Ask students to read the story "The Life of a Drop of Water" as a springboard for a creative writing exercise about the water cycle. **Note:** Direct students to the online version of the story at the following Web site:
waves.marine.usf.edu/disaster_menu/
disaster_menu_article.htm

If students do not have access to a computer, visit the Web site yourself and print out copies of the story to distribute to the class.

Procedure

1. In the story, the water drop experiences a series of natural disasters during its journey through the water cycle. Suggest that students select similar natural events to incorporate in a story of their own.
2. Have them research facts about the events (tornadoes, earthquakes, floods, wildfires, and tidal waves) they decide to include in their stories. Tell them to find out what conditions produce these events and how the water cycle is involved.

(continued on page 101)

> **Read**

Ask students to highlight words or phrases in the reading that describe the setting in which Professor Cereceda conducted her research project. ("tiny seaside village"; "the mountains above the village"; "fog, which is a regular phenomenon in the area") Ask them what natural features and conditions led Cereceda to conclude that Chungungo would be a good location to try a fog-collection system. (nearby ocean and mountains; fog very common) Use this as an opportunity to make connections with the descriptions of fog that students included in their concept webs on the previous page.

Encourage students to compare their own lives with those of the villagers. For example, how would their lives be different if fresh water were scarce? How might they try to conserve water? Does it seem likely that fog could be collected to supply water to the area where they live? Why or why not?

CHECK UNDERSTANDING
Skill: Making inferences
Ask: *Would the water recovered from the fog collectors be fresh or salty?* (fresh) *What words or phrases in the reading support your conclusions?* ("The 'miracle' of clean, fresh water . . . came about through the introduction of large fog collectors.") Have students explain their answer using what they learned about the water cycle. (When water evaporates, minerals such as salt are left behind.)

CHAPTER 9 / LESSON 26

CHAPTER 9 / LESSON 26

More Resources
The following resources are also available from Great Source and NSTA.

ScienceSaurus
Water Cycle	216
Clouds	223
Steps in Technology Design	357

SciLinks
www.scilinks.org
Keyword: Clouds and Fog
Code: GSED12

Connections
Time: 15 minutes
Materials: topographic map of Chile

GEOGRAPHY Display the map, and have one student locate the area where the village of Chungungo is located. Ask students to describe the surrounding terrain. Point out the Andes Mountains to the west, the Atacama Desert to the north, and the seacoast to the east. Discuss students' ideas about why fog might be common near the village. (An ocean air mass rises over mountains and cools. Water vapor in the air condenses to form water droplets.)

Teaching Plan pp. 98–99

▶ Explore

A FOGGY SOURCE Chungungo is very dry because of its location on Chile's northern coast. To the east, the high Andes Mountains block moist air from reaching the coast. To the west, cold-flowing ocean waters help to keep the air stable and prevent rain clouds from forming.

Use the diagram of the water cycle on page 94 and the information in this lesson to answer this question.

▶ Fog forms when water vapor condenses into droplets of water in the air. What was the source of the water vapor in the fog?

Since the land along the coast is very dry, the water must have evaporated from the ocean.

SHOW HOW IT WORKS Review the description of the fog collection system in the reading. Draw and label a diagram showing the seacoast with fog moving in, the village of Chungungo, the mountains, and the fog collectors. Show how the water gets from the collectors to the village.

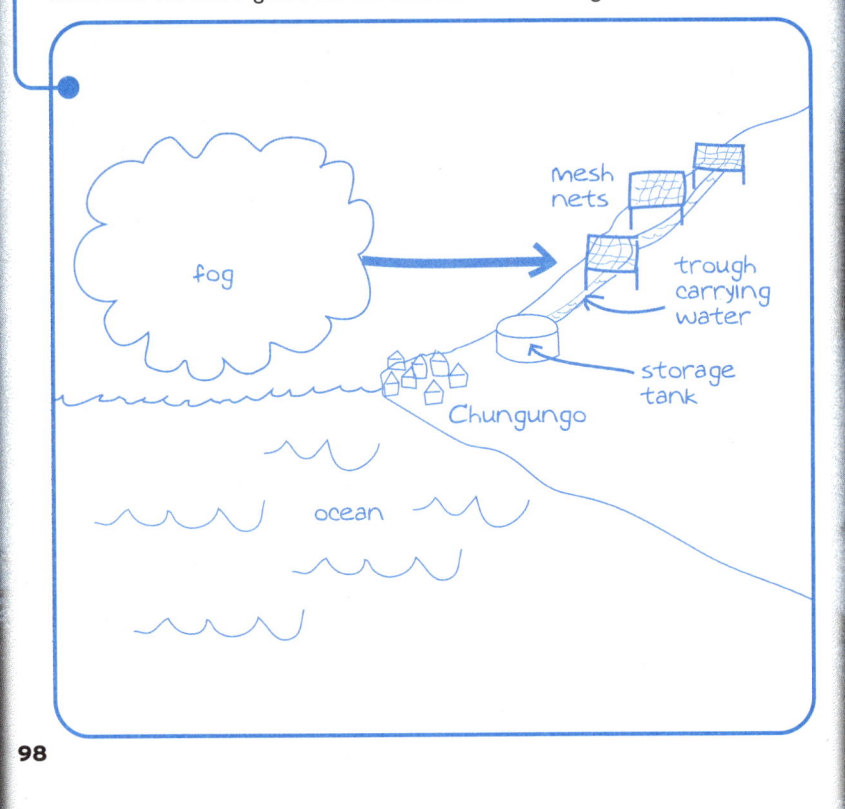

[Student diagram showing fog, ocean, Chungungo village, mesh nets, trough carrying water, and storage tank]

98

▶ Explore

A FOGGY SOURCE Students already know that the village is located in a very dry area. Direct them to look back at the map on page 96 and at the diagram of the water cycle on page 94. Since Chungungo is a seacoast village, students should infer that the source of the water vapor is the evaporation of ocean water.

SHOW HOW IT WORKS Point out that this is an opportunity for students to synthesize the information they have been reading about the fog-collection research project. First, they should orient themselves by reading the description of where the village lies in relation to the mountains and the sea. Tell students to review the photo and description of the fog-collection system in the reading. Then they can begin making a sketch of the water-collection system.

98 CHAPTER 9 / LESSON 26

▶ Propose Explanations

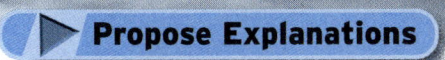

BEEN THERE, DONE THAT Before the team designed their system to collect fog, they read what other scientists had done. They found that 30 years before, another Chilean scientist had built nets to catch fog. Professor Cereceda spoke with the scientist. He told her about the work of scientists in other countries that he had read about.

▶ **How do you think the work of other scientists might have helped Professor Cereceda in her work?**

She learned what other scientists had already tried and whether or not it worked, so she did not have to try methods that did not work. Other scientists' work also gave her ideas for how to build the fog collectors.

Professor Cereceda says that science research should be used to improve people's lives. Before the villagers built the fog collection system, they had as little as one liter of fresh water per person each day—just enough to drink. Afterwards, they had about 30 liters per person each day.

▶ **Think of the ways you use water. Then list ways that the villagers might be using the additional water. How would having more fresh water improve the villagers' lives?**

With more fresh water, the villagers could cook with water, bathe, wash their clothes, grow crops, and raise animals to eat. Keeping cleaner and having more reliable food sources would improve their health.

▶ Take Action

DESIGN A FLYER Chungungo was just one of hundreds of villages in need of fresh water. On a separate sheet of paper, design a flyer to hand out to the people in other villages. Explain that villagers and scientists can work together to build a fog collection system. Briefly tell and show how the system works. Describe the benefits of the system. Include reports from villagers in Chungungo, telling how the system has helped them.

Flyers should explain that the system will capture fog and send water to the village. Students may draw a diagram or write a description to explain how the system works. The major benefit is a continued supply of fresh water once the system is built.

Enrichment

Time: 30 minutes
Materials: water faucet, bucket, large beaker (calibrated)

Encourage students to investigate how much water is wasted when a leaky faucet is allowed to drip. Instruct students as follows: Turn on a faucet very slightly so water drips slowly from it. Place a bucket underneath to catch the water. After 30 minutes, turn off the faucet. Measure the volume of the water in the bucket. Multiply by 48 to calculate how much water would be wasted in a day.

Assessment

Skill: Drawing conclusions

Use the following question to assess each student's progress:

How do Professor Cereceda's fog collectors make use of parts of the water cycle? (The fog collectors make use of the cooling effect of rising air currents on mountain slopes. The polypropylene nets act like the surface of leaves or tree trunks to provide a surface on which water droplets in the foggy air can condense. The trough provides a channel to carry the water to a storage tank in the village, just as a river or stream carries runoff naturally.)

▶ Propose Explanations

BEEN THERE, DONE THAT Encourage students to consider how working on project teams at school has often strengthened their final products. Point out that in science, researchers often share their results in journal articles and at meetings and conferences. This provides a common pool of knowledge. Ask: *How do you think Professor Cereceda's team may have benefited from the work of other scientists who carried out fog-collection projects?* (The descriptions of earlier projects would give Cereceda and her team ideas on how to build fog collectors and would help them eliminate unsuccessful designs.)

Ask students to suggest ways that the villagers might use the additional water provided by the fog-collection system.

▶ Take Action

DESIGN A FLYER Provide examples of promotional pieces describing gadgets, appliances, or technical devices designed to improve people's lives. Tell them that they can use these materials for ideas on how to word and format their own flyers. Remind them to review their notes and responses to questions in this lesson before they begin their flyers. Tell them to include drawings as well as descriptions of the system and its benefits. Allow students to use word processing programs or graphic design tools to give their work a more polished look.

UNIT 3 Water on Earth
CHAPTER 9 / LESSON 27

Point of the Lesson
Fog collection does not work everywhere.

Focus
- Structure of the earth system
- Abilities of technological design
- Science and technology in society
- Populations, resources, and environments

Skills and Strategies
- Generating ideas
- Making and using models
- Drawing conclusions
- Observing
- Recognizing cause and effect

Advance Preparation
Vocabulary
Make sure students understand these terms. Definitions can be found in the glossary at the end of the student book.
- cloud
- water cycle

Materials
Gather the materials needed for **Read** (p. 101), **Activity** (p. 102), and **Enrichment** (p. 103).

TEACHING PLAN pp. 100–101

INTRODUCING THE LESSON
This lesson challenges students to consider which locations are appropriate for fog collection.

Ask students to explain how they would decide whether to try fog collectors in an area with scarce water resources. Some students may think that fog collection would be a good idea in any dry area. Explain that this lesson will tell them whether they are right.

CHAPTER 9 / LESSON 27
The Water Cycle

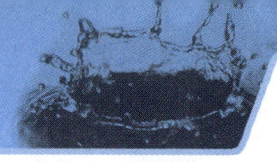

To Fog or Not To Fog

Where can fog collection work?
Fog is an inexpensive source of fresh water. But fog collection doesn't work everywhere. Scientists must consider many factors before deciding whether or not to build a fog collection system.

▶ **Before You Read**

A SUITABLE PLACE Think about what you learned in Lesson 26. Some dry, arid places could benefit from fog collectors, but not all dry places can use them.
▶ What would make one area ideal for fog collection and another area unsuitable?

Areas that do not have other water sources but that get a lot of fog would be good choices. Areas where fog is rare would not be suitable choices. It helps to have a hill so collected water can flow downhill.

WHERE WOULD YOU COLLECT FOG? Think of an area near your home or school where fog collection might work. Describe the area and what makes it a good place to collect fog. If there is no good place near you, imagine a perfect fog collection spot and describe it.

Answers will vary. Examples: an area near the ocean or a big lake, an area that is on a slope, an area where there isn't much rainfall and the land is dry

100

▶ **Before You Read**

A SUITABLE PLACE If students have difficulty answering the question, encourage them to think about why the fog-collection system worked so well for the village of Chungungo. (The area was dry with little rainfall, but fog often formed over the ocean and moved over the coast, where mountains blocked it from moving farther inland.)

WHERE WOULD YOU COLLECT FOG? Depending on your location, students may not have observed fog directly. Suggest that they try to think of foggy locations they have seen in photographs, movies, or television shows.

100 CHAPTER 9 / LESSON 27

Read

Professor Pilar Cereceda was asked if other places in the world can benefit from fog collection. Here's her answer.

Where Can Fog Collection Work?

The most important requirement, obviously, is that there be a mountain near the coast and clouds, with the appropriate characteristics, that can be intercepted by that mountain. If the cloud is at the right altitude and the prevailing winds...[are favorable], then a layer of fog will skim the ground.

"Imagine, for thousands of years, the [people living in] deserts have watched clouds pass overhead, while practically dying of thirst. What we have achieved...is a successful system for taking droplets captured by the mesh and channeling them together where they become the miracle of...[drinkable] water that flows forth from a tap in each home. Although many places appear to meet the necessary requirements, it is always essential to carry out a professional evaluation in each case to determine the most suitable terrain."

To this end, Cereceda investigates clouds, the wind, and water flows on site with her rain gauges, anemometers, and fog collectors. "What we did in Chungungo is something we certainly want to try and adapt in other areas...."

appropriate: suitable, useful
intercepted: blocked
altitude: height above Earth's surface
prevailing winds: winds that usually blow from only one direction
essential: necessary
evaluation: a careful examination
terrain: features of the land
rain gauge: an instrument that measures the amount of rainfall
anemometer: an instrument that measures wind speed

From: de Luigi, Maria. "Pilar Cereceda (Chile)." In Person. International Development Research Centre. (www.idrc.ca/library/document/102386/cereceda.html))

NOTEZONE

List the things that are necessary for fog collection to work.

a mountain near the coast, clouds that can be blocked by the mountain

FIND OUT MORE

SCIENCESAURUS
Water Cycle	216
Clouds	223
Wind	225
Steps in Technology Design	357

101

Science Scope Activity

(continued from page 97)

3. Ask students to imagine that they are a drop of water caught up in the events they have just researched. To stimulate creativity, ask questions such as: *Which event would you want to be part of? What forces would affect you? How would you get from a puddle on the ground to the cloud? What would happen to you when you were heated or cooled?*

4. Once students have finished the research, tell them to write a fictional story that explains how the weather-related event formed and where they traveled as a water drop. Encourage them to include drawings to illustrate their narratives.

Read

Time: 10–15 minutes
Materials: rain gauge and anemometer (or photographs of these instruments)

Remind students to jot down any questions that occur to them as they read about Cereceda's evaluation methods. If possible, bring in a rain gauge and an anemometer (or photographs of these instruments), and explain to students how they work. Tell students to highlight the portion of the reading that represents a persuasive argument for extending the research project to other areas of the world. (the reading's second paragraph)

CHECK UNDERSTANDING
Skill: Recognizing cause and effect
Ask: *Would fog collectors work in Chungungo if there were no mountains near the coast? Why or why not?* (No; the mountains keep the fog from moving farther inland and away from the village.)

CHAPTER 9 / LESSON 27 101

CHAPTER 9 / LESSON 27

More Resources

The following resources are also available from Great Source.

SCIENCESAURUS

Water Cycle	216
Clouds	223
Wind	225
Steps in Technology Design	357

READER'S HANDBOOK

Argument or Persuasive Writing	274

▶ Explore

MAKING DECISIONS Imagine that you are looking for places that can benefit from fog collection. The flowchart below shows that the first step is to visit the site. If it looks promising, you set up a test fog collector. Then you use the result of the test to make a decision. There are three possible decisions. For each description below, choose the best decision. Use the flowchart to see your choices.

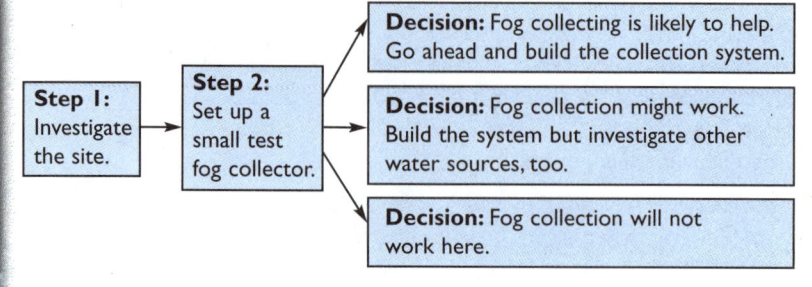

Step 1: Investigate the site. → **Step 2:** Set up a small test fog collector. →
- **Decision:** Fog collecting is likely to help. Go ahead and build the collection system.
- **Decision:** Fog collection might work. Build the system but investigate other water sources, too.
- **Decision:** Fog collection will not work here.

▶ On your first site visit, you find a village on a foggy mountain. You visit again in the next season and find no fog for several months. Should you set up a test collector? Explain the reason for your decision.

Either reject fog collection because it cannot work all year long, or set up collectors for foggy months and investigate other water sources for seasons without fog.

▶ You find that the fog collectors will have to be placed several kilometers away. Bringing water to the village will be expensive. What's your decision? Explain.

Either reject fog collection because it is too expensive or build the system if you can find a group to pay the extra cost of materials.

▶ You find a village on a mountainside that gets fog all year long. The test collectors work. A nearby spring provides just enough fresh water for drinking and cooking. What's your decision? Explain.

Build the system. Fog collection will provide additional fresh water for growing crops.

TEACHING PLAN pp. 102–103

▶ Explore

MAKING DECISIONS Remind students to use the flowchart as a guide in the decision-making process. You may want to walk students through the first problem. Call on a student to read the question. Point out that fog seems to be a seasonal or irregular phenomenon in the area described in the first example. Suggest that students go on to Step 2, setting up a test collector. Discuss possible outcomes, then have volunteers read the choices in Step 3 of the decision tree. Accept all student answers if they provide solid reasons for their decisions. Have students complete the other decisions independently. Then let volunteers explain their decision-making process to the rest of the class.

▶ Activity

Time: 25–30 minutes
Materials: large plastic bowl; water; dust and soil; dark food coloring; small, heavy drinking glass; clear plastic wrap; tape; pebble

▶ This activity is best done on a sunny day.

▶ Have students work in groups of two to four.

▶ Use a heavy glass to prevent tipping. Do not use plastic, as it will float and be unstable in water.

▶ Tell students to be sure to tape the entire edge of the plastic wrap to the bowl so no air can enter or leave the bowl.

▶ A few hours is enough time to see results if the setup is in full sunlight. Extend the time if necessary.

▶ Explain to students that they have built a simple model of a solar still, which uses the sun's heat to distill or purify water.

Activity

CLEANING WATER

Build a model to find out how water is cleaned as it moves through the water cycle.

What You Need:
- large plastic bowl
- water
- dust and soil
- dark food coloring
- small, heavy drinking glass
- clear plastic wrap
- tape
- pebble

What to Do:
1. Pour water into the bowl until it is about 3 cm deep.
2. Mix dust and soil into the water. Add a few drops of food coloring.
3. Place the clean, dry glass right-side up in the center of the bowl.
4. Cover the bowl loosely with plastic wrap. Tape the edges of the plastic wrap to the bowl.
5. Place the pebble on the plastic wrap directly over the glass. The pebble should push the plastic down a bit. The plastic must not touch the glass.
6. Leave the bowl in full sunlight for a few hours.

WHAT DO YOU SEE? Look in the glass. Describe what you see.

Clear, clean water has collected in it.

Propose Explanations

HOW DOES IT WORK?

▶ *Explain what happened in your model.*

When the dirty water was heated by the sun, water particles evaporated. The dust and soil did not evaporate with the water. When the water vapor hit the plastic, it cooled and condensed back into liquid. The drops flowed down the plastic and fell into the glass.

▶ *Explain why water that is collected from fog does not contain microorganisms.*

Fog is made of drops of water that evaporated and then condensed. When the water evaporated, microorganisms were left behind.

103

Enrichment

Time: will vary
Materials: research sources about the Namib Desert; posterboard and colored markers

Tell students that in the Namib desert, located along the southwestern coast of Africa, rain does not fall for years. However, sand dunes run parallel to the coast. Fog moves in from the ocean several times a month, leaving water flowing along the dunes. Ask students to think about the adaptations that living things would need to survive in such a place. Have them use the Internet and library resources to investigate the Namib Desert. Students could share what they have learned through posters or oral reports.

Assessment

Skill: Sequencing

Use the following question to assess each student's progress:

What are the main steps that Professor Cereceda and her team must complete in order to evaluate a possible new location for a fog-collection system? (Research the area's water problem; visit the site to see whether it has suitable terrain and other characteristics; build and test a small-scale fog-collection system; evaluate the success of the system; build the system; make improvements, or decide that the area is not a suitable site for a full-scale system.)

▶ Students may leave the setups overnight to see how much more water is collected. Water will continue to collect in the glass, although more slowly than in sunlight.

Propose Explanations

HOW DOES IT WORK? Encourage students to explain their models in terms of the water cycle. Ask: *Do you think this system could be used economically on a larger scale to remove salt from seawater? Why or why not?* Guide students to consider the amount of energy that is necessary to obtain a small amount of fresh water from a large amount of seawater. However, both seawater and solar energy are easily obtainable resources in many locations, so it could be possible to use such a system economically.

Students should recognize that a similar process is going on in the fog collectors. Just as "pollutants" are left behind in the solar still, microorganisms are also left behind when ocean water evaporates and then condenses in the fog collectors.

CHAPTER 9 / LESSON 27

CHAPTER 10
Overview

Bountiful River

LESSON 28
Coming Together

Point of Lesson: *A watershed is an area of land that catches precipitation and channels it into a river, lake, or marsh.*

This lesson describes the Russian River watershed in northwestern California. Students then create a map of the watershed in their area, identifying the major river, lake, or marsh, the tributaries that feed into it, the headwater of each tributary, and the boundary of the watershed.

Materials
Activity (p. 105), for each group:
- map of local area that shows streams, creeks, rivers, lakes and ponds
- tracing paper
- masking tape
- clear tape
- blue, red, and black pencils

LESSON 29
Flooding a River

Point of Lesson: *Some dams are built across rivers to create water reservoirs for distant communities.*

This lesson discusses the creation of the Quabbin Reservoir in Massachusetts, which stores water for the city of Boston. Students read about the decision in 1927 to dam the Swift River and the efforts involved in accomplishing this task. They examine photographs showing the area before, during, and after the project and infer how knowledge of the area's topography helped engineers plan the work. Students then analyze the costs borne by people who made their homes in the river valley, the benefits realized by residents of Boston and surrounding communities, and the impact on wildlife.

Materials
Enrichment (p. 107), for the class:
- research sources about reservoirs

LESSON 30
Restoring a River

Point of Lesson: *Sometimes a compromise can resolve conflicting needs for water.*

The Walla Walla River in Washington supports human economic activity as well as wildlife. As in so many other places, the needs of humans conflicted with those of the wildlife that depend on the Walla Walla. In this lesson, students learn how environmentalists and farmers agreed to restore the Walla Walla River in order to save local fish species while still allowing water to be used for agricultural purposes.

Materials
Introducing the Lesson (p. 110), for the class:
- promotional materials from a local state park

Enrichment (p. 111), for each pair or group:
- (for physical models) sand, rocks, and water, or a river modeling kit

Connections (p.112), for the class:
- research sources about the Lewis and Clark expedition to the Pacific Northwest

Take Action (p. 113), for the class:
- research sources about local water issues

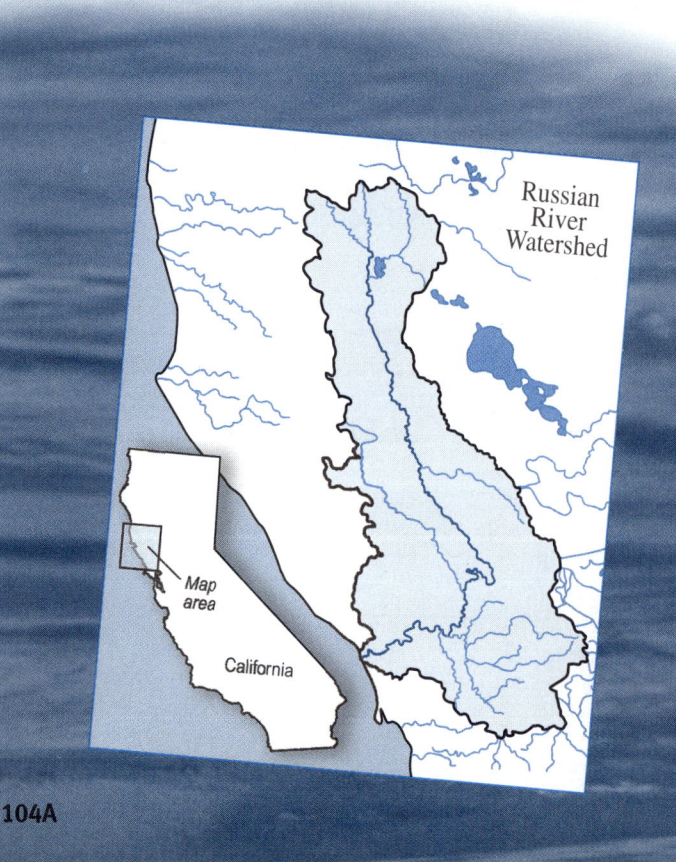

Background Information

Lesson 28

Watersheds catch rain and snow melt and channel it into creeks, streams, and rivers. Eventually, all the water of every watershed flows into the ocean. A watershed can be very small or extremely large. For example, the Mississippi River watershed drains much of North America. The boundaries of watersheds are often mountain ridges. Water on one side of a ridge flows downhill into one watershed, and water on the other side of the ridge flows downhill into a neighboring watershed.

Lesson 29

The Quabbin Reservoir's name is a Native American word meaning "many waters." The reservoir covers 39 square miles (100 square kilometers) and supplies drinking water to as many as 2.5 million people. Although the project had a profound effect on people in the area (four entire towns had to be moved), many animals have thrived in and around the Quabbin reservoir. It is home to many varieties of birds, fish, and mammals.

1927

1937

1987

104B

UNIT 3 Water on Earth
CHAPTER 10 / LESSON 28

Point of Lesson
A watershed is an area of land that catches precipitation and channels it into a river, lake, or marsh.

Focus
- Structure of the earth system
- Populations, resources, and environments

Skills and Strategies
- Interpreting scientific illustrations
- Making inferences
- Making and using models

Advance Preparation

Vocabulary
Make sure students understand these terms. Definitions can be found in the glossary at the end of the student book.
- map legend
- map scale
- precipitation

Materials
Gather the materials needed for *Activity* (p. 105).

TEACHING PLAN pp. 104–105

CHAPTER 10 / LESSON 28
Bountiful River

COMING TOGETHER

One trickling stream doesn't hold much water. But water from a hundred trickling streams can add up.

Where does all the water in lakes and rivers come from? In most cases, it comes from rain that falls on the land around the lake or river. A *watershed* is an area of land that catches precipitation and channels it into a large body of water, such as a lake, river, or marsh. Since water runs from higher places to lower places, rain that falls on a mountain will run down the mountain until it reaches flat ground. Water that moves downhill across the land surface is known as *runoff*.

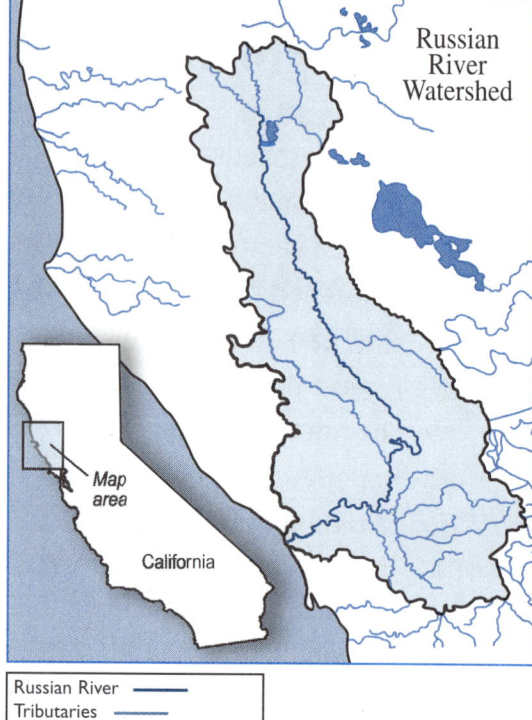

FIND OUT MORE

SCIENCESAURUS
Divides and Drainage Basins 193
Water Pollution 352

SCILINKS
www.scilinks.org
Keyword: Watersheds
Code: GSED13

Russian River Watershed map

Russian River ———
Tributaries ———
Watershed boundary ———

▶ **Explore**

INTERPRETING A MAP The map above shows the watershed of the Russian River in northern California. The Russian River is shown in dark blue. All the streams and smaller rivers are shown in light blue. The streams and smaller rivers that feed into a larger river are known as *tributaries*.

▶ Use a red pen or pencil to color the tributaries that feed into the Russian River.

Students should color all the streams and smaller rivers within the watershed boundary.

INTRODUCING THE LESSON
In this lesson, students will learn that precipitation is channeled into rivers, lakes, and marshes. They will also investigate the watershed in their area.

Ask students to identify the locations of streams, rivers, ponds, and other bodies of water in your area. Have them name various materials that runoff might pick up as it moves over the land.

Some students may think that all water pollution is caused by factories and other commercial businesses. Point out that runoff also collects other wastes such as motor oil, pesticides, herbicides, fertilizers, and animal waste.

▶ **Explore**

INTERPRETING A MAP Make sure students can identify the Russian River and the smaller streams and rivers that flow into it. After they have marked the tributaries on the map, ask: *Which way is the water flowing in all these streams and small rivers?* (toward the Russian River) *Where does all the water in the Russian River end up?* (in the ocean) Challenge students to identify areas of higher elevation on the map and explain how they know the elevation is higher there. (Higher elevation is found at the beginning, or headwater, of each tributary. Water always flows from higher areas to lower areas.) Ask students if they think there is always the same amount of water being collected in the watershed and to explain why. (No; there is more water during heavy precipitation and less water during dry seasons.)

Activity

IDENTIFY YOUR WATERSHED

Get to know your own watershed.

What You Need:
- map of local area that shows streams, creeks, rivers, lakes, and ponds
- tracing paper
- masking tape
- clear tape
- blue, red, and black pencils

What to Do:
1. Find your school on the map.
2. Place the tracing paper over your school and the area of land around it. Hold the tracing paper in place with small pieces of masking tape at the corners.
3. Find the stream nearest to your school. Use a blue pencil to trace its entire length. Follow it upstream to its head (the place where it starts) and downstream until it reaches a river, lake, or marsh.
4. Use the blue pencil to trace all the smaller streams that also feed into that stream and into the river, lake, or marsh.
5. Use a red pencil to mark a dot at the head of each stream you traced. Then connect the dots.
6. Use the black pencil to label your school and the bodies of water on the map.
7. Add arrows to show the direction of water flow in the streams.
8. Add a legend to show the scale of your map. (Copy the legend from the map.)

What Do You See?
▶ What does the red line connecting the dots show?
   the boundary of the watershed

Think About It:
▶ In what ways do people use the land in your watershed?
   Answers will vary but may include homes and schools, industry, parks, landfills, and farming.

▶ What might pollute runoff as it flows over the land?
   Answers will vary. Examples: fertilizers, weed killers, pesticides, motor oil, animal wastes, industrial waste

▶ How can pollutants dumped into small streams near your school or home affect a larger stream many miles away?
   The small streams would carry the pollutants to the larger streams.

105

More Resources
The following resources are also available from Great Source and NSTA.

ScienceSaurus
Divides and Drainage Basins	193
Water Pollution	352

Reader's Handbook
Elements of Textbooks: Maps	163
Elements of Graphics: Map	555

Math On Call
Scale Drawings	377
Scale	440

SciLinks
THE WORLD'S A CLICK AWAY

www.scilinks.org
Keyword: Watersheds
Code: GSED13

Assessment
Skill: Sequencing

Use the following task to assess each student's progress:

Have students describe the path taken by a drop of water that falls as rain on a mountain and travels through the watershed to a large river. (The drop of water moves downhill as runoff, joins with other drops, flows into a small stream, then into larger and larger streams until it finally runs into the large river.)

Activity

Time: 45 minutes
Materials: map of local area that shows streams, creeks, rivers, lakes, and ponds; tracing paper; masking tape; clear tape; blue, red, and black pencils

- Have students work in small groups.
- Use a map of the smallest region that contains the entire watershed.
- Alternatively, students can draw a more precise map by tracing topographical maps with elevation data, such as those available from the United States Geological Survey (USGS) or from Web sites that create customized maps. Maps of all watersheds in the United States can be created at: www.nationalatlas.gov
- Students may need to tape sheets of tracing paper together for a large or oddly shaped watershed.
- When students have connected the dots with a red line showing the boundary of the watershed, point out that the red line also shows a high point in the local topography and that the other side of the red line represents other watersheds.

CHECK UNDERSTANDING
Skill: Generating questions
Ask students to suggest questions for further study they could do using their watershed maps. Then have them suggest a plan for studying each question. (Questions will vary. Examples: How has the watershed changed over time? What communities does water pass through before it reaches us? What communities does our runoff water run through?)

CHAPTER 10 / LESSON 28   105

UNIT 3 Water on Earth
CHAPTER 10 / LESSON 29

Point of Lesson
Some dams are built across rivers to create water reservoirs for distant communities.

Focus
- Populations, resources, and environments
- Risks and benefits
- Science and technology in society

Skills and Strategies
- Generating ideas
- Comparing and contrasting
- Making inferences
- Recognizing cause and effect

Advance Preparation

Vocabulary
Make sure students understand this term. The definition can be found in the glossary at the end of the student book.
- watershed

Materials
Gather the materials needed for *Enrichment* (p. 107).

TEACHING PLAN pp. 106–107

INTRODUCING THE LESSON
This lesson describes how the Quabbin Reservoir in Massachusetts was created to provide water for the city of Boston and encourages students to consider the cost-benefit analysis that led to the decision. Ask students how much water they think they use every day. Students may be surprised to learn that each person in the United States uses an average of 100 gallons (379 liters) of water per day, according to the Federal Citizen Information Center.

CHAPTER 10 / LESSON 29
Bountiful River

Flooding a River

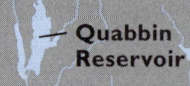

Map of Massachusetts showing Quabbin Reservoir and Boston

How do you turn a river into a lake?

In the early 1900s, the Swift River wandered through a valley in western Massachusetts. Along its banks were the towns of Enfield, Greenwich, Prescott, and Dana. People in these towns enjoyed their lives in the valley. But the valley that held these towns could also hold something else, and the water-hungry residents of the city of Boston knew it.

▶ Before You Read

THINK ABOUT IT When European settlers arrived in North America, they lived in small communities. Each community needed a water supply, so the settlers chose to live near a river, lake, or stream. As more settlers arrived, some small communities grew into large towns. As more people moved to the towns, some towns grew into cities. Soon the people in the cities did not have enough clean water to meet their needs.

▶ What do you think a growing city could do to get enough clean water for its residents?

Answers will vary. Examples: bring in water by truck or train; divert a river; move the city

106

▶ Before You Read

THINK ABOUT IT Ask students to share their answers to the question on this page. Then ask: *How would city officials decide which method to use?* Discuss the decision-making process, and have students list all the groups they think would be involved in the decision, such as citizens' groups, city planners, elected officials, and engineers. Lead students to realize that these groups will compare the costs and the benefits of each solution.

In addition to the issues surrounding Boston's water supply, you might want to discuss other water supply issues in the United States. In the southwestern states, for example, the use of water in the Colorado River Basin is a major political issue. Point out that southwestern states tend to be dry and that they also have some of the fastest-growing cities in the country.

---

106   CHAPTER 10 / LESSON 29

> **Read**
>
> Here is how one growing city turned to its neighbors to get enough clean drinking water.
>
> ## QUABBIN RESERVOIR
>
> In the late 1800s, the Swift River Valley was an isolated but prosperous farming and industrial area as well as a vacation destination. The valley was a beautiful...spot.
>
> In the 1890s, rumors began to circulate that Boston needed more water to slake the thirst of its ever-increasing population. As more and more people flowed into Boston, its existing water supply simply could not keep up with demand. More water would have to be found. The Swift River Valley fit all the criteria for a large reservoir. Boston would get the water it needed. But what would the cost be to the people of the Swift River Valley?
>
> The cost would be the total annihilation of the valley. All homes, industries, and farms would have to be sold, moved, or destroyed. Everyone would have to leave. Even the graves would be dug up and the bodies reburied elsewhere. Thirty-nine square miles [101 km^2] of land would be cleared, burned, and flooded....
>
> In 1927, the Massachusetts State Legislature officially declared [that] the valley would become the source of Boston's water supply, the Quabbin Reservoir. In 1933 and 1935, construction of [a dam] began. By 1939, the new reservoir began to fill, erasing four towns from the map.
>
> ---
>
> **isolated:** set apart
> **prosperous:** successful
> **slake:** satisfy
> **criteria:** requirements
> **reservoir:** a human-made lake where water is stored for use by people
> **annihilation:** destruction
>
> From: "The Quabbin Reservoir," *The Connecticut River Homepage*. University of Massachusetts Department of Biology. (www.bio.umass.edu/biology/conn.river/quabbinres.html)

NOTEZONE
What do you want to learn more about after reading this?

FIND OUT MORE
SCIENCESAURUS
Habitat Loss 341
Tradeoffs 369
Risk-Benefit Analysis 371

SCILINKS
THE WORLD'S A CLICK AWAY
www.scilinks.org
Keyword: Rivers
Code: GSED14

Enrichment

Time: will vary
Materials: research sources about reservoirs

Encourage interested students to research the history of towns that have been flooded to create reservoirs. Some suggestions are listed below.

- to create the Quabbin Reservoir: Enfield, Greenwich, Prescott, Dana
- to provide water to New York City: West Hurley, Brown's Station, Olive Bridge, Brodhead, Rock Rift, Rock Royal, Neversink, Bittersweet, Arena, Union Grove, Eureka, Lackawack, Gilboa
- to create the International Falcon Reservoir on the border of Texas and Mexico: Lopeño, San Pedro, San José, Santa Fé, El Tigre
- to create the Mossyrock Dam in Washington State: Kosmos, Nesika, Riffe

Ask students what they find most interesting about the "lost" towns. Have them present their findings in the form of a magazine or newspaper article or a brief radio or TV report.

> **Read**
>
> Have students create a K-W-L organizer like the example below. Their questions can be used for the NoteZone activity.
>
> Encourage students to create a time line of the events mentioned in the reading. Ask: *How many years passed from the time the decision was made until the time the reservoir began to fill?* (12 years)

What I **K**now	What I **W**ant to Know	What I **L**earned
Growing cities need water.	How did the growing city of Boston get enough water?	The Quabbin Reservoir was built to provide water to Boston.

CHECK UNDERSTANDING
Skill: Generating questions
Ask: *What questions do you think were asked to help identify the costs and benefits of building the Quabbin Reservoir?* (Answers will vary. Examples: How much money will it cost to build the reservoir? How much will it cost to move the towns? How much water will the reservoir provide for the people of Boston? What are the benefits of creating a large lake?)

CHAPTER 10 / LESSON 29

More Resources
The following resources are also available from Great Source and NSTA.

SCIENCESAURUS
Habitat Loss	341
Tradeoffs	369
Risk-Benefit Analysis	371

READER'S HANDBOOK
Read with a Purpose:	
K-W-L Chart	92
Elements of Graphics:	
Photograph	557

SCILINKS
THE WORLD'S A CLICK AWAY

www.scilinks.org
Keyword: Rivers
Code: GSED14

Connections
MATH Have students locate the Quabbin Reservoir on the map on page 106. Then provide the following statistics:
- The Quabbin Reservoir holds 412 billion gallons of water.
- 155 million gallons are taken from the Quabbin Reservoir each day.
- 118 million gallons are taken from the Wachusett Reservoir each day.

(continued on page 109)

TEACHING PLAN pp. 108–109

▶ **Explore**

BEFORE AND AFTER Ask students how they can tell all three photos are of the same area. (The mountains and other landscape features are the same.) Ask what the photographers did to make sure people would know these photos were of the same area. (All were taken from approximately the same spot.)

Tell students that although there are no buildings still standing in the area, visitors to the Quabbin Reservoir can still see traces of the towns that used to be there. In some places, there are cellar holes, stone walls, and stone foundations of houses that once stood in the area. Some American Indian sites have also been preserved. A visitor center offers tours and other educational activities, and there is an observation tower with views of the surrounding countryside and three other states.

If your school is near the Quabbin watershed area, contact the visitor center to arrange a visit for your class. In other states or regions, contact nearby reservoirs or dams to find out what educational opportunities they offer. Consider taking a field trip to the site or asking a representative from the facility to visit your class.

108   CHAPTER 10 / LESSON 29

▶ **Explore**

BEFORE AND AFTER These photos of the Swift River Valley were all taken from the same location in different years. The first photo was taken in 1927 just after the decision was made to flood the valley. The second was taken in 1937 once preparations were complete and the valley was ready to flood. The third shows the reservoir filled with water years later in 1987.

1927

1937

1987

▶ What things can you see in the 1927 photo that are absent in the 1937 photo?

buildings, roads, and trees on the valley floor

▶ On the 1937 photo, draw a curved line that separates the trees from the bare ground.

Compare the line you drew and the water line in the 1987 photo.

▶ How do you suppose engineers decided where to remove trees and where to leave them standing?

They removed all the trees that would be under water when the valley was flooded.

108

▶ Propose Explanations

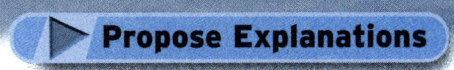

GOOD AND BAD RESULTS Most decisions faced by communities have both costs and benefits. Costs are the bad—or negative—things that are results of the decision. Benefits are the good—or positive—things that are results of the decision.

▶ According to the reading, what was the benefit of creating the Quabbin Reservoir? Who benefited?

The benefit was a supply of clean drinking water for the city of Boston. The residents of Boston benefited.

▶ According to the reading, what were the costs? Who felt the costs the most?

The costs were four towns being completely eliminated and people losing their homes, their land, their work, and their cemeteries. The towns' residents felt the costs the most.

The Quabbin watershed is protected from most human uses. Hunting, hiking, fishing, and some boating are allowed. Camping is not.

▶ How does protecting the watershed protect the water in the reservoir?

Water in the reservoir collects from runoff that flows over the land around it. Protecting the land from most human use reduces the risk of runoff becoming polluted.

▶ How do you think creating the reservoir might have harmed wildlife?

Answers will vary. Example: The animals and plants that live in rivers but cannot live in a lake might have died. Animals that lived in forested areas were displaced.

▶ How do you think creating the reservoir benefited wildlife?

Answers will vary. Examples: The animals and plants that can live in a lake but not a river would be able to survive there. Protecting the land around the reservoir also protected wildlife.

▶ What activities should not be allowed in or around a reservoir? Why?

Any activities that could pollute the water, such as using motorboats. Water in a reservoir must be clean so it won't harm people who drink it.

109

(continued from page 108)

▶ The Quabbin Reservoir and the Wachusett Reservoir supply water for 2.5 million people in 46 cities and towns each day.

Have students use the statistics to write word problems. Let them exchange and solve the problems. Then ask: *What elements did the successful problems have?* (They were clearly worded and had enough information to solve the problem.)

Assessment
Skill: Sequencing

Use the following question to assess each student's progress:

How was the Quabbin Reservoir created? (Four towns in the Swift River Valley were demolished, and the land was cleared. A dam was built across the Swift River, flooding the valley.)

▶ Propose Explanations

GOOD AND BAD RESULTS Make sure students' responses to the first two questions are based on information from the reading. Some students may recognize that there were also financial costs associated with creating the Quabbin Reservoir and transporting the water to Boston, but they may not know who paid those costs. Explain that some of the costs were covered by doubling the price of water to customers from $50 to $100 per million gallons. Also explain that the landowners in the towns that were flooded were paid for their property.

If students have difficulty answering the last four questions, briefly discuss their ideas about what the reservoir area is like today, using the 1987 photograph as a basis for the discussion.

CHAPTER 10 / LESSON 29   109

UNIT 3 Water on Earth
CHAPTER 10 / LESSON 30

Point of Lesson
Sometimes a compromise can resolve conflicting needs for water.

Focus
- Understanding about science and technology
- Populations, resources, and environments
- Risks and benefits
- Science as a human endeavor

Skills and Strategies
- Predicting
- Generating ideas
- Making inferences
- Generating questions

Advance Preparation

Vocabulary
Make sure students understand these terms. Definitions can be found in the glossary at the end of the student book.
- conservation
- reproduce

Materials
Gather the materials needed for *Introducing the Lesson* (p. 110), *Enrichment* (p. 111), *Connections* (p. 112), and *Take Action* (p. 113).

TEACHING PLAN pp. 110–111

INTRODUCING THE LESSON
Time: will vary
Materials: promotional materials from a local state park

This lesson describes how water flow in the Walla Walla River was restored and describes the issues surrounding the uses of the river. Ask students how different groups use rivers in their area.

Students may think that a river preserved in its natural state cannot be used for irrigation or recreation. Bring in promotional materials from a local state park or material obtained from Internet sites to show students that rivers designated as "wild and scenic" can be used for irrigation, industry, and recreation provided those uses do not harm the protected wildlife and water quality of the river.

CHAPTER 10 / LESSON 30
Bountiful River

RESTORING A RIVER

Sometimes a river can be brought back to what it once was.

The need for water in any community is great. People use water for drinking, cooking, washing, and growing plants for food. Factories use large amounts of water. Farmers often get the water they need for crops by diverting it from nearby rivers. (Diverting a river means changing its direction of flow.) But this often harms wildlife that depends on the river. Groups that want river water for cities or farms and groups that want to protect rivers for wildlife argue about what to do.

One river that groups argued over is the Walla Walla River in Washington state. The river is home to many fish and other wildlife. But over the past hundred years, much of the river's water has been diverted and used to water crops. An environmental group called WaterWatch was interested in restoring the river.

▶ Before You Read

GOODBYE TO WATER Think about a river you have seen—either a river in your area or one you have seen on TV. Now imagine that about half the water in the river will be diverted to supply farms and factories.

▶ **What changes in the river would you expect to see?**

Answers will vary. Example: The water level in the river would drop. The water might not be deep enough for swimming or boating. Fish might die in the shallower water. New plants might grow on land that had been covered by water.

▶ Before You Read

GOODBYE TO WATER In addition to the issue of diverting rivers for agricultural or industrial use, you might want to talk about other water use issues that affect the environment. For example, in many places rivers have been dammed to produce hydroelectric power. Land areas are submerged, and fish that used to migrate upriver to reproduce can no longer do so. Have students suggest as many examples as they can, and have the class brainstorm a list of all the possible environmental consequences they can think of.

▶ **Read**

NOTEZONE

Underline three main ideas in this reading.

A member of WaterWatch talks about the day he saw the Walla Walla River flowing again and what it took to get there.

Bringing Back the River

A few weeks ago I...witnessed something that has rarely...been seen [in] the past century: water flowing in the Walla Walla River on a hot August day.

What's so remarkable about water flowing in a river? In this case, plenty. Throughout the 20th century, the Walla Walla was completely dried up...at the town of Milton-Freewater every summer by irrigation diversions.... At the start of summer irrigation the river would dry up so abruptly that fish were left stranded in isolated pools. For 40 years, biologists would stun these fish with electric shockers, scoop them up in buckets and move them to wet parts of the river. [Then we discovered that] a few of those unlucky stranded fish were protected by the Endangered Species Act.

[Rather than fight each other in court,] WaterWatch and other conservation groups went to the Walla Walla [watershed] in April of 2000 to meet with the irrigators, and they made us feel welcome. We all shook hands, sat down at a table... and talked for several hours.

...The irrigators have committed to [return enough water to] permanently maintain flows in the river.... The river kept flowing all summer [this year], and... the fish didn't need to be rescued. This would be the first plan of its kind to restore river flows under the Endangered Species Act, and it won't be easy.

irrigation diversions: redirecting water from the natural path of the river to places where it can be used to water farm crops

abruptly: suddenly
isolated: set apart
permanently: all the time
maintain: keep

From: Benson, Reed. "Stream of Consciousness." *WaterWatch.* (www.waterwatch.org/instream.html#STREAM)

FIND OUT MORE
SCIENCESAURUS
Freshwater
 Ecosystems 148
Habitat Loss 341
Tradeoffs 369
Risk-Benefit
 Analysis 371

111

Enrichment

Time: will vary
Materials: (for physical models) sand, rocks, and water, or a river modeling kit

Explain that scientists, engineers, and environmentalists all use models to show what will happen to a river if its water is diverted or restored. These may be computer models, mathematical models, artistic representations, or three-dimensional physical models. Emphasize that although there are many different types of models, all good models include enough relevant information to help people understand what will happen in a given situation.

Encourage interested students to create a model showing what will happen to a river when it is diverted or what will happen when a river that has been diverted is partially or completely restored to its original flow. For example, students could create a mathematical model describing the depth and speed of the river in its original state and when it has been diverted, or they could create a physical model using sand, rocks, and water or a river modeling kit from a scientific supply company. You may want students to work in pairs or small groups to create their models. Provide class time for students to work on their models, or assign this as a long-term project. Have students present their models to the class and explain what the model represents and how it works.

▶ **Read**

After students complete the NoteZone activity, ask volunteers to read the sentences they underlined. For each underlined sentence, ask students to find details in the text that support the main idea. If some students underlined different sentences, ask them to use the text to support their choices. Discuss how identifying main ideas can make it easier to understand the point of a reading.

Ask students to describe how the conservationists and biologists took care of the fish when the river was dried up. (They would stun the fish and move them to wet parts of the river.) Point out that fish were probably not the only wildlife affected when the river dried up every year. Ask students to brainstorm a list of other wildlife that may have been affected. Ask whether they think the biologists may have helped those plants and animals too and, if so, what they did to help. (Example: River birds, reptiles, amphibians, and insects were also affected, but they could probably get to the wet parts of the river by themselves. River plants were also affected; the biologists helped make sure the plants did not die out.)

CHECK UNDERSTANDING
Skill: Organizing information
Ask: *What does it mean to divert a river?* (change its direction of flow) *What are some benefits of diverting a river?* (The water can be used by farmers or factories.) *What are some costs?* (Wildlife can be harmed.)

CHAPTER 10 / LESSON 30   111

CHAPTER 10 / LESSON 30

More Resources

The following resources are also available from Great Source.

ScienceSaurus

Freshwater Ecosystems	148
Habitat Loss	341
Tradeoffs	369
Risk-Benefit Analysis	371

Reader's Handbook

Reading Know-How: Finding the Main Idea	50

Write Source 2000

Using Gathering Strategies	54

Connections

Time: will vary
Materials: research sources about the Lewis and Clark expedition to the Pacific Northwest

SOCIAL STUDIES The Walla Walla River played an important role in American history during the Lewis and Clark Expedition from 1804 to 1806. Have students research the connection between the Expedition and the Walla Walla River region of Oregon and Washington. Explain that Lewis and Clark were hired by Thomas Jefferson to explore the Pacific Northwest and find a passage to the

(continued on page 113)

TEACHING PLAN pp. 112–113

▶ Explore

CONFLICTING INTERESTS After students have answered the questions in this section, divide the class into two groups. Have one group represent the conservationists and the other group represent the irrigators. As a class, hold a panel discussion on how the Walla Walla River water should be used. Make sure students support their positions with facts from the lesson.

Encourage each group to represent its position while looking for opportunities to compromise. After the discussion, work as a class to develop a proposal that works for both sides. Compare this proposal with the compromise described in the lesson. Could there be more than one solution that would be acceptable to both sides? Discuss how having people with different views work together to solve a problem can lead to more creative solutions.

WHAT DO YOU THINK? Another effect seen in the Walla Walla River was the increase in illegal fishing when fish became concentrated in certain locations in the river because they could not move farther. Also, there had been a general weakening of species of fish in the river. For example, the population of bull trout in the main part of the river was in danger of extinction from inbreeding because it was not able to breed with the healthier population above the barrier.

▶ Explore

CONFLICTING INTERESTS

▶ What two groups argued over the Walla Walla River?
   the conservationists (WaterWatch) and the irrigators

▶ Describe each group's position on how Walla Walla River water should be used. What did each group want?
   The conservationists wanted to keep the water in the river for the fish and other wildlife. The irrigators wanted to use the water to grow crops.

▶ Why was it a problem that both groups wanted to use the river?
   There is only so much water in the river. If the irrigators took all they wanted, there wouldn't be enough to keep the river flowing. If all the water were left in the river, the irrigators wouldn't have any water for their crops.

A few species of wild fish managed to live in the river even with so little water. Two of these species were identified as being threatened with extinction. These fish were protected by law. The environmentalists could have taken the farmers to court for breaking the law protecting the fish. But they didn't.

▶ How did the two groups find a compromise?
   They sat down and talked it out. The irrigators diverted less water and made sure the river flowed permanently. Both groups got some water.

WHAT DO YOU THINK? Fish can be very choosy about where they lay their eggs. Many travel the length of a river to find the right spot.

▶ How might diverting river water affect fish's ability to reproduce? How would the total number of fish be affected over time?
   The fish were stuck in isolated pools and couldn't travel the length of the river, so they might not have been able to lay eggs. Without eggs, no new fish would be born and the fish population would decrease.

▶ **How might leaving water in the river affect farmers? How would it affect consumers?**

The farmers wouldn't have enough water to grow crops. Then there wouldn't be enough food for people, and the farmers wouldn't be able to make a living.

▶ Take Action

DO RESEARCH Is there a water battle going on in your area? Do some research to find out. Which body of water is in question? What is the issue about that water—water use, water quality, or another concern? Which groups are fighting about the water? What is each group's position?

In the space below, take notes about the issue in your area. List questions you'd like to ask local water specialists, wildlife experts, farmers, politicians, town planners, and business owners.

NOTES
Local issues will vary.

QUESTIONS
Questions might include where people stand on the issues and why.

(continued from page 112)

Pacific Ocean. Their journals indicate that they were in the Walla Walla River area in the fall of 1805 and again in the spring of 1806. Have students present their findings to the class in the form of a campfire story, an adventure ballad, an annotated map, or a poster.

Assessment

Skill: Designing an experiment to test a hypothesis

Use the following task to assess each student's progress:

Ask students to suggest experiments that would reveal whether restoring the Walla Walla River solved the environmental problems caused by diverting the river in the first place. (Sample experiments: Measure the water level over time; count the fish in different parts of the river.)

▶ Take Action

Time: will vary
Materials: research sources about local water issues

DO RESEARCH Water issues vary regionally, but some of the following issues may affect your area: rights of use and water consumption; rights of public access; water quality and pollution; industrial use of water for cooling or other purposes; dam building; dam removal; water-use agreements between municipalities; and building fish ladders on dams. Help students find resources to conduct their research.

If possible, identify people involved on different sides of the local issue and invite them to visit the class. Have students prepare questions before the visit. You may want to invite people from opposing sides to visit at the same time and participate in a campaign-style debate, with each person taking turns and following time limits as they answer questions.

CHAPTER 10 / LESSON 30   113

CHAPTER 11
Overview

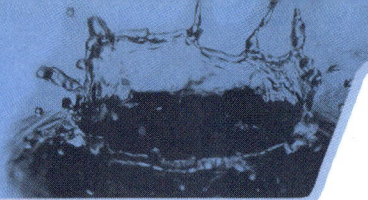

Water Watch

LESSON 31
Freshwater Worries
Point of Lesson: *People around the world have problems with their supply of fresh water.*

A reliable supply of fresh water is essential for human life. Most of the water on Earth is salt water, and most of the fresh water on Earth exists as ice. Water pollution and climate variations can make fresh water difficult to obtain. In this lesson, students learn about challenges people face in obtaining and using fresh water.

Materials
Read (p. 115), for the class:
- globe or world map

Science Scope Activity (pp. 114B and 115), for each group:
- 1 L water
- 100-mL graduated cylinder
- funnel
- two 1-L plastic bottles
- dropper
- blue food coloring
- marker
- masking tape
- 2 small test tubes
- test tube rack
- 30-mL calibrated cup

Connections (p. 116), for each pair:
- protractor
- calculator

Laboratory Safety
Review these safety guidelines with students before they do the Science Scope Activity in this lesson.
- Wipe up spills immediately to avoid risk of slips and falls.
- Immediately report any broken glass to your teacher. Stay out of the area until it has been cleaned up.

LESSON 32
Hold the Salt
Point of Lesson: *Desalination can be used to obtain fresh water from salt water.*

Most of Earth's surface is covered with salt water. In this lesson, students learn advantages and disadvantages of different methods of desalination and build a model desalination device to investigate the process.

Materials
Enrichment (p. 119), for each group:
- 2 small plastic cups
- masking tape
- marker
- two 1-cm cubes raw, peeled potato
- salt
- teaspoon
- metric ruler

Activity (p. 120), for each group:
- two 2-L plastic bottles
- black acrylic spray paint
- 30 cm clear plastic tubing, 1–2 cm in diameter
- duct tape
- 120 cm^3 table salt
- 1 L water
- large bowl
- small bowl
- spoon
- funnel
- block of wood

for each student:
- lab apron
- safety goggles

Laboratory Safety
Review these safety guidelines with students before they do the activities in this lesson.
- Do not taste any substances in the laboratory.
- Wipe up spills immediately to avoid risk of slips and falls.
- *Activity:* Wear safety goggles and a lab apron while spraying the paint.

LESSON 33
One Cool Idea
Point of Lesson: *Towing icebergs is an unusual solution to water shortages.*

Most of Earth's fresh water is frozen in Antarctica. Scientists are studying ways to use icebergs as a source of fresh water for human use. In this lesson, students learn about one attempt to move an iceberg to a drought-stricken area in northeast Africa.

Materials
Propose Explanations (p. 123), for the class:
- large world map
- map of major ocean currents (see *ScienceSaurus* section 205)

Enrichment (p. 123), for each student or group:
- ice cubes
- plastic bags
- rectangular tank or other container
- water

Laboratory Safety
Review these safety guidelines with students before they do the Enrichment activity in this lesson.
- Wipe up spills immediately to avoid risk of slips and falls.
- Immediately report any broken glass to your teacher. Stay out of the area until it has been cleaned up.

UNIT 3: WATER ON EARTH

Science Scope Activity

Water, Water, Everywhere?

NSTA has chosen a Science Scope *activity related to the content in this chapter. You'll find the activity's procedure in Lesson 31, page 115.*

Time: 40–45 minutes

Materials: 1 L water; 100-mL graduated cylinder; funnel; two 1-L plastic bottles; dropper; blue food coloring; marker; masking tape; 2 small test tubes; test tube rack; 30-mL calibrated cup

Many students assume that there is an unlimited amount of water available for human consumption because fresh water seems very abundant. However, the amount of fresh water available is very small—only about 1 percent of the world's water. Through this investigation, students will gain a better understanding of how much water is actually available for human consumption.

Have students work in small groups.

(continued on page 115)

Background Information

Lesson 31

In 1997, a United Nations study found that one-third of the world's people live in countries facing potentially serious water shortages. Around the world, water usage is increasing at a rate faster than the population is increasing, while supplies of fresh water remain limited. Water pollution continues to be a major factor contributing to the lack of usable water for many people around the world.

Lesson 32

Every day, more than 8 million cubic meters (2 billion gallons) of fresh water are produced by desalination. The largest desalination plants are in the Arabian Peninsula. Most water is desalinized using the process of distillation. Other methods of desalination include freezing and thawing, reverse osmosis, and electrodialysis. All methods of desalination are expensive because they require large amounts of energy.

Lesson 33

People have been investigating the idea of using icebergs to provide fresh water for over 100 years. Studies in the 1980s concluded that the idea was not practical due to the high cost of fuel used to tow the icebergs and the fact that most of the ice dissolved or melted on the way to its final destination. Using new technology, experts predict that icebergs will become an important source of fresh water in the next 50 years.

UNIT 3 Water on Earth
CHAPTER 11 / LESSON 31

Point of Lesson
People around the world have problems with their supply of fresh water.

Focus
- Structure of the earth system
- Populations, resources, and environments
- Natural hazards
- Personal health
- Abilities of technological design

Skills and Strategies
- Predicting
- Comparing and contrasting
- Creating and using graphs
- Generating ideas
- Solving problems

Advance Preparation

Vocabulary
Make sure students understand these terms. Definitions can be found in the glossary at the end of the student book.
- glacier
- pollution

Materials
Gather the materials needed for *Read* (p. 115), *Science Scope Activity* (p. 114B and p. 115), and *Connections* (p. 116).

TEACHING PLAN pp. 114–115

INTRODUCING THE LESSON In this lesson, students learn that fresh water is a limited resource not equally available to people in all parts of the world. Ask students: *How does ocean water differ from the water you use in your home?* (Ocean water contains salts and is not suitable for drinking, cooking, and bathing.) Then ask them to identify the source of their water. If students do not realize where their fresh water comes from, identify the source for them—surface water from a lake or reservoir, or groundwater from a public or private well.

114   CHAPTER 11 / LESSON 31

CHAPTER 11 / LESSON 31
Water Watch

FRESHWATER WORRIES

Clean clear water. We all need it—but for some, it's not easy to get.

Most of Earth's water (97%) is salt water, which people cannot drink. Only a tiny percentage is fresh water. Most of that is locked up in ice at the North and South poles and in glaciers. The little fresh liquid water that remains is not always available where and when people need it. An area may have no rain for months or even years. Then suddenly the area may be drenched by heavy downpours that cause floods.

Water pollution is also a concern around the world. Waste water from factories can pollute rivers, streams, lakes, and groundwater. (Groundwater is water in the ground that supplies wells.) Human and animal wastes can also pollute sources of fresh water.

▶ Before You Read

THINK ABOUT YOUR WATER Does your community ever experience water shortages? Try to imagine what it would be like not to have enough clean, fresh water to meet your needs. Think about all the ways that you and your family use water.

▶ Which water uses should you stop during a water shortage? Which water uses are too important to stop?

Answers will vary. Examples: Stop watering lawns, washing cars, and filling swimming pools. Continue using water for drinking, cooking, and washing clothes.

114

▶ Before You Read

THINK ABOUT YOUR WATER Discuss students' responses to the questions. Ask them to explain the reasoning behind their choices of which uses to stop and which to continue. You may want to discuss ways water is used outside the home—for example, in industry, both in the making of products and as a cooling agent. Ask students to explain the importance of water to farming and ranching.

Read

Too Little, Too Much

Hajara lives in Niger, West Africa, where the rainy season doesn't always bring enough fresh water to last the whole year.

It was one of the worst years my parents could remember. Each day, I had to walk 20 kilometers to find a well to fill my bucket. The walk back was the worst—the bucket was so heavy on my head that I swear my neck had shrunk by the time I got home.

One day, the well dried up and I had to look for water in the ponds. My mum had to boil it to get rid of the…microbes. This takes ages and you have to wait until it cools down before you can use it. But it's OK. It's what you have to do if you live in a dry, hot country.

— Hajara Kader, Niger

Julie lives in the east African country of Kenya. Although Kenya is often dry, in 1997–1998 it had too much rain.

The rains started in October 1997 and ended in mid-April, 1998: six months of disaster in Kenya. People and animals drowned, crops were flooded, and bridges and roads were spoiled by the deluge of water. Even today, many of the roads have not been repaired in the poorer areas of the country. Waterborne diseases such as cholera, dysentery, typhoid and bilharzia increased due to the rains. In a developing country such as Kenya, people have a hard time finding the money to rebuild their homes. Where crops and farms were destroyed, others also lost their jobs.

— Julie Nailantei, Kenya

microbes: organisms too small to be seen without a microscope; some cause disease
deluge: a heavy downpour
waterborne: carried by water

From: "Fresh Water." *Pachamama*. United Nations Environment Programme. (www.unep.org/geo2000/pacha/fresh/fresh2.htm)

NOTEZONE
Underline the water sources Hajara uses.

Africa ▲

NOTEZONE
If you could talk to Julie, what would you ask her?

FIND OUT MORE
SCIENCESAURUS
Water Pollution 352
Surface and Groundwater Pollution 353

SCILINKS
www.scilinks.org
Keyword: Water Conservation
Code: GSED15

115

Science Scope Activity
(continued from page 114B)

Procedure:
Give students these instructions:

1. Measure and pour 100 mL of water into one 1-L plastic bottle. Repeat this process nine more times so the bottle contains 1,000 mL (1 L) of water.
2. Add 1 drop of blue food coloring to the bottle. Gently swirl the bottle to mix the coloring with the water. This water represents all of Earth's water.
3. Put the funnel in the mouth of the other, empty bottle. Measure and pour 30 mL of the blue water into the empty bottle.
4. With tape and a marker, label the first bottle (the one that contains the larger amount of water) *Ocean Water* 970 mL. Label the second bottle *Fresh Water*.
5. Label the test tubes *Groundwater* 4 mL and *Surface Water* 0.4 mL.
6. Pour 4 mL of water from the *Fresh Water* bottle into the 30-mL cup. Then pour that water into the *Groundwater* test tube.
7. Use the dropper to remove 2 drops of water from the *Fresh Water* bottle. Put that water into the *Surface Water* test tube.
8. Make a label that reads *Frozen in Icecaps and Glaciers* 25.6 mL. Tape the label below the *Fresh Water* label that is already on the bottle.

Read

Time: 10 minutes
Materials: globe or world map

After students complete the reading, point out that flooding does not cause disease, but it does contribute to diseases that are spread in contaminated water. Bacteria, protists, and other microbes are the main causes of this contamination.

You may want to briefly discuss factors that affect how much rainfall an area receives. Have students use a globe or world map to find where the equator transects the African continent. Tell them to draw the equator on the map in their book. Have students note Kenya's proximity to both the ocean and the equator. Explain that heavy rains occur along Kenya's coast but that the climate is much drier inland. Also explain that much of Niger is desert. Challenge students to explain how Niger's location may contribute to its dry climate. (Niger is close to the equator and is not bordered by an ocean or other large body of water.)

CHECK UNDERSTANDING
Skill: Comparing and contrasting
Have students make a two-column chart titled *Earth's Fresh Water*. Tell them to head one column *Usable Sources* and the other *Unusable Sources*. Then ask students to complete the chart by listing sources of fresh water in the appropriate columns. (Usable Sources: groundwater in wells; surface water in rivers, streams, lakes, ponds, and marshes Unusable Sources: water frozen in glaciers and icecaps; water that is accessible but too polluted for use)

CHAPTER 11/ LESSON 31

CHAPTER 11 / LESSON 31

More Resources
The following resources are also available from Great Source and NSTA.

ScienceSaurus
Water Pollution	352
Surface and Groundwater Pollution	353

Reader's Handbook
Elements of Graphics: Pie Chart	558

Math on Call
Circle Graphs	296
Understanding Percent	442

SciLinks
THE WORLD'S A CLICK AWAY
www.scilinks.org
Keyword: Water Conservation
Code: GSED15

Connections
Time: 10–15 minutes
Materials: protractor, calculator

MATH Ask students what type of data can be appropriately shown in circle graphs. (data that show the relative sizes of the parts making up a whole) Have students examine the

(continued on page 117)

TEACHING PLAN pp. 116–117

▶ **Explore**

COMPARING DROUGHTS AND FLOODS Hajara's family suffered when their area had a drought, a long period of very dry conditions. Julie and her family suffered from floods.

▶ **What clues in each reading tell you that farming was difficult because of too little or too much water?**
   Hajara said she lives in a dry country. Julie said that crops were flooded.

▶ **How can having too little or too much water both contribute to the spread of disease?**
   When there's not enough water to fill the well, people have to take water from a pond. The water might contain microbes that cause disease. Floodwater can carry microbes into people's homes, gardens, and wells.

INTERPRETING GRAPHS The two circle graphs show how much of Earth's water can be used by people. Use the information in the graphs to answer the questions.

▶ **According to the first graph, what percentage of all water on Earth is usable by humans?**
   0.3%

▶ **What makes 99.7 percent of Earth's water unusable by humans? (Hint: Think about what you read at the beginning of this lesson.)**
   The water is salty or is frozen near the poles or in glaciers.

▶ **According to the second graph, where is most of the usable water?**
   underground, as groundwater

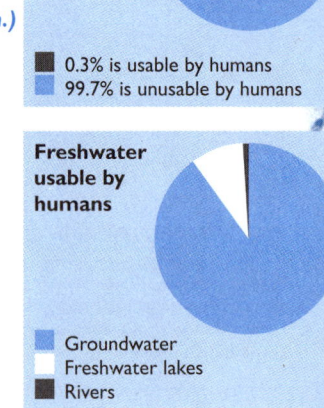

All water on Earth
- 0.3% is usable by humans
- 99.7% is unusable by humans

Freshwater usable by humans
- Groundwater
- Freshwater lakes
- Rivers

116

▶ **Explore**

COMPARING DROUGHTS AND FLOODS
Students should recognize that because plants require water for growth, a drought makes it difficult to grow crops. Explain that flooding can wash away soil and that waterlogged soil prevents air from getting to the roots, causing the plants to rot and die.

Be sure students understand that during extreme droughts, people may be forced to use water (from ponds, lakes, or other sources) that they know is unsafe for drinking. Boiling such water prior to use may kill any harmful microbes that live in the water. However, boiling may not protect people from other harmful substances such as chemicals.

INTERPRETING GRAPHS Review with students the various uses people make of water. (drinking, cooking, washing, farming, industry) Before students answer the questions relating to the first graph, ask them to explain what properties water must have in order to be usable by people. (The water must not be salty or polluted and must be in liquid form.)

116 CHAPTER 11 / LESSON 31

▶ **USING PRECIOUS WATER** People need water to drink. They also need it to irrigate crops and to use in manufacturing. The adjacent circle graph shows how fresh water is used around the world. Use the information in the graph to answer the questions below.

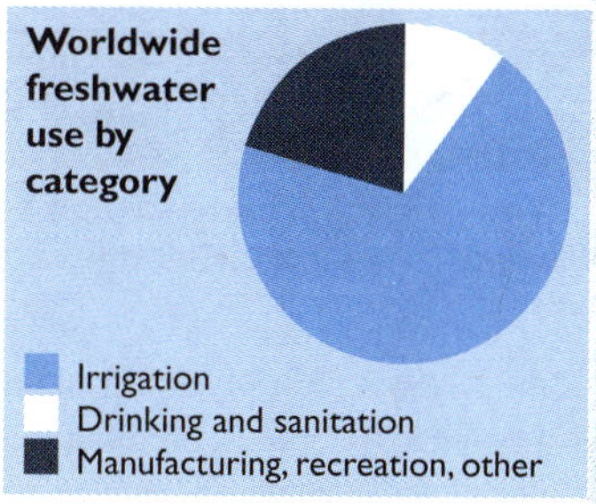

Worldwide freshwater use by category

- Irrigation
- Drinking and sanitation
- Manufacturing, recreation, other

▶ What is the largest use of fresh water? The smallest?

largest—irrigation

smallest—drinking and sanitation

▶ The world's human population is growing. Scientists are looking for ways to conserve water—that is, reduce the water used for certain needs. Which category of use do you think they should try to conserve first? Explain your answer.

Answers will vary. Example: irrigation, because that is the category that

uses most of the world's water

▶ **Take Action**

IMPROVE A TECHNOLOGY Some irrigation systems are simple canals dug next to crops. Water is pumped into the canals. As the water flows down the canals, nearby plants take in the water. The water in the canals is exposed to the hot sun. As water is heated, much of it evaporates and thus does not reach the plants.

▶ How could this canal irrigation system be improved so that less fresh water is lost through evaporation? Draw, label, and write your ideas.

• _Answers will vary. Examples: Cover the canals to shade the_

water from sunlight and trap evaporating water; run the water

through underground pipes to the individual plants; allow the

water to flow only at night when there is less evaporation.

117

(continued from page 116)

circle graphs on these two pages. Ask them to analyze the differences in how the data in the first graph are presented compared with the data in the other two graphs. (The key for the first graph indicates the percentages represented by each category; the keys for the other two graphs do not.) Have students work in pairs to determine the percentage represented by each wedge of the second and third graphs using a protractor and calculator.

Assessment
Skill: Concept mapping

Use the following task to assess each student's progress:

Have each student develop a concept map that identifies where Earth's freshwater resources are located and classifies these sources as usable or unusable by humans. A sample concept map is shown below.

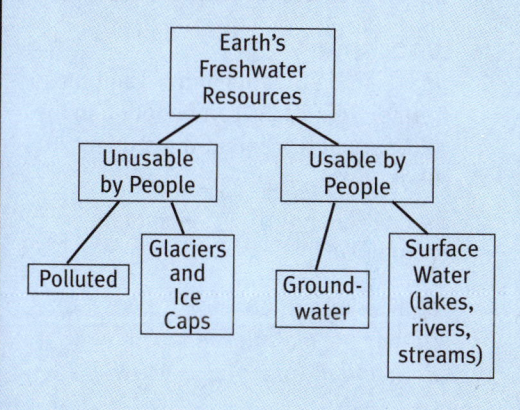

Earth's Freshwater Resources
- Unusable by People
  - Polluted
  - Glaciers and Ice Caps
- Usable by People
  - Groundwater
  - Surface Water (lakes, rivers, streams)

USING PRECIOUS WATER The graph on this page shows the relative amounts of water used in three different categories. Extend the discussion by asking students to identify the types of activities that are considered recreational uses of water. (swimming, boating, fishing, water skiing, sailing)

Discuss students' responses to the second question. Then have them work in small groups to brainstorm a list of ways they and their family members could reduce the amount of water they use at home. (Possible responses: Take shorter showers; wash only full loads of laundry and dishes; wash cars less often; reduce watering of lawns; fix leaky plumbing fixtures.)

▶ **Take Action**

IMPROVE A TECHNOLOGY Before students begin drawing their ideas, discuss how a canal irrigation system carries water to plants and the drawbacks of this system. After students complete the task, have them share their ideas.

CHAPTER 11 / LESSON 31   117

UNIT 3 Water on Earth

CHAPTER 11 / LESSON 32

Point of Lesson
Desalination can be used to obtain fresh water from salt water.

Focus
- Structure of the earth system
- Science and technology in society
- Abilities of technological design
- Properties and changes of properties in matter
- Populations, resources, and environments

Skills and Strategies
- Comparing and contrasting
- Observing
- Creating and using tables
- Making and using models
- Making inferences
- Drawing conclusions

Advance Preparation

Vocabulary
Make sure students understand these terms. Definitions can be found in the glossary at the end of the student book.
- heat energy
- volume
- molecule

Materials
Gather the materials needed for *Enrichment* (p. 119) and *Activity* (p. 120).

TEACHING PLAN pp. 118–119

CHAPTER 11 / LESSON 32

Water Watch

HOLD THE SALT

You might sprinkle salt on your food. But you wouldn't want it in your drinking water!

Over 70 percent of our planet is covered by oceans. Unfortunately, the water is too salty for drinking, irrigation, and manufacturing. Long ago, people figured out that if they could remove the salts from ocean water, they'd have plenty of usable water. *Desalination* is the removal of salts and other substances from ocean water. It's a great idea—but it's not cheap.

▶ **Read**

NOTEZONE
Jot down a question about desalination to ask your teacher.

There's more than one way to get the salts out of ocean water.

Fresh Water from Salt Water

People have been pulling fresh water out of the oceans for centuries using technologies that involve evaporation, which leaves the salts and other unwanted [substances] behind. Salty source water is heated to speed evaporation, and the evaporated water is then trapped and distilled. This process works well but requires large quantities of heat energy, and costs have been [too high] for nearly all but the wealthiest nations…. To make the process more affordable, modern distillation plants recycle heat from the evaporation step.

A potentially cheaper technology called membrane desalination may expand the role of desalination worldwide…. [In] membrane desalination,…a thin, semipermeable membrane [is placed] between a volume of saltwater and a volume of fresh water. The water on the salty side is highly pressurized to drive water molecules, but not salt and other [substances], to the pure side…. This process pushes fresh water out of salt water.

FIND OUT MORE
SCIENCESAURUS
Ocean Water 202

INTRODUCING THE LESSON

This lesson explains that the vast amount of water covering Earth's surface is too salty to use for drinking, irrigation, and manufacturing. Ask students if they know what distillation is. (the process of purifying water by boiling it, capturing the steam, and cooling the steam to condense pure water) Then ask students to suggest methods that are commonly used for separating the components of mixtures and solutions. (Examples: evaporating liquid to leave solids behind; adding a chemical to precipitate solids; straining) Discuss the processes involved in each method. Ask students: *Which method do you think would be most useful for separating the salts out of ocean water?* (evaporating the water to leave the salts behind)

▶ **Read**

Review the process by which evaporating water leaves behind salts and other impurities. Then have students read the passage. After they have completed the reading, ask them to explain how salt is removed from ocean water through distillation. (The water is heated to cause evaporation—a change from the liquid state to the gas state. As the water evaporates, salts are left behind. The water vapor is collected and cooled, resulting in fresh water.) Then ask students to explain how membrane desalination removes salts from ocean water. (A semipermeable membrane is placed between salt water and fresh water. Pressure is applied to the salt water to force water molecules through the membrane and into the fresh water. The salts and other substances are left behind.)

Discuss the questions students wrote for the NoteZone activity.

118 CHAPTER 11 / LESSON 32

Although…[membrane desalination] plants can offer energy savings, the earliest membranes…were fragile,…had short life spans, [and were damaged by] contaminants in the source water…. Pretreatment [steps], such as filtering out sediments and bacteria, must be extremely rigorous…. A new generation of so-called thin composite membranes…are sturdier, provide better filtration, and may last up to 10 years.

distilled: purified a liquid by boiling it and then letting it condense
membrane: an extremely thin sheet of material
semipermeable: lets some materials through but not others
pressurized: placed under pressure
contaminants: substances that make another substance unclean
sediments: tiny particles that settle out of water
bacteria: one-celled organisms that do not have a nucleus; some cause disease
rigorous: strict
composite: made of more than one material

From: Martindale, Diane, and Peter Gleick. "Seeking New Sources: Sweating the Small Stuff." *Scientific American.*

▶ Explore

ANALYZE PROS AND CONS Identify the advantages and disadvantages of the two desalination methods described in the reading. Record your ideas in the chart.

DISTILLATION		MEMBRANE DESALINATION	
Advantages	Disadvantages	Advantages	Disadvantages
1) this method works well	1) requires large amounts of heat energy	1) could be cheaper than distillation	1) early membranes were damaged by contaminants
2) heat can be recycled and used for another purpose	2) costs are too high for most nations	2) energy savings	2) early membranes required pretreatment filtering
3) can take a long time		3) newer membranes are sturdier and provide better filtration	

119

▶ Explore

ANALYZE PROS AND CONS Suggest that students reread the passage, underlining advantages for each method of desalination and circling disadvantages. Once they have reread the material, students should be able to successfully complete the chart using the information they identified.

Enrichment

Time: 25 minutes
Materials: (per group) 2 small plastic cups, masking tape, marker, 2 potato cubes, salt, teaspoon, metric ruler

Note: Before students begin, cut (or have reliable volunteers cut) raw, peeled potatoes into 1-cm cubes.

Students can observe the effects of osmosis by doing the following activity.

1. Measure both potato cubes and record their size.
2. Label one plastic cup *Fresh Water* and the other *Salt Water*. Half-fill each cup with warm tap water.
3. Add two teaspoonfuls of salt to the *Salt Water* cup and stir.
4. Place one potato cube into each cup. Let the the cups stand overnight.
5. Remove the potato cube from each cup and measure it. Record each cube's size.

The cube in the fresh water will increase slightly in size; the cube in salt water will decrease slightly in size. Explain to students that the size changes are the result of a process called *osmosis*. In this process, molecules move from an area of higher concentration to an area of lower concentration. In the *Fresh Water* cup, water molecules moved from the surrounding water into the potato cube. In the *Salt Water* cup, water molecules moved from the potato cube into the surrounding salt water.

CHECK UNDERSTANDING
Skill: Drawing conclusions
Ask students to define the term *desalination* in their own words and explain when desalination might be necessary. (Desalination is the removal of salts from ocean water. The process is most likely to be used in places where fresh water is scarce but ocean water is plentiful.)

CHAPTER 11/ LESSON 32   119

CHAPTER 11 / LESSON 32

More Resources
The following resources are also available from Great Source.

ScienceSaurus
Ocean Water   202

Reader's Handbook
Reading Know-how:
   Comparing and Contrasting   42
Focus on Science Concepts   132

Connections

LITERATURE Discuss with students the meaning of *irony*— the use of words to express something different from and often opposite to the literal meaning. Tell students that irony often adds a dramatic effect or humor to stories or cartoons. Tell students to imagine a newspaper headline that reads: "Man in Boat at Sea Dies of Thirst!" Challenge students to explain why this statement is ironic. (The man is completely surrounded by water, but the water is not suitable for drinking.)

Activity

BUILD A DESALINATION DEVICE

Evaporative distillation is one way to get fresh water from salt water. But burning fuels to heat the water costs money. Sunlight is a cheaper source of heat. See how sunlight can be used to purify water.

What You Need:
- two 2-L plastic soda bottles, one painted black
- 30 cm clear plastic tubing, 1–2 cm in diameter
- duct tape
- 120 cm^3 table salt
- 1 L water
- large bowl
- small bowl
- spoon
- funnel
- block of wood

What to Do:
1. In the large bowl, mix the salt in 1 liter of water. Stir with a spoon until the salt is dissolved.
2. Pour about 5 mL of the salty water into the small bowl. Leave it overnight.
3. Put the funnel in the mouth of the black bottle. Pour in the remaining salt water. Rinse and dry the large bowl.
4. Put one end of the tubing in the black bottle. Use duct tape to seal the opening. Put the other end of the tubing in the clear bottle. The setup should look like the diagram on this page.
5. Put both bottles near a window where sunlight will hit them. Place the block under the black bottle. Leave both bottles alone for several days.

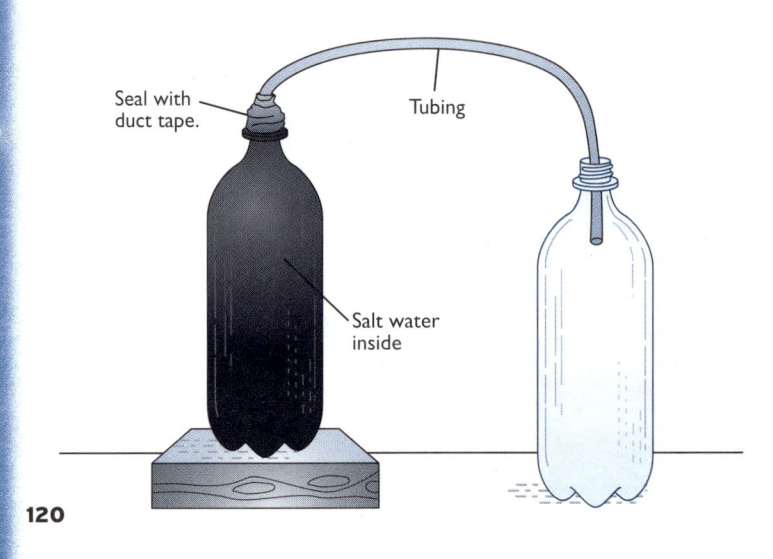

Seal with duct tape.   *Tubing*
Salt water inside

120

TEACHING PLAN pp. 120–121

Activity

Time: *Day 1:* 10–15 minutes for initial setup; *Day 2:* 15–20 minutes for completion of setup; *several days later:* 10–15 minutes for follow-up observations and responses

Materials: two 2-L plastic bottles; black acrylic spray paint; 30 cm clear plastic tubing, 1–2 cm in diameter; duct tape; 120 cm^3 table salt; 1 L water; large bowl; small bowl; spoon; funnel; block of wood; lab aprons; safety goggles

Note: To save time, paint the outside of half of the 2-L plastic bottles black prior to the day of the activity, or have reliable volunteers do so under your direct supervision. *Caution:* Spray the paint in a well ventilated area.

Caution Students should wear lab aprons and safety goggles during this activity.

▶ Have paper towels available for cleanup of spills, should they occur.

▶ Have students work in groups of two to four.

▶ In step 2, identify a suitable location for students to place their bowls overnight.

▶ In step 5, identify a location near a window where students can place their bottles for several days. The bottles should remain undisturbed during this time.

120   CHAPTER 11 / LESSON 32

What Do You See?

▶ **What do you notice after several days?**

There are drops of water in the tubing and some water in the clear bottle.

Examine the small bowl.
▶ **What was left in it after the water evaporated?**

salt

Pour the water from the clear bottle into a bowl. Leave the water in the bowl to evaporate overnight.
▶ **What is left in the bowl? What can you infer about the water?**

The bowl is empty. There was no salt in the water.

▶ **What do you think happened to the salt you dissolved in the water for the black bottle?**

The salt was left behind in the black bottle.

In Lesson 31, you read about water worries in Niger and Kenya. Look at the map on page 115 to see where each country is located.
▶ **Could this desalination method be useful in Niger? In Kenya? Explain.**

It would not be useful in Niger because that country is not next to the ocean. It could be useful in Kenya because it is next to the ocean.

Assessment
Skill: Recognizing cause and effect

Use the following questions to assess each student's progress:

What natural processes are involved in the use of distillation to obtain fresh water from ocean water? (evaporation and condensation) *Why is salt not present in the water collected following distillation of salt water?* (The salts do not evaporate with the water; they are left behind.)

Students should understand that as water evaporated from the small bowl and the black bottle, salt was left behind. Water that evaporated from the small bowl dissipated into the air. Water that evaporated from the black bottle condensed in the tubing and trickled into the clear bottle.

UNIT 3 Water on Earth

CHAPTER 11 / LESSON 33

Point of Lesson
Towing icebergs is an unusual solution to water shortages.

Focus
- Structure of the earth system
- Science and technology in society
- Science as a human endeavor

Skills and Strategies
- Interpreting scientific illustrations
- Interpreting data
- Using space/time relationships

Advance Preparation

Vocabulary
Make sure students understand this term. The definition can be found in the glossary at the end of the student book.
- continent

Materials
Gather the materials needed for *Propose Explanations* (p. 123) and *Enrichment* (p. 123).

More Resources
The following resource is also available from Great Source.

SCIENCESAURUS
Ocean Currents	203
Surface Ocean Currents	204

TEACHING PLAN pp 122–123

INTRODUCING THE LESSON
This lesson explores the use of icebergs near Antarctica as possible sources of fresh water in dry areas such as Africa. Ask students to describe Antarctica's location and general climate.

Students may think that Antarctica is made up entirely of ice. Ask them to explain what a continent is. (a large landmass) Use this definition to emphasize that Antarctica is a large landmass, covered with ice.

CHAPTER 11 / LESSON 33

Water Watch

ONE COOL IDEA

How do you move the world's biggest ice cube?

Antarctica, the continent around the South Pole, holds about 70 percent of the world's fresh water. The water is trapped in the form of a thick sheet of ice that covers the continent. Every so often, a large chunk of this ice breaks off and floats on the ocean's surface as an iceberg. The sight of a giant chunk of fresh water was too tempting for Professor Patrick Quilty. He had to figure out a way to get it to where it was needed most.

▶ Read

NOTEZONE
Circle the place where the ice is now.

Underline the place where Professor Quilty wants it to go.

FIND OUT MORE
SCIENCESAURUS
Ocean Currents 203
Surface Ocean Currents 204

Look out, icebergs! Patrick Quilty is a man with a plan.

ICEBERGS TO AFRICA

Australian polar scientist Professor Patrick Quilty thinks he has a pretty cool idea. He wants to move Antarctic icebergs around the world for use as a source of [fresh] water.

Yes, icebergs.

Professor Quilty reckons it can be done by wrapping icebergs in huge, and he means HUGE, plastic bags and towing them to places like Africa where water is… scarce.

…[Professor Quilty] says if an iceberg [were] towed behind a ship, it would [melt] as it reached warmer waters. But…if it [were] wrapped in plastic, that could be avoided. The professor says a [fiber]-reinforced plastic is available that would hold the iceberg and the water as it [melts]. "You could actually get [the iceberg]…up to north-eastern Africa where there are drought areas, and then potentially provide a base for their food source…," he says.

polar: having to do with the North or South Pole
reckons: believes
scarce: in short supply
potentially: possibly

From: Fry, Sandra. "Icebergs to Africa." *Australian Broadcast Corporation.* (www.abc.net.au/news/features/antarctica/)

▶ Read
After students complete the reading, ask a volunteer to summarize Professor Quilty's idea. Then ask students to explain why the icebergs must be wrapped in plastic before being moved to warmer regions. (The plastic bags collect the fresh water produced as the iceberg melts. This collected water can then be made available to people living in drought areas.)

122 CHAPTER 11 / LESSON 33

▶ Propose Explanations

RIVERS OF WATER Professor Quilty has an idea about how nature can help move the icebergs. Look at the map below. It shows the pattern of currents—rivers of water—that move through Earth's oceans. These currents carry floating objects along with them. "Aha!" thinks Professor Quilty.

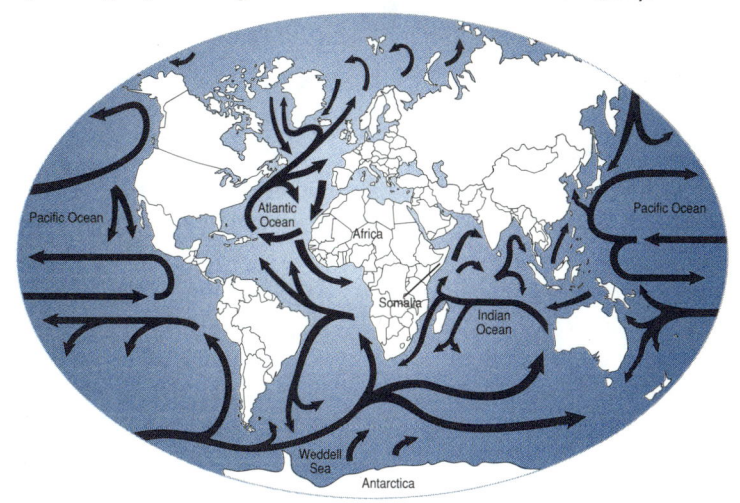

▶ Look at the ocean currents that flow between Antarctica and Africa. Explain how a combination of drifting and towing could be used to move an iceberg from Antarctica to drought-stricken Somalia in northeast Africa.

If an iceberg were wrapped up in the Weddell Sea, currents could take it to somewhere in the south-central Indian Ocean. There, it could drift along with the current that circles counterclockwise toward the east coast of Africa. Then a ship could tow it north to Somalia.

▶ To what other places could an iceberg be moved using ocean currents and towing?

the west coasts of South America and Australia

Enrichment
Time: will vary
Materials: ice cubes, plastic bags, rectangular tank or other container, water

Encourage interested students to design a model to test the procedure suggested by Professor Quilty. Have students prepare a detailed plan that includes a list of materials and the steps needed. After submitting their plans to you for approval, allow students to carry out their tests and report their findings to the class.

Assessment
Skill: Comparing and contrasting

Use the following questions to assess each student's progress:

What advantages does Professor Quilty's method of obtaining fresh water have over desalinating ocean water? (The water frozen in an iceberg is fresh water. If an iceberg can be moved to a desired location, obtaining liquid fresh water from it would be much simpler and less expensive than trying to obtain fresh water from ocean water.) *What are the disadvantages of Professor Quilty's method?* (For the idea to work, a means of containing the water obtained from the melting iceberg must be developed.)

▶ Propose Explanations

Time: 15 minutes
Materials: large world map, map of major ocean currents (see *ScienceSaurus* section 205)

RIVERS OF WATER To make sure students understand the role of currents in moving the iceberg, use a large world map to trace the path suggested by students. Have students identify the portions of the path that would require the ship to tow the iceberg and those that would rely on ocean currents.

Tell students that ocean currents can carry objects over very long distances.

Tell students to imagine that a bottle containing a note is placed in the ocean off the east coast of the United States. Ask them to identify where the bottle will likely travel if it is picked up by the Gulf Stream—the warm current that moves northeast along the east coast. Provide a map with Earth's major surface currents labeled so students can use the names as they describe possible routes. (Several different routes are possible, depending on the other currents that might pick up the bottle and their directions of flow.)

CHECK UNDERSTANDING
Skill: Recognizing cause and effect
Ask students: *Why did Professor Quilty think of Antarctica as a source of fresh water?* (Antarctica's ice holds about 70 percent of the world's fresh water.)

CHAPTER 11 / LESSON 33   123

CHAPTER 12
Overview

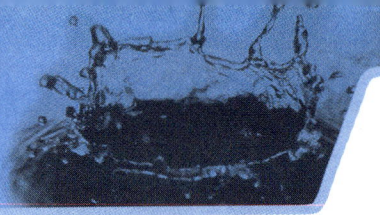

Current Events

LESSON 34
Ocean Rivers
Point of Lesson: *Surface ocean currents flow in predictable paths.*

Every year thousands of containers on cargo ships are lost at sea during heavy storms. The materials or merchandise that were in the containers usually sink, but sometimes they float on surface currents and find their way to land. Such accidents provide data about surface ocean currents.

Materials
Before You Read (p. 124), for teacher demonstration:
- clear plastic tank (aquarium or terrarium)
- cork
- water
- spoon

Science Scope Activity (p. 124B and p. 125), for each group:
- clear plastic tank (aquarium or terrarium)
- water
- 10 mL salt
- food coloring
- 3 foam cups
- paper clip
- metric ruler
- pencil
- 6 ice cubes

Explore (p. 126), for the class:
- atlas or globe

Connections (p. 126), for teacher demonstration:
- pie pan
- water
- pepper
- drinking straw
- marble
- clay

LESSON 35
Beachcomber Scientist
Point of Lesson: *Science ideas and tools sometimes come from unexpected places.*

Being a scientist sometimes means taking advantage of unexpected events. When surface currents carried thousands of sneakers around the Pacific Ocean, oceanographer Curtis Ebbesmeyer saw an opportunity to use the sneakers to track ocean currents.

Materials
Assessment (p. 129), for the class:
- map of North Atlantic gyre (see *ScienceSaurus* section 205)

LESSON 36
Electricity From the Sea
Point of Lesson: *Ocean currents can be harnessed to generate electricity.*

In Norway, scientists and engineers have designed water mills that generate energy from the ocean's currents. These turbines will be placed on the bottom of the sea-bed near the coast of Norway. This type of ocean water mill creates much more energy than wind-driven turbines are able to because ocean currents are much more powerful than wind. Each water-mill generates 300–800 kW of electricity.

Materials
Enrichment (p. 131), for each group:
- 2-L plastic bottle
- scissors
- clay
- drinking straw
- sink with running water

Connections (p. 132), for the class:
- research sources about the Gulf Stream

Laboratory Safety
Review these safety guidelines with students before they do the Enrichment activity in this lesson.
- To prevent the scissors from slipping on the curved surface of the plastic bottle, puncture the bottle first with the point of the scissors, then cut starting at the puncture.
- Use only cold water from the faucet to avoid accidental burns.

Science Scope Activity

Why Is There a Current?

NSTA has chosen a Science Scope activity related to the content in this chapter. You'll find the activity in Lesson 34, page 125.

Time: 20–30 minutes

Materials: clear plastic tank (aquarium or terrarium), water, 10 mL salt, food coloring, 3 foam cups, paper clip, metric ruler, pencil, 6 ice cubes.

This activity models vertical ocean currents within a body of water. Students see that both the temperature and the salinity of water contribute to current circulation.

(continued on page 125)

Background Information

Lesson 34

A storm in the North Pacific Ocean swept several cargo containers of Nike sneakers off of the ship *Hansa Carrier* as it traveled between Korea and the United States on May 27, 1990. Six months later, the shoes began to appear on the coast of Washington, and up to a year later the ocean and wind currents of the North Pacific gyre continued to distribute shoes from the spill to the shores of Hawaii, Wake Island, the Philippines and Japan. Oceanographer Jim Ingraham is credited with the creation of the Ocean Surface Current (OSCURS) simulation model mentioned in the excerpt on page 125.

Lesson 36

Engineers continue to improve their designs for ocean turbines to address any issues they have experienced or problems they can foresee. The designs allow small marine life forms to pass harmlessly through the slowly turning turbine paddles. Screens divert larger marine animals.

Other advantages of producing energy with ocean currents are that this hydro-technology does not create toxic byproducts and does not change the landscape, disturb the local ecology, or uproot communities.

UNIT 3 Water on Earth

CHAPTER 12 / LESSON 34

Point of Lesson
Surface ocean currents flow in predictable paths.

Focus
- Structure of the earth system
- Science as a human endeavor

Skills and Strategies
- Interpreting scientific illustrations
- Using space/time relationships
- Making inferences
- Predicting
- Making and using models
- Generating questions
- Communicating

Advance Preparation

Vocabulary
Make sure students understand this term. The definitions can be found in the glossary at the end of the student book.
- ocean current

Materials
Gather the materials needed for *Before You Read* (p. 124), *Science Scope Activity* (p. 125), *Explore* (p. 126), and *Connections* (p. 126).

CHAPTER 12 / LESSON 34

Current Events

OCEAN RIVERS

It's strange, but true—rivers run through oceans. And some surprising things are floating around.

Each year, ships carry more than 100 million containers across Earth's oceans. The containers are the size of large trucks and sit on the ships' open decks. Many are filled with products that are made in one place and sold in another. Doll heads, bath toys, and sneakers are some of the items that make the long voyage across the ocean. Sometimes a cargo ship runs into stormy weather. Then containers can fall off a ship and be lost at sea. But that doesn't stop some of this cargo from reaching shore!

▶ **Before You Read**

OCEAN IN MOTION Did you ever see a movie about a storm at sea? Watch the waves at the shore? Go deep-sea fishing? Seen people surfing, live or on TV?

▶ **List all the kinds of motion you can think of that take place in the ocean.**

Students may mention waves moving water up and down at sea, tides, waves crashing on shore, undertows, swells, and so on. They may have noticed that the waves were larger on windy days.

124

TEACHING PLAN pp. 124–125

INTRODUCING THE LESSON
This lesson introduces the concept that ocean water is in constant motion with currents that flow like rivers. Ask students what they know about ocean currents and how they affect the movement of water in the oceans. Ask students to describe any experiences they may have had with ocean currents. For example, have they ever been in a boat or on a raft that drifted for some distance? Were they ever not allowed to swim at a beach because of a riptide? Students may not realize that some ocean currents can move over very long distances. Point out that there are different kinds of currents and that they can cover a variety of distances.

▶ **Before You Read**

Time: 10–15 minutes
Materials: clear plastic tank (aquarium or terrarium), cork, water, spoon

OCEAN IN MOTION Some ocean currents are deep below the surface, while others are at the surface. Surface currents could easily be confused with waves. Currents involve the actual flow of water from one part of Earth to another. Waves involve the transfer of energy.

Set up a simple demonstration to show students how the water molecules in a wave move. Fill a clear tank with water. Float a cork in the water. Lightly tap the water at one end with a spoon to generate waves. Tell students to watch the cork very closely and observe how it moves. Ask: *Does the cork travel across the water surface, or does it just bob up and down?* (It bobs up and down.) *What does the cork's motion tell you about the movement of water in a wave?* (The wave moves across the surface, but each water molecule actually moves in a circular path, ending up right about where it started.)

124 CHAPTER 12 / LESSON 34

Read

What happens when 60,000 sneakers fall into the ocean? Here's the story of their wet journey from Asia to North America.

These Shoes Just Did It

Surface currents in the oceans move in large slow circles called gyres. That explains the story of 60,000 Nike shoes [that] spilled from a storm-tossed cargo ship in the northeastern Pacific in May 1990.

Six months to a year later, beachcombers from British Columbia to Oregon began to find shoes. Oceanographers constructed a computer model that predicted the shoes' route. In 1993, shoes were found in Hawaii….

The shoes…were wearable after a scrubbing to remove barnacles, algae, and tar.

surface current: a river of water pushed along the ocean's surface by winds

beachcomber: a person who looks for objects that have washed ashore on a beach

oceanographer: a scientist who studies the ocean

barnacle: a hard-shelled ocean animal that attaches itself to surfaces

algae: plant-like organisms that live in water and carry out photosynthesis

From: "Staying On Top: These Shoes Just Did It." *Ocean Planet*. Smithsonian Institution. (seawifs.gsfc.nasa.gov/OCEAN_PLANET/HTML/oceanography_currents_2.html)

NOTEZONE

What carried the sneakers to shore?
surface currents

What kinds of lost cargo might make it to shore?
items that float

What kinds might not make it?
items that sink

FIND OUT MORE

SCIENCESAURUS
Ocean Currents 203
Surface Ocean Currents 204
Coriolis Effect 205

SCILINKS
THE WORLD'S A CLICK AWAY
www.scilinks.org
Keyword: Ocean Currents
Code: GSED16

125

Science Scope Activity
(continued from page 124B)

Procedure
Give students the following instructions.
1. Fill the tank with tap water.
2. Mix a saltwater solution by combining 10 mL of salt with 250 mL of water. Stir until the salt dissolves. Add a few drops of food coloring.
3. With a pencil, mark the position of two holes in one cup's side just above each other—one at 1.25 cm from the bottom, the other at 2.5 cm from the bottom.
4. Pour the colored saltwater into the cup. Lower the cup so it is submerged in the water with its top just above the water's surface.
5. Clip the cup to the side of the tank.
6. With a pencil point, punch two holes in the cup at the marks.
7. Record what you observe. (The colored water streams downward.)
8. Empty and refill the tank.
9. Add 6 ice cubes to 250 mL of water. Add a few drops of food coloring. Let the water cool a few minutes.
10. Fill a new cup with the colored ice water. Attach the cup to the side of the tank as before. Again, make two holes in the side of the cup.
11. Record your observations. (The colored water streams to the bottom of the tank.)

Note that the waves will hit the opposite end of the tank and refract back toward the cork. Waves will then be coming from two directions, and the water will be choppy, making the circular motion more difficult to see. Let students repeat the activity themselves after the water has calmed.

Read

Ask students if they have ever found an object that has washed up on a beach. Ask them if they wondered where the object might have come from. The reading presents a puzzling mystery that can only be explained by learning more about the motions of ocean currents and where they carry floating objects.

CHECK UNDERSTANDING
Skill: Making inferences
Ask students: *Why do you think the oceanographers' computer model was able to predict the route of the sneakers?* (Students should infer from the reading that surface currents move in predictable patterns.)

CHAPTER 12 / LESSON 34   125

CHAPTER 12 / LESSON 34

More Resources

The following resources are also available from Great Source and NSTA.

SCIENCESAURUS

Ocean Currents	203
Surface Ocean Currents	204
Coriolis Effect	205

SCILINKS
THE WORLD'S A CLICK AWAY

www.scilinks.org
Keyword: Ocean Currents
Code GSED16

Connections

Time: 20 minutes
Materials: pie pan, water, pepper, drinking straw, marble, clay

GEOGRAPHY Tell students that three factors affect the direction of surface currents: Earth's wind patterns (prevailing winds), the location of the continents, and Earth's rotation. Do the following demonstration to model the effects of winds and bodies of land. Fill the pie pan with water and sprinkle pepper over the surface. Use a straw to blow over the surface of the water. Ask: *In which direction do the currents travel?* (In the same direction as the wind)

(continued on page 127)

TEACHING PLAN pp. 126–127

▶ **Explore**

INTERPRETING A MAP The map below shows the movement of the North Pacific gyre, a system of surface currents in the Pacific Ocean. The numbers show where Nike sneakers from the lost container were found on different dates in the early 1990s.

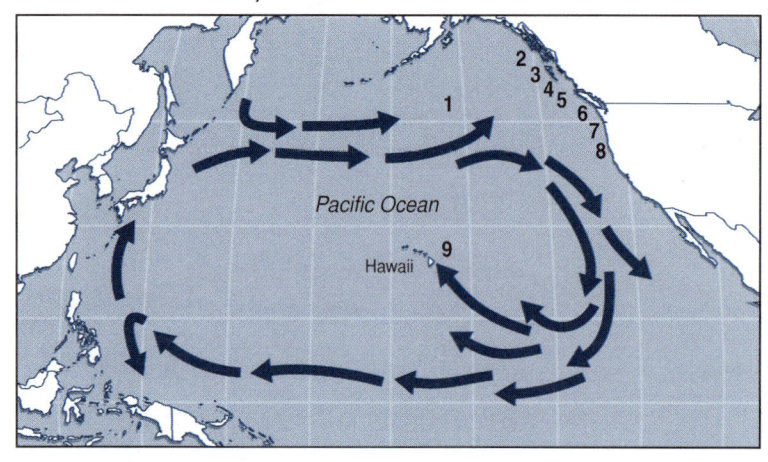

❶ shoe spill	May 27, 1990	❻ 150 recovered	April 4, 1991
❷ 200 recovered	Nov.–Dec. 1990	❼ 200 recovered	May 9–10, 1991
❸ 100 recovered	Jan.–Feb. 1991	❽ 200 recovered	May 18, 1991
❹ 200 recovered	Feb.–March 1991	❾ several recovered	Jan.–March 1993
❺ 250 recovered	March 26, 1991		

MAKE INFERENCES Where do you think the sneakers landed next? (If you need to, refer to a world map or globe.) Explain.

Following the path of the currents, the sneakers might have landed in

Japan, the Philippines, or New Guinea.

▶ The map shows that about 1,300 sneakers were found. What do you think happened to the almost 59,000 other sneakers lost at sea?

Students may think that some sneakers sank, others were eaten

by sea animals, some people did not report what they found, and

many sneakers are still floating in the currents.

126

▶ **Explore**

INTERPRETING A MAP Ask students to recall what a gyre is. (a large circular surface current in the ocean) Point out that gyres move clockwise in the Northern Hemisphere and counter-clockwise in the Southern Hemisphere due to Earth's rotation and the Coriolis effect. This effect exists because places on Earth's equator travel faster than places in the higher or lower latitudes (since Earth's circumference is greatest at the equator). The differences in speed cause the moving streams of water to bend (deflect) the flow.

MAKE INFERENCES
Materials: atlas or globe
Allow students to refer to an atlas or globe to find the names of the land masses around which the illustrated currents flow. Students should be able to predict that the sneakers will continue to be carried by the currents shown with arrows on the map. Encourage students to combine the facts that they learned about ocean currents with their own experiences to figure out what might have happened to the sneakers that have not yet been found or reported.

126   CHAPTER 12 / LESSON 34

▶ **Take Action**

GENERATE QUESTIONS The paths of ocean currents change direction slightly from season to season and from year to year. Whatever sneakers are still out there may be found in the future.

Imagine you are an oceanographer who is using the sneakers to study ocean currents in the northern Pacific. Design a poster to put up at beaches. On it, ask people to look out for sneakers. Tell them why the sneakers are there. (Make sure they know they can keep the sneakers!) Include some questions that will give scientists studying ocean currents more information to add to the map. Ask people to send answers to the questions. Write your message and questions below.

Answers will vary. Examples: How many sneakers did you find? On what date did you find them? Where did you find them? Do you know anyone else who found sneakers? Where and when did the person find them?

127

(continued from page 126)

Empty and dry the pan. Use clay to represent continents. Make a slightly sloping mound about 2 cm wide in the pan's center. Refill the pan with water and sprinkle with pepper. Blow over the surface again. Ask: *How does the land affect the surface currents?* (They go around the land.) The third factor is Earth's rotation, which causes the Coriolis effect. Currents bend in a clockwise direction north of the equator and counter-clockwise south of the equator. To demonstrate, empty the pan, put a marble in the center, have a student slowly turn the pan, and give the marble a light push to start it moving toward the pan's side.

Assessment
Skill: Concept mapping

Use the following task to assess each student's progress:

Have students make a concept map about ocean currents. Tell them to put the key concept, ocean currents, in the center and to add details, definitions, and examples around the key concept. (Student maps may include the following: travel in predictable paths; caused by wind; temperature and density differences cause movement; gyre in Pacific Ocean, changes direction from season to season, changes direction from year to year; Gulf Stream in Atlantic Ocean)

▶ **Take Action**

GENERATE QUESTIONS Emphasize that the purpose of the sneaker study is to add to scientists' knowledge about ocean currents. Encourage students to think about the kinds of information oceanographers would be interested in learning from the people who found the sneakers. Ask: *Why would reporting floating objects be useful?* (Examples: The objects could help predict the movement of oil spills or locate missing vessels or people.)

Suggest that students explore the Beachcombers' and Oceanographers' International Association Web site at the following: www.beachcombers.org

This site provides information on other Internet sites and club meetings dedicated to matching up the sneakers into pairs.

CHAPTER 12 / LESSON 34   127

UNIT 3 Water on Earth

CHAPTER 12 / LESSON 35

Point of Lesson
Ideas for science investigations sometimes come from unexpected places.

Focus
- Structure of the earth system
- Nature of science
- Understanding about scientific inquiry
- Science as a human endeavor

Skills and Strategies
- Communicating
- Making inferences

Advance Preparation

Vocabulary
Make sure students understand this term. The definition can be found in the glossary at the end of the student book.
- ocean current

Materials
Gather the materials needed for *Assessment* (p. 129).

CHAPTER 12 / LESSON 35
Current Events

BEACHCOMBER SCIENTIST

Can a sneaker be a tool of scientific research? Ask an oceanographer!

Quick! Think of all the things you can do with a sneaker. Chances are that doing scientific research didn't come to mind. It wasn't on oceanographer Curtis Ebbesmeyer's mind either. But sometimes doing scientific research is simply a matter of observing something that's already out there—like hundreds of sneakers that wash up on beaches all around the Pacific Ocean.

▶ Before You Read

EVERYDAY SCIENCE Not all science is done in a laboratory. And scientific discoveries don't always require fancy equipment. Sometimes things that happen right around you can lead to new discoveries. You just need to keep an open mind to new ideas.

▶ Write about a time when you made an interesting discovery about the natural world. What were you doing? What did you notice? What new ideas did you have?

Student ideas should reflect knowledge about the natural world derived from a non-laboratory setting.

TEACHING PLAN pp. 128–129

INTRODUCING THE LESSON
This lesson describes how oceanographer Curtis Ebbesmeyer took advantage of an accident at sea to develop not only a long-term research project but also a new way to study surface currents.

Ask students to identify ways that scientists learn about the world around them. Make a list of their responses on the board. Encourage students to add to the list as they read through the lesson.

Some students may think that science is done only in a laboratory. To get an idea of how students think science is done, ask them whether there is only one scientific method or whether there are many ways of doing science. (many) Can scientific discoveries be made by accident? (yes)

▶ Before You Read

EVERYDAY SCIENCE Allow class time for students to share their responses to the questions. Then ask them if they would like to add to the list you started in the Introducing the Lesson discussion.

▶ Read
In addition to the NoteZone task, students could underline the types of cargo that are cast adrift as a result of accidents. (shoes, hockey gloves, Legos) Ask them to predict which items would float and make good markers to track surface currents.

128 CHAPTER 12 / LESSON 35

▶ **Read**

New scientific ideas often come from unexpected places. Meet a beachcomber scientist who still learns from his mom.

Tracking Currents With Sneakers

Every year, more than 10,000 containers fall overboard and spill their cargo into the ocean. Storms are often to blame. An 8-foot by 40-foot [2.43-meter by 12.1-meter] container, which can carry up to 58,000 pounds [26,308.4 kilograms] of cargo, might hold 10,000 shoes, 17,000 hockey gloves, or a million Legos.

[Oceanographer Curtis] Ebbesmeyer and his partners... design and manufacture instruments that measure ocean currents.... Until 1990, Ebbesmeyer dropped (buoys), (drift cards), and (markers) into the sea to track current flows without giving much thought to what was already adrift. But when his mom quizzed him about where beach junk comes from, he realized that the ocean was filled with readymade markers whose course he could plot from ship to shore.

buoy: a marker, often with a bell or light, designed to float on the ocean's surface

drift cards: floating cards used to track the paths of currents

plot: locate on a map

From: Podsada, Janice. "Beach: Nike Shoes Wash Up." *The Daily Herald* (Everett, WA)

NOTEZONE
Circle all the items that Ebbesmeyer used to track ocean currents.

▶ **Propose Explanations**

THINKING LIKE A SCIENTIST Ebbesmeyer listened to his mom's question and thought about it carefully, even though she is not an oceanographer. How is this an example of good scientific habits?

Answers will vary. Example: He has an open mind and is willing to consider the ideas of other people. A good habit for scientists is being willing to hear what others have to say, because it might help the scientists do their work.

FIND OUT MORE
SCIENCESAURUS
Surface Ocean Currents 204

129

More Resources
The following resources are also available from Great Source.

SCIENCESAURUS
Surface Ocean Currents   204

READER'S HANDBOOK
Focus on Science Concepts   132

WRITE SOURCE 2000
Making Your Narrative Work   157

Assessment
Materials: map of North Atlantic gyre (see *ScienceSaurus* 205)

Skill: Predicting

Use the following questions to assess each student's progress.

Display a map of the North Atlantic gyre. Ask students:

▶ *Where would you put objects to study ocean currents?* (Good locations for the objects include the Gulf Stream waters off the East Coast of the United States and the North Atlantic Equatorial Current off the north coast of South America.)

▶ *Where would the objects travel?* (The objects would most likely move across the Atlantic to Europe or up into the Gulf of Mexico.)

▶ **Propose Explanations**

THINKING LIKE A SCIENTIST Ask students whether their family members or friends have played a role in helping them form fresh insights. Encourage them to consider how using such insights not only solved Ebbesmeyer's immediate problem of how to track currents but also helped raise new questions.

Use the question as an opportunity to discuss examples of scientific methods and attitudes, such as making observations; asking questions and proposing answers, explanations, and predictions; using logical thinking; respecting accuracy; and being willing to consider alternative ways of solving problems. Ask: *What does the word "science" mean?* Students may consider it to be a body of knowledge. If so, ask: *What sets people like Ebbesmeyer apart?* Lead students to understand that science is as much a way of thinking and an attitude as it is a body of knowledge.

CHECK UNDERSTANDING
Skill: Organizing information
Ask students to imagine that they are going to write an article about Ebbesmeyer's research project. Ask them to list Who, What, When, Where, Why, and How questions on a sheet of paper and then write a corresponding fact after each word.

CHAPTER 12 / LESSON 35   129

UNIT 3 Water on Earth
CHAPTER 12 / LESSON 36

Point of Lesson
Ocean currents can be harnessed to generate electricity.

Focus
- Structure of the earth system
- Science and technology in society
- Science as a human endeavor
- Transfer of energy
- Motion and force

Skills and Strategies
- Creating and using tables
- Interpreting scientific illustrations
- Making inferences
- Communicating

Advance Preparation

Vocabulary
Make sure students understand these terms. Definitions can be found in he glossary at the end of the student book.
- coal
- electrical energy
- natural gas
- ocean current
- surface current
- wind

Materials
Gather the materials needed for **Enrichment** (p. 131) and **Connections** (p. 132).

TEACHING PLAN pp. 130–131

CHAPTER 12 / LESSON 36
Current Events

Electricity From the Sea

How can we get useful electrical energy from ocean currents? Some scientists are coming up with ideas!

Windmills can change the energy of steady winds into electrical energy. Can the steady force of water currents do the same thing? A group of scientists and engineers in Norway think so. Currents move through the ocean in many parts of the world. In some places, the water is shallow enough so that a "wind mill" can be placed on the seabed to reach the current. So if it works in Norway, it might work in other places, too.

▶ Before You Read

ENERGY RESOURCES There are lots of ways to produce electrical energy. Some are listed in the following chart. What other ways can you think of? Add them to the chart. Then list the advantages and disadvantages of each one. Maybe you'll have an idea that no one has thought of yet!

Ways to Produce Electrical Energy	Advantages	Disadvantages
From wind	Wind is free and cannot run out.	Many places don't get steady winds.
From burning coal	Coal is cheap and plentiful.	It causes lots of pollution.
From burning oil and natural gas	These fuels burn cleaner than coal.	The U.S. has to import oil. Natural gas can explode.
Solar energy	It's free and won't run out.	It's usable only in places that are usually sunny.
Releasing water from a dam	Water power is free once a dam is built.	A dam cuts off the water supply downriver where farmers may need it.

INTRODUCING THE LESSON
This lesson introduces the possibility of using ocean currents to drive a turbine-generator similar to those found in hydroelectric power plants. Ask students where we get energy to light and heat our homes. (Most students will say that energy comes from power plants, but some will not know the source that supplies energy to the power plants.) Then ask students if they think that the energy contained in ocean currents could be harnessed to produce electric power.

▶ Before You Read

ENERGY RESOURCES As students complete the chart, remind them to add other ways of producing electricity to the first column. Have volunteers read their ideas aloud.

▶ Read

As background for the reading, explain to students how wind turbines generate electricity. Wind turbines are machines that capture the wind's energy, just as these new "water mills" are designed to trap the powerful force of ocean currents.

A wind turbine's rotor blades convert wind energy to mechanical energy. A shaft attached to the blades turns a coil in the generator, which produces an electric current. Suggest that students draw a diagram to help them visualize the process, then check the diagram against one in a book or on the Internet.

Encourage students to highlight any unfamiliar terms or phrases in the reading. Then tell them to look for context clues that will help them understand the meaning of these terms.

130   CHAPTER 12 / LESSON 36

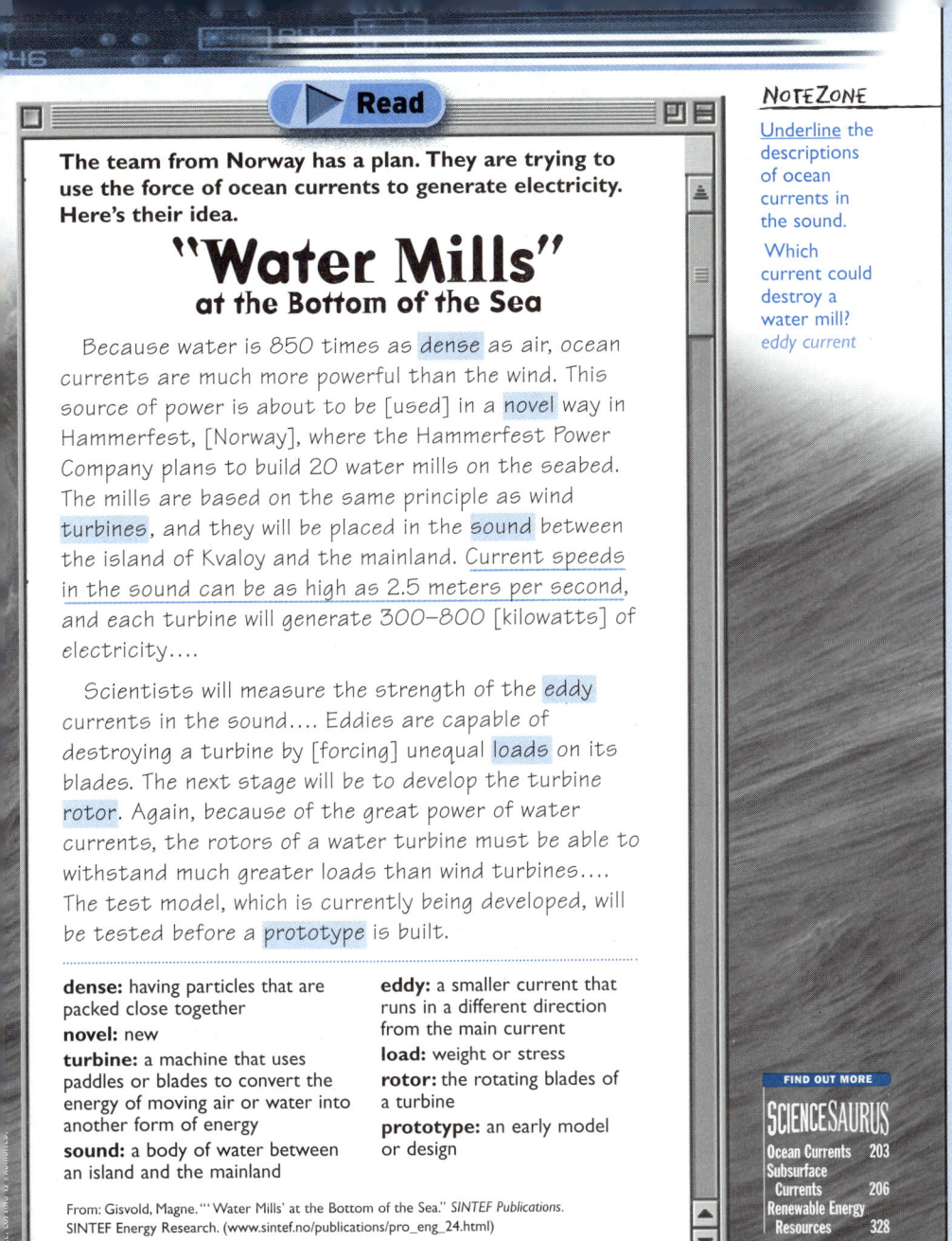

▶ Read

The team from Norway has a plan. They are trying to use the force of ocean currents to generate electricity. Here's their idea.

"Water Mills" at the Bottom of the Sea

Because water is 850 times as dense as air, ocean currents are much more powerful than the wind. This source of power is about to be [used] in a novel way in Hammerfest, [Norway], where the Hammerfest Power Company plans to build 20 water mills on the seabed. The mills are based on the same principle as wind turbines, and they will be placed in the sound between the island of Kvaloy and the mainland. Current speeds in the sound can be as high as 2.5 meters per second, and each turbine will generate 300–800 [kilowatts] of electricity....

Scientists will measure the strength of the eddy currents in the sound.... Eddies are capable of destroying a turbine by [forcing] unequal loads on its blades. The next stage will be to develop the turbine rotor. Again, because of the great power of water currents, the rotors of a water turbine must be able to withstand much greater loads than wind turbines.... The test model, which is currently being developed, will be tested before a prototype is built.

dense: having particles that are packed close together
novel: new
turbine: a machine that uses paddles or blades to convert the energy of moving air or water into another form of energy
sound: a body of water between an island and the mainland
eddy: a smaller current that runs in a different direction from the main current
load: weight or stress
rotor: the rotating blades of a turbine
prototype: an early model or design

From: Gisvold, Magne. "'Water Mills' at the Bottom of the Sea." SINTEF Publications. SINTEF Energy Research. (www.sintef.no/publications/pro_eng_24.html)

NOTE ZONE

Underline the descriptions of ocean currents in the sound.

Which current could destroy a water mill?
eddy current

FIND OUT MORE
SCIENCESAURUS
Ocean Currents 203
Subsurface Currents 206
Renewable Energy Resources 328

Enrichment

Time: 40–45 minutes
Materials: 2-L plastic bottle, scissors, clay, drinking straw, sink with running water

Modern paddle wheels use the power of flowing water to generate electricity. Students can work in small groups to make a simple model to harness this energy source. Provide them with the following instructions and a copy of the diagram below.

1. Cut off the top third of the bottle to make a top section and a bottom section.
2. Make two small V-shaped notches at opposite sides of the bottom section's edge.
3. Mold clay into a ball around the middle of the straw.
4. Cut four paddle blades from the top section of the bottle.
5. Insert the blades into the clay at equal intervals so they align with the straw.
6. Put the paddle wheel in the notches. Make sure it turns freely.
7. Hold the model under a running faucet in the sink with the paddle blades in the stream of water.
8. Find a way to use the model to do work, such as lifting a small weight hanging on a string.

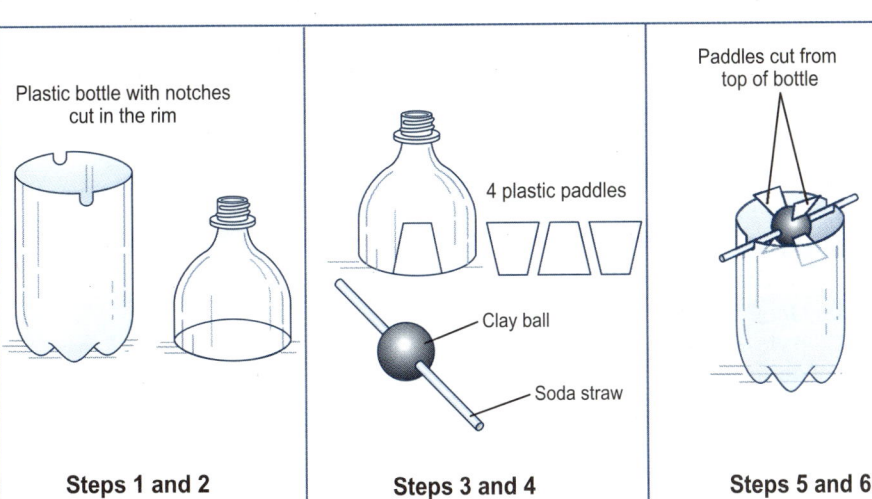

Plastic bottle with notches cut in the rim

Steps 1 and 2

4 plastic paddles
Clay ball
Soda straw

Steps 3 and 4

Paddles cut from top of bottle

Steps 5 and 6

CHECK UNDERSTANDING
Skill: Organizing information
Ask students to make a list of the potential problems scientists might face in trying to build and use water mills. (They must find a suitable location for the water mills and make the turbine blades and rotors strong enough to withstand the force of the ocean currents.)

CHAPTER 12 / LESSON 36

CHAPTER 12 / LESSON 36

More Resources

The following resources are also available from Great Source.

ScienceSaurus

Ocean Currents	203
Subsurface Ocean Currents	206
Renewable Energy Resources	328

Reader's Handbook

Summarizing	232
Elements of Graphics:	
Map	555
Table	559
5 W's Organizer	672

Write Source 2000

Writing News Stories	167

Connections

Time: will vary
Materials: research sources about the Gulf Stream

GEOGRAPHY Have students research the climate of Ireland and England and find out how the Gulf Stream affects it. Tell them to compare the weather and rainfall in those countries with the weather and rainfall of a location at the same latitude in North America. Ask them to predict what would happen to the climate in these two regions of the world if the path of the Gulf Stream were altered.

Teaching Plan pp. 132–133

▶ Propose Explanations

ANALYZE ADVANTAGES A team of American scientists is designing its own water mill to convert the energy of an ocean current into electrical energy. The Gulf Stream is a surface current in the western Atlantic Ocean. It carries water north along the eastern coast of the United States. At its fastest, the Gulf Stream current moves at more than 2 meters (6.5 feet) per second.

Although it officially starts off the coast of North Carolina, the Gulf Stream is fed by water from the Florida Current. On the map you can see the start of the Florida Current between the southern tip of Florida and Cuba. The arrows show the direction and speed of the current. The longer the arrow, the faster the current moves. The closer a current is to shore, the shallower the water.

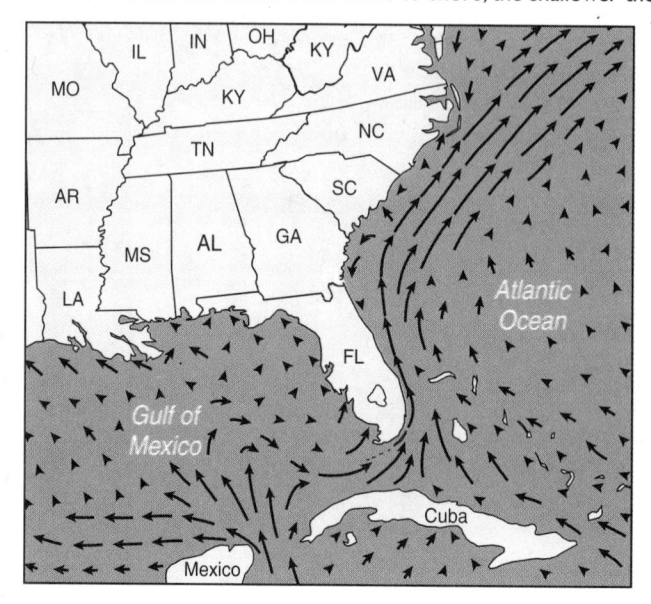

▶ The American team chose to test its water mill off the southeast coast of Florida. Why do you think they chose that location?

The current comes very close to the east coast of Florida. It should be easier to try their prototype closer to shore. Also, the long arrows show that the current is very fast near the southern tip of Florida. This means there is more energy available to convert into electrical energy. Being close to shore reduces the cost of bringing the energy to its point of use.

132

▶ Propose Explanations

ANALYZE ADVANTAGES Before students begin their analysis, draw a side view of the ocean floor showing how it drops off sharply at the edges of the continents. Explain that when choosing sites for water mills, the team of scientists must be aware of potential dangers. Point out that the scientists need to suspend and then anchor the water mills offshore; otherwise the mills will drift in the currents.

Remind students that the speed and direction of the current are indicated on the map by the length and direction of the arrows. Students will need to correctly interpret these data to explain their choice of sites.

Tell students that in addition to American scientists designing water mills off the coast of Florida, Canadian scientists are carefully choosing sites where they might develop Ocean Energy projects at sites off the coast of British Columbia, in San Francisco Bay, and in Washington state. The scientists hope to convert ocean currents to emission-free electricity.

132   CHAPTER 12 / LESSON 36

▶ Once the Gulf Stream moves past North Carolina, how does it change direction? What would this mean for scientists looking for places to put their water mills?

It moves eastward away from the coast. The electricity would have to travel a greater distance to reach shore. The ocean may be deeper, and it would be harder to place water mills that ran off a surface current on the ocean floor.

▶ **Take Action**

GIVE A NEWS REPORT You are a television science reporter. Your boss gives you two minutes of airtime to report on the water mill plan for the Gulf Stream. Write a script of what you will say. First, write an outline of your script below. Decide what pictures you will need. Remember to include Who, What, When, Where, Why, and How. Make your report interesting and accurate. When you have written your draft, have someone time you as you read it. Make sure your report is two minutes long.

Student scripts should reflect the style of television news reports while covering the "five W's" and "How."

Assessment
Skill: Generating ideas

Use the following task to assess each student's progress.

Tell students to examine the map on page 132, choose another location to test water mills, and mark the location on the map. (Other locations with a fast current close to land are north of western Cuba and between western Cuba and the Yucatan Peninsula of Mexico.)

▶ **Take Action**

GIVE A NEWS REPORT Explain that the American scientists work for a company called Gulfstreamhydro, Inc. Encourage students to do further research. For additional information and photo sources about this and similar projects, direct them to Web sites such as the following:
searider.net/waterpower.htm
www.palatkadailynews.com/pages/07162001/power.html

Students may want to incorporate this information into their news reports. Remind them to evaluate Internet sources just as critically as any written source. Suggest that they use an organizing device such as a "5 W's" chart to ensure that their script outlines are complete. (See *Reader's Handbook,* page 672.)

CHAPTER 12 / LESSON 36   133

UNIT 4 Weather and Climate

About the Photo
This dramatic lightning storm over the city of Seattle and the blizzard shown in the small photo are just two examples of severe weather conditions that students will learn about in this unit.

About the Charts
A major goal of the *Science Daybooks* is to promote reading, writing, and critical thinking skills in the context of science. The charts below describe the types of reading selections included in this unit and identify the skills and strategies used in each lesson.

How does weather affect our lives?
We consult a weather report to prepare ourselves for the day ahead—to find out if we'll need an umbrella or sunscreen or snow boots. What happens in the air above us to cause different kinds of weather? And how do people handle severe weather conditions, such as a hurricane or blizzard?

In this unit you'll explore weather and climate. Air pressure—the weight of the air pushing down on you—plays a major role in determining the weather. You'll learn how differences in air pressure produced one of the most violent storms ever to hit the Northeast and how weather forecasters tried to protect fishing boats out at sea. You'll read about other kinds of severe weather—tornadoes, hailstorms, and blizzards. You'll find out how trees can tell scientists what the climate was like thousands of years ago. Then you'll travel to the Arctic to study ice conditions that may tell scientists whether our global climate is changing.

SELECTION	READING	WRITING	APPLICATION
CHAPTER 13 • THE ATMOSPHERE			
37.	• Background information • Read a diagram	• Label a diagram	
38. "High Flyers" (science article)	• Use prior knowledge • Read a data table	• Make and analyze graphs • Make inferences	• Critical thinking—problems/solutions
39. "Riding the Wind" (NASA press release)	• Examine a satellite image • Directed reading	• Label a map • Draw conclusions	• Research • Draw and label a map
CHAPTER 14 • STORMY WEATHER			
40. "Collecting Weather Data" (fictionalized account)	• Quickwrite • Questioning	• Read air pressure maps • Defend answer	• Collect air pressure data • Analyze air pressure data
41. "Hurricane Grace" (fictionalized account)	• Relate to personal experience • Draw a sketch	• Interpret and label an air pressure map • Read a graph • Cause and effect	• Generate questions
42. "The Perfect Storm" (fictionalized account)	• Directed reading • Read for detail	• Read and interpret a map • Defend answer	• Risk analysis

THE CHAPTERS IN THIS UNIT ARE...

CHAPTER 13:
The Atmosphere
Find out: Why did James Glaisher pass out as he rode in a hot-air balloon?

CHAPTER 14:
Stormy Weather
Find out: Why was "the perfect storm" of 1991 so violent?

CHAPTER 15:
Weird Weather
Find out: On average, how many tornadoes occur each year in your state?

CHAPTER 16:
Climate Change
Find out: Why is hunting seals on the Arctic ice more dangerous now than in the past?

Answers to *Find Out* Questions

CHAPTER 13
Glaisher passed out from lack of oxygen as the balloon approached a record-breaking altitude of 7 miles (11.3 km). (pp. 138–139)

CHAPTER 14
"The perfect storm" resulted when three weather systems—a low-pressure system, a high-pressure system, and a hurricane—collided to produce unusually violent weather conditions. (pp. 147–148, 151–152)

CHAPTER 15
To answer this question, students will need to consult the map on page 158, which shows the average number of tornadoes that occur in different areas of the United States each year.

CHAPTER 16
The Arctic ice has been thinning in places where the Inuit safely hunted seals in the past. (p. 170)

SCILINKS
THE WORLD'S A CLICK AWAY

www.scilinks.org
Keyword: Current Research
Code: GSSD04

? Did You Know?
How fast a tree cricket chirps is affected by temperature. Listen to a cricket chirp. Count how many chirps it makes in 15 seconds, then add 37 to that number. Your result will be close to the actual air temperature in degrees Fahrenheit.

SELECTION	READING	WRITING	APPLICATION
CHAPTER 15 • WEIRD WEATHER			
43. "A Survivor's Story" (eyewitness account)	• Use prior knowledge • Directed reading	• Interpret a map	• Research • Create a flier
44. "The Summertime Hazard of Eastern Colorado" (climate center article)	• Brainstorming • Directed reading	• Read and interpret a histogram • Make inferences	• Make a list of scientific questions
45. "The Blizzard of 1888" (personal narrative in writing project publication)	• Directed reading • Cause and effect	• Compare and contrast • Make inferences	
CHAPTER 16 • CLIMATE CHANGE			
46. "What Trees Know" (science magazine article)	• Use prior knowledge • Sketching • Directed reading	• Use prior knowledge • Sketching • Directed reading	• Research climate change
47. "Arctic Changes" (science magazine article)	• Directed reading • Identify evidence	• Directed reading • Identify evidence	
48. "Melting Above, Melting Below" (newspaper article)	• Write a description • Main ideas	• Write a description • Main ideas	• Write a research proposal

UNIT 4 WEATHER AND CLIMATE

CHAPTER 13
Overview

The Atmosphere

LESSON 37
Feeling the Pressure?
Point of Lesson: *A barometer measures the pressure of air on objects.*

In this lesson, students learn about air pressure and study the design of Torricelli's barometer. They infer which diagram of a barometer shows higher and lower air pressure, based on the effect of air pressure on the height of a column of mercury.

Materials
Introducing the Lesson (p. 136), for the class:
▶ scale

LESSON 38
Up, Up, and Away
Point of Lesson: *Air pressure and temperature decrease as altitude increases.*

This lesson offers a graphic description of a historical balloon flight in which two men discovered firsthand that air pressure and temperature both decrease as altitude increases. Students use tables and graphs to analyze data describing conditions at high altitudes and relate those conditions to the dangerous effects on the human body, which were experienced by the two men before they returned to Earth.

Materials
Activity (p. 140), for each student:
▶ two colors of pencils
Connections (p. 140), for the class:
▶ research sources about traditional hot air balloons
▶ materials to create posters
Take Action (p. 141), for the class:
▶ PBS Nova video "Danger in the Jet Stream" (available for purchase through the ShopPBS Web site www.pbs.org)

LESSON 39
Thar She Blows!
Point of Lesson: *Differences in air pressure produce winds.*

In this lesson, students relate differences in air pressure to development of local winds, the Santa Ana winds of southern California. They examine a satellite image of the area as well as a map showing the conditions of barometric pressure that lead to these winds. Finally, they explore the interactions of the Santa Ana winds with the landscape.

Materials
Science Scope Activity (p. 143), for teacher demonstration:
▶ 250-mL flask
▶ paper towel
▶ pail or other container
▶ hot water (26°C to 40°C)
Take Action (p. 145), for the class:
▶ local almanacs or newspapers
▶ local maps

Laboratory Safety
Observe the following safety guideline when you do the Science Scope Activity demonstration in this lesson.
▶ Be very careful with the hot water to avoid burning yourself.

Science Scope Activity

Bubbles in a Bottle

NSTA has chosen a Science Scope activity related to the content in this chapter. You'll find the activity in Lesson 39, page 143.

The activity will provide observable evidence that air moves from areas of higher pressure to areas of lower pressure.

Background Information

Lesson 37

Evangelista Torricelli (1608–1647) assisted Galileo during the last three months of that scientist's life. After Galileo's death, Torricelli was invited to stay on by Galileo's employer.

Torricelli was investigating the nature of a vacuum when he developed the mercury barometer in 1643. His experiment touched off an academic controversy, as most thinkers of the day agreed with Aristotle that a vacuum was not possible in nature.

Lesson 38

Glaisher and Coxwell had made previous attempts that same year to explore the upper atmosphere, including one that took them higher than 25,000 feet.

Whether they actually reached an altitude of 37,000 feet is disputed by some. Glaisher's value was based on his estimate of the time elapsed between his last measurement while ascending (at 29,000 feet) and his first measurement while descending, as well as the rates of ascent and descent. He was unconscious for part of the period included in his estimate, and neither man knew the precise moment when the balloon stopped rising and began to fall. Nevertheless, their confirmed altitude of 29,000 feet—without oxygen—remains remarkable and is well known among both scientists and balloonists to this day.

UNIT 4 Weather and Climate
CHAPTER 13 / LESSON 37

Point of Lesson
A barometer measures the pressure of air on objects.

Focus
- Properties and changes of properties in matter
- Structure of the earth system
- History of science
- Abilities of technological design

Skills and Strategies
- Interpreting scientific illustrations
- Interpreting data
- Making and using models

Advance Preparation

Vocabulary
Make sure students understand these terms. Definitions can be found in the glossary at the end of the student book.

- air pressure
- molecule
- altitude
- temperature
- atmosphere

Materials
Gather the materials needed for *Introducing the Lesson* (p. 136).

CHAPTER 13 / LESSON 37
The Atmosphere

Feeling the Pressure?

On some days, the air presses on you with greater force, on other days with lesser force.

You may think air is just empty space, but it's actually made of molecules that have weight. Because air has weight, it pushes down on everything it touches—including people! The more air there is above you, the more it pushes down on you. As a result, air pressure is lower the higher you go in the atmosphere. At higher altitudes, air molecules are spread farther apart.

Air pressure is measured with an instrument called a barometer. The first barometer was built by Italian scientist Evangelista Torricelli in 1643. He filled a bowl with mercury, a metal that is liquid at room temperature. Then he also used mercury to fill a thin glass tube that was closed at one end. He turned the tube upside down with the open end in the bowl of mercury. The mercury did not run out—it stayed at a certain height in the tube. Above the mercury, at the top of the tube, was a vacuum—a space with no air in it. When the air pressure outside the tube increased, it pushed down more on the mercury in the bowl. As a result, the mercury went up higher in the tube. When the outside air pressure decreased, it pushed down less on the mercury in the bowl, and the mercury in the tube dropped down lower in the tube. (Caution: Do not try to repeat Torricelli's experiment! Mercury is poisonous.)

Torricelli barometer ▶

136

TEACHING PLAN pp. 136–137

INTRODUCING THE LESSON
Time: 25 minutes
Materials: scale

In this lesson, students learn that air exerts pressure on objects and how barometers measure air pressure. Ask students to define the term *air pressure* in their own words.

Some students may think that air pressure adds to the force of gravity and increases the weight of objects or holds objects down. Explain that objects do not weigh more on days with higher air pressure and less on days with lower air pressure. To illustrate this, you could have students weigh objects on days when air pressure is high and on days when it is low.

To help students understand the description of Torricelli's barometer, suggest that they refer to the diagrams on the next page as they read.

136 CHAPTER 13 / LESSON 37

▶ Explore

GET AIR Air pressure changes from day to day in the same place. These changes are measured and used in weather forecasts. Look at the two diagrams of Torricelli barometers below.

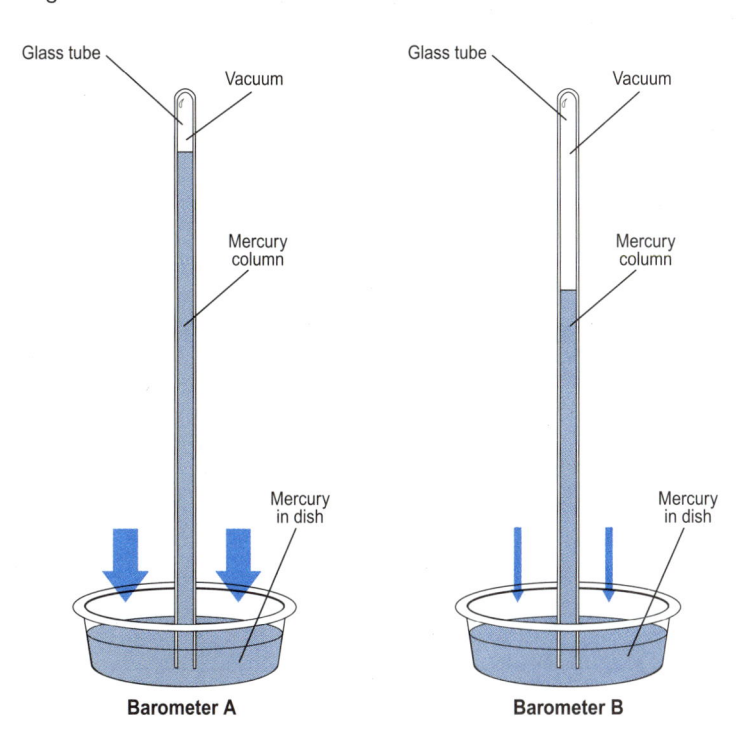

Barometer A

Barometer B

▶ Which barometer shows higher air pressure?
   Barometer A

▶ Which barometer shows lower air pressure?
   Barometer B

▶ Draw arrows on both diagrams to show how strongly the air is pushing down on the mercury. Use thick arrows for higher air pressure and thin arrows for lower air pressure.

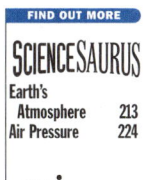

FIND OUT MORE

SCIENCESAURUS
Earth's
 Atmosphere   213
Air Pressure   224

www.scilinks.org
Keyword: Atmospheric Pressure and Winds
Code: GSED17

137

More Resources
The following resources are also available from Great Source and NSTA.

SCIENCESAURUS
Earth's Atmosphere   213
Air Pressure   224

READER'S HANDBOOK
How to Read a Diagram   602

www.scilinks.org
Keyword: Atmospheric Pressure and Winds
Code: GSED17

Assessment
Skill: Recognizing cause and effect

Use the following question to assess each student's progress:

How did Torricelli's mercury barometer measure air pressure? (Air pushing down on the mercury caused it to rise in a sealed tube. When air pressure was higher, it pushed down harder, and the mercury rose higher in the tube. When air pressure was lower, it pushed down less, and the mercury dropped down lower in the tube.)

▶ Explore

GET AIR Help students interpret the diagram by asking them to explain where the air is pushing on the mercury. (on the surface of the mercury in the open dish) Then ask them to explain how this pushes mercury up the tube. (The downward force of the air pressure on the mercury's surface pushes more mercury into the open end of the tube, and the mercury level in the tube rises.)

Have students compare their annotated diagrams to see whether they all used the arrows the same way. Point out that the arrows represent something that cannot be seen. Explain that scientific diagrams often use arrows to represent physical interactions such as pressure and speed.

CHECK UNDERSTANDING
Skill: Recognizing cause and effect
Have students draw two simple diagrams of Torricelli barometers, label one diagram *Lower Air Pressure* and the other *Higher Air Pressure,* then mark the tubes to show the mercury level in each case. (higher air pressure—higher mercury level in tube; lower air pressure—lower mercury level in tube)

CHAPTER 13 / LESSON 37   137

UNIT 4 Weather and Climate
CHAPTER 13 / LESSON 38

Point of Lesson
Air pressure and temperature decrease as altitude increases.

Focus
- Science as a human endeavor
- Structure of the earth system
- Risks and benefits
- Science and technology in society
- History of science
- Regulation and behavior

Skills and Strategies
- Making inferences
- Creating and using graphs
- Comparing and contrasting
- Interpreting data
- Predicting

Advance Preparation
Vocabulary
Make sure students understand these terms. Definitions can be found in the glossary at the end of the student book.

- air pressure
- altitude
- gas
- horizontal axis
- temperature
- vertical axis

Materials
Gather the materials needed for **Activity** (p. 140), **Connections** (p. 140), and **Take Action** (p. 141).

TEACHING PLAN pp. 138–139

CHAPTER 13 / LESSON 38
The Atmosphere

UP, UP, AND AWAY
Ride a balloon into the skies with two explorers.

In 1783, people began trying to fly by filling balloons with hot, light air. The first balloons rose only about 100 meters, but scientists kept trying. Later balloons were filled with hydrogen and other "lighter-than-air" gases. Scientists wanted to know what was above the layer of air we live in, now called the troposphere. In 1862, scientist James Glaisher and pilot Henry Coxwell had the courage to explore this high frontier.

▶ Before You Read

THE AIR UP THERE You've probably read reports or seen TV shows about people who climb Mount Everest, the highest mountain in the world at 29,028 feet (8,845 meters, 8.845 kilometers).
▶ What problem does high altitude create for mountain climbers? What do you think causes this problem?

Mountain climbers have trouble breathing at high altitudes. The air at the top of a high mountain is "thinner" than the air at the base of the mountain.

▶ Read

In 1862, Henry Coxwell and James Glaisher flew a balloon 1.5 miles (2.5 kilometers) higher than the summit of Mount Everest.

HIGH FLYERS

As Glaisher patiently recorded what his instruments told him, the four mile [6.4 km] and five mile [8 km] marks were passed. Both men knew they were in line for a record. As Coxwell climbed into the rigging to free the valve line, Glaisher's eyesight began to deteriorate. He began to lose the power to move his arms and legs. His voice goes, his hearing fades. He passes out....

138

INTRODUCING THE LESSON
This lesson describes how air pressure and temperature vary with altitude and the physiological effects of high altitude on the human body. Lead a class discussion about hot air balloons. Explain that "lighter-than-air" gases are those for which a given volume of the gas weighs less than the same volume of air under the same conditions. Students may think that cooler air is always "heavier" or more dense than warmer air. Explain that this is true only when both the cooler air and the warmer air are under the same conditions.

▶ Before You Read
THE AIR UP THERE Encourage students to discuss what they know about the effect of high altitude on mountain climbers. If your school is located at high altitude, ask students how people who come from lower altitudes can be affected by visiting your area. Otherwise, have students who have lived in or visited places at high altitude describe the differences between high altitude and low altitude. For example, students may report that visitors to high altitude may have trouble catching their breath and may have to be careful to avoid "altitude sickness."

▶ Read
Have students compare the height reached by the balloonists and the height of Mount Everest with distances they are familiar with, such as the distance between their home and the school or a shopping center. Students probably will know such distances in miles. Let them convert miles to feet,

138 CHAPTER 13 / LESSON 38

Coxwell, in the rigging, is frozen almost helpless with the cold. His hands are turning blue and black. He tumbles, rather than climbs down into the basket. The balloon is still rising. Coxwell seizes the gas valve rope in his teeth and pulls. The valve opens and the balloon begins to descend.

Neither man appreciates the situation until afterwards when the instruments are read. But they have reached the 37,000 feet [11,300 m] mark. They are the first men in the stratosphere.

Without oxygen, without pressure suits, without a protective cabin, seven miles [11.3 km] high, they have penetrated into Jumbo Jet country.

rigging: the ropes that tie the balloon to its basket
valve line: the tube that opens the balloon to release hot air
deteriorate: become worse
basket: the open compartment at the base of the balloon that carries the balloonists
seizes: grabs
descend: move downward
stratosphere: the layer of the atmosphere above the troposphere
pressure suits: special clothing worn to provide oxygen at a safe air pressure
penetrated: entered

From: Marion, Fulgence. *Wonderful Balloon Ascents: or the Conquest of the Skies.*

NOTEZONE
Underline the words that tell how one of the explorers suffered from a lack of oxygen.

FIND OUT MORE
SCIENCESAURUS
Earth's Atmosphere 213
Composition of the Atmosphere 214
Layers of the Atmosphere 215
Kinds of Graphs 390
Line Graphs 394
Making a Line Graph 395–399

Enrichment
Ask students to draw a design for a hot air balloon using common household materials. For example, students could design a hot air balloon using a plastic dry cleaning bag and a hairdryer. Students' designs should reflect an understanding of how air temperature and pressure enable balloons to rise. If students' designs can be constructed and operated safely, let students build and demonstrate their balloons.

▶ Explore

READ A DATA TABLE This table shows the measurements you might make if you went up in a balloon. The abbreviation *hPa* stands for hectopascals, a unit used to measure air pressure.

▶ **Which altitude on the data table is closest to the highest point that Glaisher and Coxwell reached?**
11,000 m

▶ **What would the temperature have been at that altitude?** −56.5°C

▶ **Where on Earth's surface do you think you might find temperatures that low?**
near the North and South poles or on Mt. Everest

Altitude	Air Temperature	Air Pressure
0 m	15°C	1,013 hPa
1,000 m	8.5°C	900 hPa
2,000 m	2°C	800 hPa
3,000 m	−4.5°C	700 hPa
4,000 m	−11°C	620 hPa
5,000 m	−17.5°C	540 hPa
6,000 m	−24.5°C	470 hPa
7,000 m	−30.5°C	410 hPa
8,000 m	−37°C	360 hPa
9,000 m	−43.5°C	310 hPa
10,000 m	−50°C	260 hPa
11,000 m	−56.5°C	230 hPa
12,000 m	−56.5°C	190 hPa

---

meters, and kilometers for comparison with the heights given in Before You Read and the excerpt. (1 mile = 5,280 feet; 1,609 meters; 1.6 kilometers)

Check students' responses to the NoteZone task to make sure they did not identify the problems Coxwell suffered as a result of the freezing temperatures. Then ask students why a lack of oxygen caused Glaisher's problems. (The brain needs oxygen to function properly.)

▶ Explore

READ A DATA TABLE Explain that standard air pressure at sea level is defined as 1,013 hPa, the value given in the table for the pressure at 0 m. Explain that air pressure can also be measured in other units, such as atmospheres (atm), inches or millimeters of mercury, millibars, or pounds per square inch.

Students may need to convert −56.5°C to °F to answer the last question with confidence. Show students how to calculate the conversion: °F = $\frac{9}{5}$(°C) + 32. (−56.5°C = −69.7°F) Encourage students to convert all the temperatures in the table so they have a better understanding of the temperatures faced by the balloonists.

CHECK UNDERSTANDING
Skill: Comparing and contrasting
Ask students to describe the relationship between altitude and air pressure. (As altitude increases, air pressure decreases.)

CHAPTER 13 / LESSON 38

CHAPTER 13 / LESSON 38

More Resources

The following resources are also available from Great Source.

ScienceSaurus

Earth's Atmosphere	213
Composition of the Atmosphere	214
Layers of the Atmosphere	215
Kinds of Graphs	390
Line Graphs	394
Making a Line Graph	395–399

Math On Call

Interpreting Data	307
Temperature	567

Connections

Time: will vary
Materials: research sources about traditional hot air balloons; materials to create posters

SOCIAL STUDIES Hot air balloons are used in celebrations by different cultures around the world. Paper balloons called sky lanterns are used in Taiwan to celebrate events such as high school graduation and the Yuan Hsiao Festival that occurs at the end of the Chinese New Year celebration. These balloons are powered by hot air produced by igniting fuel-soaked fabric that has been tied to the bars

(continued on page 141)

Teaching Plan pp. 140–141

▶ Activity

Time: 30–40 minutes
Materials: two colors of pencils

- ▶ Make sure students understand which is the horizontal axis and which is the vertical axis.
- ▶ If students have difficulty creating appropriate titles for their graphs, emphasize that each graph shows a relationship between altitude and one other variable.

ANALYZE YOUR GRAPHS Review students' answers in a class discussion. Draw two sets of axes on the board, and have students tell you how to draw the line that represents the data on each graph.

MAKE INFERENCES To help students visualize why low air pressure means that there is more space between the air molecules, draw a model on the board. First, draw two boxes of equal size. Explain that the boxes represent the same volume of air. In the first box, draw several small circles to represent molecules of air. Then ask students what the drawing would look like if the air pressure were lower and there were more space between the molecules. Draw this in the second box. Point out that increasing the space between the molecules but keeping the volume the same means that there are fewer air molecules in that volume of space.

▶ Activity

MAKE A GRAPH

Have you ever plotted two kinds of data on the same type of graph? Try it with air pressure and temperature. Use the two grids below to graph the data in the table on page 139.

What You Need:
- two colors of pencils

What to Do:
1. On both graphs, label the horizontal axis "Altitude (meters)."
2. On the horizontal axis, find the highest point that Coxwell and Glaisher reached. Write "highest point" below this altitude.
3. Label the left graph's vertical axis "Air Temperature (°C)."
4. Label the right graph's vertical axis "Air Pressure (hPa)."
5. While plotting one graph, place a strip of paper over the data for the other graph to avoid confusion.
6. Use one color pencil on the left graph. Plot a point for the temperature at each altitude listed in the table. Then draw a line to connect the points.
7. Use a second color pencil for the right graph. Plot a point for the air pressure at each altitude. Then draw a line to connect the points.
8. Add a title to each graph.

Relationship Between Altitude and Air Temperature

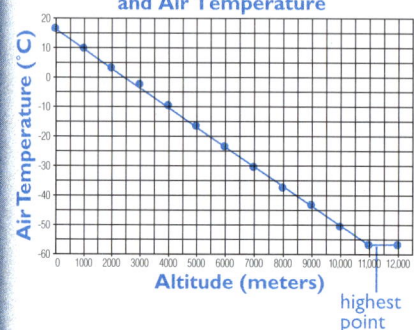

Relationship Between Altitude and Air Pressure

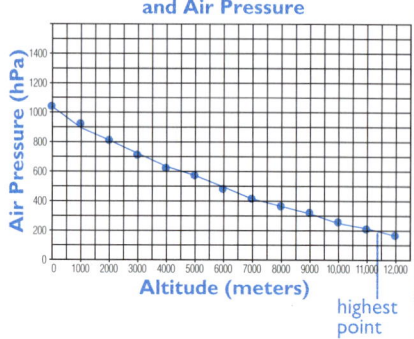

ANALYZE YOUR GRAPHS

▶ How does air pressure change as you go higher into the atmosphere?

Air pressure decreases as you go higher.

▶ How does air temperature change as you go higher into the atmosphere?

Air temperature also decreases as you go higher.

MAKE INFERENCES During their balloon ride, Glaisher suffered from altitude sickness. Altitude sickness is caused by not enough oxygen in the air that a person is breathing.

▶ *Was it the change in air temperature or the change in air pressure that caused Glaisher's altitude sickness? Explain your answer. (Hint: Recall what you learned in the previous lesson about air molecules at higher altitudes.)*

It was the change in pressure. As the balloon rose, the air pressure around the men became lower. Low air pressure means the air molecules were farther part. Each lungful of air contained less oxygen.

▶ Take Action

REAL WORLD PROBLEMS Glaisher and Coxwell had many problems on their balloon ride. Imagine taking a high-altitude balloon ride today.

▶ *What problems would you want to avoid? What do you think you could do to prevent those problems? Fill in the graphic organizer below.* *Answers will vary. Examples are shown below.*

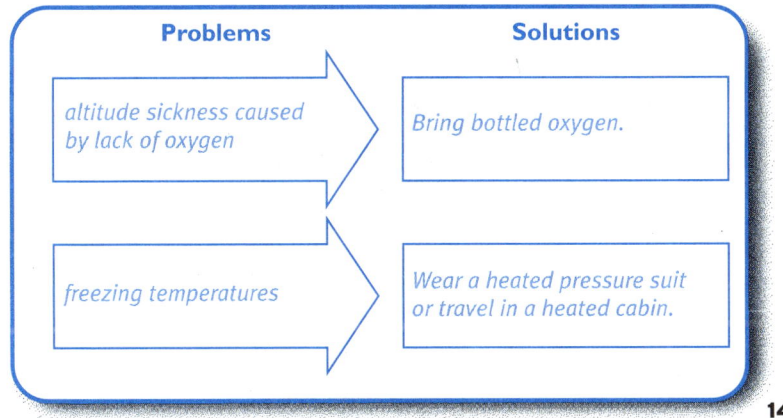

Problems	Solutions
altitude sickness caused by lack of oxygen	Bring bottled oxygen.
freezing temperatures	Wear a heated pressure suit or travel in a heated cabin.

(continued from page 140)

that hold the balloon open; the balloon glows and rises into the night air. In Greece, the same type of flying lantern, called an aerostat, is used to celebrate Easter. Encourage students to research these festivals and find pictures of the balloons and of the celebrations in which hundreds or thousands of balloons are launched at the same time. Have students create a poster or other visual display to share their findings with the class.

Assessment
Skill: Making inferences

Use the following questions to assess each student's progress:

How does the air pressure at the base of a mountain compare with the air pressure at the top of the mountain? (The air pressure at the base of the mountain is higher.) *How do you think the air temperatures compare?* (The temperature at the base of the mountain is higher.)

▶ Take Action

Time: 45 minutes
Materials: PBS Nova video "Danger in the Jet Stream" (available for purchase through the ShopPBS Web site www.pbs.org)

REAL WORLD PROBLEMS Have students watch the video and identify the problems faced by the balloonists as well as their solutions. As an alternative to the video, students could do Internet research on the great balloon race of the late 1990s, when different teams of balloonists attempted to be the first to travel around the world. The following PBS Nova Web site is a good place for students to begin their research:
www.pbs.org/wgbh/nova/balloon/

UNIT 4 Weather and Climate

CHAPTER 13 / LESSON 39

Point of Lesson
Differences in air pressure produce winds.

Focus
- Structure of the earth system
- Understanding about science and technology
- Transfer of energy

Skills and Strategies
- Interpreting scientific illustrations
- Making inferences
- Interpreting data
- Drawing conclusions
- Communicating

Advance Preparation

Vocabulary
Make sure students understand these terms. Definitions can be found in the glossary at the end of the student book.
- air mass
- air pressure
- atmosphere
- cloud
- satellite
- wind

Materials
Gather the materials needed for *Science Scope Activity* (p. 143) and *Take Action* (p. 145).

TEACHING PLAN pp. 142–143

INTRODUCING THE LESSON
In this lesson, students learn that wind is produced by differences in air pressure. They examine typical wind patterns in southern California and in their own area. Ask students to describe their own experiences with high winds, including what the weather was like at the time. Students may think that cold temperatures produce fast winds. Explain that wind is caused by differences in air pressure, which in turn are caused by the uneven heating of Earth's surface.

CHAPTER 13 / LESSON 39
The Atmosphere

Thar She Blows!

Hot-air balloon rides, kite flying, sailing—all these activities depend on wind.

Heat from the sun warms Earth's surface. Heat from the surface radiates into the air above it, heating the atmosphere. As the atmosphere warms, the air becomes less dense. This less dense air rises. As a result, the place it rose from becomes an area of lower pressure. Cooler air—which is more dense—flows into the lower pressure area. Air moving from an area of higher pressure to an area of lower pressure produces wind. When the difference in air pressure between the two areas increases, the wind blows stronger from the higher to the lower pressure areas.

▶ Before You Read

EXAMINE A SATELLITE IMAGE This photograph taken from a satellite shows the California coast and Pacific Ocean. The wispy grey areas extending out from the coastline are clouds of airborne dust. The bright white areas at the bottom of the photograph are regular clouds of water droplets.

▶ Where do you think the dust comes from? What moves the dust out over the ocean?

The dust comes from the land areas. Wind blows the dust out over the ocean.

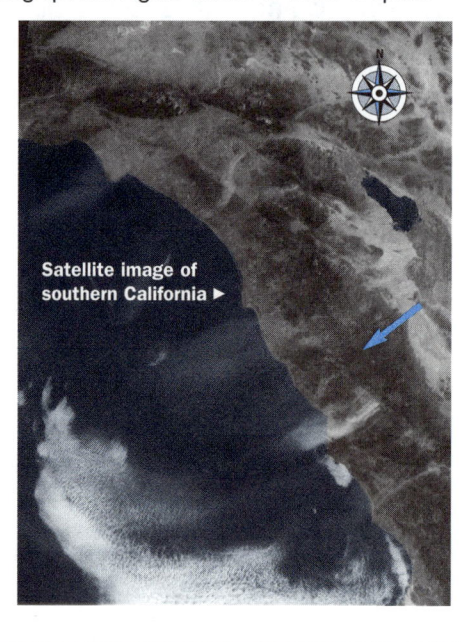

◀ Satellite image of southern California ▶

▶ Before You Read

EXAMINE A SATELLITE IMAGE To orient students to the satellite image, have them first identify the locations of the water and land areas in the photograph. Then have them identify the dust clouds.

Students may enjoy seeing satellite images of their own area. You can obtain USGS images of most parts of the United States at the following Web site: terraserver.homeadvisor.msn.com

Have students identify local landmarks such as lakes, mountains, or other geographic features.

> **Read**

Winds whip through the narrow canyons along the coast of southern California.

Riding the Wind

Any allergy-stricken southern Californian can tell you when the Santa Ana winds are blowing. Recently, Santa Anas blew through the southland at speeds [greater than] 80 kilometers (50 miles) per hour.

A new image from [a satellite camera] on NASA's *Terra* spacecraft shows the pattern of airborne dust stirred up by Santa Ana winds on February 9, 2002. These dry, northeasterly winds usually occur in late fall and winter when a high pressure system forms in the Great Basin between the Sierra Nevada and Rocky Mountain ranges. The strength of the winds enables them to pick up and relocate surface dust.

allergy: extreme sensitivity to certain substances
Santa Ana winds: local winds that blow from the northeast in southern California
southland: the area in the south of a region
high pressure system: a large mass of dense air

From: "Santa Ana Winds Swirl Over Southern California."
NASA Jet Propulsion Laboratory. California Institute of Technology.
(www.jpl.nasa.gov/releases/2002/release_2002_43.html)

NOTEZONE

Winds are named for the direction they blow from. Draw an arrow on the photo on page 142 to show the direction that the Santa Ana winds blow.

Santa Ana winds blow from the northeast, so the arrow should point to the southwest.

FIND OUT MORE
SCIENCESAURUS
Air Pressure 224
Wind 225

Science Scope Activity

Bubbles in a Bottle
Time: 45 minutes
Materials: 250 mL flask, paper towel, pail or other container, hot water (26°C to 40°C)

Procedure
Do this activity as a demonstration.

1. Fill the flask approximately halfway with hot water.
2. Fold a paper towel in half and lay it flat on a level desktop or tabletop.
3. Swirl the water in the flask several times and empty it into the container. Immediately turn the flask upside down and set it down on the paper towel.
4. Have students carefully observe the setup and record their observations. (After 20–30 seconds, bubbles will appear inside the flask. Then the paper towel will begin to rise inside the flask.)

Ask students to explain their observations. (As the warm air inside the flask cooled, the molecules slowed, creating an area of low pressure inside the flask. The higher-pressure air outside the flask then pushed air into it. The air entering the flask formed the bubbles. Eventually, the pressure difference became so great that the towel itself was pushed inward.)

Area shown in satellite image

> **Read**

Encourage students to jot down questions as they read. Then have them share their questions and help each other find answers. For example, students might ask: *How can allergy sufferers tell when the Santa Ana winds are blowing?* (The winds blow dust or other allergens into the area.)

Ask students what they learned about high pressure systems from the reading. (A high pressure system is a large mass of dense air. In late fall and winter, a high pressure system forms in the Great Basin between the mountain ranges and produces winds.) Ask students what they think a low pressure system is. (Students should reason that a low pressure system is a large mass of less-dense air.)

To help students complete the NoteZone activity, point out the compass rose in the upper right corner of the photograph on page 142.

CHECK UNDERSTANDING
Skill: Making inferences
Ask: *What produces wind?* (air moving from an area of higher pressure to an area of lower pressure) *What do you think causes a very strong wind?* (a greater difference in air pressure between two areas)

CHAPTER 13 / LESSON 39

CHAPTER 13 / LESSON 39

More Resources
The following resources are also available from Great Source.

ScienceSaurus
Air Pressure	224
Wind	225

Reader's Handbook
Elements of Graphics:
Diagram	552
Map	555

Write Source 2000
Using Maps	491

Connections

LITERATURE Winds have been portrayed as characters in folktales and literature of many cultures. For example, the Four Winds are common characters in the folktales of Nordic cultures and Native American tribes. Encourage students to read folktales that describe how the winds got their names, where they came from, or what roles they played in the lives of humans. The Native American tales *The Wind-Blower* and *How the Four Winds Were Named* and the Nordic tales *The Lad Who Went to the North Wind* and *East o' the Sun West o' the Moon* are available online through the Baldwin Project at: www.mainlesson.com

TEACHING PLAN pp. 144–145

▶ **Explore**

AIR PRESSURE AND THE SANTA ANAS The map below shows air pressure readings. Locations with the same air pressure are connected with lines called *isobars*. The isobars outline large air masses and show whether the air pressure in the masses is high or low.

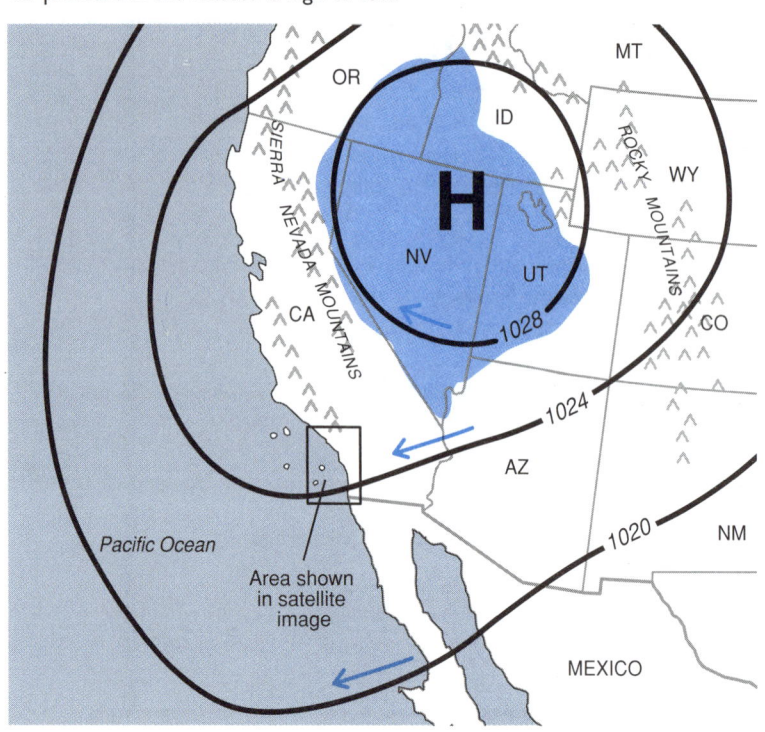

The Great Basin area of the United States lies between the Sierra Nevada Mountains and the Rocky Mountains. It includes all of Nevada and parts of the surrounding states.

▶ Use a colored pencil to lightly shade the Great Basin.

A high pressure system, like the one over the Great Basin on the map, is a large mass of dense air. The dense air sinks and moves outward from the center of the high in a clockwise direction. This flow of air causes wind.

▶ Draw an arrow on each isobar line to show the direction in which the wind is moving in the Great Basin high pressure system.

   The arrows should show a clockwise direction of flow.

144

▶ **Explore**

AIR PRESSURE AND THE SANTA ANAS
After students have drawn arrows on the isobars, tell them that in the Northern Hemisphere, air moves in a clockwise direction around areas of high pressure. In the Southern Hemisphere, it moves in a counter-clockwise direction. Explain that this weather pattern is known as an *anticyclone*, and it usually results in clear, sunny weather.

▶ **Propose Explanations**

DUST IN THE WIND You may want to give students more background on the Santa Ana winds as they work on this section. The Santa Ana winds are dry, usually hot winds that carry dust westward through the canyons in the spring and again late in the fall. The high-pressure weather system over the Great Basin, called the Great Basin High, is usually quite stable; energy from the sun maintains the high air pressure in the system. However, the stability of this system can change whenever there is a low-pressure system over the Pacific Ocean off the coast of California. The difference in air pressure between the low-pressure system off the coast and the high-pressure system over the Great Basin causes air to move through the mountain passes and toward the coast.

Explain that the relationship between wildfires and the Santa Ana winds is complex. The hot, dry winds help create the conditions for the fires by drying out the vegetation as they blow toward the coast. The winds also speed up as they move through tight, twisting canyons, which fans the flames. When

144   CHAPTER 13 / LESSON 39

▶ Propose Explanations

DUST IN THE WIND Look again at the satellite image on page 142. The darker areas are mountains covered with trees and other plants. Areas of the Great Basin east of the mountains look lighter because they have few or no trees and other plants.

▶ Did the dust shown in the photograph come from the mountains or from the Great Basin? Explain your reasoning.

From the Great Basin; the soil there is not protected and held down by trees and other plants, so winds blowing over the soil can easily pick up dust and carry it away.

▶ Santa Ana winds move through narrow canyons. As they do, they pick up speed. How would the Santa Ana winds affect any wildfires in that area?

The winds would make the fires flare up and spread quickly.

▶ Take Action

INVESTIGATE YOUR LOCAL WINDS The Santa Ana winds are called local winds because they occur in a small area. Sea breezes are another type of local wind. They occur in areas near the ocean. Mountain breezes and valley breezes are other examples of local winds.

Research local winds in your area. Find out what kind of wind it is (a sea breeze or valley breeze, for example) and when it blows—the time of day or season of the year. Find out what causes the wind. Draw and label a simple map of your area to show the direction and pattern of your local winds.

145

---

the gusty winds change direction, flames are sent into new areas. In addition, the fires have an effect on the winds. The flames heat the air, and the warmer air rises so that more air moves in to replace the rising air. This creates more gusts, which cause the fire to spread even farther and faster.

▶ Take Action

Time: 40–45 minutes
Materials: local almanacs or newspapers, local maps

INVESTIGATE YOUR LOCAL WINDS To help students get started on this activity, have a brainstorming session in which students try to remember wind patterns in your area during the previous year. Use the following questions to prompt students' ideas: *Do you remember any especially windy days during the last year? When were they?*

Assessment

Skill: Recognizing cause and effect

Use the following questions to assess each student's progress:

What does an isobar on a weather map represent? (all the points with the same air pressure) *Why are the air pressure readings important?* (Differences in air pressure cause winds.)

What else was happening with the weather? Did the wind affect what you were doing? How?

Help students find resources, such as local almanacs, newspapers, or Internet weather sites. If possible, invite a local meteorologist to visit the class and answer students' questions about local winds. You may want to provide students with copies of local maps that they can use as the basis for their own maps.

CHAPTER 13 / LESSON 39   145

CHAPTER 14
Overview

Stormy Weather

LESSON 40
Predicting a Storm
Point of Lesson: *Meteorologists use many forms of data to forecast weather.*

In this lesson, students examine the kinds of weather data that were used in predicting and tracking "the perfect storm" of October 1991. They describe the location of Hurricane Grace on a satellite image and interpret an air pressure map of conditions leading up to the storm to identify where strong winds may develop. Students have the opportunity to collect their own air pressure readings and relate changes in air pressure to changes in weather.

Materials
Read (p. 147), for the class:
- map that includes the eastern United States, Canada, and the western Atlantic Ocean

Science Scope Activity (p. 147 and p. 149), for each pair:
- Web-Based Hurricane Investigation Sheet (copymaster pages 228–229)
- Internet access

Explore (p.148), for the class:
- map used in Read (p. 147)
- local weather maps

Connections (p.148), for the class:
- copy of Sebastian Junger's *The Perfect Storm, A True Story of Men Against the Sea*

Propose Explanations (p.149), for the class:
- barometer

Take Action (p.149), for the class:
- barometer (optional)

LESSON 41
A Storm Like No Other
Point of Lesson: *When weather systems collide, unusually powerful storms can form.*

When Hurricane Grace collided with a cold front, the hurricane changed direction, producing 80-knot (148 km/h) winds and 9-meter (39-foot) waves. The fast-moving hurricane then ran into a storm off Sable Island, near Nova Scotia. The combination of these three weather systems created one of the most violent storms of the century. In this lesson, students examine the causes for the extreme wind speeds and the relationship between wind speed and wave height.

Materials
Read (p. 151), for the class:
- 100-ft tape measure

Explore (p. 152), for the class:
- map used in Read (p. 147)
- research sources about Hurricane Grace

LESSON 42
At Sea in a Storm
Point of Lesson: *Many factors influence how people react to dangerous weather.*

In this lesson, students consider the pressures on the crew of the *Andrea Gail* and the options they had for dealing with the weather conditions, as recreated by the author of *The Perfect Storm*. Although the weather was extremely dangerous, the captain, crew, and their families also faced the risk of unbearable financial loss if the swordfish spoiled on the way home. Students compare the last known location of the *Andrea Gail* with the path of "the perfect storm" and speculate, with the author, on the fate of the boat.

Materials
- none

Science Scope Activity

Science on the Web: Exploring Hurricane Data

NSTA has chosen a Science Scope *activity related to the content in this chapter. You'll find the activity in Lesson 40, pages 147 and 149.* This activity helps students understand complex relationships in science and involves them in current events. Students use actual scientific data to complete a three-part, inquiry-based activity about hurricanes—how they are formed, how they are categorized, and where they are occurring today.

Have students compare and contrast their hurricane data to look for patterns. Then ask them to generate some questions of personal interest. For example: How have the worst hurricanes affected people? What areas experience the most hurricanes? How are hurricanes related to El Niño?

(continued on page 147)

Background Information

Lesson 40

Until the mid-20th century, hurricane reports were available only from ships that had escaped them in the ocean. In 1943 an airplane flew through a hurricane for the first time and recorded wind speed, temperature, and the location of the eye. Now weather data are collected by satellites and weather buoys and are interpreted by supercomputers, allowing time for preparation in areas that may lie in a storm's path.

Lessons 41 and 42

Bob Case, the now-retired meteorologist who named "the perfect storm," estimates that the conditions creating the storm occur only once every 50–100 years. If the timing or tracking of any of the three weather events that came together to form the storm had been different, the storm would not have reached the epic proportions it did. Another unusual aspect of the storm was its path. Storms generally travel from west to east across the Northeast; "the perfect storm" moved from east to west, as shown on page 155 of the student book.

UNIT 4 Weather and Climate

CHAPTER 14 / LESSON 40

Point of Lesson
Meteorologists use many forms of data to forecast weather.

Focus
- Natural hazards
- Structure of the earth system
- Science as a human endeavor
- Change, constancy, and measurement
- Understanding about science and technology

Skills and Strategies
- Interpreting scientific illustrations
- Interpreting data
- Comparing and contrasting
- Making inferences
- Collecting and recording data
- Predicting
- Creating and using tables

Advance Preparation

Vocabulary
Make sure students understand these terms. Definitions can be found in the glossary at the end of the student book.
- air pressure
- atmosphere
- hurricane
- prediction
- satellite
- weather

(continued on page 147)

TEACHING PLAN pp. 146–147

CHAPTER 14 / LESSON 40
Stormy Weather

Predicting a Storm

Weather is more predictable if you have the right tools.

A meteorologist studies the atmosphere and weather and makes weather predictions. Once in a while, a prediction will surprise a meteorologist. Meteorologist Bob Case worked for the National Weather Service back in 1991, when "the perfect storm" hit. In fact, he came up with the phrase "the perfect storm." Case's job was to forecast the weather for the New England states and the ocean alongside them. Reports came from a powerful computer in Maryland. Case read the data and knew what was coming. In spite of the sunny weather along the coast, a big storm was forming out at sea.

At the same time, fishing boats, huge ocean cargo ships, and sailboats were out on the ocean. All used weather reports to plan their routes and stay out of a storm's way. They depended on Bob Case's forecasts to make those decisions.

▶ **Before You Read**

WEATHER REPORT Meteorologists use many kinds of information to make their predictions. These predictions are used for weather forecasts on television, the radio, the Web, and in newspapers.

▶ *Think about the weather forecasts you have seen, read, or heard. List all the kinds of weather information presented. Describe the sorts of weather images that are used.*

Information—temperature, wind speed and direction, precipitation,

air pressure, humidity, dew point. Images—satellite images of clouds,

precipitation, weather maps using symbols, radar images.

▼ An approaching storm off Newport, RI

146

INTRODUCING THE LESSON
This lesson explains how meteorologists go about collecting and interpreting weather data, including satellite images and air pressure maps. The lesson also investigates how barometric pressure readings are used in weather forecasts.

Ask students if anyone has seen the movie *The Perfect Storm*. Ask: *Why was the storm called "the perfect storm"?* (The conditions at sea came together to form the perfect conditions for such a storm.) *How does the movie depict the author's ideas about what might have happened?* (by portraying the conversations between the men on the *Andrea Gail* and other everyday details)

Ask: *How accurately can scientists predict large and dangerous storms?* Students may believe that advanced technology is able to pinpoint the exact path of a storm. Explain that in the hours before a hurricane makes landfall, an accurate forecast can predict the storm's position only to within 50 miles (31 km) and the wind speed within 8 miles (5 km) per hour.

▶ **Before You Read**

WEATHER REPORT To help students describe weather forecasts, you may want to have weather reports on hand from local newspapers or printouts from www.weather.com for your area. The DataStreme Project from the American Meteorological Society at www.amet.soc.org/dstreme/ provides detailed daily weather maps that highlight a wide range of weather data.

146   CHAPTER 14 / LESSON 40

Read

Here's how Bob Case got the information he needed to predict what he later named "the perfect storm."

Collecting Weather Data

October 28th is a sharp, sunny day in Boston, temperatures in the fifties with a stiff wind blowing off the ocean. A senior meteorologist named Bob Case is crisscrossing the carpeted room, consulting with the various meteorologists on duty that day. Most of them are seated at heavy blue consoles staring...at columns of numbers—barometric pressure, dew point, visibility—scrolling down computer screens....

A satellite photo of a hurricane about to clobber the coast of Maryland hangs in...[Case's] office. He is responsible for issuing regional forecasts based on satellite imagery and a nationwide system...[of weather] data-collection points....

Since early the previous day, Case has been watching something called a "short-wave trough aloft" slide eastward from the Great Lakes. On satellite photos it looks like an S-curve in the line of clear dry air moving south from Canada....The trough moves east at forty miles [64 km] an hour, strengthening as it goes. It follows the Canadian border to Montreal, cuts east across Northern Maine, crosses the Bay of Fundy, and traverses Nova Scotia throughout the early hours of October 28th. By dawn an all-out gale is raging north of Sable Island.

console: a monitor and keyboard that are connected to a computer system
barometric pressure: a measure of the pressure that air exerts in a certain place at a certain time
dew point: the temperature at which water vapor changes to liquid water
visibility: the clearness of the atmosphere
satellite imagery: pictures produced with data collected by satellites
trough: an elongated area of low barometric pressure
traverses: goes across
gale: a strong wind with speeds up to 87 km/h

From: Junger, Sebastian. *The Perfect Storm: A True Story of Men Against the Sea.* Harper Collins.

NOTEZONE
Jot down a question about the reading to ask your teacher.

FIND OUT MORE
SCIENCESAURUS
Meteorology	212
Weather	218
Collecting Weather Data	219
Weather Maps and Symbols	220
Air Pressure	224
Wind	225

147

(continued from page 146)

Materials
Gather the materials needed for *Read* (p. 147), *Science Scope Activity* (p. 147 and p. 149), *Explore* (p. 148), *Connections* (p. 148), *Propose Explanations* (p. 149), and *Take Action* (p. 149).

Science Scope Activity

Science on the Web: Exploring Hurricane Data
Time: 45 minutes
Materials: Web-Based Hurricane Investigation Sheet (copymaster pages 228–229), Internet access

Procedure
Give each pair of students a copy of the Web-Based Hurricane Investigation Sheet and the following instructions:

Part 1 investigates what a hurricane is. Log onto www.usatoday.com/weather/video/whurdev.htm and observe the animated simulations. Record the answers in Part 1 of the Investigation Sheet.

Part 2 investigates how scientists categorize hurricanes using charts that summarize hurricanes for the season. Log onto www.weather.unisys.com/hurricane/index.html, investigate the scientific data, and record the answers in Part 2 of the Investigation Sheet.

(continued on page 149)

Read

Time: 5–10 minutes
Materials: map that includes the eastern United States, Canada, and the western Atlantic Ocean

Have students find the hurricane's location and the trough's path on the map. Point out the location of Sable Island. Explain to students that the term "trough aloft" means that at that time, the trough did not reach the ground.

As students read through the passage, have them underline examples of weather data that Bob Case studied as he tracked the storm. (barometric pressure, dew point, visibility, satellite imagery, and the movement and position of the trough) Ask students what additional data might help Case monitor and predict the storm. (wind speed, temperature, speed at which the storm is moving)

CHECK UNDERSTANDING
Skill: Concept mapping
Have students make a concept map titled "Weather Predicting." Have them write the kinds of information that Bob Case used in predicting "the perfect storm." (Students' maps may include barometric pressure, dew point, visibility, temperature, wind speed and direction, precipitation, satellite images, and humidity.)

CHAPTER 14 / LESSON 40   147

CHAPTER 14 / LESSON 40

More Resources
The following resources are also available from Great Source.

ScienceSaurus
Meteorology	212
Weather	218
Collecting Weather Data	219
Weather Maps and Symbols	220
Air Pressure	224
Wind	225

Reader's Handbook
Elements of Textbooks: Maps	163

Math on Call
Temperature	567

Connections
Time: will vary
Materials: copy of Sebastian Junger's *The Perfect Storm, A True Story of Men Against the Sea*

LITERATURE Obtain a copy of Junger's book. Have students search for excerpts that describe the weather conditions leading up to the storm. Ask volunteers to give a dramatic reading of the excerpts they chose.

▶ Explore

INTERPRETING SATELLITE IMAGERY
The satellite image at the right shows Hurricane Grace off the coast of the eastern United States.

▶ **What does Hurricane Grace look like on this satellite image?**
It looks like a spiral or pinwheel of white clouds.

▶ **Describe the location and size of Hurricane Grace. Use a U.S. map as a reference.**
Hurricane Grace is over the Atlantic Ocean to the east of North Carolina.
It is about as large as all of the southeastern states together.

READING AIR PRESSURE MAPS
Barometric pressure is an important factor in predicting the weather. If barometric pressure is high or rising, there usually will be sunny skies and dry weather. If barometric pressure is low or falling, there usually will be clouds and stormy weather.

Study the map. Each line, called an *isobar*, connects places with the same barometric pressure. When the line makes a complete circle, the area inside the line is labeled either H or L. H stands for the center of a high-pressure area. L stands for the center of a low-pressure area.

▶ **Where on the map do you see lows?**
over the Atlantic Ocean east of Georgia and over Nova Scotia

▶ **Where on the map do you see highs?**
over the Atlantic Ocean far to the east of New England and over Quebec

Air flows from areas of higher pressure into areas of lower pressure. The closer the isobars are, the stronger the wind.

▶ **Where are the isobars very close together on this map?**
between the high over Quebec and the low over Nova Scotia

148

TEACHING PLAN pp. 148–149

▶ Explore

Time: 25 minutes
Materials: map used in Read (p. 147)

INTERPRETING SATELLITE IMAGERY
Have students note the location and size of Hurricane Grace by drawing a circle on the map they used in Read. Have students use the distance scale to determine the size of Hurricane Grace. In addition to the Web sites listed for the Science Scope Activity on pages 147 and 149, list the following Web sites that show additional satellite imagery:

www.usatoday.com/weather/satpic/wsatcar.htm
www.usatoday.com/weather/satpic/wsatusae.htm

Ask students to compare the satellite pictures on the Web sites with the photo of the hurricane on page 148.

Time: 20 minutes
Materials: local weather maps

READING AIR PRESSURE MAPS Have students locate the isobars and note the high and low pressure zones on local weather maps. Explain that the numbers at the end of the isobars represent the recorded air pressure data. You may want to point out other weather map symbols such as those that indicate warm and cold fronts and wind speed and direction. Weather maps also show areas of cloud cover and precipitation.

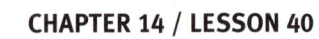

148   CHAPTER 14 / LESSON 40

▶ Propose Explanations

THINK IT OVER

▶ How does having outlines of U.S. states and Canadian provinces make it easier for meteorologists to interpret the satellite images?

Outlining the states and provinces lets meteorologists see where clouds and storms are located and how big a storm is.

Surface barometric pressure readings come into government weather offices several times a day. In the Atlantic Ocean there are floating buoys with instruments that measure and transmit pressure readings every two hours. Weather forecasters like Bob Case watch these readings looking for changes. From his Boston office, Case watched the barometric pressure drop over the ocean near Nova Scotia, Canada.

▶ What kind of weather would a meteorologist have predicted for boats and ships in that area of the ocean? Explain.

They would have predicted bad weather, since falling barometric pressure usually means stormy weather.

▶ Take Action

ANALYZE AIR PRESSURE DATA

Collect a barometric pressure reading at about the same time every day for one week. Also note the weather each day. You can obtain the measurements by using a barometer, listening to radio weather reports, or going online. Record the day, time, and reading in the table. Include units of barometric pressure as part of your reading.

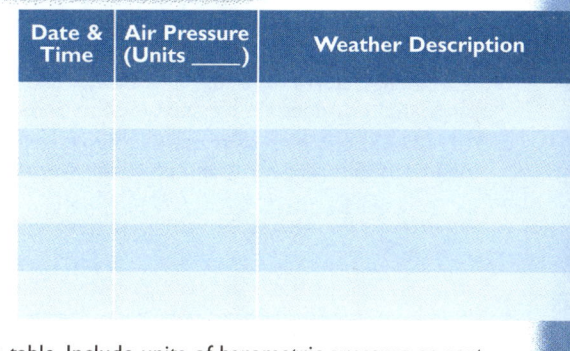

Date & Time	Air Pressure (Units ____)	Weather Description

▶ Did the barometric pressure rise, fall, or stay about the same from one day to the next?

Answers will vary.

▶ If the barometric pressure stays about the same from day to day, what can you predict about the weather?

There won't be much change in the weather.

149

Science Scope Activity
(continued from page 147)

Part 3 investigates the major storms and hurricanes happening today. Log onto www.usatoday.com/weather/hurricane/whuro.htm and investigate today's storm activity. Then log onto www.usatoday.com/weather/wtrack.htm to plot and track one storm's activity. Record the answers in Part 3 of the Investigation Sheet.

Assessment
Skills: Interpreting scientific illustrations

Use the following questions to assess each student's progress:

What do isobars represent on a weather map? (Isobars are lines on a weather map that connect places with the same barometric pressure.)

What letters are used to show the air pressure in the center of an air mass? (H stands for an area of high pressure. L stands for an area of low pressure.)

▶ Propose Explanations

Time: 10 minutes
Materials: barometer

THINK IT OVER Make sure students understand that air pressure is caused by the weight of the atmosphere pressing down on Earth. Point out that air pressure changes from day to day along with the temperature and the amount of moisture in the air. Obtain a barometer and have students note the barometric pressure reading. Ask students what might happen if the current barometric reading begins to fall. (There will most likely be a change in the weather, becoming stormy or cloudy.)

▶ Take Action

Time: 5 minutes per day for 1 week
Materials: barometer (optional)

ANALYZE AIR PRESSURE DATA Explain that meteorologists use several different units to measure air pressure, including inches of mercury (often abbreviated as just "inches"), millibars (mB), and hectopascals (hPa). Point out that 1 mB is equal to 1 hPA. Caution students to collect readings using the same unit of measurement every day so they can compare the values.

When students have completed their tables, have them relate the changes in air pressure to the changes in weather. Ask: *What does a rapidly falling barometric reading usually indicate?* (a storm approaching) *What does a rising barometric reading represent?* (fair weather approaching)

CHAPTER 14 / LESSON 40   149

UNIT 4 Weather and Climate

CHAPTER 14 / LESSON 41

Point of Lesson
When weather systems collide, unusually powerful storms can form.

Focus
- Natural hazards
- Structure of the earth system
- Change, constancy, and measurement
- Understanding about science and technology

Skills and Strategies
- Communicating
- Interpreting scientific illustrations
- Creating and using graphs
- Recognizing cause and effect
- Generating questions

Advance Preparation

Vocabulary
Make sure students understand these terms. Definitions can be found in the glossary at the end of the student book.

- air pressure
- hurricane
- speed
- tornado
- wave
- weather
- wind

Materials
Gather the materials needed for *Read* (p. 151) and *Explore* (p. 152).

CHAPTER 14 / LESSON 41

Stormy Weather

A STORM LIKE NO OTHER

A small fishing boat is no match for a violent storm.

The cold ocean waters off the coast of eastern Canada are home to thousands of swordfish during the warmer half of the year. Swordfishing boats go out for weeks at a time to catch this valuable fish. Unfortunately, these waters are located on one of the worst storm paths in the world. Weather there can change quickly. Storms can be powerful and dangerous—especially when three weather systems collide.

The swordfishing boat *Andrea Gail* sailed from Gloucester, Massachusetts, on September 20, 1991. It was last heard from at 6 P.M. on October 28, 1991. At that time, the boat was in the low-pressure area near Sable Island and Nova Scotia. This Sable Island storm was one of the three weather systems that helped form "the perfect storm."

▶ **Before You Read**

SEVERE WEATHER Depending on where you live, the word *storm* may bring different pictures to mind. Hurricanes, hailstorms, thunderstorms, blizzards, and tornadoes are common in some places and rare in others.

▶ *Write about one kind of storm you know well. Describe the weather conditions before, during, and after the storm.*

Students' answers will depend on their personal experiences.

_____
_____
_____
_____
_____
_____
_____
_____

TEACHING PLAN pp. 150–151

INTRODUCING THE LESSON
This lesson explains how "the perfect storm" formed, including a study of fronts and pressure systems.

Find out what students already know about how storms form by asking them to make a list of the weather conditions necessary for the formation of a storm.

Some students may believe that the same storms are in existence all the time, simply moving from place to place. Explain that a number of factors are necessary for the formation of a storm. When a mass of warm or cool air meets the right atmospheric conditions, a storm can be created.

▶ **Before You Read**

SEVERE WEATHER Have students share their descriptions of storms. Most paragraphs should include accounts of any type of severe weather, including precipitation, strong winds, and extreme temperatures. You may want to talk about the differences between various types of storms. For example, blizzards are characterized by high winds, freezing temperatures, blinding snowfall, and drifting snow. High winds and rainfall characterize hurricanes, while high winds in the shape of a funnel are characteristic of tornadoes. Students should also note the location and general climate of their weather storms.

While discussing hurricanes, point out that some hurricanes (notably Hurricane Hugo in 1989) do affect areas that are well inland.

▶ **Read**

While the *Andrea Gail* fights to stay afloat in huge waves, things get worse for all ships in the area.

HURRICANE GRACE

Hurricane Grace...has been quietly slipping up the [U.S.] coast. At 8 A.M. on the 29th, Grace collides with the cold front, as predicted, and goes reeling back out to sea. She's moving extremely fast and packing eighty-knot [148 km/hr] winds and thirty-foot [nine-meter] seas.... Grace crosses the 40th parallel that afternoon. At 8 P.M. on October 29th, Hurricane Grace runs into the Sable Island storm.

The effect is instantaneous....The wind starts rushing into the low at speeds up to a hundred miles [160 km] an hour. As a NOAA disaster report put it...a year later, "The dangerous storm previously forecast was now fact...."

The bulk carrier *Zarah*, just fifty miles [81 km] south of the *Andrea Gail* takes ninety-foot [27-meter] seas over her decks that shear off the steel bolts holding her portholes down. Thirty tons of water flood the...crew's sleeping quarters...and kill the ship's engine. The *Zarah* is 550 feet [168 meters] long.

cold front: the leading edge of a mass of cold air; cold fronts can bring violent storms
reeling: spinning
knot: a measurement of speed at sea or in the air; one nautical mile (1.852 km) per hour
parallel: also called line of latitude; an imaginary line that shows distance north or south of the equator
NOAA: National Oceanic and Atmospheric Administration (the National Weather Service)
bulk carrier: a large ship used to carry loose cargo such as coal or grain
shear: cut
porthole: a window in the side of a ship

From: Junger, Sebastian. *The Perfect Storm: A True Story of Men Against the Sea.* Harper Collins.

The Fisherman's Memorial at Gloucester ▶

THEY THAT GO DOWN TO THE SEA IN SHIPS 1623 — 1923

NOTEZONE

The *Andrea Gail* was 70 feet (22 meters) long. Sketch how big it would look next to the *Zarah*.

Sketch should show the Andrea Gail about one eighth the length of the Zarah.

FIND OUT MORE

SCIENCESAURUS
Weather Collecting 218
Weather Data 219
Weather Maps and Symbols 220
Air Masses 221
Weather Fronts 222
Air Pressure 224
Wind 225

SCILINKS
THE WORLD'S A CLICK AWAY
www.scilinks.org
Keyword: Storms
Code: GSED18

151

Enrichment

Have students collect the current day's weather data for your area, including satellite images and barometric pressure readings. Ask them to predict what the weather in their area will be like in the coming days. Have them describe what information they used to make these predictions.

Ask students to compare their predictions with those of the DataStreme Project from the American Meteorological Society at: amet.soc.org/dstreme

▶ **Read**

Time: 10–15 minutes
Materials: 100-ft tape measure

After students complete the reading and the NoteZone activity, let them measure the lengths of the two ships along a sidewalk or in a parking lot or ball field.

Explain to students that a cold front is formed when a cold air mass meets and pushes under a warm air mass. The cold front forces the warm front upward, resulting in a violent storm. Ask students why the collision of the cold front and Hurricane Grace resulted in a violent storm. (A hurricane is a low-pressure area that contains rising warm air. The collision of the cold front and the warm air would produce the severe weather.)

CHECK UNDERSTANDING
Skill: Recognizing cause and effect
Ask students to list the factors that contributed to the formation of "the perfect storm." (Hurricane Grace collided with a cold front and turned back out to sea. Grace then crossed the 40th parallel and ran into a storm around the Sable Island area.)

CHAPTER 14 / LESSON 41   151

CHAPTER 14 / LESSON 41

More Resources
The following resources are also available from Great Source and NSTA.

SCIENCESAURUS
Weather	218
Collecting Weather Data	219
Weather Maps and Symbols	220
Air Masses	221
Weather Fronts	222
Air Pressure	224
Wind	225

WRITE SOURCE 2000
Interviewing Tips	170

MATH ON CALL
Scatter Plots	305
Coordinate Geometry	318

SciLINKS
THE WORLD'S A CLICK AWAY

www.scilinks.org
Keyword: Storms
Code: GSED18

▶ Explore

INTERPRETING MAPS Over several days, three weather systems collided to create violent weather conditions. The first weather system was the low-pressure system that formed over the Great Lakes and moved east to Nova Scotia. The second system was the high-pressure system that formed over Quebec. The third system, Hurricane Grace, had formed over the Atlantic east of Florida.

▶ Look at the air pressure map on page 148 again. Label the map with the number 1 where the first weather system formed, 2 for the second system, and 3 for the third system.

READING A GRAPH
Water waves are usually caused by wind pushing the water in front of it. The graph at the right plots many measurements of wave height and wind speed during one year on Lake Michigan. Each plot looks like a circle. By reading the graph, you can see the wind speed and wave height when each measurement was taken.

▶ When wind speed was less than 5 meters per second, how high were most waves?

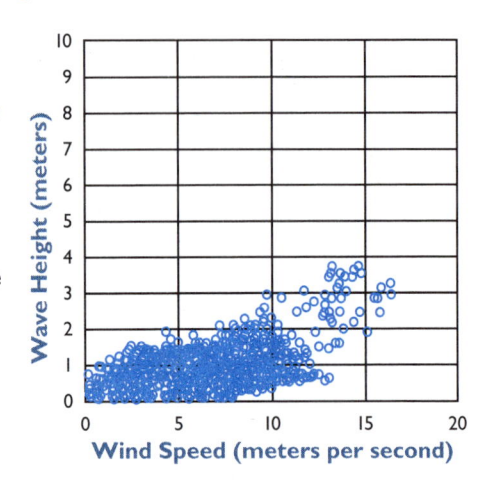

Most were less than 1 meter high.

▶ What was the height of the tallest waves that were measured?

almost 4 meters

▶ Did a wind speed of 10 m/s always produce waves of the same height? Explain your answer.

No; according to the graph, waves were from 0.5 to 3 meters high.

152

TEACHING PLAN pp. 152–153

▶ Explore

Time: 20 minutes
Materials: map used in Read (p. 147); research sources about Hurricane Grace

INTERPRETING MAPS Encourage students to figure out ways they might trace the path of Hurricane Grace as it moved northward up the Atlantic. Using research sources, have students predict where the three weather systems may have collided and find that area on the map.

READING A GRAPH Explain that the readings plotted on the graph were taken from a buoy in Lake Michigan. Point out that the scatter of the points is not as drastic as the scatter of points that would occur in an ocean because Lake Michigan is a much smaller, enclosed body of water. Waves do not occur on as large a scale in these small bodies of water as they do in the open ocean.

Students may want to know why a certain wind speed can produce waves of different heights. Two other variables also affect wave height: the length of time the wind blows (its duration) and the distance it blows across open ocean (its fetch). Have students find examples on the scatter plot where the same wind speed produces waves of different heights. (A wind speed of 10 m/s can produce waves of 2 or 3 m.)

▶ **Propose Explanations**

UNDERSTANDING CAUSE AND EFFECT
▶ What is the usual relationship between wind speed and wave height?
  As wind speed increases, wave height increases.

Some buoys at sea automatically collect weather data. One buoy is very near the *Andrea Gail*'s last known position. By the evening of October 28, when the *Andrea Gail* was last heard from, the buoy was sending startling data. Wind speed was more than 100 miles (161 km) per hour. Waves were 70 feet (21 m) high. The *Andrea Gail* was lost at sea.

▶ Based on what you've read, how do you think weather conditions might have caused the *Andrea Gail* to sink?
  High waves and strong winds may have swamped the boat or flipped it
  over. Then it would have filled with water and sunk.

▶ **Take Action**

GENERATE QUESTIONS
▶ You are investigating the disappearance of the *Andrea Gail*. What questions would you ask meteorologist Bob Case? What would you ask another swordfish boat captain? What would you ask the boat's builder? What would you ask a Coast Guard rescue officer?
  Answers will vary. Examples: I would ask Bob Case if he's seen a
  stronger storm since "the perfect storm." I would ask a swordfish boat
  captain if he/she was on the water that day, and if so, what did he/she
  see and experience. I would ask the boat's builder if there was a way the
  boat could have been made stronger. I would ask the Coast Guard rescue
  officer why rescuers couldn't save the *Andrea Gail*'s captain and crew.

153

Connections

MATH Remind students that a coordinate grid like the one on page 152 is a way to locate points on a plane. The horizontal axis (*x*-axis) and the vertical axis (*y*-axis) divide the plane into four quadrants. Points are plotted using *x* and *y* coordinates. Ask students to name the coordinates for some of the small circles on the graph.

Assessment

Skill: Recognizing cause and effect

Use the following question to assess each student's progress:

What are some factors that may cause a violent storm, particularly at sea? (A cold front colliding with another weather system such as a hurricane can produce a violent storm. Also, high winds result in increased wave heights.)

▶ **Propose Explanations**

UNDERSTANDING CAUSE AND EFFECT
Explain to students that hurricanes have maximum sustained winds of at least 75 miles (120 km) per hour. Point out that the winds surrounding the *Andrea Gail* were of hurricane force and that the height of the waves was at least equal to the length of the boat.

▶ **Take Action**

GENERATE QUESTIONS Have students form small groups and share their questions. Then pose this question: *A meteorologist has received some readings from a buoy in the Atlantic Ocean. Wind speeds are currently 15 miles (24 km) per hour and wave heights are about 3 meters (9.9 ft). A cold front is approaching from the west and the wind is increasing. What can the meteorologist expect to happen? Why?* (A violent storm may occur when the cold front collides with another weather system, and wave heights will increase.)

CHAPTER 14 / LESSON 41 153

UNIT 4 Weather and Climate
CHAPTER 14 / LESSON 42

Point of Lesson
Many factors influence how people react to dangerous weather.

Focus
- Natural hazards
- Risks and benefits
- Structure of the earth system

Skills and Strategies
- Interpreting scientific illustrations
- Predicting
- Making inferences

Advance Preparation

Vocabulary
Make sure students understand this term. The definition can be found in the glossary at the end of the student book.
- weather

CHAPTER 14 / LESSON 42
Stormy Weather

At Sea in a Storm

What do you do when your boat is filled with tens of thousands of dollars worth of fresh swordfish, your ice machine is failing, and a storm is on the way?

Sebastian Junger, author of *The Perfect Storm*, wondered about the same thing. As he wrote about the storm, Junger imagined what the captain of the *Andrea Gail* might have been thinking.

Of the many swordfishing boats at sea during "the perfect storm," only one—the *Andrea Gail*—sank in the storm. The tragic outcome was that captain Billy Tyne and his crew—Bugsy Moran, Dale Murphy, Alfred Pierre, Bobby Shatford, and David Sullivan—all lost their lives.

NoteZone
Underline the main reasons why the captain might have decided to head for home instead of sailing away from the storm.

FIND OUT MORE
SCIENCESAURUS
- Weather 218
- Collecting Weather Data 219
- Weather Maps and Symbols 220
- Air Masses 221
- Weather Fronts 222
- Air Pressure 224
- Wind 225

Read
Here's what Junger believes captain Billy Tyne was thinking.

The Perfect Storm

Billy finishes up his last haul around noon on the 25th and—the crew still stowing their gear—turns his boat for home. They'll be one of the only boats in port with a load of fish, which means a...high price.... Billy has a failing ice machine and a twelve hundred mile [1,900 km] drive ahead of him. He'll be heading in while the rest of the fleet is still in mid-trip....

Billy...has undoubtedly heard the forecast, but he's...[not] inclined to do anything about it.... Weather reports are vitally important to the fishing, but not so much for heading home. When the end of the trip comes, captains generally just haul their gear and go.

haul (noun): a load of fish that has been caught
stowing: putting away
inclined: willing
haul (verb): take aboard a boat

From: Junger, Sebastian. *The Perfect Storm: A True Story of Men Against the Sea.* Harper Collins.

TEACHING PLAN pp. 154–155

INTRODUCING THE LESSON
This lesson discusses possible reasons why the captain of the *Andrea Gail* did not seek safe shelter from "the perfect storm." Ask students what they know about the fate of the *Andrea Gail* and why they think the ship became caught in such a violent storm.

Some students may think that all events described in the book actually took place. Emphasize that Sebastian Junger could only make inferences about why the *Andrea Gail* sailed the path that it did. No one knows exactly what happened on board.

Read
Discuss the possible reasons that students underlined in the reading. Encourage them to suggest other reasons that the *Andrea Gail* may have headed straight into a storm.

Explore

HEADING HOME This map shows the last known location of the *Andrea Gail* at 6 P.M. on October 28. After that, radio contact was lost. The boat and crew were never found.

The *Andrea Gail* was heading to its home port of Gloucester on the coast of Massachusetts. Gloucester was almost 1,900 kilometers away.

▶ What places were closer than Gloucester? Why do you think captain Billy Tyne didn't try to head there?

Sable Island, Nova Scotia, Newfoundland, and Maine were closer. Captain Tyne probably wanted to sell his fish in his home port of Gloucester.

The line on the map shows the path, or track, of "the perfect storm."

▶ Do you think the *Andrea Gail* would have sailed into the storm as it tried to get home? Explain your answer.

Yes. It might have sailed into the storm on October 29 near Sable Island, and it might have met it again after November 2 south of Nova Scotia.

UNDERSTANDING RISKS Captain Billy Tyne had heard the weather service forecasts. He knew that a violent storm was forming.

▶ Why do you think he didn't drive his boat to the east, which is where the rest of the swordfishing boats waited out the storm?

He wanted to reach home port to sell his fish before the other boats could get there.

▶ The crew and their families depended on the money made from the fish they caught. What risk did they face if the ice machine failed?

The fish would rot, and the captain and crew wouldn't make any money.

More Resources
The following resource is also available from Great Source.

SCIENCESAURUS
Weather	218
Collecting Weather Data	219
Weather Maps and Symbols	220
Air Masses	221
Weather Fronts	222
Air Pressure	224
Wind	225

Enrichment
Ask students to write a dramatic reading or a poem about the fate of the *Andrea Gail*. Encourage them to use vivid language to describe the images of the storm and what the crew might have been thinking, doing, or feeling during their struggle at sea. Let students give dramatic readings of their writing.

Assessment
Skill: Recognizing cause and effect

Use the following question to assess each student's progress:

What factors led to the sinking of the Andrea Gail? (Instead of seeking a safe harbor or heading east like the other swordfishing boats, the *Andrea Gail* headed west, straight into the area where the three weather systems collided.)

Explore

HEADING HOME Help students find Massachusetts on the map and the approximate location of the city of Gloucester, noting its location in relation to the area where the storm occurred. Ask students if they think it is safe to assume that the *Andrea Gail* went down in the area where the storms collided.

UNDERSTANDING RISKS Ask students if they think that it was worth the risk of trying to make it back to Gloucester with the day's catch. If the *Andrea Gail* had made it back to Gloucester, would that change students' opinion of the risk involved?

Ask students to reassess their reasons for why this violent storm was named "the perfect storm." (Weather conditions were perfect to create a violent storm.)

CHECK UNDERSTANDING
Skill: Making inferences
Ask: *If the Andrea Gail had headed east, would the crew's chances of surviving the storm have been better?* (Yes, the ship might have gotten out of the path of the storm and into safer waters.)

CHAPTER 15
Overview

Weird Weather

LESSON 43
Down Tornado Alley
Point of Lesson: *Most tornadoes occur in a specific region of the United States.*

In this lesson, a 13-year-old student describes his encounter with a tornado. Students identify the descriptive terms Allen Nelson uses for the weather leading up to the tornado and compare the frequency of tornadoes in different parts of the country by interpreting a map.

Materials
Science Scope Activity (pp. 156B and 157), to construct each tornado machine:
- Tornado Machine Instruction Sheet (copymaster p. 230)
- two 50 × 45-cm pieces and one 50 × 25-cm piece of ¼ inch plywood
- one 45 × 42-cm piece of pegboard
- two 45-cm long strips and two 50-cm long strips of 1 × 1 inch white pine
- nails or wood screws
- box fan
- tray
- small fan
- warm water
- dry ice
- tongs for handling dry ice
- safety goggles

Laboratory Safety
Transport the dry ice for the Science Scope Activity in a foam-plastic ice chest with a loose fitting lid. Review these safety guidelines with students before they do the activity.
- Dry ice is frozen carbon dioxide gas and is extremely cold. Do not touch the dry ice with your hands. Use tongs.
- Do not inhale the carbon dioxide gas.
- Wear safety goggles throughout the activity.

LESSON 44
Hail Hail!
Point of Lesson: *Hailstorms can occur anywhere but pose the greatest risk in the Plains states.*

In this lesson, students evaluate data about severe hailstorms in Colorado, and think of reasons why data on hailstorms, as reported by observers, do not match data on hailstorms from the National Weather Service. Students then use a map to compare the frequency of hailstorms with the frequency of tornadoes in different states and suggest reasons why both types of storms are common in some areas.

Materials
Enrichment (p. 161), for the class:
- earth science textbooks

Explore (p. 162), for each student:
- drawing compass

Connections (p. 162), for the class:
- newspapers
- magazines

LESSON 45
Digging Out
Point of Lesson: *Snowstorms were more difficult to predict and deal with in the past than they are today.*

The blizzard of 1888 paralyzed the northeastern United States and left hundreds of people dead. In this lesson, students read a first-hand account of the storm as recalled by a man who lived through it. They then compare and contrast today's storm prediction and snow removal methods with those available in the late 1800s.

Materials
none

UNIT 4: WEATHER AND CLIMATE

156A

Science Scope Activity

Tornado Machine

NSTA has chosen a Science Scope *activity related to the content in this chapter. The activity begins here and continues in Lesson 43, page 157.*

To build the "tornado machine," students will first need to assemble a wooden box as described below. The instructions for using the "machine" are on page 157.

Time: ongoing
Materials: see page 156A
Procedure
Give each group a copy of the Tornado Machine diagram and the following instructions.

1. Put on safety goggles. Use nails or screws to attach the two larger pieces of plywood to the smaller piece of plywood along their 50-cm edges to form three sides of a box.
2. Nail two 20-cm strips of pine to both edges of the box for support.
3. Nail the pegboard to the bottom of the box.
4. Nail a pine strip to each side of the bottom of the box for support.

(continued on page 157)

When students have completed the activity, ask the following questions: *What effect does the box fan setting have on tornado formation?* (When the fan setting is higher, more air will be sucked upward.) *What effect does the position of the small fan have on tornado formation?* (Correct positioning deflects air against the walls of the box.) *How can you produce different kinds of funnel?* (by manipulating the angle and speed of the little fan and the speed of the box fan.)

Background Information

Lesson 43

Three conditions are necessary for tornadoes to form: unstable air, moist air near the ground, and a source of uplift. Such conditions are common in the central states during the spring months, when warm, moist air from the Gulf of Mexico sweeps up and meets cool, dry air from the north.

A severe thunderstorm develops first, then the funnel cloud.

Lesson 44

The main cause of hail is atmospheric instability that produces updrafts strong enough to lift heavy hailstones as they grow. Both hailstorms and tornadoes develop in thunderstorms, so it is no coincidence that both are common wherever conditions for severe thunderstorms exist.

The largest hailstone recorded in the U.S. fell in Kansas in 1970. It weighed 758 g (1.67 lbs) and measured 44 cm (17.5 in.) in circumference.

Lesson 44

The blizzard of 1888 resulted in a transportation crisis that crippled the Northeast. High winds created snow drifts 12–15 m (40–50 ft) high. This crisis helped convince city leaders to create the New York subway system. Construction was approved in 1894 and began in 1900.

UNIT 4 Weather and Climate
CHAPTER 15 / LESSON 43

Point of Lesson
Most tornadoes occur in a specific region of the United States.

Focus
- Structure of the earth system
- Natural hazards

Skills and Strategies
- Interpreting scientific illustrations
- Comparing and contrasting
- Generating ideas
- Organizing information
- Communicating

Advance Preparation

Vocabulary
Make sure students understand these terms. Definitions can be found in the glossary at the end of the student book.

- cloud
- histogram
- tornado
- weather

Materials
Gather the materials needed for *Science Scope Activity* (p. 156B and p. 157).

TEACHING PLAN pp. 156–157

INTRODUCING THE LESSON
This lesson presents the average numbers of tornadoes that occur annually in different areas of the United States, including the states that are located in the area known as "Tornado Alley."

Find out what students already know about tornadoes and where they occur in the United States. Ask: *What are the characteristics of a tornado? How is a tornado different from a hurricane? Where do you think most tornadoes occur in the United States?*

Many students may confuse tornadoes with hurricanes. Tell students that while both are intense and destructive storms characterized by low pressure centers, there are differences between the two. Point out that tornadoes form over both land and (as waterspouts) over water, whereas hurricanes form only over water. A tornado is characterized by a long funnel-shaped spout, while a hurricane is a much wider mass of winds that blow counterclockwise in a circle around an "eye."

CHAPTER 15 / LESSON 43
Weird Weather

Down Tornado Alley

Tornado—coming to a cloudy sky near you!

Tornadoes are one of the deadliest forms of severe weather. Strong winds rushing into a funnel cloud can pull cars, livestock, and even buildings into the air and deposit them miles away.

▶ Before You Read

TORNADO WATCH Tornadoes can occur anywhere in the United States, but they're more likely to occur in some places than in others.

▶ What would you do if you thought there might be a tornado heading toward your area? How would you find out for sure if a tornado was on the way?

Answers will vary. Examples: First question—Go to a safe place such as a basement; stay away from windows, which might shatter. Second question— Listen to or look for reports on television, radio, or the internet.

▶ Before You Read

TORNADO WATCH Students who do not live in a tornado area may need assistance in answering these questions. Prompt them by asking: *What do you do to obtain information about approaching weather?* (listen to or watch a weather channel, listen to local radio stations, read newspaper warnings)

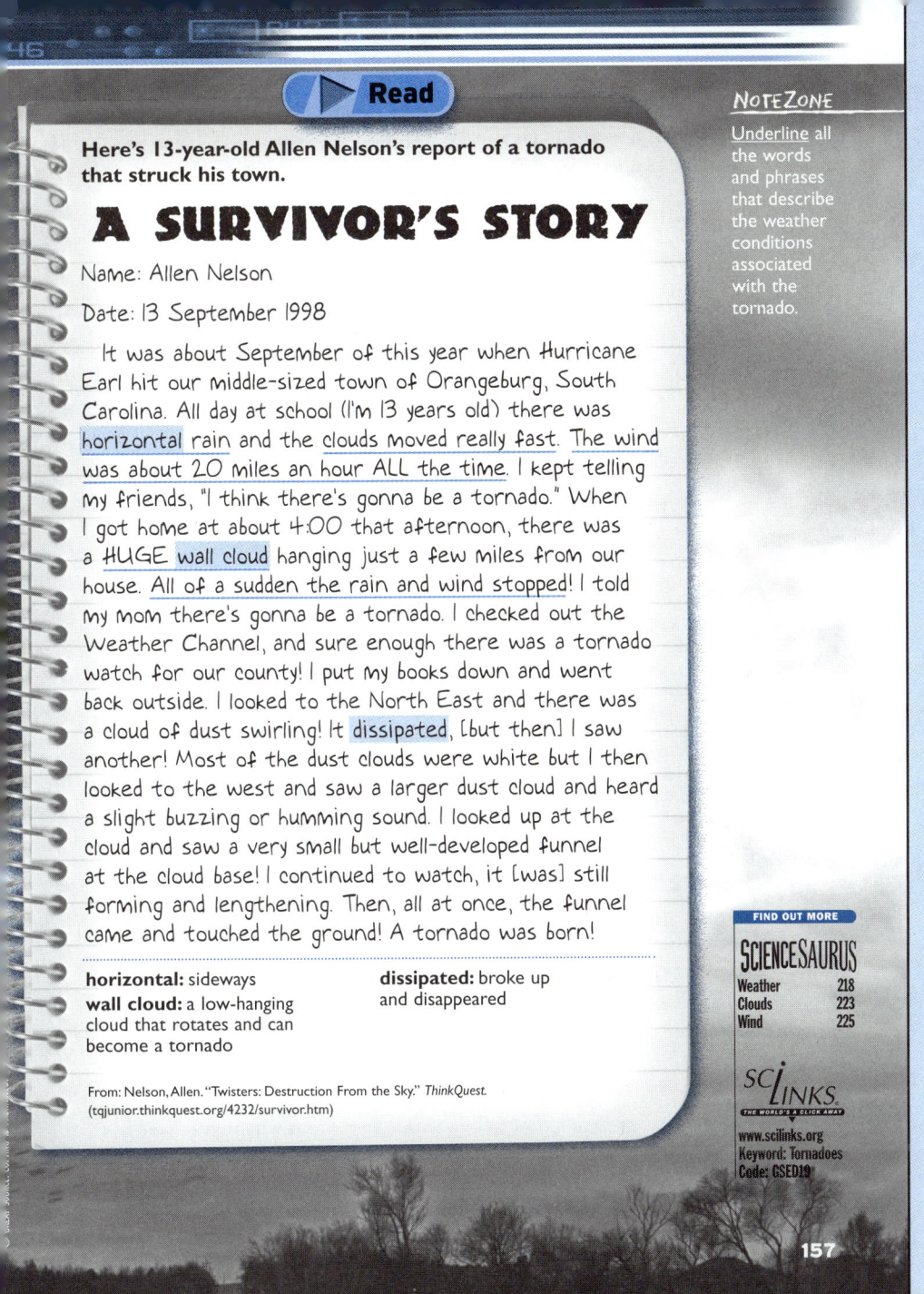

Read

Here's 13-year-old Allen Nelson's report of a tornado that struck his town.

A SURVIVOR'S STORY

Name: Allen Nelson

Date: 13 September 1998

It was about September of this year when Hurricane Earl hit our middle-sized town of Orangeburg, South Carolina. All day at school (I'm 13 years old) there was horizontal rain and the clouds moved really fast. The wind was about 20 miles an hour ALL the time. I kept telling my friends, "I think there's gonna be a tornado." When I got home at about 4:00 that afternoon, there was a HUGE wall cloud hanging just a few miles from our house. All of a sudden the rain and wind stopped! I told my mom there's gonna be a tornado. I checked out the Weather Channel, and sure enough there was a tornado watch for our county! I put my books down and went back outside. I looked to the North East and there was a cloud of dust swirling! It dissipated, [but then] I saw another! Most of the dust clouds were white but I then looked to the west and saw a larger dust cloud and heard a slight buzzing or humming sound. I looked up at the cloud and saw a very small but well-developed funnel at the cloud base! I continued to watch, it [was] still forming and lengthening. Then, all at once, the funnel came and touched the ground! A tornado was born!

horizontal: sideways
wall cloud: a low-hanging cloud that rotates and can become a tornado
dissipated: broke up and disappeared

From: Nelson, Allen. "Twisters: Destruction From the Sky." ThinkQuest. (tqjunior.thinkquest.org/4232/survivor.htm)

NOTEZONE

Underline all the words and phrases that describe the weather conditions associated with the tornado.

FIND OUT MORE

SCIENCESAURUS
Weather 218
Clouds 223
Wind 225

SCILINKS
www.scilinks.org
Keyword: Tornadoes
Code: GSED19

157

Science Scope Activity

(continued from page 156B)

To complete this activity, students first need to assemble the box as described on page 156B. Give students the following instructions.

5. Lay the box fan flat on top of the box so it will pull air upward.
6. Put warm water and dry ice in a tray to produce "clouds."
   Caution: Dry ice is frozen carbon dioxide gas and is extremely cold. Do not touch the dry ice with your hands. Use tongs.
7. Put the tray underneath the box so the gaseous carbon dioxide (the "clouds") can escape through the holes in the pegboard.
8. Turn the box fan on low to pull the "clouds" upward.
9. To produce wind shear, hold the small fan to the right of the open side of the box, pointed toward the middle of the left wall. Adjust the small fan's position until the wind shear and updraft combine to produce a miniature tornado.

Read

Encourage students to highlight any parts of the reading that may change their ideas about tornadoes. Ask students who may have witnessed a tornado to share their experiences with the class. Most students will be familiar with tornado scenes they have seen on television or in the movies. Have them compare Allen Nelson's description—and their real-life experiences—with what they have seen on film.

Make sure students understand that as in the Science Scope Activity, weather conditions must be just right to produce a tornado. Explain that most tornadoes occur during severe thunderstorms when warm, moist air is pushed upward by a mass of cold air. This updraft is what causes a tornado to form.

CHECK UNDERSTANDING
Skill: Concept mapping
Have students create a concept map for the characteristics of a tornado. (Students' concept maps might include the following: wall cloud, severe storm, strong winds, funnel shape, buzzing or humming sound.)

CHAPTER 15 / LESSON 43   157

CHAPTER 15 / LESSON 43

More Resources

The following resources are also available from Great Source and NSTA.

SCIENCESAURUS

Weather	218
Clouds	223
Wind	225

READER'S HANDBOOK

Elements of Textbooks:	
Maps	163

WRITE SOURCE 2000

Personal Narrative	154

SCILINKS
THE WORLD'S A CLICK AWAY

www.scilinks.org
Keyword: Tornadoes
Code: GSED19

▶ **Explore**

INTERPRET A TORNADO MAP This map shows the average number of tornadoes that occur in different areas of the United States each year.

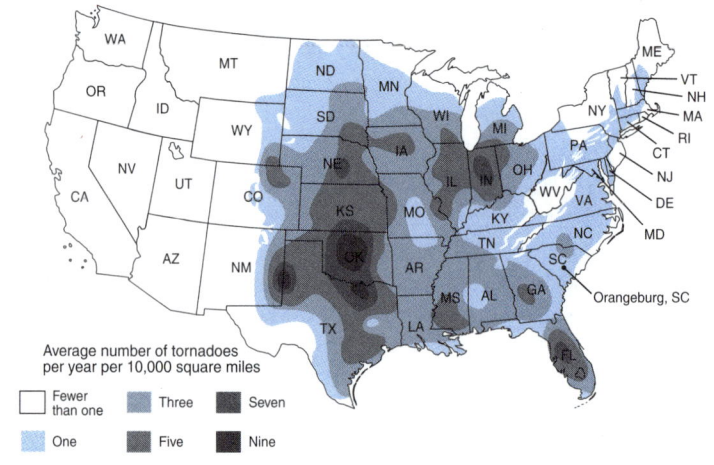

Average number of tornadoes per year per 10,000 square miles
- Fewer than one
- One
- Three
- Five
- Seven
- Nine

▶ According to the map, which states have at least seven tornadoes per year?

Texas, Oklahoma, Indiana, Nebraska, and Florida

▶ Which area of the country deserves the nickname "Tornado Alley"? Why?

The area down the central part of the country. This is where the greatest number of tornadoes occur.

▶ How common are tornadoes in Orangeburg, South Carolina, where Allen Nelson lives?

Orangeburg is in an area that gets an average of one tornado per year.

▶ According to the map, how common are tornadoes where you live?

Answers will vary.

158

TEACHING PLAN pp. 158–159

▶ **Explore**

INTERPRET A TORNADO MAP Direct students' attention to the map key. Have them identify which shading represents the greatest number of tornadoes per year (the darkest shading) and which represents the lowest number (the lightest shading or no shading).

If students are unfamiliar with the term *alley*, define it for them as "a narrow street." Ask students to suggest reasons why tornadoes occur most frequently in the area known as "Tornado Alley." (Cool, dry air moving in from the west collides with warm, moist air moving up from the Gulf of Mexico, producing the weather conditions necessary for funnel formation.) Point out that the United States gets more tornadoes than any other country in the world. The weather conditions suitable for tornado formation occur most frequently in the spring and summer.

158   CHAPTER 15 / LESSON 43

▶ Take Action

COMMUNICATE TORNADO SAFETY Would you know what to do if a tornado alert were broadcast for your area?
- Do some research to find out what you can do to be prepared for a tornado and what you should do during the tornado to be safe. Create a flier with a list of tornado safety rules. Add pictures to get your points across. Use the space below to plan your flier.

Fliers should include how to conduct safety drills, what safety equipment to have on hand, how to recognize the weather signs of a tornado, where to go and how to position yourself in a building when a tornado is near, what to do if you are outdoors, and what to do after the tornado until emergency personnel arrive.

159

Assessment
Skill: Communicating

Use the following task to assess each student's progress:

Ask students to describe their own personal plan of action to take if a tornado alert were broadcast for your area. (Students should describe the safety measures they would take in their own homes, the kinds of emergency supplies they would have on hand, and where the supplies would be kept. Most students should report seeking shelter in an underground area such as a basement or storm cellar or in a doorway or bathtub. Emergency supplies would include water, flashlights, batteries, and a battery-operated radio kept in the area of shelter.)

▶ Take Action

COMMUNICATE TORNADO SAFETY

Students can go online (www.fema.gov) or contact a local office of the Federal Emergency Management Agency (FEMA) for tornado safety brochures. Information is also available on the Web site of the Storm Prediction Center (www.spc.noaa.gov). Have students post their fliers around the school or at home.

Make sure students understand that the safety procedures they would follow for a tornado would differ from safety procedures for other kinds of severe weather.

To conclude the lesson, have students generate a list of questions for further study about tornadoes. For example: *What is the average wind speed in a tornado? How wide is the funnel? What is the length of the tornado's path? How long does a typical tornado last?* Then have students suggest how and where they might find answers to their questions.

CHAPTER 15 / LESSON 43

UNIT 4 Weather and Climate
CHAPTER 15 / LESSON 44

Point of Lesson
Hailstorms can occur anywhere but pose the greatest risk in the Plains states.

Focus
- Structure of the earth system
- Natural hazards

Skills and Strategies
- Generating ideas
- Comparing and contrasting
- Making inferences
- Generating questions

Advance Preparation

Vocabulary
Make sure students understand these terms. Definitions can be found in the glossary at the end of the student book.
- cloud
- diameter

Materials
Gather the materials needed for *Enrichment* (p. 161), *Explore* (p. 162), and *Connections* (p. 162).

TEACHING PLAN pp. 160–161

INTRODUCING THE LESSON
This lesson deals with the severity of hailstorms, their frequency, and the sizes of hailstones.

Ask students to tell you what they know about hailstorms, how hail is formed, and how it affects the people and places where it falls. Ask: *In what type of weather does hail normally fall?* (hot, humid weather, when thunderstorms are likely)

Students may think that because it is made of ice, hail falls only in cold weather. Explain that hail usually falls during summer thunderstorms.

CHAPTER 15 / LESSON 44
Weird Weather

Hail Hail!

How much damage can a ball of ice do? When it's falling from the sky at high speeds, a lot!

If you cut a hailstone in half, you'd see layers of ice. Each layer forms as the hailstone falls through a cloud, gathers water on its surface, and then is blown back high enough into the cloud for the water to freeze. Some hailstones are smaller than a pea. Others can be as large as golf balls—or even softballs! When the hailstones grow too large for the updrafts to lift them, they all start falling at once. So most hailstorms last only a few minutes.

▶ Before You Read

GENERATE IDEAS Imagine that you are riding in a car during a thunderstorm one summer day. Suddenly hail starts pounding down.

▶ *What might you observe around you? List your ideas.*

Answers will vary. Examples: hailstones bouncing on the ground and pounding on the car, people running for cover, cracked windshields, ground covered with hailstones, cars stopped on the road, plants being beaten down

▶ Before You Read

GENERATE IDEAS Before students begin writing, ask volunteers to describe any experiences they may have had with hailstorms. Ask them to describe the weather conditions that accompanied the hailstorm, the size of the hailstones, and what effect the hail had on the surrounding environment.

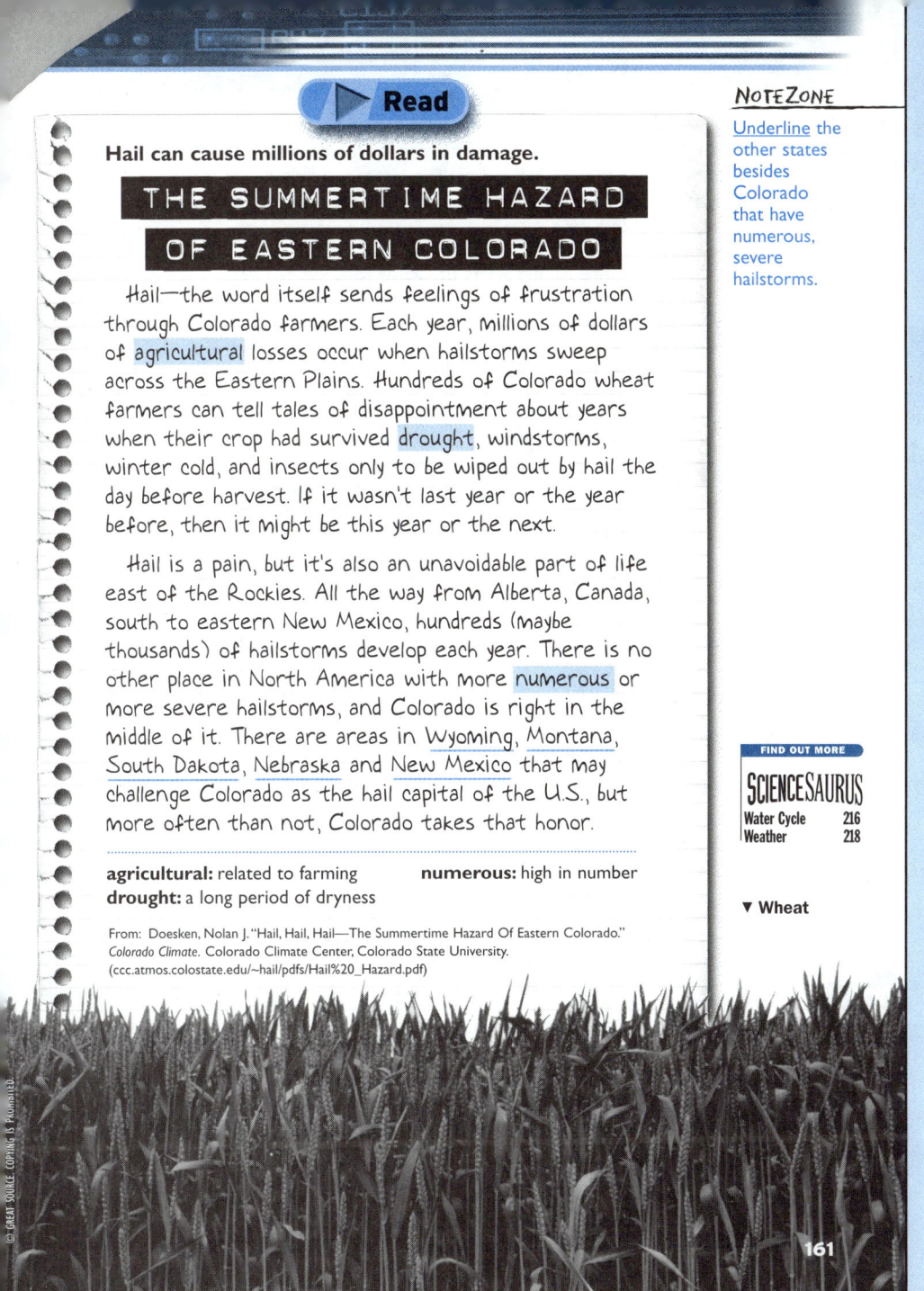

▶ Read

Hail can cause millions of dollars in damage.

THE SUMMERTIME HAZARD OF EASTERN COLORADO

Hail—the word itself sends feelings of frustration through Colorado farmers. Each year, millions of dollars of agricultural losses occur when hailstorms sweep across the Eastern Plains. Hundreds of Colorado wheat farmers can tell tales of disappointment about years when their crop had survived drought, windstorms, winter cold, and insects only to be wiped out by hail the day before harvest. If it wasn't last year or the year before, then it might be this year or the next.

Hail is a pain, but it's also an unavoidable part of life east of the Rockies. All the way from Alberta, Canada, south to eastern New Mexico, hundreds (maybe thousands) of hailstorms develop each year. There is no other place in North America with more numerous or more severe hailstorms, and Colorado is right in the middle of it. There are areas in Wyoming, Montana, South Dakota, Nebraska and New Mexico that may challenge Colorado as the hail capital of the U.S., but more often than not, Colorado takes that honor.

agricultural: related to farming
drought: a long period of dryness
numerous: high in number

From: Doesken, Nolan J. "Hail, Hail, Hail—The Summertime Hazard Of Eastern Colorado." *Colorado Climate.* Colorado Climate Center, Colorado State University. (ccc.atmos.colostate.edu/~hail/pdfs/Hail%20_Hazard.pdf)

NOTEZONE

Underline the other states besides Colorado that have numerous, severe hailstorms.

FIND OUT MORE
SCIENCESAURUS
Water Cycle 216
Weather 218

▼ Wheat

161

Enrichment

Time: will vary
Materials: earth science textbooks

Have students use earth science textbooks to find out about the process by which hailstones are formed. They may accompany their research with diagrams and should note that hailstones are generally formed in cumulonimbus clouds, the clouds normally associated with thunderstorms.

▶ Read

Encourage students to highlight any new or surprising information in the reading about hail and hailstorms. Ask students if this information changes their ideas about hailstorms and their effects. Then discuss the damage that a hailstorm can cause. (Fruit trees that are in blossom in the spring can be damaged, reducing fruit crops. Large hailstones can kill livestock. The same large-size hail can also damage cars, including all the cars in a dealer's lot. People who work outdoors are at risk of injury.) Make sure students understand that like tornadoes and other kinds of severe weather, hailstorms can cause many thousands of dollars in damage every year.

CHECK UNDERSTANDING
Skill: Sequencing

Ask students to describe the characteristics of a hailstone and the steps involved in hailstone formation. (Hailstones consist of layers of ice. The hailstone falls through a cloud and gathers water on its surface. Then it is blown back up into the cloud, where the water freezes. This process is repeated to form layers of ice.)

CHAPTER 15 / LESSON 44   161

CHAPTER 15 / LESSON 44

More Resources
The following resources are also available from Great Source.

SCIENCESAURUS
Water Cycle	216
Weather	218

MATH ON CALL
Graphs That Compare	291
Histograms	295

Connections
Time: 30 minutes
Materials: newspapers, magazines

MATH Remind students that a histogram is a pictorial representation of numerical data that fall into different ranges or intervals. Stress that histograms are a good way to organize and display information, measurements, and other numerical data. Ask: *How does a histogram make it easy to see data?* (Putting the data in a histogram makes it easier to see how large or small the quantities are and how they compare.) Ask students to look through newspapers and magazines for examples of histograms. Allow class time for students to display the histograms and discuss the kind of information they represent.

TEACHING PLAN pp. 162–163

▶ Explore

HAILSTONE SIZES Meteorologists depend on the reports of citizens for information on hailstorms. The histogram below shows the number of hailstorms and the sizes of hailstones reported in Colorado during a seven-year period.

Severe Hailstorms in Colorado, 1986–1993

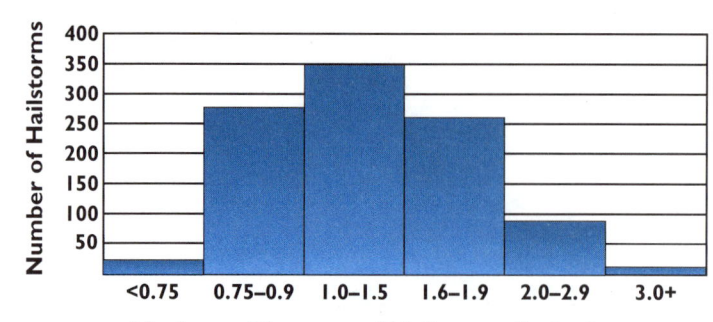

[Histogram: Number of Hailstorms vs. Maximum Diameter of Hailstones (inches)]
- <0.75: ~25
- 0.75–0.9: ~280
- 1.0–1.5: ~350
- 1.6–1.9: ~260
- 2.0–2.9: ~90
- 3.0+: ~20

▶ Which size hailstones were most often reported in Colorado?
1.0–1.5 inches in diameter

▶ Which size was least often reported?
3.0+ inches in diameter

▶ The National Weather Service says that 95 percent of hailstorms involve hailstones less than 0.5 inches in diameter. What are some reasons why the bar for less than 0.75 inches is so short?
Answers will vary. Examples: People probably didn't bother to report small hailstones. Maybe that size of hail is less common in Colorado.

▶ Explore

Time: 10 minutes
Materials: drawing compass

HAILSTONE SIZES Discuss the labels on the histogram's axes. Make sure students understand that the number of hailstorms can be found by looking at the height of each vertical bar. Point out the approximate decimal-to-inch equivalents on the horizontal axis. For example, 0.75 would be equal to $\frac{3}{4}$; 1.6 would be a bit more than $1\frac{1}{2}$. You might want to provide students with the approximate metric equivalents of these measurements: 0.75 in. = 1.9 cm; 0.9 in. = 2.3 cm; 1.5 in. = 3.8 cm; 1.9 in. = 4.8 cm; 2.9 in. = 7.3 cm; and 3.0 in. = 7.5 cm.

To help students visualize the sizes of the hailstones, have them use a compass to draw circles with the diameters given on the histogram's horizontal axis.

Ask students how a similar histogram of the hailstorms in your state might compare with the one shown for Colorado. (Students who live in Wyoming, Montana, South Dakota, Nebraska, or New Mexico should suggest that the histograms would have numerical data similar to Colorado's. Other states would have less frequent hailstorms and possibly smaller hailstones.)

▶ Propose Explanations

THINK ABOUT IT The hailstorm data in the graph is based on reports from people who call weather services and insurance companies to report hail falling in their area. Insurance companies will pay for damage on insured property caused by the weather.

▶ *Imagine you live and own property in Colorado. When would you report hail falling? Why? When would you not bother to report it? Why not?*

Answers will vary. Examples: I would report hail falling if it caused damage that my insurance company would pay for. I would not bother to report hail that is too small to cause damage.

Turn back to the tornado map on page 158. Use the information in the reading on page 161 to shade the states on the map that have a lot of hailstorms.

▶ *Which of those states also have an average of one or more tornadoes each year?*

All of them—Colorado, Wyoming, Montana, South Dakota, Nebraska, and New Mexico

Hailstorms and tornadoes both form out of severe thunderstorms.

▶ *What can you infer about the states that have both hailstorms and tornadoes?*

It is likely that severe thunderstorms are more common in those states than in other states.

▶ Take Action

GENERATING QUESTIONS Make a list of questions about hailstorms that scientists could investigate—for example, *What weather conditions exist when hailstorms occur?* Think about ways that scientists could investigate these questions. Remember: Scientific questions must be testable.

Students' questions will vary.

Assessment
Skill: Predicting

Use the following task to assess each student's progress:

Ask students to imagine they live in a farm town in Colorado. It is summertime and a hailstorm has just dropped hailstones that range in size from $1\frac{1}{2}$ to 2 inches (4–5 cm). Ask students to describe the kind of damage they might expect to see in their town. Ask them to predict the long-term effects of this damage. (Students might predict that the large-size hail will damage crops and cause other types of minor damage to outdoor objects such as cars and trucks. They might also predict injury to both people and animals outdoors at the time of the storm. Long-term effects might include financial losses due to crop damage.)

▶ Propose Explanations

THINK ABOUT IT For the third question, tell students that their inferences must be based on the information in the reading and the tornado map on page 158. Ask: *During what time of year are hailstorms the most frequent?* (summer, when severe thunderstorms are also most likely to occur) Then ask students to speculate why most severe hailstorms occur in these midwestern states. (The weather in these states has the conditions that form hailstorms.)

▶ Take Action

GENERATING QUESTIONS Remind students that scientific questions are *testable*. Scientific inquiry begins with a question, which may be the basis for a hypothesis. Information is gathered through observation or experimentation. From this, conclusions are drawn.

After students have compiled their list of questions, call on volunteers in turn to read their questions aloud and suggest at least one way that scientists could investigate the question. Let other students add their own ideas as well.

UNIT 4 Weather and Climate
CHAPTER 15 / LESSON 45

Point of Lesson
Snowstorms were more difficult to predict and deal with in the past than they are today.

Focus
- Structure of the earth system
- Natural hazards
- Science and technology in society

Skills and Strategies
- Making inferences
- Comparing and contrasting
- Recognizing cause and effect

Advance Preparation
Vocabulary
Make sure students understand this term. The definition can be found in the glossary at the end of the student book.
- weather

CHAPTER 15 / LESSON 45
Weird Weather

DIGGING OUT

A fierce surprise snowstorm can leave people trapped indoors or stranded far from home.

A blizzard is not just your average snowstorm. It's a severe storm with high wind speeds, temperatures well below freezing, and snow falling fast enough to make seeing difficult. The snow piles up rapidly and gets so high that it can take days to clear away. In one of the most famous storms, the blizzard of 1888, more than 400 people lost their lives.

NOTEZONE
Underline the words that explain why no one expected the storm.

▶ **Read**

A man living in Connecticut when the blizzard hit remembered the storm 50 years later.

The Blizzard of 1888

I couldn't see ten feet ahead of me... Snow was up to my waist. It kept snowin' all day Tuesday, and Wednesday...when I went up to town there was a drift way over your head clear from the town hall across to Woodruff's house.
Warren Westwood and Bill Woods, who...used to drive... [a horse-drawn wagon]...to work...started out Monday noon. They bought a snow shovel.... They got stuck in a big drift miles from home. One of them got the horse out and got on his back and the other took hold of the horse's tail. They hadn't got very far this way when the horse dropped dead. They plodded on, makin' their way the best they could by what landmarks they could recognize. They climbed over stone walls, and dead trees, and fell down I don't know how many times, and they was near exhausted.
...That was the worst snowstorm there ever was. And it was such beautiful weather before—nobody could realize what was comin'.

plodded: walked slowly **landmark:** an object that marks a location

From: "Weatherlore." Federal Writers' Project. Library of Congress.

FIND OUT MORE
SCIENCESAURUS
Water Cycle 216
Weather 218

TEACHING PLAN pp. 164–165

INTRODUCING THE LESSON
This lesson introduces blizzards as another type of severe weather and gives one person's account of the devastating blizzard of 1888.

Ask students to relate what they know about blizzards and the conditions that define a snowstorm as a blizzard. Tell them to consider factors such as wind speed, temperature, and visibility.

Many students will not realize that a blizzard is a special type of snowstorm with particular characteristics—freezing temperatures, large amounts of falling and blowing snow, winds of at least 56 km (35 mi) per hour, and poor visibility.

▶ **Read**

Have students find examples of ungrammatical and informal language in the reading. ("went up to town," "took hold of," "hadn't got very far," "they was near exhausted") Explain that quoted personal accounts such as this reading are referred to as oral history. Part of the tradition of an oral history is to keep true to the language used at that time and the wording used by the person telling the story. An oral history often includes grammar that is incorrect because that is how the person actually told the story. You may want to have a student with drama experience read the story aloud as the actual person might have spoken it.

Ask students to share their personal experiences with snowstorms and blizzards. Point out to students that when they tell their stories, their descriptions are their own oral histories.

▶ Propose Explanations

COMPARE AND CONTRAST
What tools did people use to clear the snow from the blizzard of 1888? Look for clues in the reading and in the photograph.

shovels, horse-drawn wagons

▼ 1888: Snow removal in Connecticut

▶ What tools do we have today for clearing large amounts of snow?

snowplows, dump trucks,
snowblowers, shovels

▶ How do people today find out about blizzards that are on the way? Why couldn't people be warned about the coming blizzard in 1888?

Today, meteorologists have the technology to gather weather data
and predict upcoming storms days ahead, but they did not have the
tools to collect and analyze weather data in 1888. Even if the storm
could be predicted, people back then could not get weather
information by radio, television, and the Internet like we can today.

MAKE INFERENCES
▶ How did the tools available in 1888 affect how well people could clear the snow from the storm?

It took a long time to clear the snow using shovels and horse-drawn
wagons. People could be trapped inside for days.

165

More Resources
The following resources are also available from Great Source.

SCIENCESAURUS
Water Cycle   216
Weather   218

WRITE SOURCE 2000
Personal Narrative   154

Enrichment
Have students interview an older person who has experienced a severe storm such as a blizzard, tornado, or hurricane. Tell students to ask about the conditions leading up to the storm and what happened during and after the storm. Students could also ask if the person made preparations for the storm or was caught off guard.

Assessment
Skill: Classifying

Use the following question to assess each student's progress:

What conditions are necessary to classify a snowstorm as a blizzard? (A blizzard has high wind speeds, poor visibility, large amounts of falling and blowing snow, and freezing temperatures.)

▶ Propose Explanations

COMPARE AND CONTRAST Ask: *How does today's technology enable people to prepare for severe weather?* (Today's weather forecasts alert people ahead of time, so fewer people are likely to be trapped in situations that may cause injury, illness, or death.)

MAKE INFERENCES Point out that in some states, severe snowstorms can trap people for a long time if they are not careful. Ask students to give examples of how people might become trapped during a blizzard. (People could be trapped in their cars if they are traveling in a blizzard, or in a building—a house, a school, or an office building—if the snowfall is extreme and they have no way to shovel themselves out.)

Discuss with students the importance of heeding weather forecasters' warnings of severe weather.

CHECK UNDERSTANDING
Ask students what kind of preparations they might make if meteorologists were predicting a blizzard for their area. (Have supplies on hand in case of power outages and loss of heat: candles or lanterns, flashlights, extra batteries, water, canned or dry food that will not spoil, a battery-operated radio, and blankets.)

CHAPTER 15 / LESSON 45   165

CHAPTER 16
Overview

Climate Change

LESSON 46
Ancient Climates
Point of Lesson: *Tree rings can provide information about climate conditions in Earth's past.*

Trees growing in temperate climates form annual growth rings whose width depends on growing conditions. Dendrochronology involves analyzing growth rings for clues about climate conditions during the time the tree was alive. The recent discovery of a stand of 50,000-year-old trees in South America provides a snapshot of climate conditions at that place and time.

Materials
Before You Read (p. 166), for the class:
- short section of board (optional)
- short log (optional)

Enrichment (p. 167), for the class:
- PBS video "Secrets of the Dead: Catastrophe!" (available for purchase through the ShopPBS Web site www.pbs.org)

Explore (p. 168), for each student:
- 3 strips of paper

Connections (p. 168)
- research sources about humans 50,000 years ago

LESSON 47
On Thin Ice
Point of Lesson: *The Inuit people are experiencing the effects of climate change.*

Warmer temperatures are threatening the traditional Inuit way of life by causing the spring melt to happen at an earlier date. Scientists are asking Inuit elders and students to assist in making observations to explore this phenomenon.

Materials
none

LESSON 48
Meltdown?
Point of Lesson: *Scientists disagree about whether global warming is affecting Arctic ice.*

A report about thinning Arctic sea ice offers an example of scientists disagreeing about the meaning of data. Such disagreements are inherent to the nature of scientific inquiry. In this case, some scientists challenge the validity of the data while others offer differing explanations for the observation of thinning ice.

Materials
Introducing the Lesson (p. 172), for the class:
- Earth globe

Science Scope Activity (p. 173), for each group:
- 3 clear plastic shoeboxes with lids
- masking tape (for labels)
- seltzer tablet
- duct tape (2 rolls total may be shared by groups)
- beaker, 500-mL
- 3 desk lamps with 100-watt bulbs
- 3 small thermometers (metal- or plastic-backed)
- water

Connections (p. 174), for the class:
- Earth globe or a map centered on the North Pole

Laboratory Safety

Review these safety guidelines with students before they do the Science Scope Activity in this lesson.
- Because water is involved, make sure to use only GFCI outlets for the lamps.
- Do not taste or eat the seltzer tablet.
- Both the 100-watt bulbs and the shades of the desk lamps may become hot enough to burn the skin. Let lamps cool completely before putting them away.
- Immediately report any broken glass to your teacher. Stay out of the area until it has been cleaned up.

UNIT 4: WEATHER AND CLIMATE

Science Scope Activity

Greenhouse Effect or Natural Cycle?

NSTA has chosen a Science Scope *activity related to the content in this chapter. You'll find the activity's procedure in Lesson 49, page 173.*

Time: 15–20 minutes for initial set-up; 3 hours for follow-up observations at 30 minute intervals

Materials: 3 clear plastic shoeboxes with lids; masking tape (for labels); seltzer tablet; duct tapes (2 rolls total); 500-mL beaker; 3 desk lamps with 100-watt bulbs; 3 thermometers; water

Human activities are adding carbon dioxide to the atmosphere. One hypothesis holds that global warming is occurring because of the greenhouse effect (carbon dioxide bonding with water vapor in the atmosphere).

In this activity, students create a model to test the effect of atmospheric carbon dioxide and water vapor on air temperature. If water vapor alone can increase atmospheric temperature, then human beings are not necessarily responsible for global temperature increases.

Results probably will support the hypothesis that the greenhouse effect contributes to global warming. Students may be tempted to say that their experiment proves "for a fact" that the hypothesis is true. Use this opportunity to reinforce that a hypothesis can only be supported or disproved—never proved. Remind students that they controlled conditions in the shoeboxes. In the real world, there are many more variables (such as wind and air pressure) that must be considered. These variables are the reason that hypotheses about global warming generate such controversy.

Have students work in small groups.

(continued on page 173)

Background Information

Climatology

A major concern in the science of climatology is whether Earth's climate is changing at present and if so, how it is changing and whether those changes are natural or are induced by human activities. Investigating these questions includes examining evidence of past climates—paleoclimatology—as well as collecting data about current climate conditions.

Climatology can be controversial because of the implications of one of its best-known hypotheses: that the greenhouse effect is causing global warming. The greenhouse effect is a supposed increase in atmospheric temperatures due to an increase in carbon dioxide and other so-called "greenhouse gases" released into the atmosphere by human activities, especially the burning of fossil fuels. The greenhouse effect is controversial because if human activity is causing an unnatural change in global climates, then, some believe, humans have an obligation to limit or halt the production of greenhouse gases. Doing so would require additional expense on the part of both businesses and individuals.

UNIT 4 Weather and Climate

CHAPTER 16 / LESSON 46

Point of Lesson
Tree rings can provide information about climate conditions in Earth's past.

Focus
- Earth's history
- Nature of science
- Science as a human endeavor
- Change, constancy, and measurement

Skills and Strategies
- Comparing and contrasting
- Making inferences
- Interpreting scientific illustrations

Advance Preparation

Vocabulary
Make sure students understand these terms. Definitions can be found in the glossary at the end of the student book.
- circumference
- data
- earthquake
- weather

Materials
Gather the materials needed for *Before You Read* (p. 166), *Enrichment* (p. 167), *Explore* (p. 168), and *Connections* (p. 168).

TEACHING PLAN pp. 166–167

CHAPTER 16 / LESSON 46
Climate Change

Ancient Climates

What can ancient trees tell us about ancient climates? A lot.

Climate is the average weather conditions—temperature and precipitation—in a particular place over a long period of time. Scientists are trying to find out if climates around the world are changing. They need to compare conditions in recent years with conditions hundreds and even thousands of years ago. One way to do this is to study ancient trees.

▶ Redwood forest

Trees that live in areas with seasonal changes form growth rings in their trunks. Each year a new ring forms. The thickness of a ring depends on the weather conditions during the year it formed—thicker rings in wet weather and thinner rings in dry weather. Over a tree's lifetime, the rings form a year-by-year record of the climate. *Dendrochronology* is the study of how tree ring patterns relate to climate changes in the past.

▶ Before You Read

INSIDE A TREE Have you ever looked at the end of a log that had been sawed straight across? Draw what the inside of the tree trunk looked like.

Students should draw a series of concentric rings.

INTRODUCING THE LESSON
In this lesson, students learn about the use of ancient tree rings to study climate changes.

Ask students to list the things a tree needs to grow. (water and other nutrients, soil, sunlight, and warm temperatures) Ask: *What does a variation in the width of tree rings indicate?* Students may think that tree ring width indicates only variations in water—that a wide ring means a wet year and a narrow ring means a dry year. Explain that narrow rings can be caused by other factors, such as insect attacks or pollutants in the soil.

Students may be interested in knowing that the first use of dendrochronology was for dating archaeological sites. Wood from ancient structures provides the rings used in dating these sites of former human habitation.

▶ Before You Read

Time: 10 minutes
Materials: (optional) short section of board, short log

INSIDE A TREE Students who have not viewed a cut tree may have noticed the "grain" of wood products. Wood grain is caused by the pattern of tree rings.

The long side of a board does not show the rings, but the cut end will show part of a set of rings. You may want to bring in a short section of a board and a short log for students to examine.

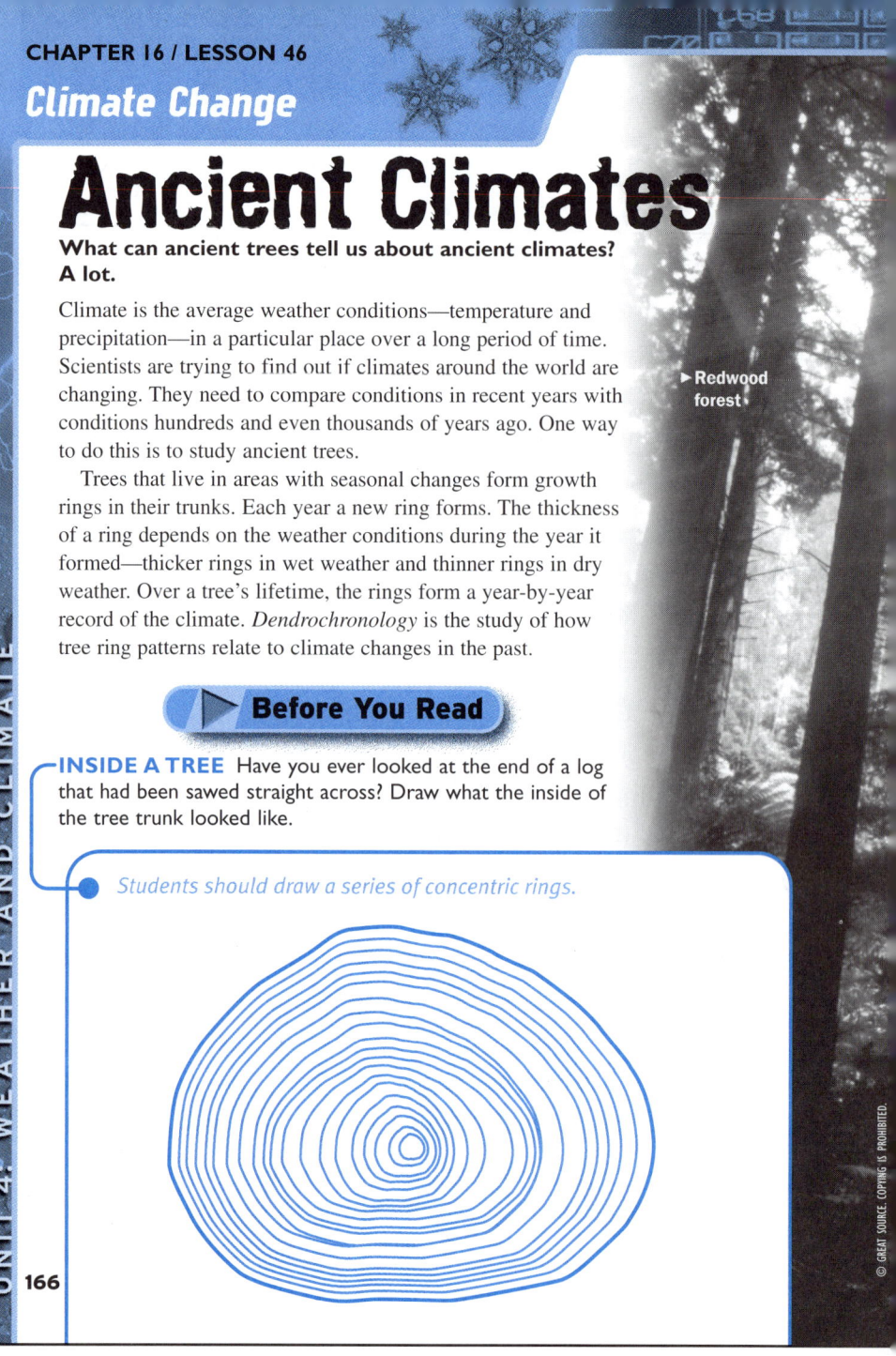

▶ **Read**

Fidel Roig found thousands of years of climate data in ancient South American tree stumps.

What Trees Know

Fifty millennia ago, volcanic ash and mud buried a forest of conifers along a Pacific shoreline in what is now southern Chile. Now, by examining the tree rings of the remaining stumps, an international team of scientists has reconstructed the earliest year-to-year record yet of climate [conditions].

The stumps of the tree species *Fitzroya cupressoides* are roughly 50,000 years old, says lead scientist Fidel A. Roig.... Data from these trees "provide a year-by-year indication of general climate [patterns]...," says team member Keith R. Briffa.... Using annual growth-ring patterns in trees, some researchers have inferred temperatures dating back about 10,000 years, or to the end of the last ice age....

In the new analysis...scientists took cross sections of 28 of the ancient stumps and measured the width of each tree ring. By averaging the data, they produced a growth record of the 1,229 years before the trees were buried, the researchers say....

Connie A. Woodhouse, a paleoclimatologist...cautions that the new data provide only a "snapshot" of an ancient climate. She says she hopes researchers will uncover more trees that can bridge the gap between old and new climate records.

---

conifer: a tree that has needle-like leaves and produces seeds in cones
reconstructed: built something again
ice age: a time period when Earth's climate was cooler and sheets of ice covered large areas of land
paleoclimatologist: a scientist who studies ancient climates

From: Wang, Linda. "Ancient Tree Rings Reveal Past Climate." *Science News.*

NOTEZONE

Underline the procedure that the scientists used to produce a growth record.

FIND OUT MORE

SCIENCESAURUS
Climate 227
Factors Affecting Climate 228
Pattern of World Climates 230

SCILINKS
THE WORLD'S A CLICK AWAY
www.scilinks.org
Keyword: Changes in Climate
Code: GSED20

167

Enrichment

Time: 30 minutes
Materials: PBS video "Secrets of the Dead—Catastrophe!" (available for purchase through the ShopPBS Web site www.pbs.org)

This PBS video describes evidence of a two-year period of unusually cold weather that occurred about 535 A.D. and explores hypotheses about what caused it. The video includes a visit to the Tree Ring Lab at Lamont-Doherty Earth Observatory, where a scientist describes the information that can be obtained from tree rings as well as how tree rings are sampled, processed, and interpreted. Show the tree-ring segment, then ask students to compare the demonstration in the video with the description of methods on pages 168–169. The video also includes segments on ice cores and carbon-14 dating.

▶ **Read**

Help students understand and expand on the idea of a climate "snapshot." Draw a time line on the board. Mark *50,000 years ago* at the left end, *10,000 years ago* about four-fifths of the way along the line, and *Today* at the right end. Invite a student to color the area of the time line for which scientists have climate data, according to the reading. The colored areas should indicate a span equal to about 1,200 years around the 50,000-year mark and the entire length from 10,000 years ago to today. Emphasize that we do not have any climate data for the period from 50,000 years ago to 10,000 years ago. The buried trees provide a "snapshot" of a long-ago era.

CHECK UNDERSTANDING

Skill: Interpreting scientific illustrations

Ask students to sketch and label a series of five tree rings that would result from the following five years, in this order:
Year 1: wet
Year 2: dry
Year 3: dry
Year 4: wet
Year 5: dry
(Students' sketches should show wide rings for Years 1 and 4, narrow rings for Years 2, 3, and 5.)

CHAPTER 16 / LESSON 46   167

CHAPTER 16 / LESSON 46

More Resources
The following resources are also available from Great Source and NSTA.

ScienceSaurus
Climate	227
Factors Affecting Climate	228
Pattern of World Climates	230

Reader's Handbook
Elements of Graphics: Diagram 552

www.scilinks.org
Keyword: Changes in Climate
Code: GSED20

Connections
Time: will vary
Materials: research sources about humans 50,000 years ago

SOCIAL STUDIES Have students do research to find out where humans were living 50,000 years ago. Were any humans living in South America, near where the trees described in the reading were buried? If not, where were humans living? How did humans live at that time—did they farm, or hunt? Did they build cities? Do experts agree about where and how humans were living at that time?

Teaching Plan pp. 168–169

Explore

HOW ARE DATA COLLECTED? A tree trunk grows in circumference each growing season. How much it grows depends on conditions such as temperature, rainfall, and sunlight. For example, a tree grows more in a rainy year than in a dry year. A ring forms as each growing season comes and goes. While the tree is growing quickly, a light-colored band of new growth forms. When growth slows later in the growing season, a darker color band forms.

▶ Tree rings are formed every year. How does that make them good recorders of weather data?

They show what the weather was like for every year that the tree was alive.

Scientists also collect samples of an ancient tree's rings by drilling sideways into the trunk and removing a core sample. The sample contains a small piece of every ring. They measure and record the width of each ring.

▶ Suppose scientists see a thicker growth ring for one year than for others. What can they infer about weather conditions that year?

They can infer that the weather conditions were excellent for that species of tree to grow, in that place.

By studying the core sample of a tree that lived 50,000 years ago, scientists can make a year-by-year time line of weather conditions during the lifetime of the tree. (This core sample is labeled number 1 in the diagram.) Scientists also take core samples of other ancient tree stumps—some older, some younger—in the same area. (These core samples are numbered 2 and 3 in the diagram.) They then compare the ring patterns from all the samples by overlapping their matching rings. This method provides a longer time line than only one tree can provide.

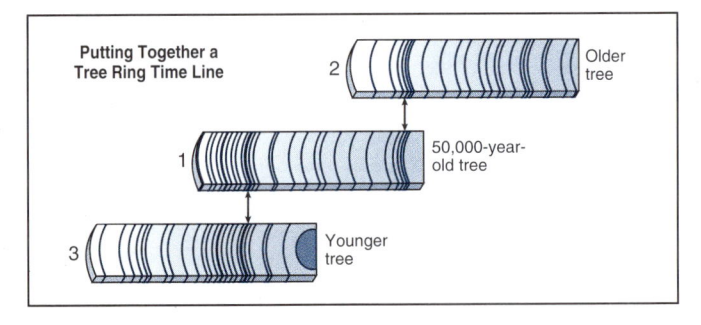

Putting Together a Tree Ring Time Line
- 2 — Older tree
- 1 — 50,000-year-old tree
- 3 — Younger tree

168

Explore
Time: 5–10 minutes
Materials: strips of paper, 3 per student

HOW ARE DATA COLLECTED? You may want to tell students that trees growing at the edge of their range provide better data than trees of the same species growing under optimal conditions. For example, a tree growing in an area that does not always have enough rainfall will show greater differences in ring width than the same species of tree growing where rainfall is plentiful.

Point out that the study described in the reading used cross-sections of trees and that core samples are another common way of gathering tree-ring data. Explain that a core sample is a long, thin piece of wood showing the rings in a tree. Core samples are collected using increment borers, which make it possible to take a sample from a living tree without cutting it down or harming it.

Students may benefit from manipulating their own "core samples." Have each student draw a series of growth rings on three strips of paper, making sure that some sections on one strip match up with sections on the other two strips, as in the illustration on this page. Have students swap core sample sets with each other and overlap the strips so the sections match up.

168 CHAPTER 16 / LESSON 46

▶ **What evidence would scientists need in order to infer that the climate had changed in an area over a thousand years?**

They would have to see if the rings got wider or narrower in trees that lived during those 1,000 years.

READING TREES A tree's growth is affected by many factors. These include soil moisture, air and soil temperatures, sunlight, and wind. Insect attacks and forest fires also affect tree growth. The width of a tree ring is the result of all these factors. For some trees, one factor may be more important than the others. If a ring is thick or thin, the dendrochronologist can infer what weather condition may have caused it.

Trees on high mountains, where it is cold, are most affected by changes in temperature. In warmer years with enough soil moisture, the trees will grow more. In colder years with the same soil moisture, they will grow less.

▶ **What climate condition could dendrochronologists study by observing rings from trees on a mountaintop? What characteristic of the rings would provide evidence of warmer or cooler years?**

temperature; thickness of the rings

▶ **What climate condition could dendrochronologists study by taking core samples from trees in dry, hot, desert-like areas?**

precipitation

▶ **Take Action**

DO RESEARCH Climate scientists find weather records in other places besides tree rings. Find out about one of the following. What makes it a good recorder of climate change?
- glacier ice
- fossil pollen
- ocean sediments
- ocean coral

Answers will vary.

Assessment
Skill: Making inferences

Use the following task to assess each student's progress:

Imagine that a volcano erupts, sending a cloud of ash into the atmosphere that partly blocks the sun around the world for two years. How might tree rings record this event? (Tree rings would probably be narrow for those two years because the trees would have less sunlight and would not grow as much.) *Note:* In fact, dry areas often have wider tree rings resulting from these events. Blocked sunlight reduces evaporation, so trees have more water for growth. However, this result is beyond what students should be expected to infer.

READING TREES Ask students to imagine a thick stand of trees. A forest fire sweeps through, leaving only a few trees alive. Those trees, which were crowded by others before the fire, now get more sunlight than they did before. Ask: *What would the growth rings on those trees look like for the years after the fire, compared with the years before the fire?* (The rings would be wider.) *How does this example show the importance of looking at more than one tree when gathering climate data?* (Any one tree might have special conditions affecting its growth, but by looking at many trees, you will have data about conditions that affected all trees in an area.)

▶ **Take Action**

Time: will vary
Materials: research sources about climate change

DO RESEARCH When students have completed their research, have them compare the various methods in a class discussion. Challenge the class to explain why no one method alone is enough to give a complete picture of climate change. Ask how having more than one kind of data for the same time period could be useful to scientists—for example, both tree rings and glacier ice. (Tree rings might show years of little growth; glacier ice data for the same period might have volcanic ash, suggesting the cause of the reduced growth.)

UNIT 4 Weather and Climate
CHAPTER 16 / LESSON 47

Point of Lesson
The Inuit people are experiencing the effects of climate change.

Focus
- Change, constancy, and measurement
- Populations, resources, and environments
- Natural hazards
- Science as a human endeavor

Skills and Strategies
- Predicting
- Making inferences
- Interpreting data
- Recognizing cause and effect

Advance Preparation

Vocabulary
Make sure students understand these terms. Definitions can be found in the glossary at the end of the student book.
- climate
- weather

CHAPTER 16 / LESSON 47
Climate Change

ON THIN ICE

Climate change may have the greatest effect on people who depend on ice.

The Inuit people live in Arctic Canada and in Alaska. Here, in one of the harshest climates on Earth, the Inuit build homes, gather food, and raise families. Their traditional diet includes fish, seals, and other mammals. Sometimes whales are hunted. Seals are the Inuit's main food source during the winter. Seals also provide food for their dogs, skins for clothing, tents, and boats, and fuel for light and heat.

The Inuit hunt seals on the Arctic Ocean ice. But lately, hunting is more dangerous than in the past. This is because the ice is thin in places where the Inuit had safely hunted seals for generations.

▲ Inuit girl

▶ Read

NOTEZONE
Underline the evidence of unusually warm weather that has been observed by the Inuit people.

Reporter Sue Armstrong visited a Canadian Inuit village in 2001. Here she describes some of the changes the villagers have been experiencing.

ARCTIC CHANGES

Unusual events are being reported across the Arctic. Inuit families going off on snowmobiles to prepare their summer hunting camps have found themselves cut off from home by a sea of mud, following early thaws. Some have discovered that the meat they cached in the ice as food for future trips has thawed and rotted. There are reports of igloos losing their insulating properties as the snow drips and refreezes; of caribou clothing clogging with ice in unusually humid weather; of lakes draining into the sea as permafrost melts...and sea ice breaking up earlier than usual, carrying seals beyond the reach of hunters.

FIND OUT MORE

SCIENCESAURUS
Climate 227
Factors Affecting Climate 228
Pattern of World Climates 230

SCLINKS
www.scilinks.org
Keyword: Changes in Climate
Code: GSED20

cached: stored in a hidden place
igloo: a temporary Inuit home made from blocks of solid snow
insulating: keeping heat in or out
permafrost: a layer of permanently frozen soil below the ground's surface

From: Armstrong, Sue. "Climate Change." *New Scientist.* (www.newscientist.com/hottopics/climate/climate.jsp?id=23154500)

170

TEACHING PLAN pp. 170–171

INTRODUCING THE LESSON
In this lesson, students learn about evidence of possible climate change in the Arctic.

Ask students to explain the difference between the terms *weather* and *climate*. (*Weather* refers to short-term changes in the atmosphere; *climate* refers to average conditions in a region over many years.)

Students may think that an unusually hot summer or warm winter is evidence of global warming. Emphasize that it is incorrect to attribute any one season's weather to long-term trends in climate change. Scientists analyze climate data from many years and from many regions before making statements about climate change.

▶ Read

After students have read the excerpt, ask them to identify the ways in which the Inuit people rely on cold weather to help them during the annual migration from the Arctic ocean ice to their summer hunting camps. (The Inuit must have snow to ride snowmobiles across, frozen storage for food supplies along the way, well-insulated igloos, warm clothing for the trip, and access to seals on the sea ice).

170 CHAPTER 16 / LESSON 47

▶ **Explore**

PREDICTING CHANGE Think about the unusual events reported by the Inuit.

▶ *How might the Arctic climate be changing?*
   The climate may be getting warmer.

▶ *How do you think this change could affect the Inuit way of life?*
   They would not be able to hunt seals on the ice, build igloos, keep
   their foods fresh, or wear clothing made from sealskin.

CONTRIBUTING TO SCIENCE With their traditions in danger, Inuit people are thinking ahead about possible climate change. Elders in Nunavut, Canada, meet to make plans for dealing with the changes. They are also sharing their lifelong knowledge of Arctic climate with scientists.

Children in Nunavut schools are also helping scientists. With their teachers, they collect weather data and check snow and ice conditions. They also record when buds open on certain plants and when insect eggs hatch. Hatching and budding are partly determined by air temperature.

▶ *If students and scientists find that insects in the same place are hatching earlier year after year, what might that tell them about the climate?*
   The climate is warming.

More Resources
The following resources are also available from Great Source and NSTA.

SCIENCESAURUS
Climate 227
Factors Affecting Climate 228
Pattern of World Climates 230

READER'S HANDBOOK
Cause-Effect Order 111

www.scilinks.org
Keyword: Changes in Climate
Code: GSED20

Assessment
Skill: Drawing conclusions

Use the following question to assess each student's progress:

What changes would the Inuit need to make if the Arctic climate is in fact warming? (Seal hunting would have to end earlier. They would need to catch more of the other animals they hunt. Not being able to freeze food would require them to hunt more often.)

▶ **Explore**

PREDICTING CHANGE Ask: *What kinds of data do you think scientists would look for to test the hypothesis that the Arctic climate is in fact warming and not just experiencing a single warm summer?* (Years of weather records going back as far as possible and additional data collected for several years into the future should be analyzed to determine whether warmer average temperatures are a long-term trend.)
Note: There is evidence that the Arctic is experiencing a warming trend, but the reading in this lesson does not address climate change.

CONTRIBUTING TO SCIENCE Challenge students to think of questions that scientists might use while interviewing Inuit elders about past weather conditions. (Examples: In what month did the sea ice start melting 20 and 40 years ago? What were weather conditions like during the annual migration? What was the last year you can remember when the meat caches were still frozen hard during the migration? Were there any years when they were partially thawed?)

CHECK UNDERSTANDING
Skill: Recognizing cause and effect
Ask students to draw a cause-effect organizer showing how warmer temperatures cause difficulty for the Inuit. An example is given below.

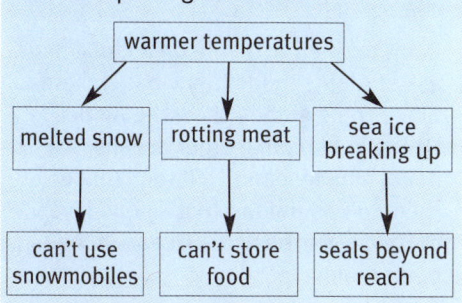

```
         warmer temperatures
        /         |          \
  melted snow  rotting meat  sea ice
      |            |       breaking up
      ↓            ↓            ↓
  can't use    can't store   seals beyond
  snowmobiles     food          reach
```

CHAPTER 16 / LESSON 47   171

UNIT 4 Weather and Climate
CHAPTER 16 / LESSON 48

Point of Lesson
Scientists disagree about whether global warming is affecting Arctic ice.

Focus
- Evidence, models, and explanation
- Understanding about scientific inquiry
- Nature of science

Skills and Strategies
- Comparing and contrasting
- Drawing conclusions
- Identifying variables
- Understanding that scientists may disagree about interpretation of evidence and even arrive at conflicting conclusions
- Generating questions

Advance Preparation

Vocabulary
Make sure students understand these terms. Definitions can be found in the glossary at the end of the student book.

- climate
- data
- precipitation
- temperature
- volume

Materials
Gather the materials needed for *Introducing the Lesson* (p. 172), *Science Scope Activity* (p. 166B and p. 173), and *Connections* (p. 174).

TEACHING PLAN pp. 172–173

CHAPTER 16 / LESSON 48
Climate Change

MELTDOWN?

Global warming is melting Arctic sea ice. Or is it?

You've probably heard the term *global warming*. Global warming is the idea that the average worldwide air temperature has risen over the past 100 years. Because air temperature is a major factor in climate, global warming may be changing climates around the world. Climate scientists are especially interested in the Arctic. Here, in the land of ice and snow, small increases in temperature can cause big changes.

▶ Before You Read

LOCAL CLIMATE Write about the climate and seasonal changes where you live.

▶ How many hours of daylight do you have in winter? How many in summer? Is there more precipitation in one season, or is precipitation about the same all year? Does the average temperature change during the year? What is the highest average temperature? What is the lowest?

Students' answers should reflect the climate conditions where they live, including any seasonal variations.

172

Time: 5 minutes
Materials: Earth globe

INTRODUCING THE LESSON
This lesson presents a disagreement among scientists about whether data provide sufficient evidence of climate change in the Arctic.

Point to the North Pole on a globe and ask students to identify what is there. Since some globes show the Arctic Ocean in blue, like other oceans, students may respond, "Water." Guide them to understand that a solid layer of ice covers the Arctic Ocean in the polar region.

Draw out misconceptions about the nature of scientific data, using this example: *Pet cats who are kept indoors live an average of 14 years. How do we know this? Did someone record the life span of every cat in the country and calculate the average?* (No. Students should realize that the life span of only some cats would be taken into account.) Explain that this method of collecting data is called *sampling*. In sampling, scientists collect a portion of all possible data and use that portion to draw conclusions. Generally, larger samples mean more reliable data. In the lesson, data about sea ice thickness are derived from a small sample.

▶ Before You Read

LOCAL CLIMATE Depending on your location, seasonal changes may be very noticeable or fairly subtle, but most students will have some idea of how average conditions vary throughout the year in their region.

Students may recall weather extremes when asked to describe averages. Remind them to describe average seasonal temperature and precipitation, not the coldest day last winter or the rainiest storm of the summer.

172 CHAPTER 16 / LESSON 48

▶ **Read**

Some scientists hypothesize that global warming is reducing the amount of ice in the Arctic. Other scientists disagree.

Melting Above, Melting Below

The great ice cover that stretches across the top of the globe has become about 40 percent thinner than it was two to four decades ago, scientists have found after analyzing data collected by nuclear submarines....

The scientists found...that from 1958 through 1976, the average thickness of the Arctic sea ice was about 10 feet [3 meters]. From 1993 through 1997, it was about six feet [1.8 meters]. In the 1990's, say the researchers, the thinning appeared to be continuing at a rate of about four inches [10 cm] a year.

There is substantial evidence that the climate of the Arctic and sub-Arctic region is warming, at least in some seasons. The area covered by sea ice has diminished and the duration of the cover has shortened in many places. Mountain glaciers in Alaska have shrunk, as has the Greenland ice cap.

The average surface temperature of the earth has risen by about 1 degree Fahrenheit [17 degrees Celsius] or a little more over the last century and by several times that amount in northern regions.

[Some scientists think] that a shift in ...natural patterns of atmospheric circulation in the Arctic may be responsible for the warmer North and the thinning sea ice. Other scientists say that the shift in natural patterns may have been touched off or enhanced by global warming....

substantial: a lot of
diminished: lessened
duration: how long something lasts
ice cap: ice and snow that cover a large area
atmospheric circulation: the movement of air masses in Earth's atmosphere
global warming: an increase in the world's average temperature, possibly caused in part by fossil fuel use

From: Stevens, William K. "Thinning Sea Ice Stokes Debate on Climate Debate." *The New York Times.*

NOTEZONE
Underline the two ideas scientists have for why the ice is thinning.

FIND OUT MORE
SCIENCESAURUS
Climate 227
Factors Affecting Climate 228
Pattern of World Climates 230

SCILINKS
THE WORLD'S A CLICK AWAY
www.scilinks.org
Keyword: Changes in Climate
Code: GSED20

Science Scope Activity
(continued from page 166B)

Procedure
Give students the following directions:
1. Label the boxes 1, 2, and 3.
2. Tape a thermometer in each box.
3. Leave Box 1 empty.
4. Add 300 mL water to Box 2.
5. Add 300 mL water to Box 3 and drop in a seltzer tablet. Then lay the lid on top, leaving a 2-cm ($\frac{3}{4}$ in.) gap to let air escape as it is replaced by carbon dioxide from the tablet's reaction with the water.
6. When the tablet in Box 3 is completely dissolved, put the lids tightly on all three boxes and seal them with duct tape.
7. Position the lamps so they shine on the boxes. Make sure all lamps are the same distance from the boxes. **Caution:** Do not put the lamps near the boxes until the lids are firmly in place and sealed.
8. Measure and record the temperature in each box every 30 minutes for 3 hours.

The greatest temperature increase will likely be in Box 3, with both carbon dioxide and water vapor in the air above the water. Explain that this result supports the hypothesis that carbon dioxide contributes to global warming, but emphasize that other factors could be affecting world climate. Point out that this is why hypotheses about global warming generate such controversy among scientists.

▶ **Read**

List the following questions on the board. Ask students to think about the answers as they reread the passage. Then discuss the answers as a class.

▶ *In which season would the climate probably be warming?* (summer)
▶ *In which season would the area covered by sea ice probably be smallest?* (summer)
▶ *What else do you already know about Arctic seasons?* (I know from Lesson 47 that sea ice broke up earlier than usual in 2001.)

CHECK UNDERSTANDING
Skill: Understanding that scientists may disagree about the interpretation of evidence and may even arrive at conflicting conclusions
Have students list evidence that the Arctic and sub-Arctic climates are warming. Then have them identify two hypotheses that may explain the evidence. (A shift in natural patterns of atmospheric circulation may be responsible. Global warming has caused or increased the shift in natural patterns.) *Does the evidence support both hypotheses?* (yes) *How could you test the hypotheses further to find out which is the stronger one?* (Observe the natural patterns of atmospheric circulation for several years to see if they really do change.)

CHAPTER 16 / LESSON 48

CHAPTER 16 / LESSON 48

More Resources

The following resources are also available from Great Source and NSTA.

SCIENCESAURUS

Climate	227
Factors Affecting Climate	228
Patterns of World Climates	230

READER'S HANDBOOK

Reading Know-how: Drawing Conclusions	41

MATH ON CALL

Gathering Data: Taking Samples	264

SCILINKS
THE WORLD'S A CLICK AWAY

www.scilinks.org
Keyword: Changes in Climate
Code: GSED20

Connections

Time: 25 minutes
Materials: Earth globe or a map centered on the North Pole

MATH Point out the North Pole on the globe or map. Tell students they can make 10 measurements of ice thickness in the Arctic Ocean. Ask: *Where should you take measurements*

(continued on page 175)

TEACHING PLAN pp. 174–175

▶ Explore

DISTINGUISHING DATA FROM CONCLUSIONS Before students fill in the table, give them a practice example:

▶ Students are lined up at the door. (observation)
▶ Class is over. (conclusion)

Emphasize that you do not observe that class is over. This is a conclusion based on observations. Students could also be lined up for a fire drill—a different conclusion based on the same observation.

ANALYZING VARIABLES Challenge students to think of other variables that might affect the results. For example:

▶ How did submarines measure the ice? Was the same method used in both 1976 and 1996, or did the method change?
▶ Were measurements taken the same week each year? Ice thickness could vary from early to late summer.

▶ Explore

DISTINGUISHING DATA FROM CONCLUSIONS Scientists disagree about if and why Arctic ice is changing. Some scientists argue that conclusions are being drawn when there are not enough observations to support them.

▶ Based on what you learned in the reading, label each of the following sentences "observation" or "conclusion."

Sentence	Observation or Conclusion?
Air temperatures during some seasons in the Arctic have risen.	observation
The average thickness of Arctic sea ice has decreased since 1958.	observation
Global warming is causing a shift in natural climate patterns.	conclusion
Arctic ice is thinning because of natural climate patterns.	conclusion
Arctic ice showed 40% thinning in the last 2 to 4 decades.	observation
Global warming is causing the Arctic sea ice to melt.	conclusion

ANALYZING VARIABLES

▶ How might *when* the data were collected affect the results?

1993 to 1997 might have been much warmer than most years are in the Arctic.

▶ How might *where* the data were collected affect the results?

The scientists might have just happened to be only in areas where ice was thinning.

▶ Propose Explanations

EVALUATE CONCLUSIONS Greg Holloway is a scientist at the Institute of Ocean Studies in Canada. He doesn't believe there's a "big melt" in the Arctic sea. He says not enough data have been collected to draw conclusions. The submarines that took the ice thickness data, for example, looked at only a small part of the Arctic sea. Holloway thinks winds may have pushed the ice into Canadian waters for a time. The submarines never

174

▶ Propose Explanations

EVALUATE CONCLUSIONS Emphasize that scientists try to consider many different explanations for the data they collect. Rising air and water temperatures is one explanation for thinning sea ice. Wind moving the ice is another explanation. Challenge students to suggest other possible explanations and describe how they would test them. (Example: There may be "warm spots" below the two places the ice has thinned. This could be tested by measuring water temperature and ice thickness in several places.)

entered Canadian waters. He thinks the ice may be becoming thicker in some spots and thinner in others—but is not disappearing.

▶ **Why is it too soon to draw the following conclusion? Global warming is causing the total volume of Arctic ice to decrease.**

We don't know if global warming is the cause of the thinner ice. We don't have enough data to know if all the Arctic ice is thinning.

▶ **List questions you'd like answered in order to be sure about changes in Arctic ice.**

Answers will vary. Example: How thick is the ice in many locations?

▶ **Take Action**

WRITE A RESEARCH PROPOSAL Pick one of the questions you listed above. Then, on a separate sheet of paper, develop a proposal to research the question. Your proposal should include the following parts.

1. The question you want to answer
2. The data you plan to collect
3. How you will go about collecting the data
4. Why having the data is important

Students' proposals will vary.

175

(continued from page 174)
to be sure you have a good sample of data? (Students might suggest laying a sheet of graph paper over the map, choosing 10 points spaced evenly apart, and measuring the ice there. Another suggestion might be to draw five equally-spaced concentric circles around the North Pole, draw a line through the circles and the North Pole, and take a measurement at each intersection of the line with a circle. Accept all answers that show students understand that a random sample would yield the most reliable data.)

Assessment
Skill: Drawing conclusions

Use the following task to assess each student's progress:

Imagine that more data have been collected. The data include ice measurements for five places. In all five places, the ice is thinner than it was in 1996. Do the data support the conclusion that warmer air and water temperatures are causing the ice to thin? (yes) *Do the data support the conclusion that wind is blowing the sea ice from one place to another?* (Yes, but if wind is moving the ice, it is less likely that the ice in all five places would be thinner than the ice measured in 1996.)

▶ **Take Action**

WRITE A RESEARCH PROPOSAL Divide the class into small groups, explaining that scientists often work in teams on proposals and on requests for research funding. Tell students that each group can apply for only one research grant, and they need to submit a proposal for just one research question. Emphasize that it does not matter which group member's question is chosen, only that the question is strong enough and the proposal written well enough to receive funding. Tell them that it is also acceptable to revise a question based on ideas from group members.

Student proposals should include a list of equipment they would need, an estimate of how long the data collection will take, and whether the time of year they collect data is important to their question.

CHAPTER 16 / LESSON 48   175

UNIT 5 Astronomy

About the Photo
The man shown in the small photo is the brilliant theoretical physicist and cosmologist Stephen Hawking, whom some compare to Einstein. Students might find it interesting that Hawking holds the same position at England's Cambridge University that Isaac Newton did. Hawking suffers from ALS (amyotrophic lateral sclerosis, commonly known as Lou Gehrig's disease), a disease that progressively weakens muscle control. Hawking has been confined to a wheelchair for much of his adult life and must use a computerized speech synthesizer to communicate. Unable to write, Hawking constructs diagrams and manipulates complex math equations in his head. Students can learn more about Hawking and his work by accessing "A Brief History of Stephen Hawking" at: vassa.net/hawking.htm.

About the Charts
A major goal of the *Science Daybooks* is to promote reading, writing, and critical thinking skills in the context of science. The charts below describe the types of reading selections included in this unit and identify the skills and strategies used in each lesson.

How do astronomers study objects in space?
When scientists want to learn about rocks or fossils, they can just dig into Earth's surface. But even the astronomers at NASA have to think up creative methods when it comes to approaching the sky.

In this unit you'll learn about objects in space and the tools scientists use to study them. Astronomers try to predict the orbit of a comet or asteroid when it approaches Earth and are even using probes to analyze the material in a comet's tail! They have debated whether Pluto is really a planet, have discovered evidence of water on Mars in the distant past, and have analyzed what the moons in our solar system are made of. You'll also learn about the life cycles of stars and the search for planets beyond our own solar system. And finally, you'll examine the "how" and "why" of space exploration.

SELECTION	READING	WRITING	APPLICATION
CHAPTER 17 • ROCKS AND ICE IN ORBIT			
49. "Asteroid Passes Near Earth" (news service article)	• Make a sketch • Main idea	• Make predictions • Label a diagram	• Make a scale drawing
50. "A Comet Changes Course" (NASA Web site story)	• Read for details	• Draw conclusions	
51. "StarDust" (NASA news release)	• Use prior knowledge • Active reading	• Interpret a diagram • Cause and effect	• Label a diagram • Defend your answer
CHAPTER 18 • SOLAR SYSTEM NEWS			
52. "Long Live Planet Pluto!" (news service article)	• Use prior knowledge • Directed reading	• Create a graphic organizer • Identify opposing views	• Create a mnemonic
53. "The Case of the Missing Mars Water" (NASA Web site story)	• Relate to past experiences • Main idea	• Interpret a scientific image • Make a list • Make inferences	• Write a "mission plan"
54.	• Read data in a table	• Create a line graph • Calculate percentages	• Analyze data

THE CHAPTERS IN THIS UNIT ARE...

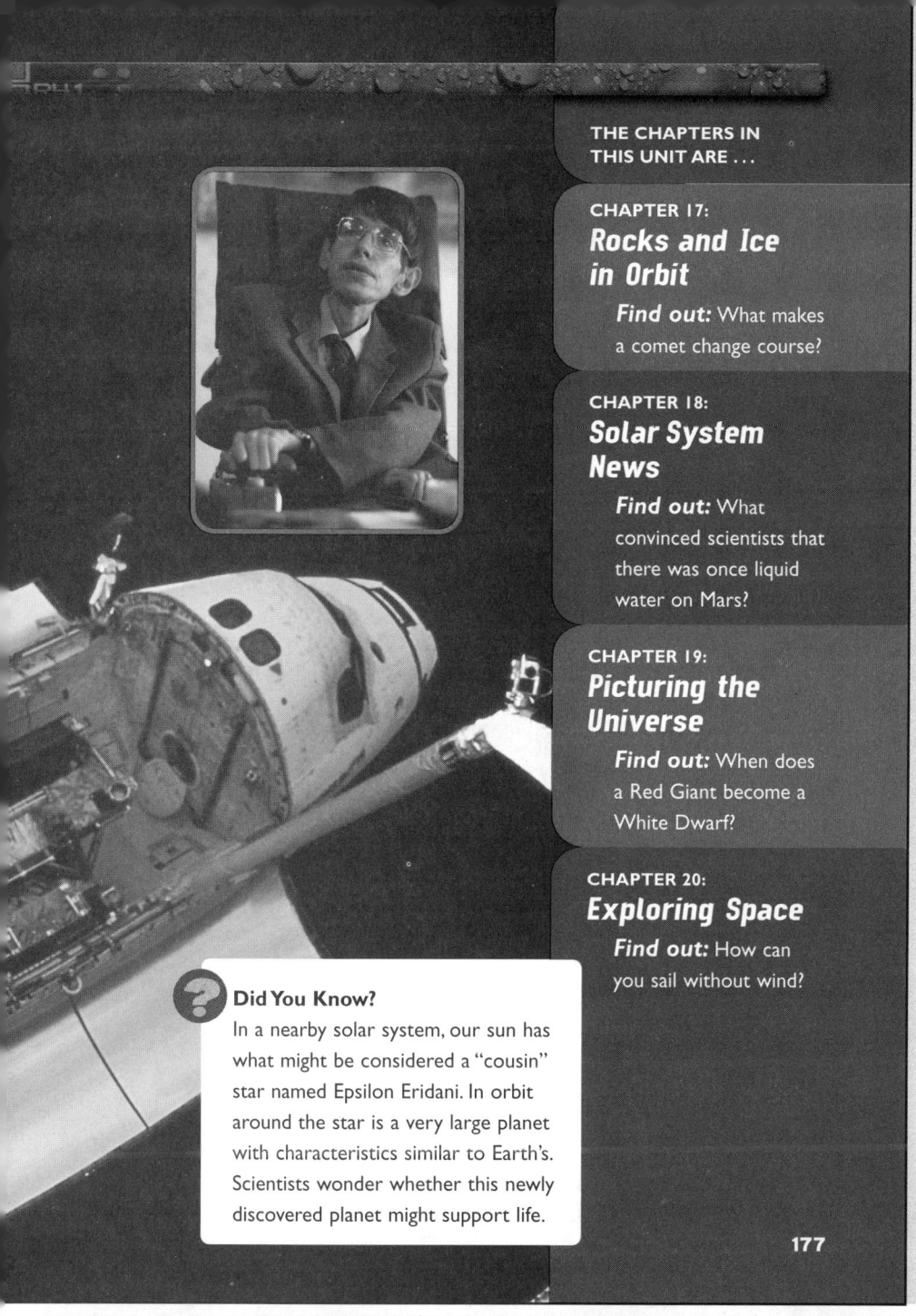

CHAPTER 17:
Rocks and Ice in Orbit
Find out: What makes a comet change course?

CHAPTER 18:
Solar System News
Find out: What convinced scientists that there was once liquid water on Mars?

CHAPTER 19:
Picturing the Universe
Find out: When does a Red Giant become a White Dwarf?

CHAPTER 20:
Exploring Space
Find out: How can you sail without wind?

? Did You Know?
In a nearby solar system, our sun has what might be considered a "cousin" star named Epsilon Eridani. In orbit around the star is a very large planet with characteristics similar to Earth's. Scientists wonder whether this newly discovered planet might support life.

Answers to *Find Out* Questions

CHAPTER 17
When a comet nears the sun and is heated, the ice in it can suddenly turn to gas. The gases shoot outward like small rocket motors, propelling the comet in a different direction. (pp. 182–183)

CHAPTER 18
Scientists have observed massive channels and eroded impact craters on Mars that are similar to features on Earth's surface produced by water erosion. (pp. 193–194)

CHAPTER 19
As a star ages, it grows larger and cooler and is known as a Red Giant. Later in its life cycle, all that is left of the star is a small white-hot core called a White Dwarf. (p. 198)

CHAPTER 20
Light exerts pressure. A solar sail will use the pressure of sunlight to propel a probe in the vacuum of space. (pp. 209–210)

SCILINKS
THE WORLD'S A CLICK AWAY

www.scilinks.org
Keyword: Developing Classroom Activities
Code: GSSD05

177

SELECTION	READING	WRITING	APPLICATION
CHAPTER 19 • PICTURING THE UNIVERSE			
55. "Young and Old Stars" (science magazine article)	• Active reading	• Interpret a diagram	• Colorize a diagram
56. "Team Sees Distant Planet" (science magazine article)	• Relate to past experiences • Read for details	• Generate questions	• Do online research
57.	• Background information	• Hands-on activity • Compare and contrast	• Draw conclusions • Defend your answer
CHAPTER 20 • EXPLORING SPACE			
58. "Sailing to the Stars" (NASA news release)	• Make a list • Directed reading	• Use analogies • Cause and effect	• Generate questions
59. "Preparing for Space" (National Geographic article)	• Pose questions • Directed reading	• Draw conclusions • Brainstorming	• Do research • Draw and label a diagram
60. "In My Opinion" (science magazine letters to the editor)	• Fact vs. sarcasm	• Cite evidence to support answer	• Debate opposing viewpoints • Write reflections

UNIT 5 ASTRONOMY   177

CHAPTER 17
Overview

Rocks and Ice in Orbit

LESSON 49
Close Encounters

Point of Lesson: *Scientists try to predict the orbits of asteroids that come close to Earth.*

Earth's close encounter with an asteroid in March 2002 sets the stage for an exploration into how asteroids are discovered, how their orbits are determined, and the reasons scientists would be interested in locating and predicting the orbits. Students use diagrams to compare the orbit of a near-earth asteroid with Earth's orbit and examine the factors that make it unlikely for an asteroid to collide with Earth.

Materials
Read (p. 179), for teacher demonstration:
▶ Earth globe
▶ grain of rice

Connections (p. 180), for the class:
▶ sheets of cardboard
▶ markers

Take Action (p. 181), for each student:
▶ graph paper
▶ drawing compass

LESSON 50
Off Track

Point of Lesson: *Sometimes a comet changes course as it orbits the sun.*

In this lesson, students read about an unusual comet, LINEAR, which did not behave as astronomers had predicted. Comet LINEAR first changed orbit, then blew up as it passed near the sun. Students compare the composition of comets with that of asteroids to understand the forces that can cause small comets, such as LINEAR, to change course.

Materials
none

LESSON 51
Capturing Comet Dust

Point of Lesson: *Studying comet dust can help us understand the history of our solar system.*

This lesson discusses NASA's StarDust probe, which was launched in 1999. StarDust is approaching comet Wild-2. It is scheduled to collect materials from the comet's tail in 2004, then return to Earth with its samples in 2006. Students interpret a diagram of StarDust's path through space to understand why the probe's round trip will take seven years. They then consider what astronomers hope to learn from StarDust's samples and use a diagram to relate predicted meteor showers with a comet's orbit.

Materials
none

Background Information

Lesson 49

Although asteroids are numerous (20,000 are known), they are small, with the total mass of all known asteroids estimated at a fraction of the mass of Earth's moon. Ceres, the largest asteroid, is about 940 kilometers in diameter (about one-quarter the diameter of Earth's moon); the smallest known asteroids are less than one kilometer across. Astronomers assume that most larger asteroids have been discovered and that many more smaller ones have yet to be found.

Most asteroids lie in the Asteroid Belt, which consists of hundreds of thousands of asteroids in a region of space lying between the orbits of Mars and Jupiter. Asteroids orbit the sun, and depending on the asteroid, can take three to six Earth years for one revolution. The location of the Belt means that asteroids are occasionally knocked out of their orbits by the gravitational pull of Jupiter or Mars. (Astronomers suspect that Mars's tiny moons Deimos and Phobos are really asteroids captured by the planet's gravity.) These asteroids are the ones that sometimes establish new orbits in the inner solar system, some of which become Near-Earth Asteroids, or NEAs.

Lesson 50

As a comet orbits the sun, it releases a tail of debris and gases that always points away from the sun. The debris and gases react with electrically charged particles travelling from the sun in so-called solar wind. The reaction causes the tail to glow, much like the gas in a fluorescent light bulb.

Lesson 51

As stated in the lesson, comets leave behind material in their orbits that Earth observers experience as meteors when the debris hits Earth's upper atmosphere. This material is too fragile to collect from the upper atmosphere and return to Earth's surface. Although this comet material cannot be collected, scientists can and do make important observations of the debris during meteor showers by using instruments aboard high-flying jets.

UNIT 5 Astronomy
CHAPTER 17 / LESSON 49

Point of Lesson
Scientists try to predict the orbits of asteroids that come close to Earth.

Focus
- Earth's history
- Earth in the solar system
- Motion and forces
- Science as a human endeavor

Skills and Strategies
- Predicting
- Using space/time relationships
- Interpreting scientific illustrations
- Comparing and contrasting

Advance Preparation
Vocabulary
Make sure students understand these terms. Definitions can be found in the glossary at the end of the student book.
- estimate
- gas
- planet
- prediction
- solar system

Materials
Gather the materials needed for **Read** (p. 179), **Connections** (p. 180), and **Take Action** (p. 181).

CHAPTER 17 / LESSON 49
Rocks and Ice in Orbit
Close Encounters

As we go about our daily lives, giant rocks are whirling around in space. Some are a little too close for comfort.

Scientists theorize that the solar system formed when a huge cloud of gases and dust came together. As these bits of material crashed into one another, they became larger and larger. Most of the dust and gas joined to form the sun. Most of the rest of the material eventually formed the planets, but there were leftover pieces.

If you could travel in a spaceship between the planets Mars and Jupiter, you might run into some leftover pieces—big rocky ones called *asteroids*. Asteroids are chunks of rock that are too small to be called planets. The area between Mars and Jupiter is called the Asteroid Belt because it contains most of our solar system's asteroids. A few asteroids, however, are closer to the sun than the Asteroid Belt. Like planets, asteroids travel around the sun along paths called *orbits*. The orbits of both asteroids and planets are ellipses (ovals) rather than circles. Asteroids' orbits usually are longer ellipses than planets' orbits. Scientists are interested in predicting the orbits of asteroids they find in space. Can you guess why?

An asteroid named Ida

▶ **Before You Read**

ROUND AND ROUND The drawing below shows the orbit of Earth around the sun. On the same drawing, show what you think the orbit of an asteroid might look like.

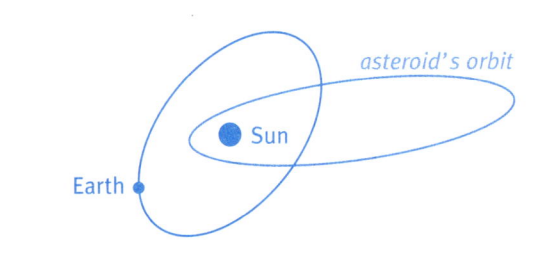

Accurate drawings would show an oval around the sun that is more elongated than Earth's orbit.

TEACHING PLAN pp. 178–179

INTRODUCING THE LESSON
This lesson discusses a recent close encounter with an asteroid and scientists' attempts to predict asteroids' orbits. Ask students if they know what an asteroid is. Students might think that asteroids are chunks of planets. Explain that most scientists think asteroids did not come from planets that broke apart but rather from material that never even came together to form a planet. Mention that astronomers think that the influences of Jupiter's gravity kept a planet from forming in what is now the Asteroid Belt between Mars and Jupiter. Asteroids are this leftover material. Have students answer the question posed at the end of the lesson introduction.

▶ **Before You Read**

ROUND AND ROUND Make sure students are familiar with the shape of an oval. Stress that some asteroids' orbits carry them closer to the sun than Earth is, but some asteroids also travel well beyond Saturn. Ask students whether they have ever seen a "shooting star" in the night sky. Explain that "shooting stars" are actually meteors and that meteors are very small asteroids. Meteors that fall to Earth are called *meteorites*.

NOTEZONE
Underline the reason why an asteroid might not be noticed as it approached Earth.

▶ Read

In March of 2002, Earth had a near miss with a passing asteroid.

Asteroid Passes Near Earth

An asteroid large enough to demolish a medium-sized city passed within 288,000 miles [460,800 km] of Earth without being noticed by astronomers until four days later.

The asteroid, about 165 feet [49.5 m] across, came from the direction of the sun, making it difficult for astronomers to spot. It passed by Earth on March 8, but wasn't seen until March 12 as it hurtled away.

Gareth Williams of the International Astronomical Union's Minor Planet Center in Cambridge, Massachusetts, helped spot the asteroid after it passed by. It was a close call in space terms. The moon is only 250,000 miles [400,00 km] away.

"The key is to detect these objects before they come out of the (sun's direction)," Williams told the Florida Today newspaper in Wednesday editions.

That way, astronomers can quickly determine an asteroid's orbit and predict whether it will hit the Earth.

▲ A telescope in New Mexico

astronomer: a scientist who studies the objects in space

From: The Associated Press. March 20, 2002.

FIND OUT MORE
SCIENCESAURUS
Solar System	
Objects	238
Asteroids	241

179

Enrichment
Have students consider the differences and similarities between asteroids and planets. Begin the discussion by asking students to list the characteristics of planets—they orbit the sun, rotate on their own axis, were formed from solar system materials, and may have moons. Go through each of these basics, and help students see if they apply to asteroids. (Most will apply; some asteroids even have their own orbiting bodies.) Lead the comparison to what is different about asteroids. Remind students that asteroids' orbits are likely to be longer ellipses than planets' orbits. Explain that most asteroids rotate on their own axis every 5 to 20 hours and that planets also vary greatly in the speed with which they rotate. For example, Jupiter rotates on its axis in about 10 hours, more than two times faster than Earth.

Help students realize that a planet's mass creates a true gravitational field. Tell students that because asteroids have less mass, they also have weaker gravitational fields, and this makes them less likely to have moons. However, in 1993 the Galileo space probe discovered a one-mile wide moon orbiting in the weak gravitational field of asteroid 243 Ida. The rock, called "Dactyl," was the first known moon of an asteroid. Dactyl may once have been knocked off of Ida in an asteroid collision and stayed in Ida's gravitational field.

▶ Read

Time: 20 minutes
Materials: Earth globe, grain of rice

Calm any fears that students may have about Earth being in any real danger of a collision with an asteroid. Explain that Earth and asteroids move in different planes, so the chances of a collision are too small to worry about. Using a globe to model Earth and a grain of rice to model an asteroid, show students how unlikely it is that two objects of such widely different sizes traveling in different planes would collide.

Explain that millions of meteors about the size of a pebble enter Earth's atmosphere and disintegrate each day. Those that do reach the ground are significantly reduced in size by friction with the atmosphere. Ask students what the terms "near miss" (in the reading's introduction) and "close call" (third paragraph) mean. Point out that although 460,800 km (288,000 miles) is "close" in space terms, it is still a tremendous distance.

CHECK UNDERSTANDING
Skill: Using space/time relationships
Ask: *Why would an asteroid be invisible from Earth as it approached and then visible after it passed Earth?* (It comes towards Earth from the direction of the sun, so the sun's brightness makes it almost impossible to see. After it passes Earth, the sun's brightness actually illuminates the asteroid when it is viewed from Earth.)

CHAPTER 17 / LESSON 49   179

CHAPTER 17 / LESSON 49

More Resources
The following resources are also available from Great Source.

ScienceSaurus
Solar System Objects	238
Asteroids	241

Math on Call
Elements of Geometric Figures: Planes	317
Scale Drawings	377

Reader's Handbook
Drawing Conclusions	41
Reading Science	100
Elements of Graphics: Diagram	552

Connections
Time: 20 minutes
Materials: sheets of cardboard, markers

MATH Explain to students that a *plane* is a flat surface that is infinitely wide and infinitely long. Asteroids, meteors, and Earth orbit the sun in different planes. Have students demonstrate planes of orbit using sheets of cardboard with an orbit drawn on each one. If necessary, assign a different plane to each student. Help students understand how unlikely it would be for orbiting objects to collide.

Teaching Plan pp. 180–181

▶ Explore

COMPARE ASTEROID ORBITS Astronomers around the world keep track of asteroids like the one in the reading. Once they have discovered an asteroid, the next step is to try to predict its orbit. Astronomers know that an asteroid's orbit is in the shape of an ellipse. They also know that the ellipse lies in an imaginary flat surface called a plane. The trick is to figure out the exact size and length of the ellipse and the angle of its plane. How do scientists do that? They use a strategy that you use to solve some math problems—estimate and check.

Astronomers begin by estimating the path the asteroid might follow and predicting its position in the sky. They then make observations of the asteroid's actual position in the sky as seen from Earth.

This diagram shows an imaginary asteroid's predicted position and its actual position. This imaginary asteroid has its orbit in the same plane as Earth. Most real asteroids would have an orbit in a different plane.

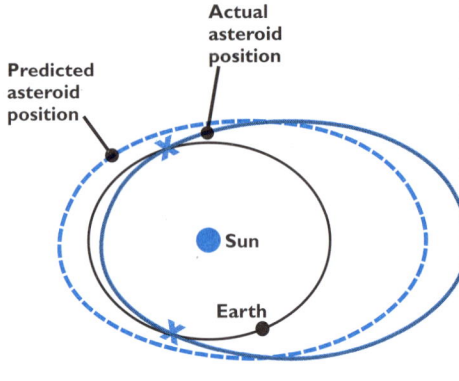

Sizes not to scale

▶ If the asteroid's predicted position and its actual position are not the same, what might astronomers conclude about their prediction?

Their prediction was not correct.

▶ If the asteroid's predicted position and actual position are not the same, what step must astronomers take next?

They must find a new and better way to predict the asteroid's orbit— gather more information, use new equipment.

▶ How will the astronomers know if their new prediction of the asteroid's orbit is correct?

when the actual locations of the asteroid they observe in the sky match the locations in their predicted orbit

▶ Mark an X on the diagram to show the places where the actual orbit of the asteroid crosses Earth's orbit.

180

▶ Explore

COMPARE ASTEROID ORBITS Use the Connections activity above to help students understand planes of orbit. Emphasize that asteroids rarely come close to Earth and hardly ever close enough to cross Earth's orbit, which makes it even more unlikely that both bodies would arrive at the same position at the same time.

Ask students to compare the asteroid's predicted and actual positions. They should note that the predicted path did not indicate the possibility of a collision. Closer observation and measurement would allow scientists to warn of any possible collision.

▶ Propose Explanations

WHY PREDICT ASTEROID ORBITS? Explain that astronomers try to predict asteroids' orbits for other reasons besides determining whether they will come close to Earth. For example, the behavior of asteroids can tell astronomers about the origins of the solar system and the gravitational forces at work. The composition of asteroids provides clues about how they formed in the early solar system. Tell students that the rock in asteroids is the oldest material in the solar system. It has never been melted like the materials that make up planets with interior heat sources.

▶ Propose Explanations

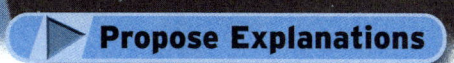

WHY PREDICT ASTEROID ORBITS?

▶ How can astronomers predict future positions of an asteroid?
by correctly predicting its orbit

▶ Why would people on Earth be interested in the orbits of asteroids, especially those that are closer than the Asteroid Belt?
People want to know if an asteroid will come close to Earth or even hit Earth. If an asteroid struck Earth, it would do a lot of damage.

▶ Look again at the actual orbit of the imaginary asteroid in the diagram. Where in its orbit would the asteroid have to be to collide with Earth? Where would Earth have to be?
The asteroid's orbit crosses Earth's orbit in two places, so there are two positions where a collision could take place. Both Earth and the asteroid would have to be in the same place at the same time for that to happen.

▶ Take Action

DRAW A DIAGRAM On a sheet of graph paper, draw a diagram that shows the positions of Earth, the moon, and the asteroid as described in the reading. Use a scale for distance of 1 square = 10,000 km. Show the asteroid's position when it passed Earth. Label the distance between Earth and the asteroid when it passed.
Student diagrams should show the distance between Earth and the asteroid labeled as 460,800 km at the position when it passed Earth.

Assessment

Skill: Predicting

Use the following question to assess each student's progress:

What steps would astronomers take if they suddenly detected a fairly large asteroid somewhere near Earth's orbit? (They would first estimate its speed and direction and try to predict its actual orbit. They would then check this estimate against actual observations made of its position in the sky as seen from Earth.)

▶ Take Action

Time: 35 minutes
Materials: graph paper, drawing compass

DRAW A DIAGRAM At a scale of 1 square = 10,000 km, the distances on students' diagrams should be as follows:

▶ between Earth and moon: 40 graph squares
▶ between Earth and asteroid: 46.8 graph squares

Students could also make a scale drawing to compare the relative diameters of the asteroid mentioned in the reading, the moon, and Earth. List the following diameters on the board:

▶ Earth: 12,800 km
▶ moon: 3,480 km
▶ asteroid: 90 m (0.09 km)

Help students select an appropriate scale for the drawing. At a scale of 1 square = 400 km, the diameters would be as follows:

▶ Earth: 32 graph squares
▶ moon: 8.7 graph squares
▶ asteroid: 0.000225 graph squares—smaller than the period at the end of a sentence!

UNIT 5 Astronomy
CHAPTER 17 / LESSON 50

Point of Lesson
Sometimes a comet changes course as it orbits the sun.

Focus
- Earth in the solar system
- Motion and forces
- Science as a human endeavor

Skills and Strategies
- Recognizing cause and effect
- Making inferences

Advance Preparation

Vocabulary
Make sure students understand these terms. Definitions can be found in the glossary at the end of the student book.
- asteroid
- comet
- gas
- orbit
- pressure
- solar system

CHAPTER 17 / LESSON 50
Rocks and Ice in Orbit

OFF TRACK

One giant snowball threw astronomers for a loop.

Most scientists believe that comets, like asteroids, are bits of material left over from the early days of our solar system. While asteroids are mostly rock, comets are made of dust, rock, and ice. Comets travel in large orbits that stretch to the far reaches of the solar system. As their orbits take them closer to the sun, they give off gases and rock particles. These materials often form comet tails that can be seen from Earth.

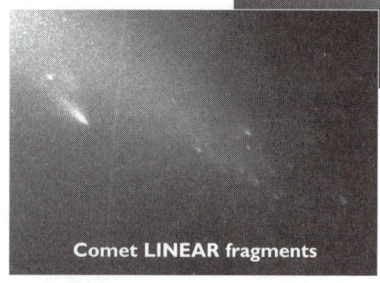

Astronomers can predict the orbits of comets, just as they can predict the orbits of asteroids. But comets are more likely than asteroids to "jump" orbit and move in a new direction. A comet named LINEAR did this. Comet LINEAR is named after the Lincoln Near-Earth Asteroid Research program. Astronomers in this program discovered LINEAR in September 1999.

Hubble NASA images

Comet LINEAR fragments

▶ **Read**

LINEAR was a surprising comet. Here is its story.

A Comet Changes Course

August 11, 2000

The astronomers measured LINEAR's movements in the sky. Using the measurements, they calculated just how they thought LINEAR would travel around the sun. But as LINEAR got closer to the sun, it didn't follow its expected path. It still **hurtled** toward the sun, but it **dodged** this way and that as it went.

The reason LINEAR bounced around so much is that a comet [is] like a "dirty snowball" [made of dust, rock, and ice]. As a comet travels in from the **outer reaches** of the solar system, the sun heats it.

FIND OUT MORE

SCIENCESAURUS
Solar System
  Objects   238
  Comets   242

SCLINKS
www.scilinks.org
Keywords: Comets, Asteroids, and Meteors
Code: GSED21

TEACHING PLAN pp. 182–183

INTRODUCING THE LESSON
In this lesson, students learn about factors that can change a comet's expected orbit. Draw students' attention to the photographs on this page, and ask them to speculate about what a comet's tail is made of. (Accept all answers without comment.) You might want to tell students that the Latin term for a comet, *stella cometa*, means "hairy star."

Some students may confuse comets with stars, thinking that comets give off light and heat as stars do. Point out the statement in the lesson introduction that comets are made of dust, rock, and ice. Explain that comets are not "burning" objects. Rather, a comet's tail glows because sunlight reflects off the dust, rock, and ice and because electrically charged particles give off light.

▶ **Read**

Make sure students understand that although both comets and asteroids formed during the early life of our solar system, only comets contain ice. This is because comets formed much farther away from the sun, in the outer, colder regions of our solar system. Like asteroids, comets orbit the sun, but their orbits are far more elliptical and their period (rate of orbiting) is far greater than that of asteroids—over 200 years in some cases.

Point out that the reading says the comet "dodged this way and that" and "bounced around." Emphasize that a comet's orbit is not determined only by the sun's gravity, as Earth's orbit is. A comet's predicted and actual paths may be quite different. Ask: *Why is this so?* (Gases shooting out of the comet can make it change direction.)

When the ice in a comet is heated quickly, it can turn to a gas suddenly. The gases shoot outward, and can move the comet just like small rocket motors. LINEAR is small for a comet, about the size of a mountain. So these jets of gas, and chunks of rocks breaking off, were able to push LINEAR off course.

...But the final surprise came when LINEAR passed close to the sun.... The sun's heat was enough to cause LINEAR to blow apart in an explosion.... Astronomers believe that most comets eventually just *disintegrate* and disappear. LINEAR was just more spectacular than most!

hurtled: sped
dodged: moved from side to side
outer reaches: the places in the solar system that are the farthest away from the sun, beyond Neptune and Pluto
disintegrate: fall apart into tiny pieces

From: "Comet Meltdown!." *NASA Kids.* Center Operations Directorate at Marshall Space Flight Center. (kids.msfc.nasa.gov/news/2000/news%2Dlinear.asp)

NoteZone
Underline the sentences that explain what caused LINEAR to move off course.

▶ Propose Explanations

▶ **What materials are comets made of?**
dust, rock, and ice

▶ **Why do these materials make small comets more likely to change course than asteroids, which are made mostly of rock?**
Comets are made partly of ice. When the ice is heated by the sun, it changes to a gas. When this gas shoots out, it can push the comet in a different direction. Asteroids don't contain ice, so they can't form gas that could push them off course.

▶ **What do you suppose might have caused the great explosion of comet LINEAR? (Hint: Think about the gas and the pressure it produces.)**
The ice might have changed to gas inside the comet. The gas could build up and create pressure. When the pressure was great enough, it would break the comet into pieces.

More Resources
The following resources are also available from Great Source and NSTA.

ScienceSaurus
Solar System Objects	238
Comets	242

Reader's Handbook
Evaluating	42
Reading Science	100

SCILINKS
THE WORLD'S A CLICK AWAY

www.scilinks.org
Keywords: Comets, Asteroids, and Meteors
Code: GSED21

Assessment
Skill: Recognizing cause and effect

Use the following question to assess each student's progress:

Imagine that astronomers are observing the sky with telescopes and detect a comet suddenly move in another direction. What probably caused this change in the comet's movement? (Gases burst out of one side of the comet.)

▶ Propose Explanations

To answer the first question, students may need to review the first paragraph at the beginning of this lesson. Explain that the ice in a comet can be heated so quickly that it instantly vaporizes and is suddenly released in a powerful burst. If necessary, remind students that a gas expands when it is heated. Ask students to relate this release of energy to the explosion of LINEAR and why it was so spectacular.

CHECK UNDERSTANDING
Skill: Recognizing cause and effect
Why might a comet orbit the sun and be seen from Earth, then leave the solar system and never be seen again? (The comet might blow apart or hit another object, or gases shooting out of the comet might change its orbit.)

CHAPTER 17 / LESSON 50

UNIT 5 Astronomy
CHAPTER 17 / LESSON 51

Point of Lesson
Studying comet dust can help us understand the history of our solar system.

Focus
- Earth's history
- Earth in the solar system
- Motion and forces
- Understanding about science and technology
- Science as a human endeavor

Skills and Strategies
- Making inferences
- Predicting
- Interpreting scientific illustrations
- Using space/time relationships

Advance Preparation

Vocabulary
Make sure students understand these terms. Definitions can be found in the glossary at the end of the student book.
- atmosphere
- comet
- gas
- orbit
- planet
- rock
- solar system

TEACHING PLAN pp. 184–185

INTRODUCING THE LESSON
This lesson presents a relatively low-cost method of studying comets to learn about the history of the solar system. Have students identify factors that make comets so difficult to study (their enormous distance from Earth; their tendency to change orbit). Ask why using a probe to gather actual cometary materials would be preferable to studying a comet from Earth. (Materials could be examined, analyzed, and compared with materials on Earth and collected from the moon.)

CHAPTER 17 / LESSON 51
Rocks and Ice in Orbit

Capturing Comet Dust

What's the best way to study a comet? Go and get a piece of it!

Astronomers think comets have changed little since they first formed at the same time as the rest of the solar system. For this reason, comets may be able to teach us about the history of the solar system. They may also contain materials like those that formed the early planets. But how can we study a comet up close?

◄ StarDust probe

▶ Before You Read

LONG WAY HOME Sometimes taking the "long way" is the best way to get to where you are going. Think of a time when traveling a longer distance made your trip easier or better. It might have been when you were walking, cycling, or even riding a bus.

▶ **Describe how the trip was longer and why this was better than taking the "short way."**

Answers will vary. Examples: (1) Taking a bus instead of having someone drive me to the mall made the trip take more time. But taking the bus saved gas and was more fun because a larger group of friends could come with me. (2) By walking around a high hill instead of straight up, I avoided steep, dangerous climbs but walked a longer distance.

▶ Before You Read

LONG WAY HOME Discuss what taking the "long way home" means. Students may offer a wide variety of personal experiences. They might also mention times when the long way saved them money, provided opportunities for them to do other things along the way, or allowed them to see things they otherwise would have missed.

▶ Read

Here's NASA's plan to get a first look at actual comet material.

STARDUST

NASA is using relatively simple low-cost probes to explore our solar system. Launched in February 1999 on a small Delta rocket, the StarDust probe will intercept and analyze the contents of a comet's tail, take close-up pictures, and then for the first time return its "catch" to Earth for complete analysis.

The mission will take a long 7 years, but by being patient, the total cost of the mission is reduced dramatically. Taking advantage of Earth's gravitational field, the craft will require a lot less...rocket fuel, and a smaller rocket can be used. After its first trip around the sun, StarDust's cleverly designed trajectory will loop it back toward Earth allowing Earth's gravitational field to slingshot the craft toward comet...Wild-2 (pronounced "vilt").

In January 2004...StarDust will finally catch up to comet Wild-2 and come within 100 kilometers of the comet's nucleus.

After another 1 billion-mile [1.6 billion-km] trip back to Earth, [part of] StarDust will...reenter Earth's atmosphere in January 2006 and parachute safely down onto the desert in the western United States.... Scientists will then be able to study the cometary... materials.... Hopefully, these studies will give us important clues about the evolution of the solar system and the origins of life on Earth.

probes: instruments used to collect data
intercept: move into
gravitational field: the force that pulls objects toward Earth and keeps them in orbit around it
trajectory: the path of a body or object through space
slingshot: in space science, using gravity to gain speed
nucleus: the solid part of a comet
cometary: related to comets

From: "Stardust." *Liftoff. Science@NASA.* Marshall Space Flight Center. (liftoff.msfc.nasa.gov/academy/space/solarsystem/comets/stardust.html)

NOTEZONE
Highlight any words you don't understand.

FIND OUT MORE
SCIENCESAURUS
Solar System
Objects 238
Comets 242

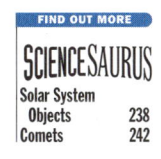

185

Enrichment
After students have completed the Explore section on the next page, suggest that they work in groups of six to create a simulation based on the diagram. Four students can play the roles of the sun, Earth, Comet Wild-2, and the StarDust probe. The fifth student could supervise the orbits of Earth and the comet, and the sixth student, the "space engineer," could supervise the probe's orbits. Tell students that they do not need to behave exactly like the space objects they are portraying—for example, the "Earth" does not have to rotate on its axis as it revolves around the "sun." The goal is to investigate some of the difficulties encountered by astronomers who plan space probes. Students should realize that intercepting a moving object with another moving object requires planning and careful coordination. Let each group demonstrate its simulation to the class.

▶ Read

To help students follow the sequence of taking the "long way" to the comet, collecting materials, then returning to Earth, you could have them number sentences and phrases in the reading.

Explain that NASA probes such as *Voyager* and *Pioneer* did not gather materials from bodies in space and did not return to Earth.

Clear up any confusion students may have about the probe collecting dust from a star, as its name suggests. Point out that popular culture has created the myth of "stardust" as a magic powder. Explain that NASA chose a catchy name for the probe simply to give people an idea of the probe's mission. Relate this to the reading by explaining that the costs of space exploration are huge, and support from taxpayers is very important.

To learn more about the StarDust project, students can visit the following NASA Web site: stardust.jpl.nasa.gov

CHECK UNDERSTANDING
Skill: Sequencing
Have students explain in their own words the steps involved in the StarDust mission and its overall purpose. (The probe is launched from Earth and orbits the sun. Its trajectory brings it back near Earth, where it gains speed as Earth's gravity affects it. Two more orbits "slingshot" the probe to intercept the comet's orbit. The probe collects material form the comet as it passes, then returns to Earth. The overall purpose of the mission is to collect cometary materials for analysis.)

CHAPTER 17 / LESSON 51 185

CHAPTER 17 / LESSON 51

More Resources
The following resources are also available from Great Source.

ScienceSaurus
Solar System Objects   238
Comets   242

Reader's Handbook
Reading Science: Reread   114
Elements of Graphics: Diagram   552

Connections
LANGUAGE ARTS Tell students that throughout history, comets have been a source of wonder and fear to humans. People in the past did not understand how a "star" could suddenly move across the sky. Students should be able to appreciate that a comet could be frightening to people who did not understand its true origins. People of different cultures created myths about comets. Encourage students to find examples of such myths in a library or on the Internet. Have them write their own myths about comets.

Teaching Plan pp. 186–187

▶ Explore

INTERPRET A DIAGRAM Review the diagram with students, focusing on the sequence of StarDust's three orbits to increase its speed and the size of each orbit. Ask a volunteer to read aloud the last sentence of the excerpt's second paragraph, which describes the "slingshot" effect of the three orbits.

To help students realize how gravitational forces can accelerate and redirect the orbit of the probe, use the analogy of a water skier speeding up as the boat turns. The attraction of Earth's gravity acts like the skier's rope, pulling the probe towards the more massive Earth. At the same time, however, the probe's speed causes it to resist being pulled completely back to Earth. Instead, the probe gains speed and is directed into a larger orbit—as would happen if the length of the water skier's rope increased as the boat circled. Emphasize, though, that the water-skier's speed and direction are affected by the friction of the water against the skis, slowing the skier down. In the vacuum of deep space, there would be no friction affecting the probe's motion.

▶ Explore

INTERPRET A DIAGRAM
This diagram shows StarDust's three orbits of the sun as the probe travels along its journey.

[Diagram showing Sun at center with Earth's orbit, 1st Orbit, 2nd Orbit, 3rd Orbit, Comet Wild-2's Orbit, and point where Probe meets comet]

▶ **How is the comet's orbit different from Earth's orbit?**
The comet's orbit is a much larger oval than Earth's orbit.

As StarDust finishes its first orbit, astronomers use remote controls to change the probe's flight path. This slight change brings the probe closer to Earth. As it flies by, the probe gets a boost from Earth's gravitational field.

▶ **Look at StarDust's second orbit around the sun. How does this boost affect StarDust's orbit?**
The orbit gets bigger, big enough to meet up with Wild-2's orbit.

▶ **How are NASA astronomers using Earth's gravitational field to reduce the cost of the StarDust project?**
They are using Earth's gravitational field to slingshot the probe toward the comet. Otherwise, they'd have to use fuel to get it there, which would cost more.

▶ Propose Explanations

THINK ABOUT IT Astronomers are excited about studying the materials found in comets.

▶ *What might they be able to learn about the solar system that they couldn't learn by studying materials here on Earth? Explain your answer. (Hint: How might Earth materials have changed over billions of years? How have comet materials changed, according to scientists?)*

Answers will vary. Example: They might be able to learn what materials were in the solar system when it formed. Earth materials from that time have probably been buried or worn away. Comet materials probably have not changed much since the solar system first formed.

WATCHING COMET BITS AND PIECES Space probes aren't the only way to observe pieces of comets. On certain nights of the year, you can just go outside and look up at the sky. For example, every October bits of Halley's Comet streak through the sky. You can see them if you live in a place with dark skies, away from city lights.

As a comet's orbit brings it near the sun, it gives off gases and rock particles. Many of the particles stay in the same orbit as the comet. As Earth crosses the part of the comet's orbit where these particles are located, the particles enter Earth's atmosphere. There they burn up in many streaks of light that can be seen on a clear night. This event is called a meteor shower.

▶ *The diagram shows the orbits of Earth and Halley's Comet. Mark the points where it might be possible to see a meteor shower made of bits of this comet.*

▶ *How many times each year would you expect a meteor shower from Halley's Comet? Explain.*

Twice a year; Earth's orbit crosses the comet's orbit twice each year.

▶ *A space probe is one way to observe comet dust. Explain how and when an aircraft could also observe bits of comets up close.*

An aircraft could travel high enough into Earth's atmosphere to observe bits of comets during a meteor shower before they burn up.

Assessment
Skill: Comparing and contrasting

Use the following question to assess each student's progress:

How would collecting materials from a comet be different from collecting materials from an asteroid? (Both objects are moving, but an asteroid does not leave a tail that could be sampled. A probe would have to actually land on an asteroid to remove materials. A comet's tail contains materials that a probe could pass through and gather.)

▶ Propose Explanations

THINK ABOUT IT Help students realize that studying comets is like looking back in time. Ask: *What forces have acted on Earth's materials that have not acted on a comet's materials?* (weathering, erosion, pressure, movements of the crust such as uplifting and faulting, and so on)

WATCHING COMET BITS AND PIECES Ask students if they have heard of other famous comets such as Hyakutake and Hale-Bopp, which recently passed near Earth. Point out that meteor showers from Halley's comet are visible in the Northern Hemisphere in October and May. The Leonid meteor showers in November and the Perseids in August also provide spectacular shows. Students may have observed the unusually profuse Leonid meteor showers in 2001 and 2002. Direct students to the Leonid MAC missions at the following NASA Web site: leonid.arc.nasa.gov/index.html

Clarify for students that trying to capture material from a comet's tail can be risky. The material consists of small rock particles, but they are travelling 21,000 km (13,000 mi) per hour—6 to 60 times the speed of a rifle bullet.

CHAPTER 18
Overview

Solar System News

LESSON 52
Planet Status

Point of Lesson: *Astronomers sometimes disagree about how to classify some objects in space.*

A move to give Pluto a number identifying it as a Trans-Neptunian Object triggered an outcry from those who thought the action was an attempt to change its status as the ninth planet. Students compare and contrast Pluto with other planets, then identify which of its properties could be used to classify it as a planet and as a comet. After that exercise, they consider why scientists disagree about Pluto's classification.

Materials
Science Scope Activity (pp. 188B, 189, and 193), for each group:
- computer with Internet access or an almanac such as *The World Almanac for Kids*
- index cards

Connections (p. 191), for the class:
- research sources about Pluto's discovery

LESSON 53
Martian Water

Point of Lesson: *Water may have once flowed freely on Mars.*

The planet Mars is now covered with dry deserts, but physical evidence on its surface suggests that water may have flowed freely across it at one time. In this lesson, students interpret a photograph of the Martian surface and relate their observations to processes that may have reshaped various structures.

Materials
Science Scope Activity (p. 193, continued from Lesson 52)

LESSON 54
Moon Make-Up

Point of Lesson: *The densities of the moons in our solar system can be used to determine the percentages of rock and ice that make them up.*

Moons in the solar system are made of rock, ice, or a combination of the two. In this lesson, students graph a line showing how the density of a moon depends on the percentage of rock it contains. They then use their graphs to analyze data about the densities of some moons to determine the percentage of rock and ice making up each moon.

Materials
Activity (p. 196), for each student:
- calculator (optional)

Science Scope Activity

Science on the Web: Technology-Based Planetary Exploration

NSTA has chosen a Science Scope *activity related to the content in this chapter. The activity begins here and continues on pages 189 and 193.*

Time: ongoing throughout chapter
Materials: computer with Internet access or an almanac such as *The World Almanac for Kids;* index cards

Procedure

1. Divide students into nine groups.
2. Assign each group a different planet in our solar system.

(continued on page 189)

Background Information

Lesson 52

Before the discovery of Pluto, astronomers had made careful calculations of the orbits of the known planets. Noticing irregularities in the orbits of Uranus and Neptune, they theorized that the irregularities might be caused by the gravitational force of a more distant, unseen planet. But because Pluto is so small, the planet was not spotted until 1930 when, through a systematic analysis of photographic plates, an astronomer at the Lowell Observatory in Arizona confirmed its existence.

Lesson 53

The two rovers mentioned in the reading's last paragraph are not the first NASA crafts to land on Mars. The Mars Pathfinder mission of 1997 landed a vehicle named *Sojourner* on the surface of Mars. After a bumpy landing, *Sojourner* rolled out to take photos and analyze the chemical composition of rocks. It also took readings from the Martian atmosphere. After 16,000 images, 15 chemical analyses of rocks, and more than a month in the frigid Mars temperatures, *Sojourner's* batteries finally wore out, completing its mission. The data *Sojourner* transmitted back to Earth encouraged scientists to plan future Mars missions focused on the search for water.

Lesson 54

Scientists calculate the density of a moon by comparing a moon's mass with its volume. But how do they determine a moon's mass? Sir Isaac Newton discovered that the mass, size, and velocity of objects in orbit are directly related. Astronomers observe a moon and its planet with a telescope and calculate the velocity of each moon and the distance between the moon and its planet. Astronomers then use these data to calculate the mass of both the moon and the planet.

UNIT 5 Astronomy
CHAPTER 18 / LESSON 52

Point of Lesson
Astronomers sometimes disagree about how to classify some objects in space.

Focus
- Earth in the solar system
- Science as a human endeavor
- Nature of science

Skills and Strategies
- Interpreting scientific illustrations
- Concept mapping
- Classifying
- Comparing and contrasting
- Making inferences

Advance Preparation
Vocabulary
Make sure students understand these terms. Definitions can be found in the glossary at the end of the student book.

- asteroid
- comet
- diameter
- gas
- orbit
- planet
- solar system
- weather

Materials
Gather the materials needed for *Science Scope Activity* (p. 188B, p. 189, and p. 193) and *Connections* (p. 191).

CHAPTER 18 / LESSON 52
Solar System News
PLANET STATUS

Is Pluto a planet or a comet? Does it matter?

Our solar system is full of objects. Some are large, some are small, some are rocky, and some are just big balls of gas. But one thing all these objects share is that they constantly orbit the sun. These objects include planets such as Earth and Mars and smaller bodies such as comets and asteroids.

Since its discovery in 1930, Pluto has been classified as a planet—the smallest and most distant planet in our solar system. But recently scientists debated whether or not Pluto should be classified as a planet. When the American Museum of Natural History in New York City opened its new space center, the exhibits did not mention Pluto as a planet. What's all the fuss about?

▲ Kitt Peak National Observatory in Arizona

▶ Before You Read

WHAT IS A PLANET?
▶ *Create your own definition of a planet.*

Answers will vary. Example: A planet is a large body in space that orbits a sun. Some planets have moons, some have rings, some have neither or both.

TEACHING PLAN pp. 188–189

INTRODUCING THE LESSON
This lesson describes the controversy surrounding the classification of Pluto as a planet.

Ask students whether they have heard of the Pluto controversy. Some students may not realize that it is possible for scientists to debate the classification of a planet or another body in space. It may surprise them that Pluto could be labeled anything other than a planet. Tell students that as they proceed through the lesson, they should think about the characteristics that define a planet and the reasons some scientists suggest reclassifying Pluto.

▶ Before You Read

WHAT IS A PLANET? If students have difficulty with this activity, suggest that they think about Earth and what it has in common with the other planets in our solar system.

Have students share their definitions and look for similarities among them. Then guide students to decide on a class definition. Write the definition on the board for students' reference as they continue through the lesson.

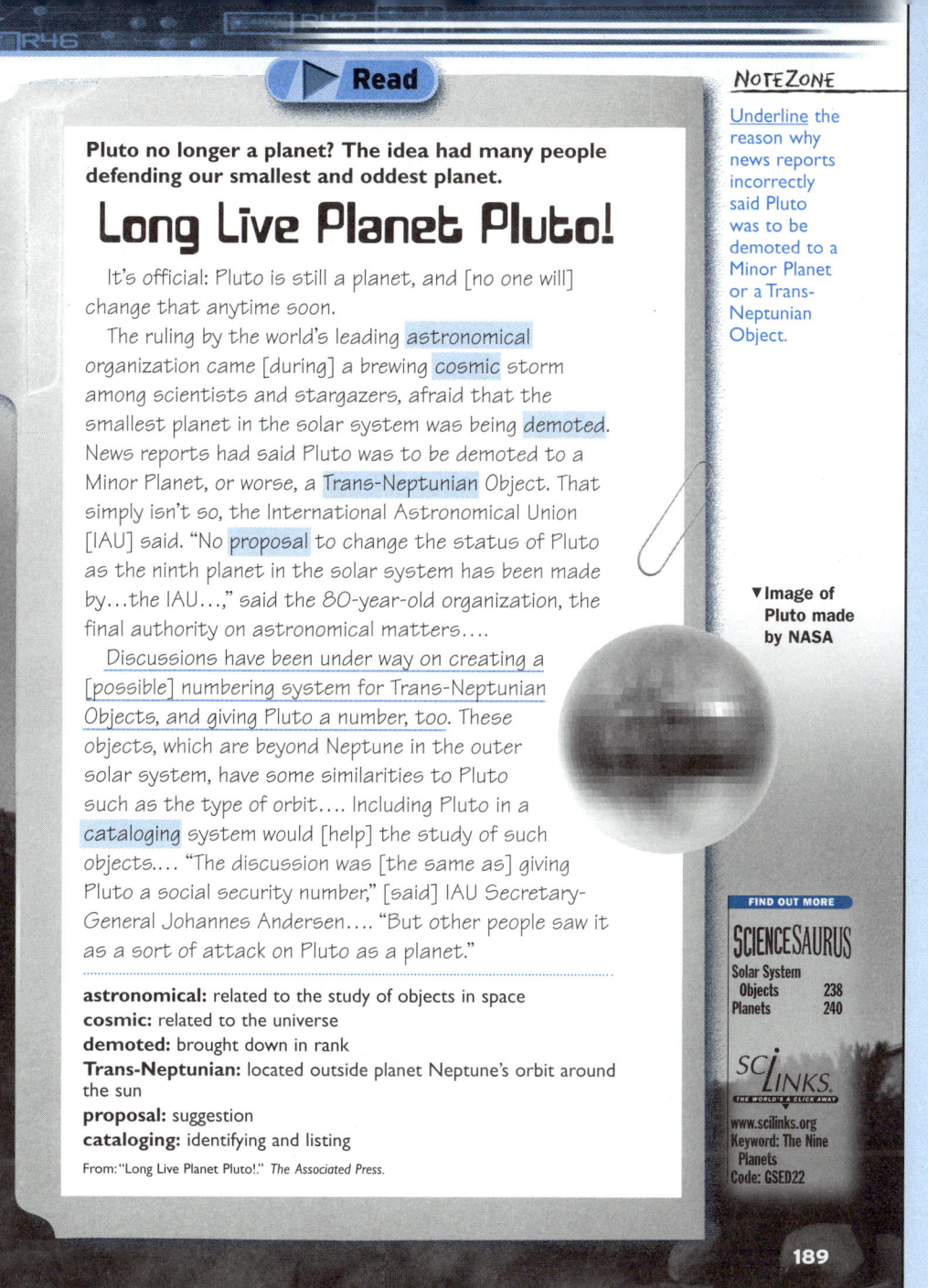

Read

Pluto no longer a planet? The idea had many people defending our smallest and oddest planet.

Long Live Planet Pluto!

It's official: Pluto is still a planet, and [no one will] change that anytime soon.

The ruling by the world's leading astronomical organization came [during] a brewing cosmic storm among scientists and stargazers, afraid that the smallest planet in the solar system was being demoted. News reports had said Pluto was to be demoted to a Minor Planet, or worse, a Trans-Neptunian Object. That simply isn't so, the International Astronomical Union [IAU] said. "No proposal to change the status of Pluto as the ninth planet in the solar system has been made by...the IAU...," said the 80-year-old organization, the final authority on astronomical matters....

Discussions have been under way on creating a [possible] numbering system for Trans-Neptunian Objects, and giving Pluto a number, too. These objects, which are beyond Neptune in the outer solar system, have some similarities to Pluto such as the type of orbit.... Including Pluto in a cataloging system would [help] the study of such objects.... "The discussion was [the same as] giving Pluto a social security number," [said] IAU Secretary-General Johannes Andersen.... "But other people saw it as a sort of attack on Pluto as a planet."

astronomical: related to the study of objects in space
cosmic: related to the universe
demoted: brought down in rank
Trans-Neptunian: located outside planet Neptune's orbit around the sun
proposal: suggestion
cataloging: identifying and listing

From: "Long Live Planet Pluto!" *The Associated Press.*

NoteZone

Underline the reason why news reports incorrectly said Pluto was to be demoted to a Minor Planet or a Trans-Neptunian Object.

▼ Image of Pluto made by NASA

FIND OUT MORE

SCIENCESAURUS
Solar System Objects 238
Planets 240

SCILINKS
THE WORLD'S A CLICK AWAY
www.scilinks.org
Keyword: The Nine Planets
Code: GSED22

189

Science Scope Activity
(continued from page 188B)

3. Tell students that each group is responsible for gathering data about its planet, such as its average distance from the sun, atmospheric composition, average density, diameter, mass, surface composition, period of rotation (how long it takes the planet to rotate one complete turn on its axis), and period of revolution (how long it takes the planet to make one complete orbit of the sun). List these terms on the board for students to copy. Instruct students to make notes on index cards with the appropriate data for each item on the list as they encounter it.

4. Data can be found at various sites on the Internet. The sites listed below are colorful, easy to navigate, and link to similar sites. Pictures and diagrams pertaining to planetary motion can also be accessed at these sites.

   ▶ The Nine Planets: A Multimedia Tour of the Solar System
   seds.lpl.Arizona.edu/nineplanets/

   ▶ Solar System Exploration
   solarsystem.nasa.gov/features/planets/planetsfeat.html

(continued on page 193)

Read

Ask: *Why did people think that Pluto was being "demoted"?* (Some astronomers suggested creating a numbering system for Trans-Neptunian objects and giving Pluto a number, too.) *Why did some people object to including Pluto in the system?* (They thought giving Pluto a number would be the same as saying that Pluto is not a planet.)

If necessary, explain to students what a social security number is. Point out that giving Pluto a number is not the same as reclassifying the planet. The number would merely make it easier to study Pluto along with Trans-Neptunian objects. It would not necessarily mean that Pluto *is* a Trans-Neptunian object or that it is no longer a planet.

Finally, point out that while the IAU continues to classify Pluto as a planet, not all astronomers agree with that decision. Explain that within the IAU, controversy about Pluto's status is ongoing, even though the possibility of reclassification has been officially settled for the time being.

CHECK UNDERSTANDING
Skill: Classifying
Ask: *What is a Trans-Neptunian object?* (an object located beyond Neptune's orbit) *Why did astronomers consider classifying Pluto as one?* (Trans-Neptunian objects have some similarities to Pluto. Including Pluto in the numbering system would help in the study of Trans-Neptunian objects.)

CHAPTER 18 / LESSON 52

CHAPTER 18 / LESSON 52

More Resources
The following resources are also available from Great Source and NSTA.

SCIENCESAURUS
Solar System Objects	238
Planets	240

READER'S HANDBOOK
Reading a Newspaper Article	218
Using Graphic Organizers	385

SCILINKS
THE WORLD'S A CLICK AWAY

www.scilinks.org
Keyword: The Nine Planets
Code: GSED22

TEACHING PLAN pp. 190–191

▶ Explore

WHAT'S IN A NAME? When Pluto was discovered in 1930, it was added to the list of planets as the ninth in our solar system. Like other planets, Pluto orbits the sun, has a rounded shape, and has weather and seasons. It is made of solid rock and ice. It also has a moon named Charon, which is half its size.

But Pluto is much smaller than the other planets in the solar system. It is even smaller than some of the moons. Its orbit is a longer oval than the other planets' orbits. Also, as you can see in the diagram, Pluto's orbit is on a different plane from those of the other planets. In these ways, Pluto is like a comet or asteroid.

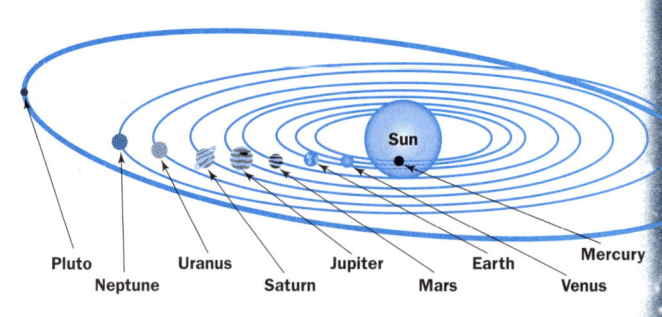

Read the following definitions of a planet and a comet.

Planet: A body in the solar system that is larger than several meters in diameter, does not produce large amounts of heat (like a star), and orbits only the sun (not another body). A planet can be mostly rock, or it can have an outer layer of gases. A planet can have its own orbiting body—a moon. Most planets have moons much smaller than they are.

Comet: A small body of rock, dust, and ice that orbits the sun in a highly oval path. Comets' orbits are very oval and not in the same plane as the planets' orbits. The diameter of the solid part of a comet is only about 15 kilometers.

MAKE A GRAPHIC ORGANIZER
▶ *Is Pluto more like a planet or a comet? Create a graphic organizer below to help you answer the question.*

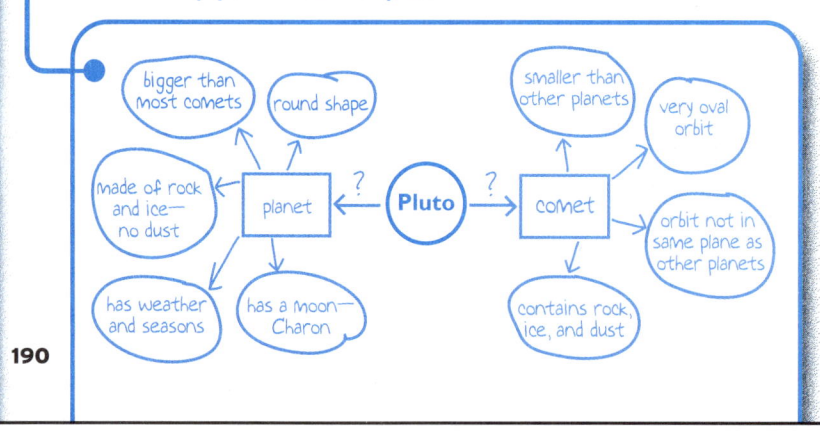

▶ Explore

WHAT'S IN A NAME? Some students may not be aware that Earth is not the only planet in our solar system that has moons. Point out that every planet except Mercury and Venus has at least one known moon and some have more than 20. Some astronomers theorize that Pluto may be a former moon of Neptune that escaped Neptune's orbit.

Explain that a plane is a flat surface that extends infinitely in all directions. Use a sheet of stiff cardboard held at different angles to demonstrate that Pluto's orbit is on a different plane from the orbits of the other planets in our solar system.

MAKE A GRAPHIC ORGANIZER
Before students begin their graphic organizers, suggest that they reread the definitions of *planet* and *comet* and highlight words to include in the organizer.

Encourage students to use their completed organizers to help them answer the text question: *Is Pluto more like a planet or a comet?* (Pluto has more in common with a planet, although it is also similar to a comet in several ways.)

▶ Propose Explanations

APPLYING KNOWLEDGE Point out that throughout the history of science, scientists have disagreed about many issues. The controversy over Pluto's classification is not an unusual occurrence. Ask students whether they can name other examples of issues that scientists disagree about. For example, students may note that not all scientists and doctors agree about the health benefits of certain foods or about the best treatment for certain diseases.

▶ Propose Explanations

APPLYING KNOWLEDGE

▶ Why do you think scientists disagree over how to classify Pluto?

Answers will vary. Example: Pluto is like a planet in some ways, but it's like a comet in other ways so it is hard to classify.

▶ The reading says a "cosmic storm" erupted when people thought Pluto was being demoted to a Trans-Neptunian Object. Why might people care about Pluto's classification?

Answers will vary. Example: People grew up learning that Pluto was a planet, and many didn't want that to change.

▶ Do you think scientists should be influenced by what the public thinks about Pluto's classification? Why or why not?

Answers will vary. Example: No. Pluto's classification should be decided by astronomers based on scientific evidence.

▶ Take Action

INVENT A MNEMONIC A mnemonic is a word clue that helps you remember some other information. To help remember the order and names of the nine planets in our solar system, many people use the mnemonic **M**y **V**ery **E**ducated **M**other **J**ust **S**erved **U**s **N**ine **P**izzas (**M**ercury **V**enus **E**arth **M**ars **J**upiter **S**aturn **U**ranus **N**eptune **P**luto).

▶ Make up as many new mnemonics as you can think of to help you remember the order and names of the nine planets.

Answers will vary. Each word of the mnemonic should begin with the first letter of the name of a planet, in order from Mercury to Pluto.

Connections
Time: will vary
Materials: research sources about Pluto's discovery

LANGUAGE ARTS Encourage interested students to find out when, where, and by whom Pluto was discovered. (It was first discovered in 1930, at the Lowell Observatory in Arizona, by Clyde Tombaugh—the only American to have discovered a planet. Tombaugh found it by taking pictures of the plane of the solar system. He took pictures one or two weeks apart, and tried to find something that looked like it moved against the background of the stars.

Then have small groups write and present a radio or television "special bulletin" broadcast announcing the discovery.

Assessment
Skill: Classifying

Use the following task to assess each student's progress:

Ask students to tell whether they think Pluto should be classified as a planet and to briefly explain their reasoning. (Students should identify characteristics that Pluto shares with other planets and tell why they think those characteristics are important.)

If students are interested in learning more about the "cosmic storm" that erupted over Pluto's classification, suggest that they search for articles and news reports on the Internet.

Let students share their answers to the third question in this section. Then discuss the potential pitfalls of allowing public opinion to influence scientists' decisions. You might use the following questions to stimulate class discussion: *Are popular ideas always good ideas? Can an unpopular idea be correct?*

▶ Take Action

INVENT A MNEMONIC Suggest to students that their mnemonics will be easier to remember if they are in sentence form, like the example in their book. Mnemonics that are funny, that are related to the topic of planets in some way, or that are based on something that really happened may also be easier to remember than a competely random or nonsensical mnemonic.

You may want to point out that Pluto is not always the ninth planet from the sun. Because Pluto's orbit is off-center in relation to the sun—and different from the orbits of the other eight planets—it sometimes crosses inside of Neptune's orbit and becomes the eighth planet from the sun. Have students look back at the diagram on page 190 to see this. Tell students that Pluto was the eighth planet from 1979 until 1999, when it crossed back outside Neptune's orbit. It will not cross inside again until 2127.

CHAPTER 18 / LESSON 52

UNIT 5 Astronomy
CHAPTER 18 / LESSON 53

Point of Lesson
Water may have once flowed freely on Mars.

Focus
- Earth in the solar system
- Science as a human endeavor
- Nature of science
- Understanding about scientific inquiry

Skills and Strategies
- Recognizing cause and effect
- Interpreting scientific illustrations
- Observing
- Comparing and contrasting
- Making inferences
- Generating ideas

Advance Preparation

Vocabulary
Make sure students understand these terms. Definitions can be found in the glossary at the end of the student book.
- atmosphere
- crater
- planet
- soil

CHAPTER 18 / LESSON 53
Solar System News
Martian Water

Did Mars once have lots of water? Scientists are beginning to think so.

When you look at Mars with binoculars or a telescope, the planet's surface appears reddish in color. You can even see the reddish color when you look at Mars at night with your naked eye. For this reason, people in the past have nicknamed Mars "the Red Planet."

Scientists have studied Mars for years. From what they could tell, the planet is very dry, like a desert. There is little moisture in its atmosphere. A closer look at the Martian surface, however, suggests that Mars might not always have been as dry as it is today.

▲ Mars

▶ Before You Read

PUDDLE JUMPING Think about an area of bare soil near your home or school where there are no plants growing. How could you tell if the area was covered by puddles recently or if rainwater has run over its surface? Describe or draw your ideas below.

Answers will vary. Example: Where puddles were, there are areas of wet or dried mud. Where rain ran over the surface, "stream" marks formed.

UNIT 5: ASTRONOMY

TEACHING PLAN pp. 192–193

INTRODUCING THE LESSON
This lesson presents the possibility that Mars once had liquid water and describes the evidence that causes scientists to think so. Ask students to think about why scientists would be interested in any form of water on Mars and what it could mean if Mars had liquid water at one time. (Liquid water in the past and even ice now could indicate that there might have been—or might be now—living organisms on Mars.)

Students may have preconceived notions about Mars and Martians from science-fiction movies and books. Lead students in a discussion of how the actual planet differs from the fictional depictions by asking them to make a list of information about Mars that is not factual.

▶ Before You Read

PUDDLE JUMPING As necessary, guide students in describing or drawing how a vacant patch of soil would look a few days after a rainfall. If students have difficulty, you might provide a few key words such as *mud, trickling water,* and *splashes* to get them started. Then ask students to tell how this activity relates to the main topic of the lesson—the search for signs of water on Mars. (Students should be able to infer that scientists look for similar signs in the terrain of Mars to tell whether liquid water once existed there.)

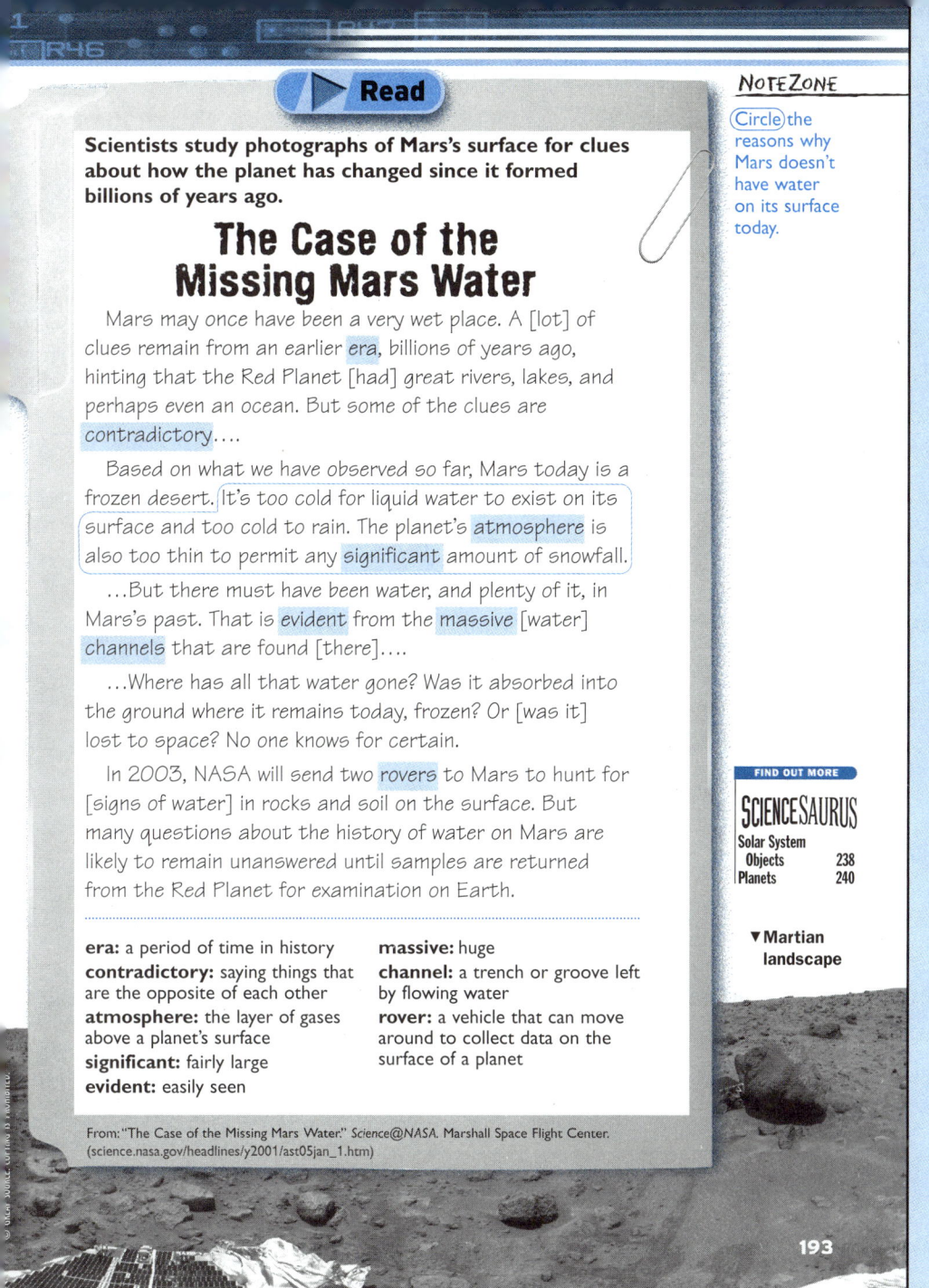

> **Read**

NOTEZONE

Circle the reasons why Mars doesn't have water on its surface today.

Scientists study photographs of Mars's surface for clues about how the planet has changed since it formed billions of years ago.

The Case of the Missing Mars Water

Mars may once have been a very wet place. A [lot] of clues remain from an earlier era, billions of years ago, hinting that the Red Planet [had] great rivers, lakes, and perhaps even an ocean. But some of the clues are contradictory....

Based on what we have observed so far, Mars today is a frozen desert. It's too cold for liquid water to exist on its surface and too cold to rain. The planet's atmosphere is also too thin to permit any significant amount of snowfall.

...But there must have been water, and plenty of it, in Mars's past. That is evident from the massive [water] channels that are found [there]....

...Where has all that water gone? Was it absorbed into the ground where it remains today, frozen? Or [was it] lost to space? No one knows for certain.

In 2003, NASA will send two rovers to Mars to hunt for [signs of water] in rocks and soil on the surface. But many questions about the history of water on Mars are likely to remain unanswered until samples are returned from the Red Planet for examination on Earth.

era: a period of time in history
contradictory: saying things that are the opposite of each other
atmosphere: the layer of gases above a planet's surface
significant: fairly large
evident: easily seen
massive: huge
channel: a trench or groove left by flowing water
rover: a vehicle that can move around to collect data on the surface of a planet

From: "The Case of the Missing Mars Water." Science@NASA. Marshall Space Flight Center. (science.nasa.gov/headlines/y2001/ast05jan_1.htm)

FIND OUT MORE
SCIENCESAURUS
Solar System
Objects 238
Planets 240

▼ Martian landscape

Science Scope Activity
(continued from page 189)

5. Alternatively, you may want to let each group conduct its own Internet search. Caution students who conduct individualized searches to think critically about the source of the information. Alert students that not all information they find will be completely accurate, and they must consider the reliability of a source when they select and evaluate data.
6. Tell students to use at least two different Internet sites to locate the data for each item on the list. Also encourage them to verify the data they have collected by consulting several independent Web sites.
7. When all nine groups have completed their research, have the class compile the data in a computer database.
8. Use the data for comparisons of the planets' characteristics.

> **Read**

Ask students to review the fourth paragraph of the reading. Tell them that data collected by the Mars *Odyssey* space probe in the spring of 2002 suggests that there might be a large amount of ice just below the surface of Mars, supporting the idea that the water was absorbed into the ground.

Ask students to predict the signs of water that the NASA rovers might look for. What evidence in the rocks and soil on Mars could show that the planet once had liquid water?

CHECK UNDERSTANDING
Skill: Making inferences
Ask: *If Mars had liquid water in the past, how must the temperature have been different then?* (The temperature must have been warmer than it is today.)

CHAPTER 18 / LESSON 53

CHAPTER 18 / LESSON 53

More Resources
The following resources are also available from Great Source.

ScienceSaurus
Solar System Objects   238
Planets   240

Reader's Handbook
Elements of Textbooks: Maps   163

Write Source 2000
Brainstorming for Ideas   10

Connections
LANGUAGE ARTS When students have completed the Take Action section on page 195, encourage them to write journal entries describing their missions to Mars. You might ask them to answer questions such as these: *What did you see? What signs of liquid water did you find? What evidence of liquid water or other documentation of the trip did you bring back to Earth?*

TEACHING PLAN pp. 194–195

▶ **Explore**

INTERPRET A SCIENTIFIC IMAGE This image of Mars's surface was taken by a camera aboard the *Viking Orbiter*—a spacecraft that orbited Mars in the late 1970s. Look closely at the different landforms in the picture. Use the line at the top of the image to get an idea of the size of the area you are looking at.

▶ List your observations of the image. Describe what you see as clearly as possible.

Answers will vary.

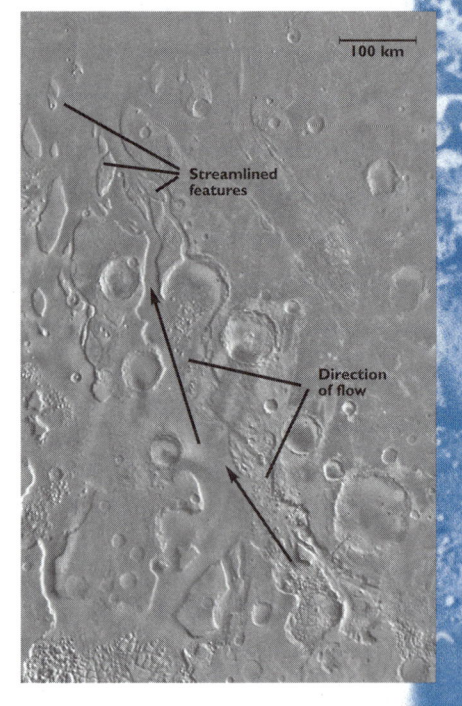

[Image labels: 100 km; Streamlined features; Direction of flow]

The circles on the surface are impact craters that formed when rocks from space hit Mars. All craters are round when they are first formed. But forces such as running water acting on the surface of the planet can change their shape.

▶ What do you notice about some of the craters near the center of the image? Are they full circles?

They are not full circles. Some are missing part of the circle or have long "tails" like rivers coming out of one end.

194

▶ **Explore**

INTERPRET A SCIENTIFIC IMAGE You may want to have students work in pairs to complete this activity, with one student in each pair writing down both students' observations.

Point out the line at the top right corner of the photograph, and explain that it is the same as the scale key on a map. Clarify that the line represents a distance of 100 kilometers. Guide students to estimate the total surface area of the section of Mars shown in the photograph and to imagine how large the craters are in real life. (The surface area of the section is about 450,500 km². The diameter of the largest circular crater, near the lower right corner, is about 100 km.)

Discuss the observations of the image that students listed. Ask: *Which landforms in the image do you think might be evidence of water on Mars?* (Students may cite the craters that are not full circles, the craters with "tails," and the areas that resemble dry riverbeds.)

194   CHAPTER 18 / LESSON 53

▶ **How does the texture of the surface vary in the image? Which parts appear rough? Which parts look smooth? What differences do you notice?**

The surface is smoother below the arrows and in the lower-left part of the image.

▶ Propose Explanations

MAKE INFERENCES Scientists who studied this image of Mars's surface compared the patterns they saw with patterns they observe on Earth's surface. Then they used the comparison to make inferences about forces acting on Mars's surface.

▶ **What processes do you think could have changed the shape of the craters in the middle of the image? (Hint: Think about the processes and actions here on Earth that move dirt around.)**

erosion by wind, running water, or ice

▶ **What conclusions might you draw about how the different textures seen in the picture were created? (Hint: Think about the processes you just identified.)**

Answers will vary. Example: Wind or water moved over the surface, smoothing it out.

▶ Take Action

MISSION TO MARS Imagine that you and two classmates are going to be the first astronauts ever to walk on the surface of Mars. How would you investigate the history of water on the planet? What clues would you look for on the surface? Where else might you look for clues? (Hint: Think about the sorts of things you'd find at the bottom of lakes and rivers here on Earth.) What clues do these materials give you that water was once present? Get together with two classmates and brainstorm some ideas. Then, on a separate sheet of paper, write your "mission plan."

Answers will vary.

195

Assessment
Skill: Comparing and contrasting

Use the following questions to assess each student's progress:

How do the Martian landforms in the image on page 194 compare with an area of dirt on Earth after it has rained? What features might you see on both Earth and Mars, and what features would you not see on Earth? (The smooth areas in the image resemble areas of dried mud on Earth and the water channels trailing from some of the craters look like marks left by water trickling over soil on Earth. The circular craters on Mars do not resemble landforms created by rainfall on Earth.)

▶ Propose Explanations

MAKE INFERENCES Guide students to understand that the same forces acting on Earth's surface—wind, running water, and ice—probably changed the shape of the craters on Mars and created the textures and patterns seen in the image.

Draw students' attention to one of the teardrop-shaped craters in the image. Tell them that one hypothesis scientists have formed is that the crater's walls protected the "downstream" side from erosion by water, causing that side to remain intact while the other side was flattened and elongated by running water. Another hypothesis is that the "tail" end of the "teardrop" consists of materials that were deposited downstream by running water.

▶ Take Action

MISSION TO MARS Have a volunteer read the hint aloud. Then ask students to tell how they might locate a former river or lake on Mars. What would it look like? (more or less like a dry riverbed or lake on Earth—a long, narrow channel or circular, bowl-shaped depression in the soil) Encourage students to think about what an empty, dried-up riverbed or lake on Earth looks like. Finally, ask students to suggest examples of things that they probably could not expect to find in a former river or lake on Mars. (shells, impressions of leaves and ferns, fish fossils, and other signs of life)

CHAPTER 18 / LESSON 53 195

UNIT 5 Astronomy
CHAPTER 18 / LESSON 54

Point of Lesson
The densities of moons in our solar system can be used to determine the percentages of rock and ice that make them up.

Focus
- Earth in the solar system
- Properties and changes of properties in matter

Skills and Strategies
- Using numbers
- Drawing conclusions
- Creating and using graphs
- Creating and using tables

Advance Preparation

Vocabulary
Make sure students understand these terms. Definitions can be found in the glossary at the end of the student book.

- matter
- moon
- planet
- rock
- solar system

Materials
Gather the materials needed for *Activity* (p. 196).

TEACHING PLAN pp. 196–197

CHAPTER 18 / LESSON 54
Solar System News
Moon Make-Up

Moons in our solar system are made of rock and ice. But how much of each moon is rock and how much is ice?

Many of the planets in our solar system have moons. Most moons are made of just rock and ice. Scientists determine what percentage of a moon is rock and what percentage is ice by using the moon's density. Density is the amount of matter in a given space. Imagine holding a rock in one hand and a piece of ice that is the same size in the other hand. The rock would feel heavier because rock is more dense than ice.

▶ Activity

DETERMINE ROCK-ICE PERCENTAGES

Use density to determine the percentages of rock and ice in the moons of the outer planets.

What You Need: pencil, calculator

What to Do:
The chart below shows how the percentage of rock in a moon determines the moon's density.

1. Use the data to make a line graph. The graph will show how a moon's density changes as the percentage of rock in it changes.

Percentage of Rock	Density of Moon (g/cm³)
100	average 3.5
80	3.0
60	2.5
40	1.9
20	1.4
0	0.9

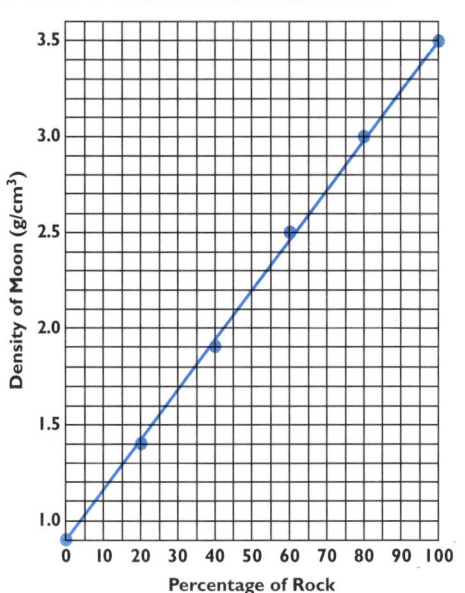

196

INTRODUCING THE LESSON
In this lesson, students graph the densities of the moons in our solar system and use that information to determine what percentage of each moon is ice and what percentage is rock. Ask students to define *density* in their own words. If necessary, explain that density is the amount of matter (mass) in a given volume of a substance.

Make sure students understand the difference between density and weight. Explain that a kilogram (2.2 pounds) of wood and a kilogram of lead weigh the same. But a kilogram of lead has a smaller volume than a kilogram of wood because lead is much denser than wood. There is more matter in any volume of lead than in the same volume of wood.

▶ Activity

Time: 30–40 minutes
Materials: calculator (1 per student, optional)

- Have students work individually or in pairs.
- Explain that g/cm³ means grams per cubic centimeter.

- Point out to students that the graph's vertical axis begins with 0.9 at the bottom, not 0. Ask them to suggest an explanation for this, based on what they see in the data table next to the graph. (No moon has a density of less than 0.9 g/cm³—the density of a moon with no rock at all.)
- Step 1: Make sure students have created their line graphs correctly before they move on to step 2.
- Step 3: Make sure students have correctly calculated the percentage of rock in the first two moons as a

196   CHAPTER 18 / LESSON 54

This chart lists the densities of the moons that orbit the outer planets in our solar system.

Planet	Moon	Density (g/cm³)	Percentage of Rock	Percentage of Ice
Jupiter	Io	3.5	100%	0%
	Europa	3.0	80%	20%
	Ganymede	1.9	40%	60%
	Callisto	1.8	35%	65%
Saturn	Mimas	1.2	12%	88%
	Dione	1.4	20%	80%
	Rhea	1.3	15%	85%
	Titan	1.9	40%	60%
Uranus	Miranda	1.4	20%	80%
	Ariel	1.7	30%	70%
	Umbriel	1.5	23%	77%
Neptune	Triton	2.1	47%	53%
Pluto	Charon	2.0	43%	57%

2. For each moon in the chart, find the point on the graph that corresponds to the moon's density.
3. Use the graph to determine the percentage of rock the moon contains.
4. Calculate the percentage of ice the moon contains. (Hint: percentage of ice = 100% minus percentage of rock)

▶ **Propose Explanations**

ANALYZE DATA

▶ *What is the average density of rock?*

   3.5 g/cm³

▶ *What is the density of ice?*

   0.9 g/cm³

▶ *Explain why Mimas has both the lowest density and the highest percentage of ice.*

   Ice has a lower density than rock, so the moon with the highest

   percentage of ice would have the lowest density.

197

practice example before they go on to calculate the percentage of ice.
▶ Step 4: Make sure students note the hint and understand that they need only subtract the percentage of rock from 100 percent to calculate the percentage of ice.

▶ **Propose Explanations**

ANALYZE DATA Review students' answers to the third question in this section. Make sure they understand the relationship between a moon's density and its percentages of ice and rock. If students need further practice with this concept, ask them to explain, for example, why Io has the highest density (it is 100% rock), why Europa is denser than Callisto (Europa is 80% rock, while Callisto is only 35% rock), and why Charon is not as dense as Triton (Charon is only 43% rock compared with Triton's 47%).

More Resources
The following resource is also available from Great Source.

MATH ON CALL
Percent   441
Understanding Percent   442

Assessment
Skill: Making inferences

Use the following task to assess each student's progress:

Tell students to imagine that all the moons on the chart were the same size. Then ask: *Which moon would be heavier, Europa or Ariel?* (Europa) *Which would be lighter, Umbriel or Rhea?* (Rhea) *Which moons would weigh the same?* (Ganymede and Titan would weigh the same, as would Dione and Miranda.) Also ask students to explain their answers. (Europa would be heavier because it is denser than Ariel. Rhea would be lighter because it is less dense than Umbriel. Ganymede and Titan would weigh the same because they have the same density; the same is true of Dione and Miranda.)

CHECK UNDERSTANDING
Skill: Using numbers
Suppose Moon A's density is 1.8 and Moon B's density is 2.2. Which moon has a higher percentage of ice? How can you tell? (Moon A; ice is less dense than rock, so the moon that is less dense must have a higher percentage of ice.)

CHAPTER 18 / LESSON 54

CHAPTER 19 Overview

Picturing the Universe

LESSON 55
A Star's Life
Point of Lesson: *The brightness and temperature of distant stars provide clues about their life cycles.*

In this lesson, students learn about the life cycle of stars and the methods astronomers use to determine a star's age. They trace the life cycle of some star types on a Hertzsprung-Russell diagram and plot the approximate location of our sun on the Main Sequence with respect to its temperature.

Materials
Enrichment (p. 199), to be shared by groups:
- almanac or astronomy text

LESSON 56
Planet Search
Point of Lesson: *Astronomers have found many planets orbiting stars beyond our solar system.*

Although scientists in popular culture are often shown working alone, most scientists today work in teams. This lesson describes how scientists in different locations worked together to confirm the existence of a planet outside our solar system, using a new technique. Students use a mental model to help understand the scientists' methods and come up with investigative questions that scientists might ask about the newly discovered planets.

Materials
Enrichment (p. 203), to be shared by groups:
- astronomy text

Explore (p. 204), for teacher demonstration:
- dime
- tape
- high-powered flashlight

Laboratory Safety
Review the following safety guideline with students before you do the Explore demonstration in this lesson.
- Do not look directly into the flashlight beam for more than a brief moment.

LESSON 57
Images From Energy
Point of Lesson: *Radio waves from space can be converted into visual images.*

In addition to visible light, other forms of electromagnetic energy travel through space. In this lesson, students learn about the forms of energy in space and how images of space objects can be derived from radio waves.

Materials
Activity (p. 206), for each student:
- Radio Telescope Data Sheet (copymaster page 231)
- 6 colored pencils or markers, including black

Background Information

Lesson 55

Stars and planets are formed from spinning clouds of dust and gases called solar nebula. In the cloud, the greater gravity exerted by bigger objects slowly pulls in smaller objects. Over hundreds of thousands of years, the bigger objects grow as they pull in more and more matter. These objects, called planetesimals, are the building blocks of planets. At the center of the cloud, gases begin to concentrate, which causes the solar nebula to spin faster and heat up. Gases at the center become so hot that fusion, the process of atomic nuclei fusing together into new elements and releasing energy, begins. It's the birth of a star.

Lesson 57

Because radio telescopes can detect the parts of the electromagnetic spectrum that light-collecting telescopes cannot, they are a crucial tool in modern astronomy. Also, because radio telescopes are very sensitive, they are ideal for observing rapidly changing phenomena such as pulsating stars.

Because radio waves are much longer than light waves and other forms of electromagnetic energy, larger radio telescopes can collect much fainter signals. Using an array of multiple telescopes, such as the Very Large Array at Socorro, New Mexico, provides better resolution. A radio telescope array now being designed by international teams of scientists, the Square Kilometer Array, or SKA, will have a total collecting area of 1 square kilometer—100 times larger than the largest present-day radio telescope—and may be spread out across a continent. The design for the SKA will be chosen in 2007.

UNIT 5 Astronomy
CHAPTER 19 / LESSON 55

Point of Lesson
The brightness and temperature of distant stars provide clues about their life cycles.

Focus
- Earth in the solar system
- Evidence, models, and explanation
- History of science
- Understanding about scientific inquiry

Skills and Strategies
- Making and using graphs
- Interpreting data
- Comparing and contrasting

Advance Preparation

Vocabulary
Make sure students understand these terms. Definitions can be found in the glossary at the end of the student book.

- energy
- gas
- horizontal axis
- life cycle
- star
- temperature
- vertical axis

Materials
Gather the materials needed for *Enrichment* (p. 199).

TEACHING PLAN pp. 198–199

CHAPTER 19 / LESSON 55
Picturing the Universe

A Star's Life

What can scientists tell about stars from their temperature and brightness? Plenty!

Birth. Infancy. Childhood. Youth. Middle age. Old age. These are some of the words used to describe the human life cycle. While stars are not living things, scientists describe them in terms of a life cycle, too. A star is born when a cloud of gas and dust comes together and begins to give off huge amounts of energy. As a star like our sun ages, it grows larger and cooler. At this stage it becomes a Red Giant. Later still, all that is left is a small white-hot core called a White Dwarf. At the end of its life cycle, a sunlike star cools even more to become a Black Dwarf.

NOTEZONE
Highlight any words or sentences you don't understand.

FIND OUT MORE

SCIENCESAURUS
Stars, Galaxies, and Constellations 244
Stars 245
Absolute and Apparent Magnitude 246

SCLINKS
THE WORLD'S A CLICK AWAY
www.scilinks.org
Keyword: What is the life cycle of a star?
Code: GSED24

▶ Read

Curious about stars, Scott Basham of Orlando, Florida, wrote to an "Ask the Expert" Web site. An astronomer (a scientist who studies objects in space) named Terry D. Oswalt answered Scott's question.

Young and Old Stars

Scott Basham: How do we determine the life cycles of stars and tag some as "young" and some as "old"?

Terry Oswalt: This is one of the most important, and interesting, problems in astronomy.... It has taken astronomers most of...[the twentieth century] to piece together the life cycles of stars, simply because we cannot live long enough to follow a single star through its life cycle. Except in a few rare cases, most stars have looked the same as they do now since before humans began looking up at the sky.

Yet stars vary remarkably in their physical characteristics.... Do stars look different from one

---

INTRODUCING THE LESSON

This lesson discusses the life cycle of stars and explains the methods employed by astronomers to determine a star's age.

Ask a volunteer to define the term "life cycle." Then ask students to explain how stars can differ from one another. Some students may believe that all stars are basically identical. On the board list the following factors that can vary from one star to another: temperature, brightness, and size. Ask questions to prompt students to think about how these factors might be related. For example: *Is a large star likely to be brighter or less bright than a small star?* (brighter) *Is a very bright star likely to be hotter or cooler than a dimmer star?* (for the most part, hotter) *Could a star's temperature and brightness tell scientists anything about its age?* (yes) Do not correct students' answers at this time, but have them make notes of their responses and check them for accuracy as they proceed through the chapter.

▶ Read

Ask volunteers to read aloud the definitions of Red Giant and White Dwarf that are given below the reading. Explain that when you are discussing stars, the terms "cool" and "hot" refer to one star's temperature compared with another star's temperature. All stars are extremely hot. Red Giants are by no means cool, merely less hot than some other stars.

Then ask: *If all stars go through stages such as Red Giant and White Dwarf, why do most stars look the same today as they did thousands of years ago?*

▼ Stars in the Milky Way

another because…they have different ages…? The key is to find a group of stars that has to be the same age….

Because it is highly unlikely that the stars in a cluster got together by accident, they must have been born at the same time…. When we compare…many different clusters, we find that those clusters which have many hot bright stars usually have some visible gas, suggesting that star formation may not be over. This type of cluster seldom has any Red Giants or White Dwarfs. In fact, the trend is that the fewer hot and bright stars a cluster has, the more Red Giants and White Dwarfs it has. The most likely cause of these differences is that different clusters have different ages—so we deduce that Red Giants and White Dwarfs are what stars become as they grow older.

tag: label
cluster: a group of stars that are close together in space
Red Giant: a large, very bright star that has cooled
White Dwarf: a small, very dense, hot, but faint star
deduce: conclude

From: "How Do We Determine The Life Cycles Of Stars And Tag Some As 'Young' And Some As 'Old?'." *Scientific American.*

(Each stage lasts an extremely long time.) *How does a star's life span compare with a human's?* (Stars have a much longer life span than people.) Be sure students understand that as with the terms "cool" and "hot," when discussing stars the terms "young" and "old" refer to one star's age compared with another's. The stars we see in the night sky are all very old.

Enrichment

Time: will vary
Materials: almanac or astronomy text

Have pairs or small groups of students choose a constellation and research a few of its stars on the Internet or in an almanac or astronomy text. Encourage students to find out what type of star each is; its temperature, brightness, and approximate age; its distance in light-years from Earth; and any interesting or unusual facts about the star. When students have completed their research, encourage them to locate each star on the modified H-R diagram. They may also want to compile their findings into a class star database.

CHECK UNDERSTANDING
Skills: Making inferences
Ask students to explain in their own words what the presence or absence of Red Giants and White Dwarfs in a star cluster tells about the age of that cluster. (Scientists have deduced that Red Giants and White Dwarfs are older stars, so a cluster with these types of stars must be older than a cluster with few or no Red Giants and White Dwarfs.)

CHAPTER 19 / LESSON 55

More Resources
The following resources are also available from Great Source and NSTA.

ScienceSaurus
Stars, Galaxies, and Constellations	244
Stars	245
Absolute and Apparent Magnitude	246

Math On Call
Graphs That Show How Data Are Clustered	300
Scatter Plots	305

SCILINKS
THE WORLD'S A CLICK AWAY

www.scilinks.org
Keyword: What is the life cycle of a star?
Code: GSED24

▶ Explore

INTERPRETING A MODIFIED H-R DIAGRAM In the early 1900s, two astronomers worked independently on the same problem. Enjar Hertzsprung worked in Denmark, and Henry Norris Russell worked in the United States. They both compared the brightness and temperature of stars. Brightness describes how much energy a star gives off. When they plotted brightness and temperature on a graph, a pattern appeared. (On the diagram below, brightness is given as a comparison with our own sun.) Today astronomers use a diagram based on their work. It is called the Hertzsprung-Russell diagram, or H-R diagram.

Notice that the temperatures on the horizontal axis go from highest on the left to lowest on the right. The numbers on the vertical axis compare the stars' brightness with the brightness of our own sun.

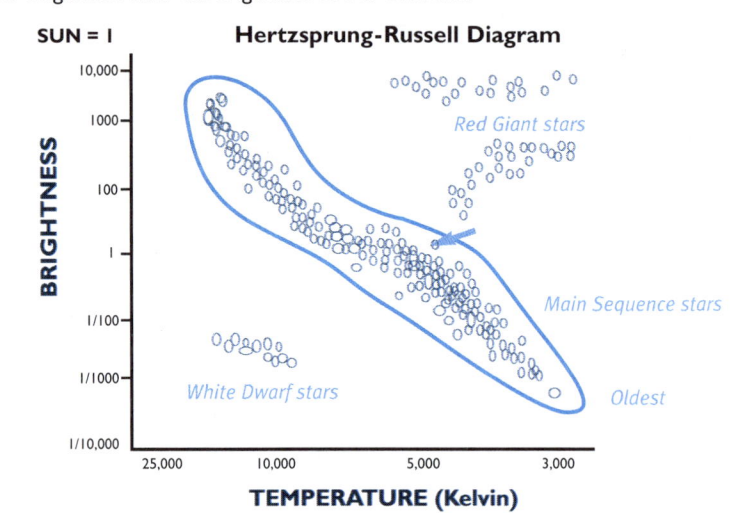

Hertzsprung-Russell Diagram
(SUN = 1; BRIGHTNESS axis from 1/10,000 to 10,000; TEMPERATURE (Kelvin) from 25,000 to 3,000)
Labels on diagram: Red Giant stars, Main Sequence stars, White Dwarf stars, Oldest

It seems logical that hotter stars would be more bright, and cooler stars would be less bright. Most stars, but not all, follow this pattern.

▶ Find the large group of stars on the diagram that fit this pattern. Circle the group and label it "Main Sequence stars."

Red Giant stars are very bright but very cool. They are bright because they are very large. Find the group of stars on the diagram that fits this description. Label them "Red Giant stars."

▶ Do Red Giant stars fit the pattern shown in the Main Sequence? Why or why not?

No; very bright Main Sequence stars are also very hot.

200

Teaching Plan pp. 200–201

▶ Explore

INTERPRETING A MODIFIED H-R DIAGRAM Point out that the temperatures on the diagram are in Kelvin, as labeled on the horizontal axis. Explain that, like Celsius and Fahrenheit, Kelvin is a scale for measuring temperature. Tell students that Kelvin is equivalent to Celsius plus 273. Emphasize that the degree symbol is not used with Kelvin readings.

Ask students to state the purpose of the diagram. (to show the relationship between a star's temperature and its brightness) Draw students' attention to the grouping of stars labeled "Main Sequence" stars, and ask: *How would you describe the relationship between the temperature and brightness of stars in this grouping?* (The hotter a star is, the brighter it is.)

Then ask: *Which of the smaller groupings of stars on the diagram could be described as bright and relatively cool?* (Red Giants) *Which grouping could be described as dim and hot?* (White Dwarfs)

200   CHAPTER 19 / LESSON 55

White Dwarf stars are very hot but very low in brightness.
▶ **Find the group of stars in the diagram that fit this description. Label them "White Dwarf stars."**

For most of their lives, stars have properties that put them on the Main Sequence part of the H-R diagram. A star stays in pretty much the same place within the Main Sequence for most of its life. At some point, its properties change and the star "moves" to a place above the Main Sequence on the diagram. Later, as it continues to change, it "moves" to a place below the Main Sequence.
▶ **Are Red Giants younger or older, compared with White Dwarfs?**
younger

Astronomers have figured out that the hotter and brighter a star is to begin with, the less time it spends on the Main Sequence.
▶ **Which stars on the Main Sequence spend the least time as Main Sequence stars?**
the ones at the upper left

ADD COLOR TO THE DIAGRAM If you live in a place away from city lights, you might notice that not all stars are the same color. Astronomers figure out the temperature of a star by analyzing the colors of light it gives off. Blue stars are hotter, and red stars are cooler.
▶ **Use a blue pencil or pen to color the stars on the H-R diagram with temperatures between 10,000 K and 25,000 K.**
▶ **Use green for stars with temperatures between 5,000 K and 10,000 K.**
▶ **Use yellow for stars between 3,000 K and 5,000 K.**
▶ **Use red for stars with temperatures lower than 3,000 K.**

▶ **Propose Explanations**

WHERE'S OUR SUN? When astronomers analyzed the color that our own sun gives off, they found it to be mostly yellowish green. Our sun's brightness places it on the Main Sequence. Its temperature is about 6,000 K.
▶ **Draw an arrow pointing to the area on the H-R diagram where our sun is located.**
▶ **What does our sun's position on the diagram tell you about where it is in its life cycle?**
Its position shows that our sun is in the main part of its life.

201

Assessment
Skill: Comparing and contrasting

Use the following questions to assess each student's progress:

How does a star's brightness change during its life cycle? (A star goes from bright to very bright to relatively dim as it ages.) *How does its temperature change as it ages?* (Its temperature goes from hot to cool to very hot.)

▶ **Explore**

Explain that it is actually a star's mass that determines its location on the Main Sequence and the point when it "moves off" to become a Red Giant. (The star's mass also determines how hot the star is.) The star moves off the Main Sequence when it has fused, or "burned," all the hydrogen in its core into helium.

Be sure students understand that while some stars have a shorter life span than others, there is no such thing as a star "dying young." Unlike plants and animals—which can die prematurely at any point in their life cycles—every star completes all phases of the star life cycle.

ADD COLOR TO THE DIAGRAM Ask whether students have seen the constellation Orion, which is visible in winter in the Northern Hemisphere. Point out that star color is easy to observe in Orion. The star Betelgeuse at the constellation's upper left appears red. The star Rigel, at its lower right, appears blue.

Based on the coloring they have just done, ask students to infer whether a star that gives off green light would be hotter or cooler than a star that gives off yellow light. (hotter) Than a blue star. (cooler)

▶ **Propose Explanations**

WHERE'S OUR SUN? Help students determine the approximate location of 6,000 K on the horizontal axis of the H-R diagram. Ask them to draw a vertical line from that location up through the Main Sequence grouping and then draw a horizontal line across from the number 1 on the vertical axis. Explain that this point represents the location of our sun within the Main Sequence.

CHAPTER 19 / LESSON 55 201

UNIT 5 Astronomy
CHAPTER 19 / LESSON 56

Point of Lesson
Astronomers have found many planets orbiting stars beyond our solar system.

Focus
- Earth in the solar system
- Evidence, models, and explanation
- Understanding about science and technology
- Science as a human endeavor

Skills and Strategies
- Comparing and contrasting
- Making and using models
- Making inferences
- Generating questions

Advance Preparation
Vocabulary
Make sure students understand these terms. Definitions can be found in the glossary at the end of the student book.

- gas
- gravity
- planet
- solar system
- star

Materials
Gather the materials needed for *Enrichment* (p. 203) and *Explore* (p. 204).

TEACHING PLAN pp. 202–203

CHAPTER 19 / LESSON 56
Picturing the Universe

Planet Search

What does it mean when a star's brightness dims? Something very interesting!

If planets form from the same gases and dust as stars do, then there are sure to be many, many planets in the universe. So the search for planets is on!

Teamwork—that's what it takes to find planets beyond our solar system. More than a dozen teams of astronomers around the world are searching for planets. They point their telescopes at nearby stars and look for signs that a star might have planets orbiting it. The signs come slowly, sometimes over years. But the results are amazing. Earth may not be the only planet in the universe suited for life!

▲ Artist's painting of a planet crossing in front of a distant star called HD 209458

▶ Before You Read

SCIENCE TEAMWORK A few scientists work alone, but most scientists work in teams. Sometimes the people on the team work in the same building. Other times they work thousands of miles apart. Each member of the team has skills, knowledge, or tools that the others don't have. Together, the team members can solve problems that one scientist couldn't solve alone.

▶ *Describe a time when you were part of a team that solved a problem. What problem did you solve? How did each member of the team help solve it?*

Answers will vary. Examples: student teams at school, sports teams, teamwork within a family, teamwork among a group of friends

202

INTRODUCING THE LESSON
This lesson describes the search for planets beyond our solar system. Ask students to tell anything they have heard or read about the search for such planets.

Students may not realize that certain conditions must be present for life as we know it to exist. Ask students what these conditions might be. (water, an atmosphere, moderate temperatures, and so on) Explain that other planets in our own solar system do not have these conditions.

Point out that like planets in our own solar system, distant planets also must revolve around sun-like stars. Astronomers hope to find planets orbiting distant stars by studying these stars through telescopes.

▶ Before You Read

SCIENCE TEAMWORK Ask: *Why do most scientists work in teams?* (Each team member has skills, knowledge, or tools that the others do not have.) Discuss students' examples of times they were part of a team. Ask: *Could you have solved the same problems or accomplished the same goals on your own? Why or why not?* (No; all the team members were needed. Each played a different role.) Encourage students to think about how their own experiences solving problems might apply to a team of scientists.

Read

In 1999 astronomers saw a planet outside our solar system for the first time.

Team Sees Distant Planet

November 1999

A planet in another star system has been seen to cross the face of its parent star. The transit, as it is called, is the most direct glimpse yet of an extrasolar planet.

Over the past 4 years, several teams [of astronomers] have discovered more than two dozen extrasolar planets orbiting sunlike stars without actually seeing a single one. The astronomers inferred [the planets'] existence from slight [back and forth] movements of the parent stars, presumably [caused by] the tug of an orbiting planet.

On November 5, [astronomers Geoffrey] Marcy, Paul Butler, and Steve Vogt reported that they had detected a new set of telltale wobbles. As always, Marcy passed the new data on to [astronomer Greg] Henry, who uses small, automated telescopes...in Arizona to study sunlike stars [and look] for...planetary transits.

"When I saw Marcy's data for the star HD 209458," [Henry said], "I realized that a transit might occur in the night of November 7.... I quickly reprogrammed one of the automated telescopes before I went home." The next day, when Henry looked at the brightness measurements, he hardly believed what he saw. Exactly at the predicted moment, the star showed a brightness drop of 1.7%.

parent star: the star that a planet orbits
extrasolar: outside of our own solar system
wobble: a side-to-side movement

From: Schilling, Govert. "Astronomy: Shadow of an Exoplanet Detected." *Science*.

NoteZone

How did Henry know when to point his telescope at star HD 209458?

The other scientists had calculated when the planet might cross in front of the star.

FIND OUT MORE
SCIENCESAURUS
Stars 245
Searching the Web 422

SCILINKS
www.scilinks.org
Keyword: Telescopes
Code: GSED23

203

Enrichment

Time: will vary
Materials: astronomy text

Students can learn more about detecting distant planets by visiting the following Web site: www.space.com/searchforlife/seti_doyle_worlds_010809.html

Have small groups use this site or an astronomy text to research methods of detecting distant planets that are not covered in this lesson. Ask students to write a paragraph describing each method. Then encourage them to identify one planet that was discovered using each method, research the planet, and create a fact file of information about it.

Read

Point out that astronomers determine whether a star has planets orbiting it by looking for certain signs. Tell students to highlight the signs mentioned in the reading.

Students may be curious about the name of the planet described in the reading. Explain that as of 2002, no permanent system had been devised for naming extrasolar planets. The temporary system is to add a lower case letter to the name or number of the star that the planet orbits. The name of the planet described in this reading is HD 209458 b.

Tell students that HD 209458 is a yellow, sun-like star 153 light-years from Earth and is located in the constellation Pegasus. Explain that in November 2001, astronomers using the Hubble Space Telescope directly observed an atmosphere on this planet—the first observation of an atmosphere on a planet beyond our solar system. Then ask students to explain the significance of this observation. (The presence of an atmosphere is one of the conditions required to sustain life.)

CHECK UNDERSTANDING
Skill: Making inferences
Ask: *Why were Geoffrey Marcy and his colleagues so excited when they detected a wobble in star HD 209458?* (The wobble indicated that the star was being pulled by a planet orbiting it.)

CHAPTER 19 / LESSON 56   203

CHAPTER 19 / LESSON 56

More Resources
The following resources are also available from Great Source and NSTA.

ScienceSaurus
Stars	245
Searching the Web	422

SciLinks
www.scilinks.org
Keyword: Telescopes
Code: GSED23

▶ Explore

WHAT DO YOU THINK? Imagine taping a dime on a car's bumper next to the headlight. One dark night you see the car approaching from several blocks away. Its headlights are on.

▸ Do you think you would be able to see the dime? Why or why not?
   You would not be able to see the dime. The headlight would be too bright to let you see an object next to it that doesn't give off light.

▸ How is this similar to astronomers looking for distant planets?
   A planet near a star would also be hard to see because the light of the nearby star is so bright and the planet doesn't give off any light of its own.

LOOKING FOR WOBBLES With the tools they had in 1999, the California astronomers could not see the planet near star HD 209458. Instead, they looked for signs that a planet was affecting the star. Even a small planet's tug of gravity pulls on the star it orbits. As the planet orbits the star, it pulls on different sides of the star. This makes the star wobble.

After many mathematical calculations, the California team predicted when the planet might pass in front of star HD 209458. They called an astronomer in Tennessee and asked him to point a telescope in Arizona at the star.

▸ What did the telescope in Arizona show?
   The star dimmed.

▸ Use the example of a dime and a car headlight as a model to explain what happened.
   If a dime were passed directly in front of a car's headlight, the light would look a bit dimmer. As the planet passed in front of the star, it blocked some of the star's light, making it look dimmer from Earth.

204

TEACHING PLAN pp. 204–205

▶ Explore

Time: 5 minutes
Materials: dime, tape, high-powered flashlight

WHAT DO YOU THINK? If students have difficulty understanding the example of the dime taped to the bumper, you might try to demonstrate the concept in a darkened classroom, using a dime taped to one side of a high-powered flashlight. (**Caution:** Do not allow students to look directly into the flashlight beam for more than a brief moment.)

LOOKING FOR WOBBLES Be certain students understand that the telescope in Arizona did not show the planet itself but showed the light from star HD 209458 dimming as the planet passed in front of it. Tell students that this method of detecting a planet is called the transit method or "wink" method because the dimming of light makes the star appear to wink.

THAT'S TEAMWORK Ask: *Why was working as a team so important?* (The California astronomers who detected the wobble in star HD 209458 could not see it dimming from their location. They needed someone to use a telescope in Arizona.)

GENERATE QUESTIONS Review the conditions necessary to sustain life that students identified in Introducing the Lesson (p. 202). Emphasize that "life" refers to all forms of life, including microscopic organisms. A life-sustaining planet would not necessarily be inhabited by any plants, animals, or other organisms that we would recognize. You also might want to discuss what scientists would need to know in order to determine whether an object is (or was) a living organism.

THAT'S TEAMWORK!

▶ **What was the team of astronomers in California able to detect? How did they use that evidence?**

They were able to detect a wobble in star HD 209458. They inferred that a planet was nearby.

▶ **How was the astronomer in Tennessee able to help the team?**

He used his telescope to directly observe dimming of the star and confirm the other astronomers' inference that a planet was present.

GENERATE QUESTIONS The planet described in the reading has a surface temperature of about 2,000°C (3,500°F). It is not likely to support life, but astronomers hope to find other planets that might. Think about the conditions that support life on Earth. List questions that scientists would need to answer in order to find out whether a far-off planet might support life.

Answers will vary. Examples: What is the planet's surface temperature? What is it made of? Is there water on the planet? Does the planet have an atmosphere? How close is the planet to the star it orbits?

▶ **Take Action**

DO ONLINE RESEARCH By the summer of 2002, astronomers had found evidence of more than 100 planets outside our solar system. Go online to find out how many planets scientists have now found beyond our solar system. Try searching by typing in these three keywords as one search: *extrasolar* (which means outside our solar system), *planet*, and *database*. What is the name and URL of a site you found? How many extrasolar planets are listed? Choose one of those planets and give its name. On a separate sheet of paper, list the information about it in the database.

Answers will vary.

Site name and URL _____

Number of extrasolar planets _____

Name of planet _____

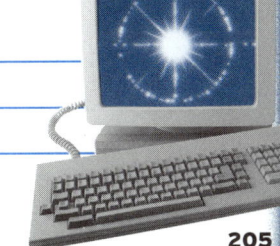

205

Assessment
Skill: Making inferences

Use the following task to assess each student's progress:

Ask students to briefly describe the two methods scientists used to detect the planet near star HD 209458. Also ask them to explain why scientists used both methods together to detect the planet. (The first method involves looking for the wobble that occurs when a planet's gravity tugs at the star it orbits. The other method involves observing and measuring how much a star's light dims as a planet passes in front of it. Students should infer that astronomers use the two methods together because the chances of observing a planet in transit across a star at random, without first predicting the event using the wobble method, are extremely slim.)

▶ **Take Action**

DO ONLINE RESEARCH Students can work in pairs or small groups to complete this activity. There are several catalogs, encyclopedias, and databases of extrasolar planets available on the Internet. If students are having difficulty locating information, you may want to direct them to the following database from NASA's Jet Propulsion Laboratory: planetquest1.jpl.nasa.gov/atlas/atlas_index.cfm

CHAPTER 19 / LESSON 56   **205**

UNIT 5 Astronomy
CHAPTER 19 / LESSON 57

Point of Lesson
Radio waves from space can be converted into visual images.

Focus
- Earth in the solar system
- Understanding about science and technology
- Science as a human endeavor

Skills and Strategies
- Comparing and contrasting
- Making and using models
- Interpreting scientific illustrations

Advance Preparation
Vocabulary
Make sure students understand these terms. Definitions can be found in the glossary at the end of the student book.
- electromagnetic spectrum
- energy
- wave

Materials
Gather the materials needed for *Activity* (p. 206).

CHAPTER 19 / LESSON 57
Picturing the Universe

IMAGES FROM ENERGY

You can't see most kinds of energy from space, but you can use them to make images.

Your eyes can see only visible light. Visible light is part of the electromagnetic spectrum. The electromagnetic spectrum also includes other forms of energy that can travel through space, such as X rays, ultraviolet light, microwaves, and radio waves. All these other forms of energy are invisible to us.

Most telescopes can detect only part of the electromagnetic spectrum. Light telescopes, like the ones used to find distant planets, collect visible light. Using computers, astronomers create visible-light images that show how the object would look to the human eye if you could see that far away. Other telescopes detect the invisible forms of energy from space. For example, radio telescopes detect radio waves. These too can be made into images you can see.

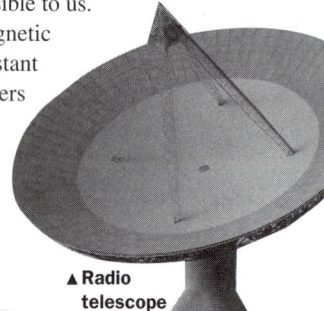

▲ Radio telescope

▶ Activity

IMAGES FROM RADIO WAVES

Try making your own image from the energy detected by a radio telescope.

What You'll Need:
- radio telescope data sheet (Your teacher will provide this.)
- 6 colored pencils or markers, including black

What to Do:
1. Line up the colored pencils or markers and compare their brightness. (Hint: Squint your eyes or put the pencils or markers in the shade to help you see the brightness of the colors.) Move the colors around until you have arranged them from darkest to brightest.
2. To keep track of the order of the colors, fill in the key below. Use black for 0, the next darkest color for 1, and so on. The brightest color should be 5.

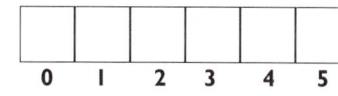

| 0 | 1 | 2 | 3 | 4 | 5 |

3. Use the key to color the boxes on the data sheet.

206

TEACHING PLAN pp. 206-207

INTRODUCING THE LESSON
This lesson discusses energy from space, some of which can be seen, the rest of which can be used to generate images.

Discuss the electromagnetic spectrum and the various types of waves it includes. Point out that a medical X-ray image is one common example of an image formed from electromagnetic waves. (You may want to have students read *ScienceSaurus* sections 305–309 before beginning the lesson.)

▶ Activity
Time: 25–30 minutes
Materials: (for each student) Radio Telescope Data Sheet (copymaster page 231); 6 colored pencils or markers, including black

▶ **Step 1:** Some students may arrange the colors in the order of the colors of the rainbow. Tell them to re-arrange the colors from darkest to brightest. If students have a hard time placing two similar colors in order, suggest that they substitute a different color for one.

▶ Do not assign one particular set of colors to the key. Arbitrary color assignment is a major point of the activity.

If students are unable to locate a picture of a spiral galaxy, suggest that they refer to *ScienceSaurus* section 247, Galaxies, which includes a small picture of a spiral galaxy. Point out that the image in *ScienceSaurus* is not a radio-wave image, but it approximates how the galaxy would actually look if you could get close enough to see it with the human eye. That is why the image is much less colorful than the images students created.

206 CHAPTER 19 / LESSON 57

What Do You See?

▶ *What kind of space object does your image look like? (Hint: Look at pictures in an astronomy book or the astronomy chapter of a science textbook.) If you are still not sure what the object is called, describe how it looks.*

a spiral galaxy (or an object shaped like a pinwheel) surrounded by dark space

▶ *How is the image you made the same as your classmates' images? How is it different?*

Students' images should all be the same shape, but the colors may differ.

▶ Propose Explanations

"TRANSLATE" YOUR IMAGE Each square you colored represents a point in space. The number in the square represents the strength of the radio waves detected by a group of radio telescopes.

FIND OUT MORE
SCIENCESAURUS
Stars, Galaxies, and
Constellations 244
Galaxies 247

▶ *What do you think 0 means? What do you think 5 means?*

0 means no waves; 5 means very strong waves.

The astronomers who make images from radio waves choose the colors they use for each image. The colors are not the colors you would see if you looked at the visible light from the space object.

▶ *Does it matter what colors you chose to create your radio telescope image? Why or why not?*

It doesn't matter because the colors are just a code. They represent radio waves, not colors of visible light.

▶ *What if you had used the brightest color for 0 and black for 5? Would you still have seen the shape of the object? Would you still know where on the image the most radio energy was? Explain.*

It wouldn't matter if I changed the colors. I would still see the same shape, and I would still know where the most radio energy came from.

207

More Resources
The following resource is also available from Great Source.

SCIENCESAURUS
Stars, Galaxies, and
Constellations 244
Galaxies 247

Enrichment
Encourage students to visit the "Behind the Pictures" pages at the following Hubble Space Telescope Web site:
hubblesite.org/sci.d.tech/behind_the_pictures

The pages present an interesting discussion of the use of color in images captured by the telescope. Students may also enjoy browsing the site's picture gallery:
hubblesite.org/gallery

Assessment
Skill: Making inferences

Use the following task to assess each student's progress:

Have students explain why each individual's choice of colors was not important in creating the images. (The colors are a code. They aren't the actual colors of space objects.) Then ask them to explain what is important about the use of color in this activity. (the brightness of each color compared with the other colors chosen)

▶ Propose Explanations

"TRANSLATE" YOUR IMAGE If students have trouble understanding why the particular colors they used in this exercise are not important, point out that filling in the data sheet is comparable to filling in a paint-by-numbers picture. No matter which colors you use, if you follow directions correctly, you will get the same image. For example, if you are coloring a picture of a dog, it will look like a dog no matter what colors you make it.

CHECK UNDERSTANDING
Skill: Comparing and contrasting
Have each student compare his or her image with a classmate's image. Tell students to identify the areas of the classmate's image where the most and least radio energy is represented.

CHAPTER 19 / LESSON 57   207

CHAPTER 20 Overview

Exploring Space

LESSON 58
Sailing Through Space
Point of Lesson: *Scientists are investigating whether sunlight could be used to push a space probe beyond our solar system.*

Solar sails are an experimental method of accelerating probes through space. Because such spacecraft would not require fuel, they have the potential to travel beyond our solar system. Major design differences between fuel-powered and solar-sail spacecraft are the result of the differences in their energy source.

Materials
none

LESSON 59
In Freefall
Point of Lesson: *Astronauts train for space travel by flying in free-falling airplanes.*

Objects in orbit are in freefall—constantly falling toward Earth without reaching it. Freefall is disorienting because objects in a spacecraft behave as if they are weightless. Astronaut training includes a ride in a freefalling aircraft. This ride helps astronauts get used to the freefall environment before they live and work in it.

Materials
Read (p. 212), for teacher's use:
▶ stopwatch or clock with second hand

LESSON 60
Why Explore Space?
Point of Lesson: *Some people think space exploration is a waste of time and money; others disagree.*

Reasonable people disagree about the costs and benefits of space exploration. Whether a person thinks space exploration is worthwhile depends on his or her own values. Whether that person can convince others to share the same view depends on the ability to craft a strong argument.

Materials
Activity (p. 217), for each group:
▶ 15 index cards

Background Information

Lesson 58

The idea of a sail pushed by sunlight dates to Jules Verne's 1860s novel *From Earth to the Moon*, which may have been inspired by J.C. Maxwell's discovery that light exerts pressure. (Kepler also imagined a solar sail, but his idea used solar wind, which turns out not to be workable.) Serious modern consideration of solar sails began in the late 1950s.

The basic premise of solar-sail design is the use of light to push an ultra-thin and extremely large reflective surface—the sail— to which an ultralight spacecraft is attached. Such a delicate arrangement would not withstand the forces involved in launching it from Earth's surface. Thus, solar-sail spacecraft would have to be deployed after being launched inside a traditional rocket. Or they could be assembled at a space station, then launched.

Several Web sites posted by both professionals and informed amateurs are available online. Most are written at a level appropriate to high school and above.

How Solar Sails Will Work
www.howstuffworks.com/solar-sail.htm

Intro to Solar Sailing
www.ugcs.caltech.edu/~diedrich/solarsails

The Planetary Society: Cosmos 1, The First Solar Sail
www.planetary.org/solarsail

Lesson 59

It is rare for anyone but an astronaut to be allowed onto NASA's freefall training flight (nicknamed the "Vomit Comet" for the effect it has on passengers), so *National Geographic* journalist Michael Long traveled to Russia for a paid ride on the Ilyushin-76.

In freefall and in outer space, the body's normal gravity-based mechanisms for balance cannot function. Before their freefall flights, astronauts undergo a series of experiences to test their reactions. Using special equipment on Earth, astronauts are rotated, centrifuged, turned upside-down, knocked off their feet, and otherwise twisted and turned, often at great speed.

Lesson 60

The letters stating positions against and for space exploration appeared in response to an opinion column, "Finish the Space Station, Head to Mars," by Richard Wassersug, which appeared in a news magazine for life science research professionals (*The Scientist* 16 [3]:60, Feb. 4, 2002). Dr. Wassersug, a Canadian space biologist, argued for completion of the International Space Station as it was originally planned, in spite of excessive cost overruns, because of its importance to biological research.

UNIT 5 Astronomy

CHAPTER 20 / LESSON 58

Point of Lesson
Scientists are investigating whether sunlight could be used to push a space probe beyond our solar system.

Focus
- Earth in the solar system
- Motion and forces
- Understanding about science and technology
- Science as a human endeavor

Skills and Strategies
- Making inferences
- Comparing and contrasting
- Generating questions
- Recognizing cause and effect

Advance Preparation

Vocabulary
Make sure students understand these terms. Definitions can be found in the glossary at the end of the student book.

- atmosphere
- galaxy
- gas
- molecule
- pressure
- solar energy
- solar system
- star
- wind

TEACHING PLAN pp. 208–209

INTRODUCING THE LESSON
In this lesson, students read about possibilities for a spacecraft propelled by a solar sail.

Find out what students know about conventional spacecraft by asking: *How do fuel-propelled rockets operate?* (As fuel burns, it gives off gases that expand rapidly. The gases push against the rocket, pushing it forward.)

Ask: *How does rocket fuel burn in space, where there is no oxygen?* Students may suggest that fuel burns only while it is still in the atmosphere.

Ask: *Where does the rocket get the fuel that it uses in space? Where does it get the oxygen to burn?* Lead students to realize that a rocket carries both oxygen and fuel.

▶ Before You Read

THE EFFECTS OF SUNLIGHT When students have completed their lists, ask them to consider the changes they identified. Ask: *Which changes are temporary? Which are permanent?*

CHAPTER 20 / LESSON 58
Exploring Space

SAILING THROUGH SPACE

How can you sail without wind?

You may have seen pictures of rocket-powered spacecraft with fire and exhaust streaming out the back. As rocket fuel burns, gases push out of the rear of the spacecraft, and the craft is pushed forward. Scientists at NASA are searching for new ways to move spacecraft through space. One idea is to use a push from the sun instead of a push from rockets.

▲ Probe with solar sail

▶ Before You Read

THE EFFECTS OF SUNLIGHT Think about the last time you went outside on a sunny day. How did sunlight affect objects on Earth? What changes did it produce? List some of the different ways that sunlight changes objects on Earth.

Answers will vary. Examples: It heats objects, lights them up so we can see them, tans skin, fades color in dyes, helps plants grow, and dries up puddles.

▶ Read

NASA scientists are investigating ways to use sunlight to move spacecraft beyond our solar system.

Sailing to the Stars

Imagine being onboard a sailing ship. You unfurl the sails, set your navigation controls, and set sail for...the stars? That's exactly what we may be doing some day soon. Engineers and scientists are working on ways to build solar sails that will be pushed by sunlight. Just as sailboats on Earth don't need a motor and fuel, spacecraft with solar sails won't need rockets and rocket fuel.

All of the rockets we launch now use chemicals for fuel. When rocket fuel burns, it creates expanding gases that push out the end of the rocket engine. That pushes the rocket forward. But you have to carry a lot of rocket fuel with you if you want to travel to another star! Les Johnson, manager of Interstellar Propulsion Research at the Marshall Space Flight Center, says, "The difficulty is that rockets need so much fuel that they can't push their own weight into interstellar space. The best option appears to be space sails, which require no fuel."

So plans are to try a solar sail on a...[space probe]. The...sail will be nearly half a kilometer wide. The sail would be unfurled in space. Then, continuous pressure from sunlight would slowly speed up the probe until it's moving about five times faster than possible with regular rockets.

---

unfurl: spread open
navigation: steering
interstellar: among the stars
propulsion: being pushed forward
option: choice
probe: an instrument used to collect data

From: "Sailing to the Stars," *NASA Kids*. Center Operations Directorate at Marshall Space Flight Center. (kids.msfc.nasa.gov/news/2000/news%2Dsolarsail.asp)

NOTEZONE

Circle an energy source that is used to push spacecraft through space.

Underline another way to push spacecraft that has not yet been tested.

FIND OUT MORE

SCIENCESAURUS

Forces in Nature	275
Friction	279
Balanced and Unbalanced Forces	280
Unbalanced Forces	282
Newton's First Law of Motion	284

Enrichment

The reading on this page describes one proposed method for pushing a solar-sail space probe. Probes may include other forms of propulsion as well, such as "slingshotting" off the sun or using the push of an Earth-based laser. Have students do online research to learn more about solar sail projects. Two places to start include:

▶ HowStuffWorks Web site
www.howstuffworks.com/solarsail

▶ Planetary Society's solar sail Web site
www.planetary.org/solarsail

▶ Read

Review Newton's Laws of Motion. (See *ScienceSaurus* sections 283–286.) Challenge students to identify examples of two laws in the reading:

▶ Newton's second law (force = mass × acceleration): "...continuous pressure from sunlight would slowly speed up the probe...."

▶ Newton's third law (action/reaction): "...rocket fuel creates expanding gases that push out the end of the rocket engine. That pushes the rocket forward...."

Students may also suggest that once the solar sail is moving, it will continue to move because there is no friction in space, an example of Newton's first law (inertia). Acknowledge their reasoning, but point out that sunlight is exerting a force on the spacecraft, causing it to accelerate.

CHECK UNDERSTANDING
Skill: Comparing and contrasting
Ask students to sketch a traditional rocket that uses fuel and a spacecraft that uses a solar sail. Then have them add arrows to the diagrams to show the forces that move each kind of spacecraft. Remind them to label each arrow with the source of the force. (rocket: expanding gases from burning fuel; solar-sail spacecraft: sunlight)

CHAPTER 20 / LESSON 58

More Resources
The following resources are also available from Great Source.

ScienceSaurus
Forces in Nature	275
Friction	279
Balanced and Unbalanced Forces	280
Unbalanced Forces	282
Newton's First Law of Motion	284
Newton's Second Law of Motion	285
Newton's Third Law of Motion	286

Reader's Handbook
Focus on Science Concepts	132

Connections

LITERATURE Some solar-sail scientists give credit to science-fiction stories for inspiring their career choice. Suggest that students read stories that feature solar sails. *Project Solar Sail* by David Brin, Arthur C. Clarke, and Jonathan V. Post (Roc/Penguin, 1990) is an anthology of nonfiction articles and short fiction, all on the theme of solar sails. It includes the classic short stories "The Wind from the Sun" by Arthur C. Clarke and "Sunjammer" by Poul Anderson. *Project Solar Sail* was published for the purpose of raising money for solar-sail research.

TEACHING PLAN pp. 210–211

▶ Explore

HOW SOLAR SAILS WILL WORK
Students may wonder, if there is no air in space, then why does the solar sail need to get the maximum push from the sunlight? Won't it keep moving anyway? Tell them that the sun's gravity also exerts a force, pulling the spacecraft back. The spacecraft needs enough acceleration from the sunlight to escape the sun's gravitational field.

Students may also wonder whether the solar sail will "run out of fuel" once it leaves the solar system. Yes, it will, but by that point it will be beyond the sun's gravitational field. It will continue to move at its maximum velocity without an unbalanced force such as friction to slow it down (an example of Newton's first law).

USING ANALOGIES Students may suggest that a sailboat uses wind, while a solar sail uses solar wind. Emphasize that the solar sail uses sunlight. It does not use solar wind, which is made up of charged particles from the sun.

▶ Explore

HOW SOLAR SAILS WILL WORK Solar sail designs use solar energy, but not the way you might think. They don't change light into electricity like a solar cell does. They use the pressure of light. Light exerts pressure? Well, not a lot, but some. As particles of light, called photons, strike a surface, they put a tiny amount of pressure on it. If the light is reflected by the surface, the pressure on the surface is twice as great.

▶ In order to get the greatest pressure, what sort of material do you think a solar sail should be made of?

a reflective surface, like a mirror

The force exerted by sunlight is very small. It doesn't push the solar sail very fast. But because sunlight will always be shining on the solar sail, the speed will slowly increase. Scientists predict that in time, the spacecraft will be traveling 90 kilometers per second (more than 200,000 mph)!

When objects such as airplanes and sailboats move through Earth's atmosphere, air resistance slows them down. Air resistance is caused by friction between the object and the air molecules it touches. But there is no air in outer space.

▶ How can even a small push from sunlight be enough to move a space probe a great distance?

With no air, there's no air resistance and no friction to slow the probe down. Even a small push can keep the probe moving.

USING ANALOGIES The reading compares solar sails with the sails used on sailboats.

▶ In what ways would a solar sail be like the sail on a sailboat?

Both sails are wide. Both sails are pushed by something, which moves the object forward.

▶ In what ways would a solar sail not be like the sail on a sailboat?

A sailboat's sail is pushed by air, but a solar sail would be pushed by sunlight (photons).

ENERGY FOR SAIL
A rocket-powered spacecraft and a spacecraft with a solar sail use different energy sources.

▶ **How does using each energy source affect the weight of the spacecraft?**

Rocket fuel is heavy, so it adds weight to the spacecraft. Sunlight does not add any weight to the spacecraft.

Objects outside our solar system are very far away. They are so far away that it would be much too expensive for a rocket-propelled spacecraft to carry enough fuel to reach them.

▶ **How might solar sails allow us to study distant stars and galaxies?**

The spacecraft would be able to travel longer distances because they would never run out of fuel. They would be able to reach distant stars and galaxies that spacecraft with rockets cannot reach.

▶ Take Action

PLANETARY EXPLORATION Scientists know that other stars besides our sun have planets orbiting them. A probe with a solar sail might be able to reach one of those distant planets at some time in the future. What would you like to know about a probe's journey to another solar system? Write your questions below.

Answers will vary. Examples: How far away is the other solar system? How long would the trip take? Would the probe send data back to Earth? What kinds of data would the probe collect?

Assessment
Skill: Comparing and contrasting

Use the following task to assess each student's progress:

Imagine that a friend is looking for a new idea to invest in, and he asks you about solar sails. All he knows is the name "solar sails" and the fact that they are pushed by sunlight. He thinks they would be a great idea to use on expensive racing boats for places where the air is often calm. (Use the terms doldrums *and* horse latitudes *if your students know them.) Explain why a solar sail would not work on a sailboat on Earth.* (A solar sail is pushed by sunlight. Sunlight exerts only a tiny bit of pressure. That pressure is nowhere near enough to push a heavy sailboat through the water or even to push a kite through the air on Earth's surface. It only works in space, where there is no air and therefore no friction.)

ENERGY FOR SAIL Once students have thought about how rocket fuel affects the weight of a spacecraft, invite them to reread the first paragraph of the passage on page 209. Then ask: *Is it likely that solar-powered spacecraft would ever carry human passengers?* (No, people weigh too much.) *If not, why would the writer use the image of a person on board unfurling a solar sail?* (to grab the reader's attention)

▶ Take Action

PLANETARY EXPLORATION Invite students to imagine what would happen if a probe with a solar sail did reach a distant star or planet. As the probe approached the planet, it would need to "put on the brakes" for a safe landing. One possible "brake" is using the light from that star to push against the solar sail and slow down the spacecraft. It may also be possible to use friction to slow the spacecraft, if it could be done without burning.

UNIT 5 Astronomy
CHAPTER 20 / LESSON 59

Point of Lesson
Astronauts train for space travel by flying in freefalling airplanes.

Focus
- Motion and forces
- Science as a human endeavor
- Abilities of technological design

Skills and Strategies
- Recognizing cause and effect
- Making inferences
- Generating questions

Advance Preparation

Vocabulary
Make sure students understand these terms. Definitions can be found in the glossary at the end of the student book.
- altitude
- atmosphere
- gravity
- orbit

Materials
Gather the materials needed for *Read* (p. 212).

CHAPTER 20 / LESSON 59
Exploring Space

IN FREEFALL
It's not exactly space travel, but it's close enough!

Being in space is not like being on Earth. Astronauts aboard a spacecraft orbiting far above Earth experience a feeling of weightlessness. This is because the spacecraft and everything inside it are in freefall—a constant falling motion in response to Earth's gravity. Before going into space, astronauts train to live and work in freefall. They do so by going into a freefall environment within Earth's atmosphere.

NOTEZONE
What questions do you have after reading this?

FIND OUT MORE
SCIENCESAURUS
Gravity 276

SCILINKS
THE WORLD'S A CLICK AWAY
www.scilinks.org
Keyword: Space Exploration and Space Stations
Code: GSED25

▶ Read

Former flight instructor Michael Long went to Russia to ride Ilyushin-76—an airplane used to create a freefall environment. On his airplane ride, Long experienced conditions like those felt by astronauts in space.

Preparing for Space

The brilliantly white aircraft surges down the runway, engines screaming. [Once we reach the right] altitude, a steep 45-degree climb begins. Bright lights come on, and the pilot...lowers the nose of the airplane to produce about 30 seconds of [what feels like] weightlessness. Magically, we all rise like smoke and float and fly around. Just like that. People wriggling, eyes wide, mouths open, faces smiling, frowning. Bodies turning upside down—a stunning sight that my eyes record but that my brain seems unable to interpret. Major Boris V. Naidyonov of the Russian Air Force, my instructor, asks, "You OK?" He is concerned about nausea, and so am I. "I think so," I reply.
...One of my companions ricochets off the ceiling. Another does [floating] gymnastics. Naidyonov tosses me around the cargo bay like a javelin, twirls me like a baton. This is serious fun....

TEACHING PLAN pp. 212–213

INTRODUCING THE LESSON
In this lesson, students read about a trip on a freefalling aircraft. Encourage students to describe any films they have seen—in either news reports or movies—of astronauts in a spacecraft, floating in freefall. Ask them to explain why the astronauts floated. Students may say "because there is no gravity in space." Address this misconception by explaining that weight is the force of gravity pulling on a mass. Earth is pulling on objects that are in orbit, including astronauts in a spacecraft, so they do have weight. As described in the introductory paragraph, the objects are in *freefall*—continually falling toward Earth but never reaching the surface.

▶ Read
Time: 5 minutes
Materials: stopwatch or clock with second hand

Point out to students that the author describes his own reactions to being in freefall but does not tell the reader what the other passengers are feeling. Instead, he describes their actions and the expressions on their faces. Ask students to identify words and phrases in the reading that suggest how the author and other passengers are feeling during freefall.

Thirty seconds may sound like a short time, but it can feel long to the person experiencing it. Tell students to close their eyes and imagine they are in freefall, while you watch the clock. Have students silently raise a hand when they think 30 seconds has passed. At the end of 30 seconds, tell students how many people had good estimates (within 5 seconds of 30 seconds).

212 CHAPTER 20 / LESSON 59

But [some of the other passengers] are silently vomiting into plastic bags.... They are experiencing the motion sickness that afflicts more than two-thirds of all astronauts upon reaching orbit....

surges: moves with a sudden burst of speed
interpret: understand the meaning of
nausea: the feeling of being sick to your stomach
ricochets: bounces
javelin: a long, thin bar designed for throwing through the air
baton: a short, thin bar designed for spinning
afflicts: affects

From: Long, Michael. "Surviving in Space." *National Geographic.*

▶ Explore

▶ **Why is it a good idea to put astronauts in a freefall environment before their real space flight?**
to let them train how to move around so they don't damage things or injure themselves during their real space flight; to make sure they can handle it and don't get too sick if they do go

▶ **Imagine that the inside of a spaceship were like a room on Earth. What are some things that could be problems in a freefall environment?**
Answers will vary. Examples: Furniture wouldn't stay on the ground, food wouldn't stay on the table, and it would be impossible to drink from a glass.

▶ Take Action

FREEFALLING Use the Internet or a library to research the inside of a spacecraft. Notice how it is built especially for a freefall environment. Draw the inside of the spacecraft below and label its special features.

● *Drawings will vary.*

213

More Resources
The following resources are also available from Great Source and NSTA.

SCIENCESAURUS
Gravity   276

WRITE SOURCE 2000
Searching for Information   260

SCILINKS
THE WORLD'S A CLICK AWAY

www.scilinks.org
Keyword: Space Exploration and Space Stations
Code: GSED25

Assessment
Skill: Recognizing cause and effect

Use the following question to assess each student's progress:

What do you think your favorite sport or other activity would be like in a freefall environment? (Answers should reflect an understanding that objects in freefall stay in place or keep moving in the same direction until something makes them change direction. They do not fall down, as a ball does when it is kicked or thrown on Earth.)

▶ Explore
Draw an analogy between swimming and the practice of putting astronauts into freefall before their first space flight. A child learning to swim starts in shallow water (or with a flotation device) until he or she has the skills and strength to be safe and comfortable in the water. Only then is the child allowed to enter water over his or her head.

One of the most common jobs during Space Shuttle missions is running scientific experiments. Challenge students to think of simple experiments that could be done in a freefall environment. In a class brainstorming session, have students write a testable question for investigation, a hypothesis, a list of equipment and materials, and a brief description of the procedure.

▶ Take Action

FREEFALLING Assign students to report on specific aspects of life in space, such as eating, sleeping, exercising, bathing, and working.

CHECK UNDERSTANDING
Skill: Drawing conclusions
Ask: *The reading states that the passengers experience about 30 seconds of freefall. What do you think happens at the end of those 30 seconds, when the pilot pulls the plane back up and freefall ends?* (The passengers fall to the floor of the plane, maybe bumping into each other as they do so.)

CHAPTER 20 / LESSON 59   213

UNIT 5 Astronomy
CHAPTER 20 / LESSON 60

Point of Lesson
Some people think space exploration is a waste of time and money; others disagree.

Focus
- Understanding about science and technology
- Earth in the solar system
- Risks and benefits
- Science and technology in society
- Science as a human endeavor

Skills and Strategies
- Comparing and contrasting
- Communicating
- Organizing information
- Writing a scientific argument

Advance Preparation

Vocabulary
Make sure students understand these terms. Definitions can be found in the glossary at the end of the student book.
- moon
- planet

Materials
Gather the materials needed for *Activity* (p. 217).

TEACHING PLAN pp. 214–215

INTRODUCING THE LESSON
In this lesson, students read conflicting opinions about space exploration and hold a class debate on the topic. Space images in popular entertainment are so realistic that some students may not recognize the difference between science fiction and fact. To find out what students know about space exploration, ask: *Which planets have been visited by people?* (no planets, only our moon) *Which have been visited by space probes?* (Mercury, Venus, Mars, Jupiter, Saturn, Uranus, and Neptune) *Which has not been visited?* (Pluto)

214   CHAPTER 20 / LESSON 60

CHAPTER 20 / LESSON 60
Exploring Space

▼ Space probe, Pioneer 10

Why Explore Space?

Is space travel worth all the money we spend on it? You decide.

The United States government spends billions of dollars every year on space exploration. This money comes from taxpayers. Some people argue that we haven't gotten much for all that money. Others think that the journey itself is what's important, even if we don't find materials of value. Are the benefits of space travel worth the costs?

NOTEZONE
Underline Mr. Blevins's main points.

FIND OUT MORE
SCIENCESAURUS
Society and Research 364
Society's Values 365
Military and Space Technology 366
Reasonable People Disagree 373

▶ **Read**

James Blevins of Wheatland, Wyoming, sent this letter to a science magazine.

In My Opinion
March 4, 2002

…The truth of the matter is that there is nothing out there [in space] that we know of that is of much value…. All of the planets are inhospitable enough that the only way a person could live on them would be in a bubble or space ship, so what is the point? We could get to Mars and maybe even find the remains of a microbe, so that we could know for sure there was life on other planets, but at what cost? If we are smart enough to get there, surely we must be smart enough to know that there is no reason to get there. There are so many problems here on Earth that the money could be used to solve.

inhospitable: unable to support life

microbe: an organism too small to see with the naked eye

From: Blevins, James R., Jr. "Concentrate on Earth." *The Scientist*. (www.the-scientist.com/yr2002/mar/let1_020304.html)

214

▶ **Read**

Choose two student volunteers to read the letters aloud to the class—one as Mr. Blevins, and the other as Mr. Collins. Encourage the volunteers to imagine what each writer is feeling and to read the letters using tones that reflect those feelings.

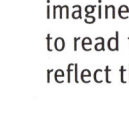

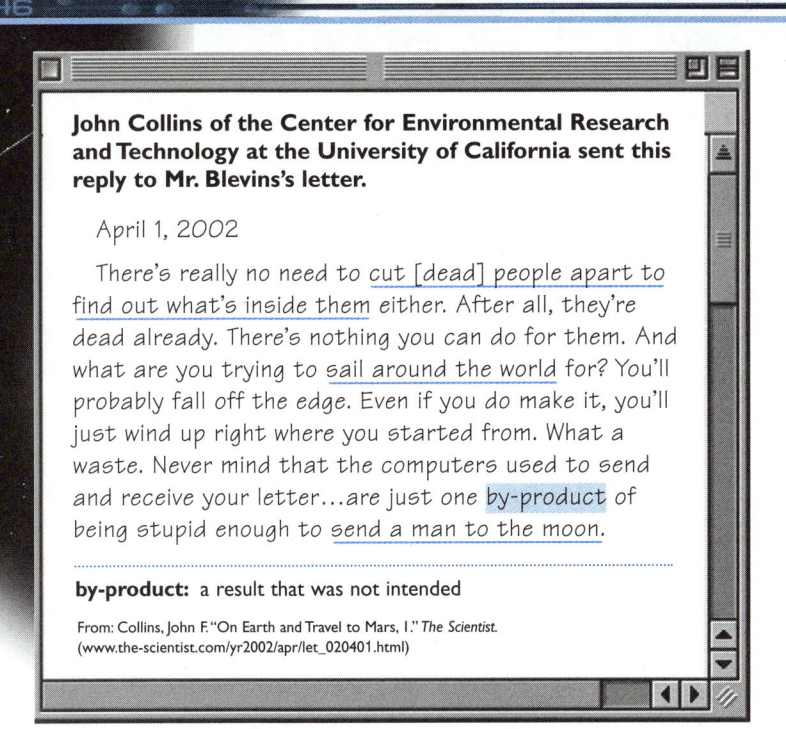

John Collins of the Center for Environmental Research and Technology at the University of California sent this reply to Mr. Blevins's letter.

April 1, 2002

There's really no need to cut [dead] people apart to find out what's inside them either. After all, they're dead already. There's nothing you can do for them. And what are you trying to sail around the world for? You'll probably fall off the edge. Even if you do make it, you'll just wind up right where you started from. What a waste. Never mind that the computers used to send and receive your letter...are just one by-product of being stupid enough to send a man to the moon.

by-product: a result that was not intended

From: Collins, John F. "On Earth and Travel to Mars, I." *The Scientist.* (www.the-scientist.com/yr2002/apr/let_020401.html)

NOTEZONE
Underline the different "explorations" Mr. Collins lists in his letter.

▶ **Explore**

COMPARE AND CONTRAST
▶ Summarize Mr. Blevins's argument in your own words.
Answers will vary. Example: There's nothing valuable in space, so why are we spending so much money to explore it? Spend the money solving problems on Earth.

▶ Summarize Mr. Collins's argument in your own words.
Answers will vary. Example: Just because there might not be valuable things to find in space doesn't mean we shouldn't explore it. Sometimes exploring leads us to new discoveries or inventions.

Enrichment
Point out to students that scientists strive to be objective, but personal opinions can affect a scientist's work. As a class, brainstorm issues that might be affected by scientists' personal opinions—for example, using animals in laboratory experiments and studying the effects of drilling for oil in a wilderness area.

Once you have a list, choose a topic and give an example of a piece of data related to that topic. For example, ask: *Suppose coral reefs are dying and that average ocean temperature is increasing. How might you interpret these data if you think that global warming is a threat?* (Warmer temperatures are killing coral reefs.) *How might you interpret these data if you think global warming is not a threat?* (The reefs are dying for another reason, such as pollution.)

▶ **Explore**

COMPARE AND CONTRAST If students have difficulty summarizing the two arguments, suggest that they start by figuring out whether each writer is for or against space exploration. Then ask them to explain how they figured that out. This approach should help them recognize the point each person is making.

CHECK UNDERSTANDING
Skill: Organizing information
Ask students to explain the difference between fact and opinion. Then have them reread the two letters. For each letter, have them identify phrases from the letter that show the author's opinion on the subject. Then have them identify facts that each author uses to support his opinion.

CHAPTER 20 / LESSON 60   215

CHAPTER 20 / LESSON 60

More Resources
The following resources are also available from Great Source.

ScienceSaurus
Society and Research	364
Society's Values	365
Military and Space Technology	366
Reasonable People Disagree	373

Reader's Handbook
Focus on Persuasive Writing	247
Focus on Speeches	256
Elements of Nonfiction: Fact and Opinion	281

Write Source 2000
Writing Persuasive Essays	115

Connections
HEALTH Prolonged periods in weightless environments can lead to loss of bone mass and other health problems. Interested students can research health risks caused by being in space and what astronauts do to keep their bodies strong while in orbit. Students could use their findings to support either position in the class debate later in the lesson.

Teaching Plan pp. 216–217

▶ Explore
TWO POINTS OF VIEW Students are probably familiar with sarcasm in everyday conversation, although they may not have heard the term for it. Give students this example: *Your big brother just ate the last slice of pizza, and you wanted it. You say, "I suppose you were just so hungry that you were going to faint unless you ate it!"* Ask: *How is this statement sarcastic?* (The person saying it did not really believe that the brother would faint.)

Students may need help in evaluating which argument is stronger. A well-written argument with a clear focus and supporting statements is stronger than one that is poorly written, disorganized, or lacking in supporting examples. Emphasize that the stronger argument is likely to be more persuasive—but a person can recognize that an argument is strong while disagreeing with it.

▶ Explore
TWO POINTS OF VIEW When people have strong ideas about an issue and are trying to convince others that these ideas are right, they often use reason or emotion to make their point. When using reason, they support their ideas with evidence. When using emotion, they try to stir up other people's feelings. Emotional arguments sometimes use sarcasm. In a sarcastic remark, a person says the opposite of what he or she means. Sarcasm is sometimes used to make fun of opposing ideas. Read the two letters again.

▶ Which writer used reason in his argument?
  Mr. Blevins

▶ Which writer used sarcasm?
  Mr. Collins

▶ How did he use sarcasm?
  He named explorations that most people would agree were useful and said they were not useful.

▶ Which person do you think made a stronger argument? (The stronger argument is not necessarily the one you agree with!) In what way was it stronger?
  Answers will vary but should include evidence from the letters to support the student's position.

216

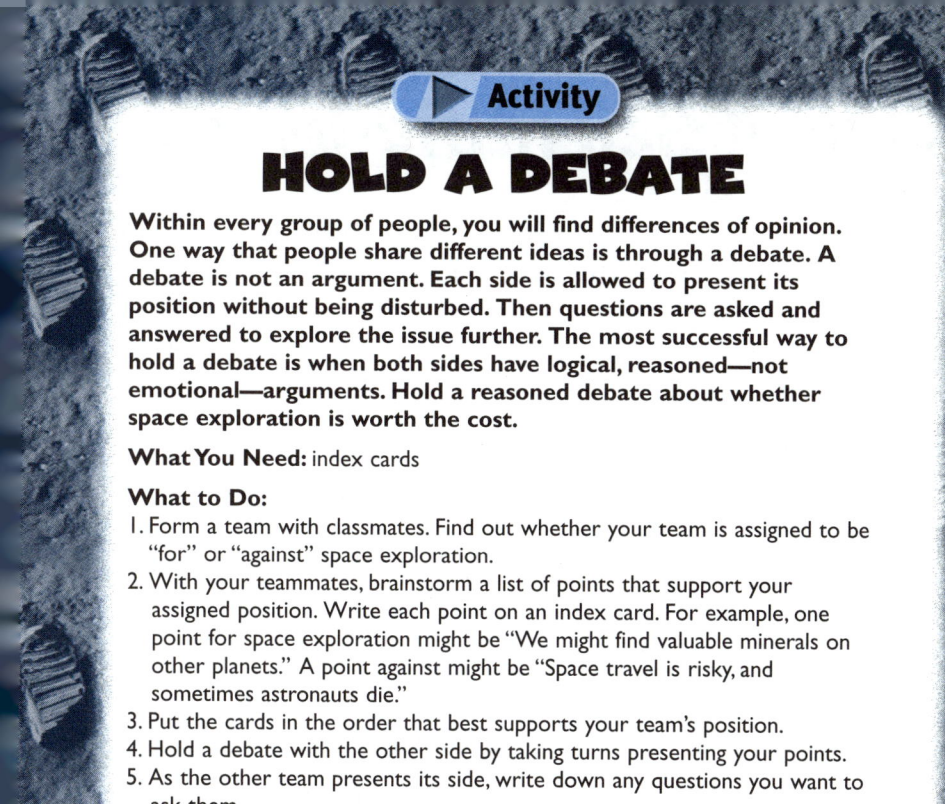

Activity

HOLD A DEBATE

Within every group of people, you will find differences of opinion. One way that people share different ideas is through a debate. A debate is not an argument. Each side is allowed to present its position without being disturbed. Then questions are asked and answered to explore the issue further. The most successful way to hold a debate is when both sides have logical, reasoned—not emotional—arguments. Hold a reasoned debate about whether space exploration is worth the cost.

What You Need: index cards

What to Do:
1. Form a team with classmates. Find out whether your team is assigned to be "for" or "against" space exploration.
2. With your teammates, brainstorm a list of points that support your assigned position. Write each point on an index card. For example, one point for space exploration might be "We might find valuable minerals on other planets." A point against might be "Space travel is risky, and sometimes astronauts die."
3. Put the cards in the order that best supports your team's position.
4. Hold a debate with the other side by taking turns presenting your points.
5. As the other team presents its side, write down any questions you want to ask them.
6. Ask the other team your side's questions. They will do the same to your team.

Write Reflections

▶ *What did you learn from the debate? Did the arguments you heard make you change your mind about anything? If so, what?*

Answers will vary.

Assessment

Skill: Organizing information

Use the following task to assess each student's progress:

For each statement listed below, ask students to identify which position (*for* or *against* space exploration) it would best support.

▶ *Technology from the space program has led to better eyeglasses, safety gear for firefighters, medical tests, and communications.* (for)

▶ *In 1999, two unmanned NASA probes, costing a total of $290 million, both failed before reaching their target, Mars.* (against)

▶ *For every dollar the U.S. spends on the space program, it receives $7 back in the form of taxes from new jobs and businesses that result from it.* (for)

Activity

Time: two 45-minute sessions, one for students to research and prepare their arguments, another for the debate
Materials: (for each group) 15 index cards

You may prefer to assign different roles to three or four teams:

▶ a team that argues for space exploration
▶ a team that argues against space exploration
▶ a team that argues in favor of robot probes but against missions that carry humans
▶ a team of moderators whose job it is to become informed on the subject and prepare incisive questions to ask each team during the debate

CHAPTER 20 / LESSON 60

Earth Science: Glossary of Scientific Terms

A

air mass: a large body of air that has about the same temperature and humidity throughout it

air pressure: a measure of the weight of the atmosphere per unit of area on Earth's surface

altitude: height above average sea level

anemometer: an instrument that measures wind speed

asteroid: object made of rock, metal, and ice that is much smaller than a planet and that revolves around the sun; Most asteroids have orbits between Mars and Jupiter.

astronomy: study of space, including stars, planets, and other objects in space, and their origins

atmosphere: the layer of gases above a planet's surface

B

bacteria: one-celled organism that lacks a true nucleus

barometric pressure: *See air pressure*

C

carnivore: an animal that feeds on other animals, such as a wolf

cementation: process that turns sediments into hard rock when a binding material, often calcite, filters into the sediment

circumference: distance around a circle or sphere

climate: the general pattern of weather in a particular part of the world over a long period of time

cloud: group of tiny liquid water droplets hanging in the air

coal: solid fossil fuel, formed deep within Earth over millions of years

cold front: the leading edge of a mass of cold air; cold fronts can bring violent storms

comet: solar system object made mostly of ice, which follows a long, narrow orbit around the sun; A comet comes near the sun only occasionally.

compaction: process by which sediments are reduced in size or volume by pressure of rock or soil lying above them

condensation: the process in which matter changes from a gas to a liquid

conservation: the wise use and protection of natural resources

continent: any of Earth's seven large land masses

continental drift: theory that continents were once part of a single landmass that broke apart and moved to their present positions; led to the theory of plate tectonics

contour interval: difference in elevation between any two contour lines on a topographic map

contour line: on a map, line that connects points of equal elevation above sea level

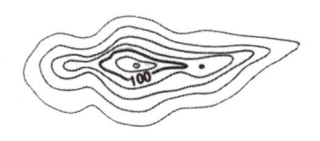

coral reef: warm ocean ecosystem based on tiny animals called coral, which build a rock-like structure (reef) that shelters other organisms

crater: bowl-shaped hollow in the ground caused by a volcano or by a meteor strike

crust: outermost, rocky layer of Earth

crystal: solid made up of molecules arranged in a regular, repeating pattern

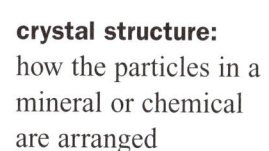

crystal structure: how the particles in a mineral or chemical are arranged

D

data: collected information, the results of an experiment or other investigation

density: a measure of mass per unit of volume; found by dividing the mass of the object by its volume

deposition: process by which wind, water, and gravity leave eroded sediments in new locations

dew point: the temperature at which water vapor changes to liquid

diameter: distance across a circle or sphere, measured through the center

dune: mound of sand that was deposited by wind

E

earthquake: energy waves passing through Earth, caused by a sudden shift along a fault line or by volcanic activity

echo: sound waves reflected off a surface

electrical energy: form of energy that consists of a flow of electric charges through a conductor

electricity: general term for interaction of electric charges

electromagnetic spectrum: full range of electromagnetic waves

elements: substances that are the building block of all matter; An element is made up of one kind of atom.

elevation: height above average (mean) sea level; also called **altitude**

energy: ability to do work

erosion: movement of weathered rock (sediment) by wind, water, ice, or gravity

estimate: an approximation or educated guess at a quantity, based on facts; also, the act of estimating

estuary: area where a river empties into the ocean and there is mixing of fresh water and salt water

evaporation: the process in which matter changes from a liquid to a gas

extinct: condition in which there are no more living members of a species

Earth Science

F

fog: a cloud close to the ground

fossil: the remains, impression, tracks, or other evidence of an ancient organism

fossil fuels: fuels such as coal, oil, and natural gas; formed over millions of years from the remains of ancient plants and animals

G

galaxy: group of millions of stars; Earth is part of the Milky Way galaxy.

gas: matter that has no definite volume or shape, such as air

geology: study of Earth's structure, composition, forces, history, and future

geothermal energy: energy obtained from thermal energy inside Earth

glacier: large mass of ice and snow that exists year-round and is involved in erosion

global warming: an increase in the world's average temperature, possibly caused in part by fossil fuel use

grassland: large land region in which the main types of plants are grasses

gravity: force of attraction between any two objects

groundwater: water that collects and flows below the ground surface

H

hardness: relative ability of a solid, such as a mineral, to resist scratching

heat energy: total kinetic energy contained in all the particles of a substance

histogram: kind of bar graph used to show the frequency of values within a set of data

horizontal axis: a horizontal line marked with a scale that is used to place data points on a graph; sometimes called the x-axis

hurricane: a huge, slowly spinning tropical storm that forms over water and has winds of at least 119 km/h (74 mph)

hypothesis: an idea that can be tested by experiment or observation

I

igneous rock: rock formed from hot melted material that cooled

inference: an explanation that is based on available evidence but is not a direct observation

isobar: line on a weather map that connects points of equal air pressure

isotopes: atoms of the same element with different numbers of neutrons in the nucleus and thus different atomic masses; for example, carbon-12 and carbon-14

L

lava: molten rock material pushed up from a volcano or crack in the Earth; magma that has reached the surface

life cycle: all stages in the life of an organism or the existence of a star

liquid: matter that has a definite volume but not a definite shape; for example, water

M

magma: molten rock that makes up Earth's mantle and becomes igneous rock when it cools

mantle: a layer of Earth's surface, lying just below the crust and above the inner core

map: flat picture of part or all of the surface of Earth or another planet

map legend: list or explanation of symbols on a map

- stream
- house
- unpaved road
- sandy area

map scale: way of showing how distances on a map relate to distances on Earth's surface

matter: the material that all objects and substances are made of; anything that has mass and takes up space

metamorphic rock: rock that has been changed over time by high pressures and temperatures inside Earth's crust

meteor: a piece of rock from space that enters Earth's atmosphere and burns, creating a bright streak of light across the sky; **meteorite** is the part of a meteor that lands on Earth

meteorology: study of Earth's atmosphere

meteor shower: particles of rock and gas from a comet that burn up in Earth's atmosphere and can be seen as many streaks of light

microscopic: too small to be seen without a microscope

mid-ocean ridge: undersea mountain range that forms where two parts of Earth's crust are pushing apart (diverging plate boundary)

mineral: element or compound, formed by nature but not formed by living things, that has a specific crystal structure and physical and chemical properties

molecule: smallest particle of a substance that still has the properties of that substance

moon: a natural object that revolves around a planet

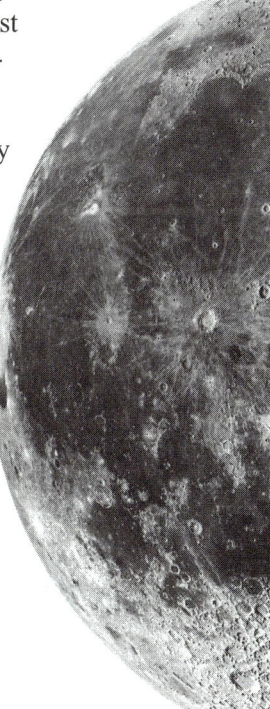

221

Earth Science

N

natural gas: a fossil fuel; flammable, odorless gas (mostly methane) found in Earth

nonrenewable resources: natural resources that cannot be replaced once used, such as oil, coal, natural gas, and minerals

nutrient: substance that an organism needs in order to survive and grow

O

ocean current: flow of water within the ocean that moves in a regular pattern

oceanography: study of the physical properties of oceans and seas

orbit: path an object in space follows as it revolves around another object, such as Earth around the sun or a satellite around Earth

organism: a living thing

P

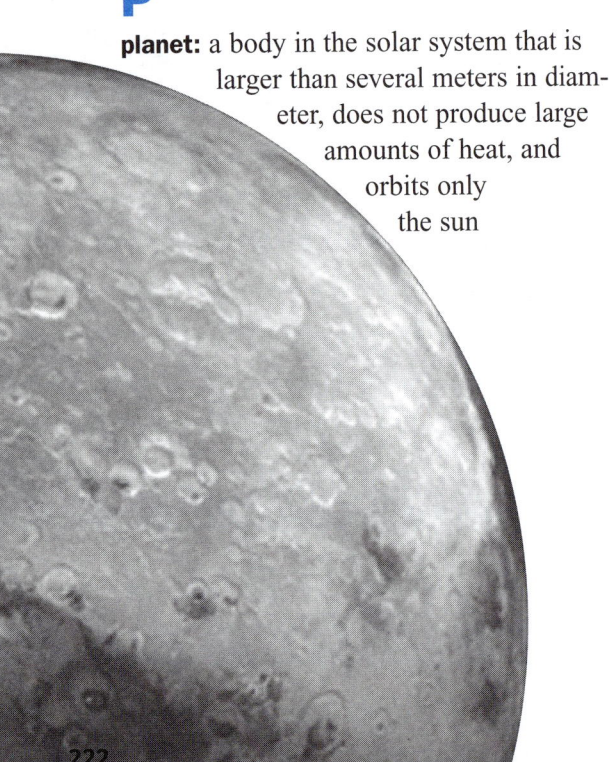

planet: a body in the solar system that is larger than several meters in diameter, does not produce large amounts of heat, and orbits only the sun

plate tectonics: theory that describes and explains the way that continents separated into today's land masses from one large ancestral land mass (Pangaea); also, the study of lithospheric plates, their movements, and Earth features that they affect

pollution: any change in the environment that is harmful to organisms

precipitation: water falling from clouds, such as rain or snow

prediction: a guess about what will happen under certain conditions, that is based on observation and research

pressure: amount of force exerted on a given area by an object or substance; SI unit is the pascal (Pa)

prevailing winds: winds that usually blow from only one direction

pyroclastic flow: ash, rocks, and similar solid material ejected from a volcano and rushing down its slope

R

radar: the use of reflected radio waves to determine the distance of an object and the direction it is moving

radioactive: giving off high-energy rays or particles

renewable resources: natural resources that can be renewed or replaced by nature, such as food crops and solar energy

reproduce: to make more individuals of the same species from a parent organism or organisms

rock: hard and compact mixture of minerals that formed naturally

rock cycle: process by which rocks, over geologic ages, are changed into different kinds of rock

runoff: water that flows over the ground surface

S

satellite: object that revolves around a larger object in space; The moon is a natural satellite of Earth; the Hubble Space Telescope is an artificial satellite.

sedimentary rock: rock formed when sediment is pressed and cemented together naturally over millions of years

sediments: tiny particles that settle out of water

soil: mixture of rock, mineral particles, and organic matter that forms at Earth's surface

solar energy: energy from the sun in the form of heat and light

solar system: the sun, its planets, and all other objects in orbit around the sun or planets

speed: distance traveled by an object in a given amount of time

star: huge object in space made up of gas and giving off light and heat from nuclear reactions; The sun is a star.

surface current: a river of water pushed along the ocean's surface by winds

T

technology: the use of scientific knowledge and processes to solve practical problems

temperature: measure of the average kinetic energy of the particles in a substance; measured in degrees Celsius (°C) or degrees Fahrenheit (°F)

theory: an idea that explains how many scientific observations are related

topographic map: map that shows the shape and elevation of the land surface using contour lines, and shows other land features using symbols and colors

topsoil: upper layer of soil, often the richest in plant nutrients

tornado: small, destructive, whirling, fast-moving storm that forms over land

transpiration: the process by which plants give off water vapor through their leaves

Earth Science

V

vertical axis: a vertical line marked with a scale that is used to place data points on a graph; sometimes called the y-axis

volcano: hill or mountain formed by material that erupts onto Earth's surface; caused by action of magma below surface

volume: amount of space an object or substance takes up; measured in liters (L) or cubic centimeters (cm^3)

W

water cycle: cycle in which water moves through the environment, through the processes of evaporation, condensation, and precipitation

watershed: area of land that catches precipitation and channels it into a large body of water, such as a lake, river, or marsh.

wave: a back-and-forth motion that travels from one place to another

wavelength: distance from any point on one wave to a corresponding point on the next wave, such as crest to crest or compression to compression

weather: conditions in the atmosphere, including humidity, cloud cover, temperature, wind, and precipitation

weathering: process by which water, wind, and ice wear down rocks and other exposed surfaces; includes chemical and mechanical weathering

wind: movement of the air caused by differences in air pressure

Teacher Assessment Rubric

Name _____ Assignment _____ Date _____

	Gold 4	**Silver 3**	**Bronze 2**	**Copper 1**
Comprehension ____%	Specific facts and relationships are identified and well-defined.	Most facts and relationships are defined.	Some facts are identified but relationships are missing.	No facts or relationships are stated.
Application and Analysis ____%	A strong plan is developed and executed correctly.	A plan is developed and implemented with some scientific errors.	Some organized ideas toward a weak plan.	Random statements with little relation to the question. No plan present.
Science Content ____%	Appropriate, complete, and correct scientific facts, ideas, and representations.	Appropriate and correct but incomplete scientific facts, ideas, and representations.	Some inappropriate, incomplete, and/or incorrect ideas, leading to further errors.	Lacking understanding of scientific facts or ideas.
Communication ____%	Strong and succinct communication of results.	Strong communication of results. Justification for outcome may be weak.	Communication of results is present, but lacks any justification.	No results are communicated. No justification is to be found. A correct answer may have appeared.
Aesthetics ____%	Exceptional. Attractive. Encourages attention. All requirements exceeded.	Neat and orderly. Requirements met.	Messy and disorganized. Some requirements missing.	Illegible and random information. Most or all requirements missing.

Chapter 2 • ROCK ON! Lesson 4 • Rock Clocks

Periodic Table of Elements

Chapter 9 • THE WATER CYCLE   Lesson 25 • Round and Round It Goes

Water Cycle Cube

1. Cut along the solid lines.
2. Fold on the dotted lines.
3. Tape the edges together to form a cube.

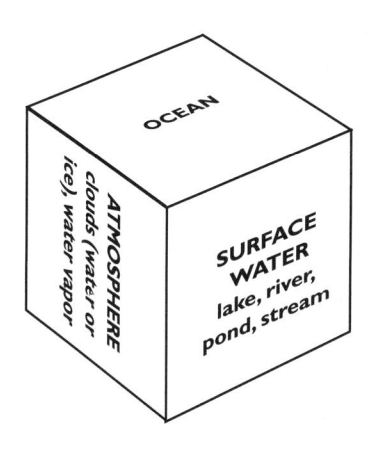

GROUNDWATER

OCEAN

PRECIPITATION
rain, snow, sleet

SURFACE WATER
lake, river, pond, stream

ATMOSPHERE
clouds (water or ice), water vapor

GLACIER

EARTH SCIENCE DAYBOOK

Chapter 14 • STORMY WEATHER   Lesson 40 • Predicting a Storm

Name _____ Date _____

Web-Based Hurricane Investigation Sheet

Part 1: What is a hurricane?

❶ What is a hurricane?
_____
_____

❷ What is the typical life cycle of a hurricane?
_____
_____

❸ How is a "storm surge" dangerous to people and property?
_____
_____
_____

Part 2: How do scientists investigate hurricanes?

❶ In what parts of the world do hurricanes occur?
_____

❷ How do scientists categorize hurricanes?
_____
_____

❸ What measurements do scientists record while investigating hurricanes?
_____

❹ What was the worst hurricane of 2001, and why do you consider it the worst?
_____
_____
_____
_____

❺ Describe Hurricane Andrew (August 16–28, 1992), which is considered the most destructive hurricane to hit the United States mainland.
_____
_____
_____
_____

228   EARTH SCIENCE DAYBOOK

Chapter 14 • STORMY WEATHER   Lesson 40 • Predicting a Storm

Name _____ Date _____

Web-Based Hurricane Investigation Sheet

Part 3: What major storms and hurricanes are happening today? How will they affect people and property?

❶ What major storms or hurricanes are there today in the eastern United States or Caribbean satellite pictures?

_____

_____

❷ Plot where one storm is now and predict where it will be 24, 48, and 72 hours from now. Check your predictions tomorrow and repeat your 24-, 48-, and 72-hour predictions.

STORM LOCATION	PREDICTION: Day 1	PREDICTION: Day 2
Now		
24 hours later		
48 hours later		
72 hours later		

❸ Where else in the world are there severe storms or hurricanes today?

_____

_____

❹ Which storms are of greatest concern to humans and why?

_____

_____

_____

❺ If a severe hurricane is predicted to travel through the area where you live, how would you prepare?

_____

_____

_____

EARTH SCIENCE DAYBOOK

Chapter 15 • WEIRD WEATHER   Lesson 43 • Down Tornado Alley

Tornado Machine Instruction Sheet

top view of wind shear and fan position

Wind moving at right angles creates the wind shear.

handheld fan

Box fan pointing up produces the updraft.

1" × 1" pine bracing

45 cm (18")

25 cm (10")

45 cm (18")

50 cm (20")

plywood

pegboard

1" × 1" pine bracing

nails or screws

dry ice and warm water

tray

230   EARTH SCIENCE DAYBOOK

Chapter 19 • PICTURING THE UNIVERSE   Lesson 57 • Images From Energy

Radio Telescope Data Sheet

0	0	0	3	3	3	3	4	4	4	3	0	0	0	0	0	0	0	0	0	3	3	3	4	3	3	0	0	0
0	0	3	3	3	3	4	4	0	0	0	0	0	0	0	0	0	0	0	0	0	3	3	3	4	3	3	0	0
0	3	3	3	3	3	4	4	0	0	0	0	0	3	3	3	0	0	0	0	0	0	0	3	3	4	3	0	0
0	3	3	3	3	3	0	0	0	0	3	3	3	3	3	4	4	3	3	0	0	0	0	0	0	3	3	4	3
3	3	3	3	0	0	0	0	3	3	3	3	4	4	3	5	5	4	0	3	0	0	0	0	0	0	3	3	4
3	3	3	0	0	0	0	3	3	3	4	4	3	3	4	5	5	4	4	3	3	0	0	0	0	0	0	3	3
3	3	3	0	0	0	0	3	3	4	4	3	3	3	3	3	3	3	4	3	3	3	0	0	0	0	0	0	0
3	3	0	0	0	0	3	4	3	3	0	0	0	0	0	0	3	3	3	4	3	3	0	0	0	0	0	0	0
3	3	0	0	0	0	3	4	4	0	0	0	0	0	0	0	0	3	3	3	4	4	3	0	0	0	0	0	0
3	3	0	0	0	3	4	4	4	0	0	0	0	0	0	0	0	0	3	3	3	5	5	3	3	3	0	0	0
3	3	0	0	3	4	4	4	0	0	0	0	0	0	0	0	0	0	0	0	3	4	3	3	3	3	0	0	0
3	3	0	0	4	3	4	4	0	0	0	0	0	0	0	0	0	0	0	0	3	4	3	3	3	0	0	0	0
3	3	0	3	3	4	0	0	0	0	0	2	2	2	2	0	0	0	0	0	0	3	4	5	3	3	0	0	0
3	0	0	3	4	3	4	0	0	0	0	0	2	1	1	2	2	2	0	0	0	0	0	3	5	3	3	3	0
3	0	3	3	4	4	0	0	0	0	2	2	1	0	1	2	3	3	3	3	3	0	0	0	3	5	5	3	0
3	0	3	3	4	4	0	0	0	0	1	1	1	0	0	1	2	3	3	3	3	0	0	0	0	3	3	3	3
3	3	0	3	4	4	0	0	0	0	1	1	0	0	0	0	1	2	3	3	3	0	0	0	0	0	3	3	3
3	3	0	0	3	3	4	0	0	0	0	1	0	0	0	0	0	1	1	0	3	3	3	3	0	0	0	3	3
3	3	0	0	3	3	0	0	0	0	1	1	1	0	3	3	0	1	1	0	0	0	3	3	4	0	0	3	3
3	3	0	0	3	3	3	0	0	0	2	2	1	0	3	3	0	0	1	0	0	0	0	3	4	3	0	3	3
3	3	0	0	0	3	3	3	0	0	0	2	1	0	0	0	1	1	1	0	0	0	0	4	3	3	0	3	3
3	3	3	0	0	3	3	3	0	0	0	0	1	1	1	1	0	1	1	0	0	0	3	4	3	3	0	0	3
3	3	3	0	0	0	3	3	0	0	0	0	0	2	2	1	1	1	0	0	0	0	4	3	3	3	0	0	3
3	3	3	0	0	0	3	3	3	0	0	0	0	1	1	2	2	0	0	0	0	0	4	4	3	3	0	0	3
3	3	3	0	0	0	0	3	3	0	0	0	0	1	1	2	2	0	0	0	0	3	3	4	3	0	0	3	3
3	3	3	3	0	0	0	3	3	0	0	0	0	4	4	3	3	0	0	0	0	3	3	3	3	0	0	3	3
3	3	3	3	0	0	0	4	3	3	3	3	3	4	4	3	0	0	0	0	0	3	3	3	3	0	0	3	3
3	3	3	3	0	0	0	3	4	4	4	3	3	3	4	3	4	0	0	0	0	5	4	3	0	0	0	4	4	3
0	4	3	3	3	0	0	0	3	3	4	4	3	0	0	0	0	0	3	5	4	3	0	0	0	3	4	3
0	4	4	3	3	0	0	0	0	0	0	0	0	0	0	0	0	3	4	5	5	4	0	0	0	0	3	4	3
0	4	5	4	3	0	0	0	0	0	0	0	0	0	0	0	0	3	3	5	4	4	3	0	0	0	0	3	4	5
0	3	5	4	3	0	0	0	0	0	0	0	0	0	0	0	0	3	3	5	4	4	0	0	0	0	3	3	4	5
0	0	5	5	4	4	3	3	3	3	3	4	3	3	3	0	0	3	3	4	4	0	0	0	0	0	3	3	5	5
0	0	0	5	3	4	3	3	3	3	3	3	4	4	3	3	3	3	3	0	0	0	0	0	3	3	3	4	0
0	0	0	0	5	4	3	3	4	3	4	3	3	3	3	3	3	3	0	0	0	0	0	0	4	3	3	0	0
0	0	0	0	0	4	3	3	4	3	3	3	3	3	3	3	0	0	0	0	0	0	0	4	4	5	3	0	0
0	0	0	0	0	0	0	3	4	3	0	0	3	3	0	0	0	0	0	0	0	0	4	5	5	3	0	0	0
0	0	0	0	0	0	0	0	0	0	0	0	0	0	0	0	0	0	0	0	4	4	4	5	3	0	0	0	0
0	0	0	0	0	0	0	0	0	0	0	0	0	0	0	0	0	0	3	3	3	4	5	3	3	0	0	0
0	0	0	0	0	0	0	0	0	0	0	0	0	0	0	0	3	3	3	3	4	5	3	0	0	0	0	0
0	0	0	0	0	0	0	0	0	0	0	0	3	3	3	3	3	3	4	4	3	3	0	0	0	0	0
0	0	0	0	0	0	3	3	3	3	3	3	3	3	3	3	3	3	3	4	4	3	3	0	0	0	0

EARTH SCIENCE DAYBOOK   231

Earth Science Index

A
Abilities necessary to do scientific inquiry, 27, 40–43, 45, 46, 48–49, 72, 73, 75, 203, 215
Abilities of technological design, 100–103, 114–117, 118–121, 136–137, 212–213, 214–217
Air mass, 142, 144, 218
Air pressure, 134, 136–137, 138–141, 142–145, 146–149, 150, 152, 218
Altitude, 136, 138–141, 212, 218
Analyzing, 13, 14, 65, 117, 119, 130, 132, 140, 149, 157, 174, 197
　See also Comparing and contrasting.
Anning, Mary, 40–43
Asteroid, 178–181, 188, 218
Astronomy, 189, 218
Atmosphere, 88, 94, 95, 218
　astronomy, 184, 187
　stratosphere, 138, 139
　troposphere, 138
　and weather, 136, 142, 146, 147

B
Bacteria, 119, 218
Background radiation, 36
Barometric pressure. See Air pressure.
Barrier beaches and islands, 63, 64, 65

C
Carbonate, 21
Carnivore, 48, 218
Cementation, 21, 218
Change, constancy, and measurement, 62–65, 66–69, 70–71, 80–81, 88–91, 94–95, 146–149, 150–153, 166–169, 170–171
Circumference, 166, 168, 218
Classifying, 21, 31, 46, 49, 53, 62, 87, 165, 188, 191
Climate, 24, 218
　ancient, 166–169
　global warming, 170–171, 172–175
Cloud, 94, 95, 100, 101, 142, 218
　wall cloud, 157
　funnel cloud, 156, 158
　and hailstones, 160
Collecting and recording data/information, 49, 70–71, 76, 125, 143, 146, 149, 151, 168, 189
Comet, 24, 218
　exploration and study, 184–187, 188, 190
　orbit, 182–183, 186, 187, 222
Compaction, 21, 218
Comparing and contrasting, 34, 39, 44, 45, 52, 53, 54, 58, 73, 74, 82, 83, 84–85, 86–87, 88, 91, 97, 106, 108, 109, 114, 115, 116, 118, 119, 123, 137, 139, 140, 146, 160, 163, 164, 165, 166, 167, 169, 172, 178, 179, 180, 188, 190, 192, 195, 198, 202, 206, 207, 208, 209, 211, 215
Composites, 119
Communicating, 17, 20, 24, 28, 29, 30, 33, 39, 49, 52, 60, 61, 64, 66, 71, 81, 88, 91, 96, 99, 103, 107, 109, 111, 113, 117, 121, 124, 128, 130, 142, 150, 153, 155, 217
Connections
　Art/Writing, 46
　Geography, 18, 22, 25, 36, 84, 90, 98, 126, 132
　Health, 58, 216
　History, 213
　Language Arts, 27, 42, 64, 68, 186, 191, 194
　Literature, 59, 120, 144, 171, 210
　Math, 79, 108, 153, 162, 174, 180
　Music, 32
　Social Studies, 18, 55, 84, 112, 140, 168
Conservation, 218
　soil, 60–61
　water, 110–113
　See also Soil conservation methods.
Contaminants, 118, 119
Continent, 72, 76, 122–123, 218
Continental drift and convergence, 72–75, 76, 79, 80, 81, 218
Coxwell, Henry, 138–141
Crater, 24, 192, 194, 219
Creative thinking
　brainstorming, 37, 110, 117, 195, 215
　using imagination, 75, 120, 169, 183
Crystal, 24, 219
Crystal structure, 24, 29, 219

D
Data vs. conclusions, 174–175
Debating, 39, 113, 217
Decay, 52
Density, 86, 87, 196, 197, 219
Deposition, 57, 62, 63, 219
Desalination, 118–121
Designing an experiment to test a hypothesis, 27, 63, 67, 77, 78, 99, 113, 123, 129, 172, 173, 173, 174
Developing hypotheses, 163, 171, 174
Diameter, 160, 188, 190, 219
Distillation, 119
　heat, 118
　semipermeable membrane, 118, 119
Drawing conclusions, 20, 24, 27, 28, 29, 56, 59, 79, 82, 85, 97, 99, 100, 118, 119, 142, 145, 171, 174, 187, 189, 195, 196, 197, 213
Drought, 52, 54, 55, 115, 161
Dune, 57, 62, 219

E
Earth in the solar system, 12–15, 16, 178–181, 182–183, 184–187, 188–191, 192–195, 196–197, 198–201, 202–205, 206–207, 208–211, 214–217
Earth's crust, 20, 21, 35, 219
　fissure, 89
　measuring movement, 80–81
　ocean floor, 76, 78–79
　rain crust, 53
　and volcano, 82
Earth's history, 20–23, 24–27, 28–29, 40–43, 44–47, 72–75, 80–81, 166–169, 178, 184, 185
Earthquake, 166, 219
Echo, 76–77, 219
Electrical energy, 30, 32–33, 219
Electricity, 30, 34, 38, 39, 219
Electromagnetic spectrum, 206, 207, 219
Elevation, 10, 11, 16, 219
Energy, 30, 33, 34, 219
　chemical, 30
　electrical, 130–131
　electromagnetic, 206–207
　fossil fuel, 30–33, 37
　heat (geothermal), 33, 34, 35, 36, 37, 39, 220
　hydroelectric, 33
　kinetic, 35
　nuclear, 33
　ocean currents, 130
　solar, 33, 37, 198, 206, 208, 223
　wind, 33, 37, 130, 211
Era, 193
Erosion, 62, 219
　caused by agricultural practices, 52–55, 56, 60
　in the Dust Bowl, 52, 53, 56
　and geology, 20, 21, 29
　prevention of, 60–61, 68–69
　of shoreline beaches, 62–65, 66–69, 70–71
　soil, 52–55, 56–59, 60–61
　wind, 57
Estimate, 178, 180, 181, 219
Estuary, 63, 219
Evaluating source material, 12, 20, 59, 101, 133, 193
Evidence, models, and explanation, 20–23, 27, 61, 67, 72–75, 80–81, 111, 172–175, 198–201, 202–205
Extinction
　of the dinosaurs, 24, 25, 219
　of fish populations, 112

F
Fertility, 53
Fog, 220
Fog collection, 96–99, 100–103

232

Forming operational definitions, 34, 37
Fossil, 40, 41, 72, 220
    ammonite, 44, 45
    fossil hunters, 48, 49
    Law of Superposition, 47
    trilobite, 44
Fossil fuels, 34, 220
    coal, 30–33, 39, 130, 218
    natural gas, 30, 31, 130, 222

G

Galaxy, 207, 208, 220
Gas
    lighter-than-air, 138
    oxygen, 139
    solar system, 178, 182, 184, 188, 190, 198, 202
Generating ideas, 12, 15, 18, 19, 34, 62, 73, 80, 81, 89, 100, 106, 110, 112, 114, 117, 127, 133, 156, 159, 160, 183, 192, 204
Generating questions, 24, 27, 39, 40, 43, 45, 80, 86, 88, 91, 101, 105, 107, 110, 113, 118, 124, 127, 143, 147, 150, 153, 160, 163, 171, 175, 202, 205, 208, 211, 212
Generator, 35
Geography, 18, 22, 25, 36, 73, 84, 90, 98, 126, 132
Geology, 20–23, 24–27, 220
Glaisher, James, 138–141
Global Positioning System (GPS), 80–81
Global warming, 134, 220
Grassland, 52, 55, 60, 220
Gratz, Andy, 25–27
Gravitational field, 185, 186
Gravity, 202, 204, 212, 220
Great Plains, 52, 53, 54, 55
Guthrie, Woodie, 57–58, 59
Gyre, 125, 126

H

Hardness, 28, 220
Hertzsprung, Enjar and Russell, Henry Norris, 200–201
Hess, Harry, 76–79
Hickam, Homer, 30–31
History of science, 72–75, 136–137, 138–141, 198–201
Horizontal axis, 138, 140, 153, 162, 196, 198, 200, 220
Hypothesis, 72–73, 220

I

Ice age, 167
Ichthyosaurus, 41, 42
Identifying and controlling variables, 172–175
Increasing awareness of safety, 35, 159, 165, 173
Interferometry or 3-D, 16–19
International Geophysical Year, 76
Interpreting data, 10, 20, 69, 80, 81, 122, 136, 137, 138, 139, 142, 146, 149, 168, 169, 170, 172, 174, 197, 200–201, 219
Interpreting scientific illustrations
    interpreting a diagram, 14, 15, 16, 18, 21–22, 30, 94, 136, 137, 166, 168, 178, 180, 186, 190, 200
    interpreting a flowchart, 102
    interpreting a graph, 116, 117, 150, 152, 200
    interpreting a histogram, 162, 220
    interpreting a map, 11, 12, 16, 31, 34, 36, 52, 54, 104, 122, 123, 126, 130, 143, 144, 146, 148, 150, 152, 154, 155, 156, 158, 163
    interpreting a satellite image, 142, 145, 146, 148, 192, 194
    interpreting a table, 16, 19, 20, 38, 39, 44, 60, 86, 87, 130, 139, 196, 197
    interpreting a timeline, 58, 167
    interpreting photos, 71, 108
    seeing patterns, 24
Interstellar travel with solar sails, 208–211
Irrigation systems, 111, 112, 117
Isobars, 144, 145, 148, 149, 220
Isotopes, 20, 21, 220

J

Jurassic period, 41

L

lamellae, 25, 26, 27
Lava, 12, 82–85, 86, 88, 221
Lava flow, 83, 85, 87
Library/internet research, 23, 48, 59, 68, 83, 87, 97, 103, 105, 107, 127, 133, 140, 141, 142, 145, 147, 151, 159, 161, 168, 193, 199, 203, 205, 207, 209, 213

M

Magma, 20, 21, 34, 35, 36, 76, 78, 82, 83, 85, 88, 90, 221
Magnetic poles, 76, 78–79
Making a decision, 38, 102, 106
Making and using models, 10, 11, 12, 61, 67, 82, 83, 95, 100, 102–103, 104, 105, 111, 118, 121, 125, 136, 137, 157, 202, 206
Making inferences, 16, 18, 29, 30, 34, 40, 41, 42, 43, 44, 45, 47, 48, 49, 52, 55, 56, 58, 61, 62, 66, 67, 70, 71, 72, 73, 80, 82, 86, 88, 95, 96, 97, 104, 106, 110, 118, 124, 125, 126, 128, 129, 130, 138, 141, 142, 143, 154, 155, 160, 164, 165, 166, 168, 169, 170, 182, 184, 188, 192, 193, 195, 197, 199, 202, 203, 205, 207, 208, 212, 220
Making scientific illustrations
    concept mapping, 38, 39, 62, 96, 99, 127, 147, 157, 190
    creating a flowchart, 19, 23
    creating a graph, 79, 138, 140, 196
    creating a table, 16, 20, 21, 38, 39, 41, 44, 69, 85, 119, 130, 146, 149, 197, 206
    drawing a diagram, 15, 30, 77, 78, 83, 88, 95, 130, 137, 141, 161, 181, 199
    K-W-L chart, 67, 107
    making a map, 11, 12, 53, 105, 117, 145
    making a timeline, 18, 68, 107
    Venn diagram, 53, 54
Mantle, 35, 221
Maps
    map legend, 11, 22, 54, 104, 158, 221
    map scale, 10, 11, 22, 104, 221
Matter, 82, 221
    gas, 82–85, 86, 87, 88–90, 94, 118, 220
    liquid, 82, 86, 87, 94, 118, 123, 221
    solid, 94, 123
Measuring, 10, 49, 80–81, 90, 113, 149, 152, 162, 168, 171, 174
Mesozoic period, 25
Meteor, 24, 221
Meteorology, 146–149, 162, 221
Meteor shower, 187, 221
Meteorites, 20, 21, 24
Microbes, 115, 116, 214
Microscopic matter, 24, 221
Mid-ocean ridge, 221
Mineral, 24, 78, 82, 85, 94, 221
Molecule, 118, 119, 136, 208, 210, 221
Moon, 196–197, 214, 221
Motion and forces, 58, 62–65, 66–69, 124–127, 130–133, 178–181, 182–183, 184–187, 208–211, 212–213, 214–217

N

National Aeronautics and Space Administration (NASA), 12, 13, 19, 185, 186
Natural hazards, 52–55, 56–59, 60–61, 70–71, 82–85, 86–87, 88–91, 114–117, 146–149, 150–153, 154–155, 156–159, 160–163, 164–165, 170–171
Nature of science, 24, 27, 40, 43, 44, 46, 48–49, 128–129, 166–169, 172–175, 188–191, 192–195
Nutrient, 52, 222

Earth Science

O

Observing, 28–29, 45, 49, 71, 82, 84–85, 95, 100, 103, 120–121, 124, 125, 126, 129, 143, 160, 173, 174, 187, 192, 193
Ocean current, 122, 123, 124–127, 128–129, 222
Oceanography, 71, 222
Oral history, 41
Orbit, 178, 180–181, 182–183, 186–187, 188, 190, 212, 222
Organism, 30, 40, 41, 94, 222
Organizing information, 12, 25, 29, 35, 38, 40, 49, 57, 65, 91, 96, 111, 117, 129, 156, 157, 162, 201, 215, 216, 217
See also Graphic organizers.
Osmosis, 119

P

Pangaea, 72
Periodic table, 21
Planet, 178, 184, 222
    cataloging, 189
    conditions to support life, 202, 205, 214
    controversy over Pluto, 188–191
    extrasolar, 202–205
    Mars, 192–195
    moons, 196–197
    solar system, 188–191
    Trans-Neptunian, 189
Plate tectonics, 20, 21, 23, 222
Pollution, 222
    air, 38, 39
    water, 104, 105, 113, 114, 115
Populations, resources, and environments, 30–33, 34–37, 38–39, 52–55, 56–59, 62–65, 96–99, 100–103, 104–105, 106–109, 110–113, 114–117, 118–121, 170–171
Prediction
    asteroid and comet orbits, 178, 180–181, 182–183
    extrasolar planet wobbles, 204, 205
    volcanic eruption, 88–91
    weather, 146–149, 152, 165
Predicting, 52, 70, 71, 80, 81, 110, 113, 114, 124, 125, 128, 132, 138, 146, 149, 154, 163, 164, 165, 170, 171, 181, 222
Pressure, 20, 21, 82–83, 182, 208, 210, 222
Properties and changes in properties of matter, 82–85, 86–87, 94–95, 118–121, 136–137, 196–197
Propulsion, 209
Pyroclastic flow, 86–87, 88, 222

Q

Quartz, 25

R

Radar, 16, 222
Radar image, 12, 13, 14, 15, 222
Radioactive, 20, 21, 37, 222
Radiometric dating, 20, 21
Reading skills
    dictionary use, 42
    main idea/supporting details, 20, 111
    summarize, 13, 20, 122, 215
Recognizing cause and effect, 24, 28, 45, 52, 53, 59, 60, 61, 62, 63, 64, 66, 70, 71, 82, 85, 86, 100, 106, 109, 123, 137, 150, 151, 153, 155, 164, 170, 171, 182, 183, 192, 208, 212, 213, 212, 213
Regulation and behavior, 138–141
Reproduction, 110, 112, 222
Research activities, 25, 45, 59, 86, 89, 97, 107, 112, 113, 126, 132, 133, 169, 175, 213
Reservoir, 106–109
Resources
    inexhaustible, 37
    nonrenewable, 30, 31, 37, 38–39, 222
    renewable, 34, 37, 38–39, 222
Risks and benefits, 88–91, 106–109, 110–113, 138–141, 154–155, 214–217
Rock, 44, 72, 184, 222
    igneous, 20, 21–22, 220
    metamorphic, 20, 21, 221
    moon, 196–197
    sedimentary, 20, 21, 223
Rock cycle, 20, 223
Roig, Fidel A., 167
Runoff, 94, 104–105, 223
Russel, Henry Norris, 200-201

S

Satellite, 80, 142, 145, 146, 147, 223
Science and technology, 16, 80, 223
    understanding, 12, 13, 16–19, 34–37, 38–39, 43, 55, 77, 110–113, 142–145, 146–149, 150–153, 184–187, 202–205, 206–207, 208–211, 214–217
    in society, 38–39, 60–61, 66–69, 70–71, 80–81, 96–99, 100–103, 106–109, 110–113, 118–121, 122–123, 130–133, 138–141, 164–165, 165, 214–217
Science as a human endeavor, 24–27, 44–47, 48–49, 72–75, 88–91, 96–99, 110–113, 122–123, 124–127, 128–129, 130–133, 138–141, 146–149, 166–169, 170–171, 178–181, 182–183, 184–187, 188–191, 192–195, 202–205, 206–207, 208–211, 212–213, 214–217
Science Scope Activities
    Bubbles in a Bottle, 143
    Greenhouse Effect or Natural Cycle?, 173
    Journeys in the Water Cycle, 97
    Making a Local Soil Map, 53
    Mapping Earth Events, 17, 115
    Pages of History, 41
    Science on the Web: Exploring Hurricane Data, 147
    Tornado Machine, 157
    What's the Connection?, 21
    Why Is There a Current?, 125
Scientific careers
    anatomist, 41
    astronomer, 176, 179, 198
    biologist, 111
    dendrochronologist, 166, 169
    forensic geologists, 9
    geophysicist, 80–81
    meteorologist, 146–149
    oceanographer, 125–127, 128
    paleoclimatologist, 167–169
    paleontologist, 48, 49
    volcanologists, 88–91
Scientific instruments
    anemometer, 101, 218
    barometer, 136, 137
    drift cards, 129
    rain gauge, 101
    seismometer, 89
    telescope, 202, 203, 204, 206
Sediment, 21, 119, 169, 223
Seafloor spreading, 76, 78–79
Sequencing, 19, 20–22, 23, 37, 66, 94–95, 103, 105, 161, 185
Shaft, 31, 35
Shale, 30
Shock, 25, 27
Silicates, 21, 82
Soil, 52, 60
    composition of, 52, 223
    on Mars, 192, 193
Soil conservation methods
    conservation tillage, 60–61
    cover crops, 60–61
    restoring wild grasslands, 60–61
    strip cropping, 60–61
    stubble mulching, 60–61
Solar system, 20, 208, 223
    Mars, 192–195
    moons, 196–197
    objects, 178–181, 182–183, 184–187, 188–191
    planets, 188–191
Solving problems, 111–113, 114, 117, 129, 141
Speed, 86, 87, 150, 152, 223
Star, 198, 223
    life cycle, 198–201
    parent star, 203

Red Giant, White Dwarf, and Black Dwarf, 198–201
temperature, 198–201, 205
Storms
  blizzard, 150, 164–165
  hailstorm, 150, 160–163
  hurricane, 70–71, 134, 146, 149, 150, 151–153, 155, 156, 220
  thunderstorm, 150, 157, 160
  tornado, 134, 150, 156–159, 223
Structure of the earth system, 10–11, 20–23, 24–27, 28–29, 30–33, 34–37, 38–39, 52–55, 56–59, 60–61, 62–65, 66–69, 70–71, 72–75, 80–81, 82–85, 86–87, 88–91, 94–95, 96–99, 100–103, 104–105, 114–117, 118–121, 122–123, 124–127, 128–129, 130–133, 138–141, 142–145, 146–149, 150–153, 154–155, 156–159, 160–163, 164–165
Surface current, 130–133, 223

T
Terrain, 17
Tertiary period, 25
Theory, 72–75, 76, 78–79, 80–81, 223
Tombaugh, Clyde, 191
Topographic map, 12, 16, 223
  contour interval, 10, 11, 218
  contour line, 10, 11, 218
Topography, 70, 71, 105
Topsoil, 52, 56, 58, 59, 60, 223
Torricelli, Evangelista, 136
Trajectory, 185
Transfer of energy, 34–37, 130–133, 142–145
Transmission wires, 35
Turbine, 35

U
Understanding about scientific inquiry, 40–43, 45, 46, 48–49, 72, 73, 75, 128–129, 192–195, 198–201, 202
Understanding that scientific findings undergo peer review, 72–75, 76–79, 172–175
Understanding that scientists change their ideas, 24, 27, 79, 81, 129, 172–175
Understanding that scientists may disagree, 72–75, 76–79, 172–175, 188–191
Understanding that scientists share their results, 24, 40, 41, 44, 72–75, 76, 99, 202
United States Geological Survey (USGS), 70, 71
Using numbers, 32, 49, 58, 116, 126, 139, 140, 152, 162, 181, 196–197, 200–201

Using space/time relationships, 10, 12, 16, 18, 40, 42, 44, 66, 68, 70, 122, 123, 124–127, 178–181

V
Vertical axis, 138, 140, 153, 162, 196, 198, 200, 224
Viscous/viscosity, 85
Visibility, 66, 147, 164
Volcano, 224
  predicting eruptions, 88–90
  seismic information, 89
  temperature, 82–83, 85, 86–87
Volume, 118, 172, 224

W
Water
  droughts and floods, 114–117, 122, 123
  fresh, 114, 115, 116–117
  glaciers, 12, 94, 95, 114, 115, 220
  groundwater, 94, 115, 220
  on Mars, 192–195
  ocean, 94, 95, 114, 115, 116
  surface, 104–105, 106–109, 115
  usable and unusable, 115–117
Water cycle, 92, 224
  condensation, 94–95, 96, 99, 101, 102, 218
  evaporation, 94–95, 101, 102, 219
  precipitation, 94–95, 104, 222
  transpiration, 94–95, 224
Waterborne diseases, 115
Watershed, 104–105, 106, 109, 224
Wave, 150, 152–153, 206–207, 224
Wavelength, 13, 224
Weather, 21, 224
  anticyclone pattern, 144
  high pressure system, 142–145, 148, 149, 152
  humidity and dew point, 146, 147, 219
  low pressure system, 143, 144, 148, 149, 152
  precipitation, 94–95, 172, 222
  predicting and reporting, 146–149, 152, 165
  severe, 150–153, 156–159, 160–163, 164–165
  temperature, 86, 87, 135, 136, 138, 139–140, 142, 146, 164, 223
  warm and cold fronts, 148, 150, 151, 218
Weathering, 20, 29, 187, 224
Wegener, Dr. Alfred, 72–75
Wind, 224
  Santa Ana, 143–145
  source of, 142–145
  speed and direction, 146, 150, 152–153, 164
  and wildfire, 145
Writing activities

description, 83
design a pamphlet, 6, 99
draw a diagram, 181
explanation, 25, 75
field notes, 29
flyer/pamphlet/brochure, 49, 64, 99, 159
imaginary dialogue, 79
interview, 43, 165
invent a mnemonic, 191
letter, 55, 64
list of questions, 91, 127, 129, 153, 163, 211
log or journal entry, 33, 68, 194
metaphor, 27
mission to Mars plan, 195
news report, 39, 64, 107, 133
paragraph, 25, 27, 47, 49, 83
plan for an explanation, 81
poem, 29
pros and cons summary, 69, 119, 130
radio or TV report, 107, 133
real world problem-solutions, 141
reflections, 217
research proposal, 175
scientific argument, 69, 215, 216
word problems, 109
write dramatically, 23

Earth Science Credits

12, 16 "Building a 3-D Map of Earth from Space!" *The Space Place.* NASA/JPL. (spaceplace.nasa.gov/srtmmka2.htm)

20 Sherlock, Sean. "How Old Is the Earth?" Online posting. *MadSci Network: Ask a Scientist.* Washington University Medical School. (http://www.madsci.org/posts/archives/mar97/858867134.Es.r.html)

24 Bird, Dr. G. Peter. "Andy Gratz, a Scientist's Eulogy." Unpublished.

28 "pebbles" from ALL THE SMALL POEMS AND FOURTEEN MORE by Valerie Worth. Copyright © 1987, 1994 by Valerie Worth. Reprinted by permission of Farrar, Straus and Giroux, LLC.

30 Hickam, Homer H., Jr. *Rocket Boys.* Delacorte Press Books for Younger Readers, a division of Random House, Inc.

30 "State by State: Percentage of Total Electricity Generation." *Nuclear Energy Institute Home Page.* Nuclear Energy Institute. (www.nei.org)

34 "Energy Story: Geothermal Energy." *Energy Quest.* California Energy Commission. (www.energyquest.ca.gov/story/chapter11.html)

40 "Mary Anning (1799-1847)." *University of California, Berkeley, Museum of Paleontology.* Regents of the University of California. (www.ucmp.berkeley.edu/history/anning.html)

48 "Dinosaur Digs" Travel Channel, copyright Discovery Communications, Inc. All rights reserved. (www.discovery.com)

52 Cather, Willa. *O Pioneers!* Houghton Mifflin.

52 From THE GRAPES OF WRATH by John Steinbeck, copyright 1939, renewed. © 1967 by John Steinbeck. Used by permission of Viking Penguin, a division of Penguin Putnam Inc.

56 DUST STORM DISASTER Words and Music by Woodie Guthrie. TRO-© Copyright 1960 [Renewed] 1963 [Renewed] Ludlow Music, Inc., New York, NY. Used by Permission.

62, 66 "Beach Erosion." *The Why Files.* Copyright 2002. University of Wisconsin Board of Regents.

70 United States. U.S. Department of the Interior. U.S. Geological Survey. "Dennis Dissipates, Work Just Begins for USGS Scientists." (http://www.usgs.gov/public/press/public_affairs/press_releases/pr979m.html)

72 Hughes, Patrick. "The Meteorologist Who Started a Revolution." *Weatherwise.*

76, 80 Vogel, Shawna. *Naked Earth: The New Geophysics.* Dutton. Reprinted by permission of Regula Noetzil Literary Agency.

82 United States. U.S. Department of the Interior. U.S. Geological Survey. "How Do Volcanoes Erupt?" *USGS Cascades Volcano Oberservatory.* (vulcan.wr.usgs.gov/Outreach/AboutVolcanoes/how_do_volcanoes_erupt.html)

86 Camp, Dr. Vic. "How Volcanoes Work: Mt. Peleé Eruption (1902)." *San Diego State University Department of Geological Sciences.* (www.geology.sdsu.edu/how_volcanoes_work/Pelee.html)

88 Wood, Chuck. "Which Method of Volcano Prediction Is The Most Useful and Reliable?" *Volcano World.* University of North Dakota. (volcano.und.nodak.edu/vwdocs/frequent_questions/grp3/question229.html)

96, 100 de Luigi, Maria. "In Person: Pilar Cereceda." *International Development Research Centre.* International Development Research Centre. (www.irdc.ca)

106 "The Quabbin Reservoir" *The Connecticut River Homepage.* Ed. Ed Klekowski and Libby Klekowski. University of Massachusetts Amherst Department of Biology. (www.bio.umass.edu/biology/conn.river/quabbinres.html)

110 Benson, Reed. "Stream of Consciousness." *WaterWatch.* (www.waterwatch.org/instream.html#STREAM)

114 "Freshwater." *Pachamama.* United Nations Environment Program. (www.unep.org/geo2000/pacha/fresh/fresh2.htm)

118 Martindale, Diane. "Sweating the Small Stuff." *Scientific American.* (www.sciam.com/2001/0201issue/0201how/htm)

122 From "Icebergs to Africa" by Sandra Fry, ABC Online, August 1997. Reproduced by permission of the Australian Broadcasting Corporation, www.abc.net.au

124 "Ocean Planet" Smithsonian Institution Traveling Exhibition Service, 1995. National Museum of American History, Behring Center. © 2002 Smithsonian Institution.

128 Posada, Janice. "Beach: Nike Shoes Wash Up." *The Herald.* 18 June 2001.

130 Grisvold, Magne. "'Water Mills' at the Bottom of the Sea." *SINTEF Energy Research.* Ed. Harald Danielsen. The Foundation for Scientific and Industrial Research at the Norwegian Institute of Technology. (www.sintef.no/publications/pro_eng_24.html)

138 Marion, Fulgence. *Wonderful Balloon Ascents.* Amazon Press. 2001

142 "Santa Ana Winds Swirl Over Southern California." *NASA Jet Propulsion Laboratory.* 22 February 2002. NASA Jet Propulsion Laboratory. (http://www.jpl.nasa.gov/releases/2002/release_2002_43.html)

146, 150, 154 From THE PERFECT STORM by Sebastian Junger. Copyright © 1997 by Sebastian Junger. Used by permission of W. W. Norton & Company, Inc.

156 Nelson, Allen. "Twisters: Destruction From The Sky." *ThinkQuest.* (http://tqjunior.thinkquest.org/4232/survivor.htm)

160 Doesken, Nolan J. "Hail, Hail, Hail—The Summertime Hazard of Eastern Colorado." *Colorado Climate.* Vol. 17, No. 7. April 1994.

164 Library of Congress, Manuscript Division, WPA Federal Writers' Project Collection.

166 "Ancient tree rings reveal past climate." http://sciencenews.org/200110331/fob2.asp. Reprinted with permission from SCIENCE NEWS, the weekly newsmagazine of science, copyright 2001 by Science Service Inc.

170 "Climate Change." Reproduced with permission from *New Scientist.*

172 Copyright © 1999 by the New York Times Co. Reprinted by permission.

179 Reprinted with permission of The Associated Press.

182 "Comet Meltdown!" *NASAKids.* Ed. Becky Bray and Patrick Meyer. August 11, 2000. NASA Marshall Space Flight Center. (http://kids.msfc.nasa.gov/news/2000/news%2Dlinear.asp)

184 "StarDust." *Liftoff to Space Exploration.* Ed. Becky Bray and Patrick Meyer. October 22, 1998. NASA Marshall Space Flight Center. (http://liftoff.msfc.nasa.gov/academy/space/solarsystem/comets/stardust.html)

188 Reprinted with the permission of The Associated Press.

192 "The Case of the Missing Mars Water," Science@NASA. NASA (science.nasa.gov/headlines/y2001/ast05jan_1.htm)

198 From "Ask The Experts," www.sciam.com. copyright © 1997 by Scientific American, Inc. All rights reserved.

202 Excerpted with permission from Schilling, Govert. *Science.* "Shadow of an Exoplanet Detected." 11-19-1999. Copyright 1999 American Association for the Advancement of Science.

208 "Sailing to the Stars." *NASAKids.* Ed. Becky Bray and Patrick Meyer. July 8, 2000. NASA Marshall Space Flight Center. (http://kids.msfc.nasa.gov/news/2000/news%2Dsolarsail.asp)

212 Long, Michael. "Surviving in Space." *National Geographic.* January 2001. (http://www.nationalgeographic.com/ngm/0101/feature1/index.html)

214 Letter to the Editor: Concentrate on Earth (http://www.the-scientist.com/yr2002/mar/let1_020304.html). James R. Blevins, Jr. The Scientist 16[5]:13, Mar. 4, 2002. © 2002, The Scientist LLC. Reproduced with permission.

214 Letter to the Editor: On Earth and Travel to Mars, 1. (http://www.the-scientist.com/yr2002/apr/let_020401.html). John F. Collins. The Scientist 16[7]:14, Apr. 1, 2002. © 2002, The Scientist LLC. Reproduced with permission.